Basic News Writing

Third Edition

Basic News Writing

Melvin Mencher
Columbia University

ᴡᴄᴃ
Wm. C. Brown Publishers
Dubuque, Iowa

Rescue, Celebration, Public Service

The photographs on the front and back covers illustrate some of the work of the media writers in *Basic News Writing*. The photo on the front by Ricardo Ferro of the *St. Petersburg Times* shows the dramatic rescue of a motorist trapped in his car after it had been struck by a truck.

In 1886, the last rivet was driven into the Statue of Liberty, and this symbol of freedom was dedicated in New York harbor. On July 4, 1986, the nation celebrated the centennial of the Statue, and journalists from around the world covered the event. Frazier Hale of the *St. Petersburg Times* caught the excitement in the large photo on the back cover.

Those who work in the media are committed to public service, and the panel from a television story board on the back cover illustrates some of the work of advertising agencies that volunteer personnel. The material here is from Young & Rubicam.

Library of Congress Catalog Card Number: 88–71079

ISBN 0–697–04284–7

Printed in the United States of America
10 9 8 7 6 5 4 3 2 1

Contents

Chapter 2 **The Reporter 20**

Part 2 **Writing 51**

Chapter 3 **Making of the Story 52**

Chapter 4 **Rudiments of the Story 88**

Chapter 5 **Structuring the Story 114**

Chapter 6 **Fine Tuning the Story 140**

Part 3 Reporting 179

Chapter 7 Finding Information and Gathering Facts 180

Chapter 8 How Reporters Work 206

Chapter 9 **Capturing the Spoken Word 230**

Chapter 10 **From the Office and On the Beat 264**

Part 4 **Specialties** 321

Chapter 11 **Broadcast Writing** 322

Chapter 12 **Visual Reporting** 338

Chapter 13 **Advertising** 370

Chapter 14 **Public Relations 384**

Part 5 **Laws and Codes 403**

Chapter 15 **Libel, Ethics and Taste 404**

Preface

This is a how-to book. It was written to help the newcomer to journalism learn how to put on paper words that accurately and clearly describe and explain ideas and events.

Basic News Writing is designed to show the beginner how to gather information, how to analyze its importance and how to put the results of this reporting and thinking into clear and accurate news stories.

The techniques recommended here are those of successful news writers, men and women who make words do their bidding. The writers who have contributed to *Basic News Writing* know that writing does not come easily. They understand how hard it is to whip words into submission so that they dance lightly or march somberly across the page. They have learned to write through patience, confidence and effort.

Patience is necessary because words have a tendency to go their own way, resisting our efforts to lock them into sentences and paragraphs. It takes time to learn to write well. Few people are born writers.

Confidence is important because sometimes it seems that the right words will never come, that the story will not blend smoothly but insists on zigzagging its way from paragraph to paragraph—no matter how patient the writer is. The newcomer should not give up.

All of us possess the creative instinct. We all want to make something of our experiences, to tell others what we have seen and heard. With confidence in ourselves, we can do that.

But it does require work. The aspiring artist who seeks to transfer a sunset to canvas does not instinctively dip his brush into the precise colors on the palette. Through study and trial and error the artist learns just how much white to mix with red for the clouds. The singer cannot turn words and musical notes into a song of lost love the first time she sees the score. It takes hours, sometimes days, before everything comes together and the performance is worth recording. The journalist is no different. Beginner or experienced news writer, effort and hard work lead to well-written stories.

Unguided effort is wasted work, however. The purpose of *Basic News Writing* is to serve as compass and sextant. It provides the directions in which the student should point his or her efforts. The techniques, principles and concepts that are suggested here come from the field, from the everyday experience of journalists on the job. Every concept and principle is illustrated with a practical example from the experience of a professional.

For the student considering a career in journalism, these illustrations serve another purpose. By watching the journalist at work, the student is able to see the many faces and facets of journalism: The young woman just out of journalism school, alone in the AP newsroom, who is called on to handle a rooming house fire that kills more than 20 people. The television network news writer who has minutes to write the story of U.S. Navy planes downing two Libyan jets. The newspaper reporter who climbs the stairs of a nearly deserted tenement to interview a family living without heat or running water.

For this third edition I have included suggestions from users of *Basic News Writing,* most of whom asked that the chapters on writing be moved forward. Also, I have combined some chapters to eliminate duplication.

In response to requests from a number of instructors, I have added chapters on advertising and public relations. This material is intended for the many students whose first news writing course surveys the communications field. I have taken the same approach to advertising and public relations as I have to news writing and reporting. Practitioners help to guide the student.

The emphasis of the textbook remains on news writing and reporting, which my colleagues inform me constitute the preparation for allied fields. The disciplined approach to material, the ability that news writing demands to distill information and to communicate it accurately, honestly and succinctly are useful in all journalistic areas.

Saul Pett of the AP said: "Behind good writing is a basic logic, a basic common sense." *Basic News Writing* takes the approach that you can't write if you can't think.

For this edition, useful contributions were made by Mark Hickson, University of Alabama, Birmingham; Carole Marshall, University of Rhode Island; Alston Morgan, Oral Roberts University, and John Rippey, The Pennsylvania State University. Kay Ellen Krane made many valuable suggestions for the content. Copyediting and proofreading for this edition were done by Merrill Perlman. Patricia Conboy prepared the index.

I also have had assistance from Maria Braden, University of Kentucky; J. Laurence Day, University of Kansas; Dick Haws, Iowa State University; Beverley Pitts, Ball State University; Howard L. Seeman, Humboldt State University; Luke Staudacker, Marquette University, and Terry Vander Hayden, Western Kentucky University.

Many of my research tasks were eased by the enthusiastic assistance of Wade Doares and Steve Toth of the Columbia University Journalism Library.

The philosophy of *Basic News Writing* is best summed up by Samuel Johnson's remark, "The end of writing is to enable the readers better to enjoy life, or better to endure it."

For all its practicality, this textbook recognizes that journalism is more calling than trade. Kin to teaching, cousin to preaching, journalism is much more than the sum of its techniques and the advice of its practitioners. Through its many examples, *Basic News Writing* seeks to demonstrate the moral underpinnings of journalism.

Journalism's hope and inspiration are its young men and women. This book was written for them and especially in memory of two young men who were killed in Vietnam, Ron Gallagher and Peter Bushey. Ron was editor of the *University Daily Kansan* when I was its adviser at the University of Kansas, and Peter was one of my students at Columbia University. They loved journalism and had faith in what it could accomplish. They wrote, they took pictures and they aspired to make the world a better place for us all through journalism. To them, journalism was a noble calling.

M. M.

Acknowledgments

Those who have provided help with the book include the following:

Jennifer J. Allen
Editor, *The Commercial Dispatch*
(Columbus, Miss.)

Mervin Block
Television writer and broadcast workshop
director

Kirk Citron
Vice president, senior writer, Hal Riney &
Partners, San Francisco

Roy Peter Clark
Associate director, Poynter Institute for
Media Studies

Claude Cookman
Photo editor

Julie Doll
Publisher, *The Hays* (Kansas) *Daily News*

Mary Ann Giordano
The Daily News

Berkley Hudson
The Providence Journal

Monica Kaufman
WSB-TV (Atlanta)

Nelda J. King
Associate creative director, Young &
Rubicam

Robert E. Kollar
Chief photographer, Tennessee Valley
Authority

Jeff McAdory
The Commercial Appeal (Memphis, Tenn.)

Mitch Mendelson
The Birmingham Post-Herald

Jack Mitchell
Vice president, Burson-Marsteller

Merrill Perlman
The New York Times

Susan J. Porter
Editor, *Scripps Howard News*

Charlie Riedel
The Hays Daily News

Neal Robbins
UPI; Roosevelt University

Rob Rose
The Blade (Toledo, Ohio)

Joel Sartore
The Wichita Eagle-Beacon

Christopher Scanlan
*The Providence Journal; St. Petersburg
Times*

Mary Voboril
The Miami Herald

Keith Warren
The Commercial Dispatch

Lindy Washburn
AP

Part One
Journalists in Action

1

On the Job

News stories can break at any time, and the reporter must be ready to handle them efficiently and intelligently. Here, Lindy Washburn of the Associated Press takes notes on a story she will soon place on the wires for newspapers and radio stations over the country.
John Titchen.

Looking Ahead

Writers attempt to give their readers, listeners and viewers an accurate, interesting, thorough account of events. The writer does this by applying his or her skills and knowledge to the tasks of research, reporting, interviewing and writing. The writer's objective is to reach people with information that is easily understood. Sometimes, the writer's purpose is to persuade the reader, listener or viewer to act.

The lights are out in the fashionable stores along Fifth Avenue, and the tall buildings in Rockefeller Center loom over the deserted streets. Patrons have made their way home from Radio City Music Hall a block away on Sixth Avenue. It is well past midnight in midtown New York.

Although the lights in one Rockefeller Center office building burn brightly, there is an unusual calm here, too. The reporters, editors and operators in the Associated Press newsroom have left for the night. The office is deserted—except for a young woman sitting at one of the desks.

Lindy Washburn is working the early shift—11:30 p.m. to 8 a.m.—in the New York City bureau of the Associated Press. She was hired as a summer vacation replacement after her graduation from journalism school.

As the newcomer in the bureau, she has been taught the ropes: the need for speed, accuracy and brevity; which wires send out sports, radio, local and national news, and the method for transmitting stories she may have to write when the operators are not on duty.

Washburn is responsible for a large area of the East Coast, and she will be on her own for most of the shift. This is her first night alone on the early shift.

As the old hands were leaving, one had stopped on his way out to re-assure her. "Looks like a quiet night," he said.

For a while it is quiet. Suddenly, at 1:40 a.m., the stillness of the office is broken by the ring of the telephone. The night city editor of the *Daily News* is calling. Washburn can sense the urgency in his voice.

Handling a Big Story—Alone

"We have a tip there's a big fire in New Jersey," he says. "Have you got anything?" No, she hasn't, she says. She asks him where the fire is. "Bradley Beach," he replies.

Washburn looks at a map and sees that Bradley Beach is a town on the Atlantic shore and is near Asbury Park, a larger city.

She calls long-distance information and asks for the telephone numbers of the Bradley Beach police and fire departments and the numbers of the departments in Asbury Park. First, she calls the Bradley Beach fire department.

"Lady, we're busy," a voice says and hangs up. He sounds frantic.

She telephones the Asbury Park fire department.

"What's happening in Bradley Beach?" she asks. "I can't get anything from the department there."

"That's some fire," the dispatcher answers. "We have departments from all over the state fighting it. It looks like a big one."

"Any deaths?" Washburn asks.

"I think it was 20 last time I checked. Could be more now."

Racing the Clock

Washburn's heart picks up a few beats. This is obviously a big story. That many deaths will have an impact on people. The story is likely to be given play around the country. She knows that at this time—nearly 2 a.m.—morning newspapers in the West are readying their front pages. She will have to hurry to catch them.

She asks the dispatcher for the address of the building, what it is used for, when the first alarm had been received. She wants to know what the building looks like—is it wood, brick, stucco? The dispatcher says it's a wooden frame building, called the Brinley Inn. No, he doesn't know the cause. Too early for that.

As she hangs up, another telephone rings. The call is from a reporter for a radio station in Asbury Park. He had called the AP's Newark bureau with information and a tape-recorded message had told him the bureau was closed for the night but that important stories should be phoned to the New York City bureau.

"Have you heard about the fire?" he asks.

"Yes," says Washburn. "How many deaths are there?" The death toll is the key to the story, and she must have it confirmed.

"The hospital spokesman on the scene says 23," the reporter replies. She gives him the address the dispatcher had provided, and he confirms that.

The radio reporter then plays for Washburn a tape of the conversation he had with a doctor from the medical examiner's office who was at the scene of the fire.

Washburn now has almost all she needs. She will have to put something on the wire at once. Then she will have to alert the AP New Jersey staff to start working on the story.

She has been typing notes from her telephone conversations, and she looks them over. The death toll clearly is the heart of the story and will go into the first sentence, her lead. She rearranges her notes with this lead in mind. Then she writes her lead. She types in the code for an all-points bulletin and starts to relay the story.

Here is her story:

```
o364
    B N ZYVVYXUIV
BNBX NR07 NR05
BNBX
BC-Bradley Beach Fire
    Bradley Beach, New Jersey (AP)--A major
fire in Bradley Beach has killed 23 people,
according to fire officials.
    The fire at Brinley Inn, 200 Brinley Ave.,
began at 11:20 P.M. and was brought under
control at midnight, according to Chief
Theodore A. Bianchi of the Bradley Beach Fire
Department.
    The cause of the fire is undetermined, he
said.
    The Brinley Inn, a three-story wood frame
building, was reportedly occupied by 36 people
at the time of the blaze. Many elderly persons
and teenagers were among those killed, the
officials said.
```

```
    Dead and injured were taken to the Jersey
Shore Medical Center and the Long Branch
Medical Center.

    More
    AP-NY-07-27 0201EDT
```

All of this is done in about 20 minutes, and Washburn is pleased by her ability to act quickly in a critical situation. (She later learns that she has beaten the opposition, the UPI, by 35 minutes.) But she is not pleased with her story. There are some flubs.

She sees that she should have abbreviated New Jersey in the dateline, and she realizes that the adjective *major* in the lead is extraneous. She also realizes that she should have used *said* instead of *according to* in the lead.

By the time her story has cleared the wire, Washburn is busy gathering more material. She learns that the Brinley Inn is a four-story rooming house, and she has obtained more details about the injured, where the dead had been trapped and the exact time the fire broke out.

She begins to write a new lead. Her focus will still be the most newsworthy fact she has, the 23 deaths. She will put next the new material she has gathered about those who were injured.

Her first story had cleared at 2:01 a.m. Her second piece clears the wire at 3:26 a.m. Here it is:

Writethru

```
    o365
    B N ZYVVYXWYF
AM-Beach Fire, Writethru, 400
Eds: Updates, Corrects Building to four-
story structure, adds color
    Bradley Beach, N.J. (AP)--At least 23
persons were killed Saturday in a fire at a
rooming house in this seaside resort, hospital
officials said.
    Two others suffered smoke inhalation and
were admitted to the Jersey Shore Medical
Center, said Hospital Administrator Ernest
Kovats. An additional 13 people were examined
at the hospital, Kovats said.
    As many as 36 people may have been inside
The Brinley Inn when the fire broke out at
11:02 P.M. and was brought under control about
midnight, authorities said.
    Witnesses said most of the victims appeared
to be elderly and appeared to be trapped on the
top floors of the four-story wood-frame
building.
    The cause of the fire was not determined,
but there were some reports of an explosion,
said Fire Chief Theodore A. Bianchi.
```

At least 35 ambulances from Bradley Beach
and several Monmouth County communities lined
up near the building, waiting to transport the
bodies, according to witnesses.

Firemen removed the victims from a third
floor exit door at the rear of the building to
a roof where they lowered the victims to the
waiting ambulances.

Two doctors, one who identified himself as
a doctor from the Monmouth County Medical
Examiner's Office, were on the scene to briefly
examine the bodies before they were transported
to Jersey Shore Medical Center.

Kovats said several bodies were transported
directly to the county morgue at Freehold Area
Hospital.

Firemen said the building was engulfed when
they arrived at the scene, making entry
impossible.

The building was badly charred on the south
and east sides of the first floor of the
building. Firemen said the fire appeared to
have started on the east side of the building
on the porch.

Local fire officials, Monmouth County Fire
Marshal Fred Leggett, the State Police Arson
Squad and Monmouth County Prosecutor Alexander
Lehrer were on the scene conducting an initial
investigation.

The Brinley Inn was the scene of another
fire in September 1979, according to the Asbury
Park Press.

AP-NY-07-27 0326EDT

In the UPI's Hong Kong Bureau

A third of the world to the west, in Hong Kong, a reporter for the UPI is going over some stories he plans to put in his files.

"Robbins," the deputy news editor calls out. He tells Neal Robbins to find a boat and track down a flotilla of Chinese junks that is approaching Hong Kong.

Chinese sneak into the British colony all the time, Robbins knows. But this is different. This is an influx by sea. It could be a big story in the United States as well as in Asia. Chinese have been leaving the mainland in small groups for political reasons, but this sounds like a large movement.

Robbins is joined by a photographer and they take off.

Packed. Crowded in a junk with all they own, 70 people watch as Robbins and a photographer approach.
Guy Liu, UPI.

Soon they are cruising the Hong Kong harbor on the 30-foot *Xinhua,* looking for a cove that the Chinese supposedly are heading for. Police boats pass them, spotter planes fly overhead and a helicopter slowly circles above the water.

They spot the cove. There before them are about 50 traditional Chinese sailing junks. "Their rust-color bat-wing sails make the flotilla seem a well-combed field of wheat," Robbins notes. The boats are anchored, and Robbins directs the captain toward a boat in the middle of the flotilla.

The photographer, a Hong Kong Chinese, calls out to some people in a Cantonese dialect. The boat people stare back. Robbins tries his college Mandarin. More stares.

The Unexpected

Finally, they locate a man who speaks Mandarin. The boat people come from South China, he says. There are 70 of them on the small wooden boat, all members of three families.

No, he replies in answer to a question from Robbins. They are not fleeing China for political reasons. They have come, he says, because the authorities warned them of a massive earthquake that is to strike their area soon.

Finding the people friendly, Robbins moves from boat to boat, asking questions. He boards some of the boats. The people are from a fishing area, he is told, and they have been informed that the earthquake is due in about a week. He is also told that gangsters invaded their area and stole valuables and commandeered some fishing boats.

A Final Check

In an hour, Robbins is ready to return to the bureau to write. On the way out of the cove, he stops to interview officials on the police boats. Police intercepted the junks and herded them into the cove, a police superintendent tells him. The police had counted 55 boats and were told that a hundred more were on the way. They estimate there are 2,000 people on the boats.

Robbins asks what the superintendent knows about the earthquake, the gangsters and whether the people will be fed and cared for. Finally, he asks whether the government will let them stay if they want to remain.

On the way back to the bureau, Robbins reads his notes. Figuring out the lead is not too hard, he thinks. Clearly, he says to himself, the point of the story, his lead, is the fact that the boats have arrived and the reason they are here.

He has arranged his notes, thought of a lead, and there is still time before they land. He starts to write his story in longhand on the boat.

In the bureau, as Robbins seats himself, the editor says, "Keep it short." As Robbins types, his editor looks over his shoulder. He asks Robbins about the gangsters.

"That's what they told me," Robbins replies. He says that the account the people gave was a bit confused.

"Bury it," the editor advises him, meaning that it should be put deep in the story.

Robbins agrees that the fear of the earthquake is the central fact.

Here is the beginning of Robbins' story as it went out on UPI's wires from Hong Kong:

```
ZCZC XHA197 NXI
00 HUP NRS
R I
     Flotilla 3-31
     By Neal Robbins
     Hong Kong, March 31 (UPI)--A flotilla of
Chinese Junks carrying some 2,000 people who
feared an impending earthquake in Southern
China, arrived in Hong Kong Tuesday, officials
said.
     Police Superintendent Bill Renahan told UPI
that a wave of 55 of the rickety wooden boats
with 2,000 men, women and children came from
Haifeng and Lufeng Counties in Guangdong
Province just north of Hong Kong. The makeshift
flotilla left home Sunday, he said.
     Another 200 to 400 vessels powered by bat-
winged sails are still out at sea carrying as
many as 10,000 residents of China, Renahan
estimated.
```

Journalists in Action

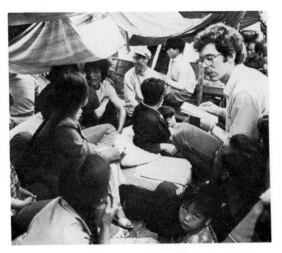

On the Scene. Neal Robbins interviews one of the Chinese families that fled the mainland. The Chinese tell Robbins that authorities had forecast a severe earthquake for their home area.
Arthur Tsang, UPI.

```
     But Hong Kong Government Sources said only
78 boats had been sighted and 48 of them
containing 1,800 people arrived Tuesday.
     Renahan said the flotilla was the largest
of its kind to hit the British Colony, which
has been flooded with hundreds of thousands of
illegal Chinese immigrants since 1978.
     Police launches corralled the 20-40 foot
(7-13 meter) boats in Joss House Bay, a small
cove surrounded by uninhabited, grassy hills
just in sight of the towering skyscrapers of
Hong Kong, but outside the main harbor.

     More
SC1755
CCCCQQE
NNNN
```

The "CBS Evening News"

In New York City, it is 5:30 p.m. according to the wall clock in the small lobby of the CBS Broadcast Center on West 57th Street. Through the lobby, down a long corridor and passageway, a set of double doors opens into a two-story studio.

It is almost an hour before air time for the "CBS Evening News," and it is quiet in the pale blue studio. At one side, behind large glass panels, is the executive producer's room. Dan Rather, the anchorman for the Evening News, is going over the program with the producer. From time to time, Rather emerges to talk to the writers who are seated next to a large desk in the middle of the studio.

They are preparing for the evening news program.

The Writers

The writers have been at work since 10 in the morning. Their first task is to read several newspapers—*The New York Times, The Washington Post, The Wall Street Journal* and the *Daily News*. Then they scan the news wires. Each writer has a different area of responsibility: one handles national news; another, foreign; a third, features, disasters and obituaries.

As they read, the writers look for the news items that make for interesting feature stories and takeouts. They are conscious of the visual possibilities of each story. A "tell" story or "reader" in which the anchor reads from a script generally is not so interesting to viewers as a story that is accompanied by videotape.

Tell stories are written tightly. But stories with good videotape may run five or six times as long. A writer may collect several thousand words for a story and reduce it to 50 words for the anchor to read as a tell story. A story that involves a correspondent in the field may require a discussion with that correspondent. The writer will want to know what Lesley Stahl in Washington will stress so he or she can write an appropriate lead-in for Rather's introduction. The lead-in is a few words that capture the essence of the story without duplicating what the reporter is going to say.

By midafternoon, the writers have a good idea of the day's news, and at 3:30 the executive producer and the editor discuss the news items for the program. The editor needs to know how much time will be needed for each item and whether it will be a tell story or will be told by a reporter on videotape.

Minutes to Go

5:58 Rather leaves the executive producer's office. He is holding a sheaf of papers, the items he will read for the Evening News. He manages to bite down on his cigar and move his lips as he reads the script. He is trim and vigorous.

6:02 Rather turns to one of his writers and asks about an item that has been inserted in the newscast, a legal suit involving Richard Nixon. "You think we should explain this?" Rather asks a writer for the program. "If we do, we'll need 10 or 15 more seconds." The writer thinks for a few seconds, nods approval to Rather, and starts writing.

6:04 Lineup item No. 22, a tell story, displeases Rather. He discusses some of the wording with a writer. The item runs for 20 seconds and is 50 words long. They agree on new wording.

6:05 "Ten is out," someone shouts, and item 10 is scratched to make room for the additional material in the Nixon story.

6:08 The camera crew begins to position itself around the room, and the two people running the prompter machines go over the script. The machines project large type directly in front of Rather so that although he appears to the viewer to be looking directly into the camera he is reading from the script projected in front of him.

6:10 Rather looks up from editing the lead-all, the first item in the newscast. "Very nice lead," he tells the writer. Rather resumes reading.

Editing Copy. Anchorman Dan Rather goes over his script minutes before broadcast and makes changes to reflect late-breaking news.
CBS News Photo.

6:11 A woman dashes out of the executive producer's office. "We have an emergency," she says. "We need something from the archives." File footage is necessary for a news item. It may not be used, but the producer wants to have it available.

6:14 Rather detects an ambiguous statement in one of the stories. The item has just been inserted in the program, and Rather wants to change some of the wording to clarify the story.

6:15 A sudden calm descends on the studio.

In the control room, there is no peace. Seven people are jammed together at a console, each one talking. In the middle front row is the director. He will cue the cameras as they focus on Rather and give other cues as the visuals, remotes and videotapes pop on and off the screen.

The goal of the control room staff is to have a tight program, to move neatly from Rather to a Washington correspondent without dead air, without cutting Rather off too soon; to synchronize the visuals that are the backdrop for Rather as he describes a spot in the Pacific (a map appears), a planet (a picture of Saturn looms over his left shoulder), a labor union (its emblem is shown).

6:23 Rather sits in front of a small mirror and is made up. He applies the lip rouge himself.

6:24 Rather shouts, "Sandy, you've got to pump that audio way up." Silence again.

6:25 "Five minutes," the stage manager calls out.

6:29 Rather settles into his chair, again reading the script. This time his lips are immobile.

"Thirty seconds." The deep voice booms in the studio and over a loud-speaker in the control room where the hubbub suddenly ceases. Countdowns are being prepared by the people at the various panels to cue the announcer, Rather, the videotape recorder, correspondents and the visuals. "Ten seconds."

Rather opens the program with a lead-in (introduction) to the big story of the day:

Dan Rather: Good evening. This is the CBS EVENING NEWS, Dan Rather reporting.

CBS News Correspondent David Martin reports tonight that a U.S. warplane has fired at what it thought was a threatening Iranian aircraft. It happened in the Persian Gulf, and word of it came after another ship was hit by a mine outside that gulf in what had been considered safe waters. Our coverage begins with Doug Tunnell.

Doug Tunnell: The Texaco Caribbean was fully loaded with Iranian crude oil and sailing alone to a deep-water anchorage just outside the gulf, when an explosion ripped a gaping 12-foot hole in its port side. Oil poured into the sea. A cloud of gas fumes filled the air for miles around the American-operated tanker, while its largely Italian crew flooded the decks to prevent a fire. The captain radioed shore that he had struck a mine. . . .

Inside a Newsroom

If we could look in on one of the 1,700 daily newspapers a few hours before press time, we might see: Telephones ringing with reporters calling in to speak to the city editor about stories they are working on. Teletype machines disgorging reams of AP and UPI copy. Copy editors reading news stories on their editing terminals, removing the word *felt* and inserting the word *said,* writing a headline for a page one story about a fatal accident.

The news editor is chatting with the managing editor about a weather story out of Florida, and reporters are writing stories on their terminals, looking up at the screen now and then to see whether the lead is just right.

A police siren pierces the evening's stillness outside, and soon the wail of an ambulance is heard. No one pays attention.

The phone on the city editor's desk rings. It is a call from the police reporter A Fatal Accident at the police station. "Bad accident at an intersection with the bypass," he says. "You want me to get out there or cover from here? They think two people have been killed."

The city editor tells the reporter to sit tight, that with the rain-slick roads and the fog there may be other accidents. The editor doesn't want the reporter to lose touch with police headquarters for a while.

"Try to get a fix on it," the editor says. "If it's as bad as you say, I think you'd better get out there. I'm sending a photographer anyway."

For the next half-hour, the police beat reporter monitors the police radio. At the same time, he goes through the notes he has taken from police reports. He spots a burglary at the First Baptist Church. He recalls that he has notes somewhere in his pad about the theft of religious scrolls from a synagogue on Maple Avenue. He decides he will put the two thefts into one story. He makes a mental note to call the lieutenant to ask whether the same people could have been involved in both burglaries.

Three blocks away in city hall, another reporter is walking into the city council At City Hall chambers. He greets the city clerk.

"Should be a good meeting tonight, Alice," he says. "The appeal on the zoning decision on Hale's will bring them out. I'm glad you gave me the background on that one."

He turns to chat with the manager of Hale's Department Store, who has entered the room with his lawyer. The reporter wants more background on Hale's plans to build a large store in a residential area outside of downtown.

In the newsroom, a young reporter is bent over several sheets of paper. They are copies of obituary notices from the advertising department. One of the notices is about the death of a retired school principal. She had taught in local schools for 30 years and was a principal for 13 years. She probably has many former students in town, the reporter thinks. She decides to obtain more information about the woman.

A telephone call interrupts her thoughts. The caller is the president of the United Way. He has the results of the fund drive just completed.

"We worked all day getting the field reports together, and I'm glad to say we've set a record," he says. The reporter asks how much was raised, what accounted for the record donations. Did any particular organization or event raise an unusually large amount of money? The questions continue.

In a corner of the newsroom, the news editor is looking over some wire service stories.

"Hurricane expected to hit Florida," he tells the managing editor. "People boarding up. Worst in a decade, they think." The managing editor tells him to put the AP and UPI stories together. It could run on page one, he says. Lots of people in town have friends and relatives who have moved to Florida.

Approaching Deadline

The news for tomorrow's newspaper is being gathered in diverse ways. Some reporters are covering events. Others are taking information from sources over the telephone. Some are digging into city files for an investigative story. News that originates outside the community is coming in on the news wires.

Not all the information and news being gathered will be used. The police reporter has had reports of two more accidents, and he knows that he will have little time to write up the minor burglaries, break-ins and arrests from his notes. He knows that he will have to spend the few hours before deadline on the accidents, rounding them up into a single story, probably for page one.

The reporter handling the obituaries has learned that a fund drive is being planned to raise money for a memorial scholarship in honor of the retired school principal who has just died. The scholarship will be called the Rose Harriet Allen Memorial Scholarship, and some of the city's leading citizens—her former students—are serving on the committee to raise money.

The reporter intends to interview these people, not only about their plans to raise money but also about their recollections of their school days in Allen's classroom.

The reporter looks at a batch of notes she has taken for several other obituaries. She shrugs. She will have no time for the calls she had planned to make for additional material for some of them. She realizes that this will displease some readers. Obituaries are among the newspaper's best-read sections, she knows. If she can, she will spend time on the other obituaries once she has finished the Allen story. She will have to work at twice the usual pace, which is twice as fast as she thought she'd work when she was studying journalism in college.

The wire editor has handed the city editor an AP story from Phoenix about the crash of a small plane. One of the three victims had owned a chain of shoe stores in town until his retirement three years ago. The city editor calls a reporter to his desk.

"Here, rewrite this. Bill Frazier died in a plane crash in Phoenix."

The reporter understands that he will have to localize the wire story so that it interests local readers. This means putting information about Frazier into the lead. He heads for the newspaper library to dig up background—the number of stores Frazier owned, his civic activities, place of birth, and other details he will need for the combination news story and obituary.

We move from this composite picture of reporters at work on a medium-sized newspaper to the newsroom of a larger daily newspaper, *The Providence Journal.*

Berkley Hudson is talking about a story he has just finished handling for his newspaper. The story—actually two stories, Hudson says—began one day in the newsroom. "This man had sneaked off the grounds of a state mental hospital, managed to get a bus and walked into the newspaper to tell his story."

The man had spent five years in the state penitentiary and 23 in a state mental hospital. Most people confined to such places believe they should be freed, but Hudson felt this story was different. Hudson let the man talk, and the longer he spoke the more Hudson felt that there had been an injustice. Reporters often act on their hunches or intuition.

Hudson decided to look into Chester Jefferds' story.

From examining hospital records and interviewing social workers and administrators at the hospital, Hudson concluded that neither justice nor compassion would be served by keeping Jefferds locked away.

"He doesn't belong here," a social worker told Hudson. That quote was underlined in Hudson's notes. It would have to go high up in the story. He remembered a point his journalism instructor had driven home relentlessly: Good quotes up high.

As angry as Hudson felt about the situation, he knew that the best way to tell the story would be to let it tell itself. The indignation would have to come from the reader. Hudson would lay out the facts and let the readers reach their own conclusions. The reporting took two weeks.

Twenty-Eight Years in Confinement

"When I had all the information I thought I needed, I decided to start writing," Hudson says. He went into the office at 10 a.m. and looked over his notes carefully. As often happens, he discovered he needed additional details.

"At 2 o'clock I had organized my notes and was ready to write." With a few breaks, he wrote until about midnight. He spent another hour with the Sunday editor, going over the story, making some changes in the copy. Here is how the story begins:

He survived inside; now he'd like to be free

By BERKLEY HUDSON
Journal-Bulletin Staff Writer

CRANSTON — Chester G. Jefferds Jr. has survived 28 years in confinement. His face has deep, bold wrinkles. His hazel eyes are murky.

He spent five years in the state prison, then 23 more in the state mental hospital. He has seen other prisoners kill themselves — and sometimes each other. His was a world of beatings and rape, strait jackets and electroshock therapy, nurse's needles and attendants' pills.

Chester Jefferds learned how a man labeled crazy stays sane in a mental institution. You keep quiet. You try to forget why you're there. You don't listen to the moans and screams around you.

"You go through the alphabet, saying the letters over and over," he says. "You go through the fraction tables. 7 into 100. 8 into 100."

He has one tooth left. The rest he lost in fights. He has a raspy voice.

"There's only one way to go in this place," he·says. "You keep your mouth shut."

Those who know him call him Jeff. He is 68. It has been 28 years since he was sentenced to life imprisonment for shooting his wife to death. Now he would like his freedom.

★ ★ ★

"HE DOESN'T belong here," says David J. Arone, a social worker at the state General Hospital. "There's plenty of evidence Chester has been able to take care of himself."

Since 1973, psychiatrists, social workers and nurses have been saying what Arone says: Jefferds is not sick, mentally or physically.

The problem, Arone says, is that Jefferds is unique among the 1,400 patients at the medical center. Like others there, he is elderly and has been in a mental hospital for many years, yet he is no longer ill. What makes him different is that he is under a life sentence for murder.

"He's still here because if he weren't here, he'd be at the prison," says Frederick Young, chief of social services at the General Hospital. Jefferds, Young says, doesn't belong in prison either. Mental-health laws require the release of anyone who is not ill, but hospital officials believe that if he were released from the hospital, he would be required to go back to prison.

"Had he been at the prison all this time as a lifer, he'd probably be free now," Young says. . . .

Six weeks after Hudson's story appeared, Jefferds was on his way to freedom. The state parole board had decided to allow Jefferds to leave the hospital for a halfway house. After three months there, he would be a free man. Hudson went to the hospital to watch Jefferds pack. He wrote a story about Jefferds' release that began:

Chester Jefferds stood next to his suitcase. It had a rope for a handle. Inside, among his few possessions, was a card from a friend. It read, "Good luck in your new venture.". . .

During the last four years, the Parole Board reviewed his case on 10 occasions. Once, in August, 1977, the board approved his removal from the locked wards for the criminally insane, but it required him to continue living at the mental institution.

The story of Chester G. Jefferds Jr., 68, was reported in the *Sunday Journal* on Feb. 8, four days after the Parole Board had considered his case once again and "continued the matter." The board wanted hospital officials to provide "concrete alternatives" on how the man could be released. . . .

Free. Six weeks after Hudson's story appeared, Jefferds was released from the state hospital where he had been confined.
Bob Thayer, The Providence Journal.

The Journalistic Process

We have been talking with and watching a few of the 47,500 reporters and editors who gather, write and produce the news that is read in the 1,700 daily newspapers and 7,000 weeklies and is heard and watched on 10,000 of the country's radio and television stations.

Veterans and newcomers, young and old, they are engaged in a process that is the same, whether for a small Massachusetts daily newspaper or for a television newscast watched by millions across the country.

From our observations, we can see that the journalistic process consists of four distinct parts:

Information gathering—Making observations, interviewing, conducting research—reporting.

Planning—Checking and verifying information, plotting the story.

Writing—Putting the story together in a form that is interesting, clear and succinct.

Production—Fitting the news into the newspaper or newscast.

In the following chapters, we will concentrate on the writing and reporting processes, how reporters write accurate and clear accounts of the events we need to know about and those we enjoy hearing about.

The job of people who report and write the news is to tell those who weren't at the event what happened. The duty of the reporter is to give an accurate, complete, impartial and timely account of what has happened or what is likely to happen.

Interview. Pat Conboy questions a source. Interviews are a major source of information for news stories.

Writing the news requires clear thinking under pressure. On her first day alone on the job, Lindy Washburn was able to handle a big story. She knew what questions to ask her sources, those the reader or listener would want answered.

Washburn was unable to cover the fire in New Jersey personally and had to rely on sources. She used the best she could locate. Neal Robbins was able to go to the event for firsthand reporting, which usually leads to a more interesting story since the written account will contain the observations that make a story ring true. He, too, sought out the official version of the event.

Before we go into any more detail about reporting and writing, let's take a closer look at the journalist. Who are these people who gather and write the news? What traits do they have in common, and what skills are they expected to have when they begin their careers? We will talk to reporters and editors for the answers to these questions.

Suggested Reading

Commission on Freedom of the Press. *A Free and Responsible Press.* Chicago: University of Chicago Press, 1947.

Halberstam, David. *The Powers That Be.* New York: Alfred A. Knopf, 1979.

Mayer, Martin. *About Television.* New York: Harper & Row, 1972.

Morris, Joe Alex. *Deadline Every Minute: The Story of the United Press.* New York: Doubleday, 1957.

Swanberg, W. A. *Citizen Hearst.* New York: Charles Scribner's Sons, 1961.

Swanberg, W. A. *Pulitzer.* New York: Charles Scribner's Sons, 1967.

2
The Reporter

"Being good in this job requires reading and writing at every opportunity, love of the work, 'round the clock commitment, fidelity to truth, leaving your personal prejudices behind, rewriting and rewriting and never hesitating to use the dictionary and to check facts over and over," says Nicholas McBride, who joined the staff of *The Christian Science Monitor* after graduating from journalism school and soon was transferred to the Washington bureau.
R. Norman Matheny, The Christian Science Monitor. Used with permission.

Looking Ahead

Journalists are curious and creative, characteristics that help them to handle assignments thoroughly and accurately and to develop out-of-the-ordinary stories. They are committed to fair play and honesty, and they keep themselves in a state of readiness, for no matter how pressing the deadline they know they must write the story in time for the next edition or newscast.

We will watch several reporters at work and then accompany a young reporter as he goes on his first assignments, performs well and then makes a mess of an assignment.

As he was reading a new biography of the American playwright Eugene O'Neill, the Boston University sophomore was struck by one of the scenes in the book. O'Neill is dying and he instructs his wife to burn the unfinished manuscripts of his plays in the fireplace of their Boston hotel room.

The student, Nick Gage, knew that the hotel had become a student dormitory. He was curious. What did the room look like now? He decided to walk across the campus to find out.

"To my surprise," he recalled later, "there was no evidence of a fireplace in the room. Out of curiosity, I looked up the blueprints of the building dating from its construction. Sure enough, there was no fireplace."

Gage, who was a reporter for his college newspaper, wrote a piece about his discovery. The authors of the biography heard about Gage's article and called him. Then they called O'Neill's widow, who said that on second thought she might have burned the manuscripts in the basement. The authors corrected the book in its next edition.

Gage was intrigued by the episode. He was, he said, "bitten by the investigative bug"—so much so that 10 years later he was interviewed for a job with *The New York Times* as an investigative reporter. The man who interviewed and hired Gage was Arthur Gelb, then metropolitan editor of the *Times* and the co-author, with his wife, of the O'Neill biography Gage had read years before.

Traits of the Journalist

You might say that Gage's curiosity made him a natural for journalism—curiosity plus a sense for what is new, interesting, different—in short, news sense.

When several members of the news staff of *The Commercial Dispatch* in Columbus, Miss., were having lunch one day they noticed a fire engine heading out of town. Naturally, the four of them jumped into a car and followed.

"A small woodworking shop had caught fire and two butane gas tanks were jeopardizing the lives of firefighters as well as the onlookers, residents of the area and the press," Keith Warren, a staff member of the newspaper, said.

The tanks caught fire, and flames shot skyward 20–30 feet. The area was evacuated, though reporters and photographers managed to stay with the firefighters. Warren took a color photo that ran across six columns of page one the next day. The paper led with the story.

Deadline. Journalists move to the speed of the clock's second hand. When a woman tried to hold up a bank in Tallahassee reporters and photographers were on the scene as quickly as law enforcement officers. The woman was captured outside the bank.

Phil Sears, Tallahassee Democrat. Used with permission.

Curiosity

The journalist often finds that curiosity pays off with good stories. What interests reporters usually interests readers and listeners.

No good reporter could pass up this handbill on the wall of a parking garage:

Missing Dog
$50 Reward

Three Legs   Blind in Left Eye
Right Ear Missing   Broken Tail
Answers to the Name Lucky

Did the owner ever find Lucky, and how could one dog be the repository of such varied misfortunes? The answers to the reporter's questions would make a good story.

Deadlines However wide the reporter's knowledge, however deep his or her talent, unless the reporter can meet deadlines, he or she is of little use in the newsroom. The deadline is an absolute demand on the journalist. For the wire service reporter, there is a deadline every minute. As Lindy Washburn was writing her fire story, she was aware that some newspapers were readying their front pages for the press. At any hour of the day or night, there is a deadline for some newspaper or broadcast station.

Sometimes the deadlines can be devastating. "I do not know of one single reporter who likes covering the World Series anymore," says Edwin Pope, the sports editor of *The Miami Herald*. The reason: deadlines. Games start at night, some as late as 8:30, in order to sell commercial spots on television. When a game runs long, there is little time between its completion and the deadlines of morning newspapers in the East.

"It drove us to our knees," said George Solomon, the assistant managing editor for sports at *The Washington Post,* of the Red Sox and Mets Series in 1986. Late starts and late endings had the sports staff pressed to the edge.

In the rush to make its deadline, *The Plain Dealer* in Cleveland, Ohio, ran a headline for a Sox-Mets game that no one noticed lacked a key word:

> **Red Sox Win,**
> **Take Series**

The headline should have read:

> **Red Sox Win,**
> **Take Series Lead**

But such blunders are rare. Journalists manage to do the job despite deadlines. In the key sixth game, the Red Sox looked sure winners of the game and the Series, and Pope started to write a column about the Red Sox winning the Series. Then the Mets came back, and he changed directions in his column. In the top of the 10th, the Red Sox took the lead. Pope switched again. It was past midnight in the East, and time was running out on Pope. He pounded away about the Red Sox. And, of course, the Mets won in the bottom of the 10th, and Pope tossed out his third effort. Against stomach-wrenching pressure, he managed to finish the column in time. The Oakland-Dodger Series posed even tougher problems for Eastern newspapers.

Baseball or board meeting, profile or police drug raid—whatever the story, there is always a deadline in journalism.

There are calmer moments, though. And when the reporter has time he or she puts it to good use by doing enterprising news and feature stories. The city hall reporter will do a feature on the mayor's hobby of raising roses, which has won him national recognition from horticultural groups. The education reporter will profile a day care center volunteer worker, and the county courthouse reporter will interview a judge about his campaign for court reforms.

Composure

"This, I think, is the essence of feature writing. You have to be passionately interested in everything. You have to want to learn about frogs or cancer or assassins, everything there is to know. You have to know five times as much as you're ever going to use in the story. The only really essential quality of a writer is crazed curiosity.— *Cynthia Gorney, The Washington Post.*

Creativity, Ingenuity

Enterprise is another word for reportorial creativity. When reporters converged on Washington for the funeral of President John Kennedy, one reporter separated himself from the pack. Jimmy Breslin of the *Daily News* went to Arlington National Cemetery and interviewed the gravedigger. His story about the man's sadness did a better job of summing up the nation's mourning than the other reporters' coverage of the funeral procession.

"Now and then the breaking news will save us from dullness and make the paper worth a quarter," says James K. Batten, president of the Knight-Ridder newspaper chain. "But most days it won't. And it's got to be our creativity, or ingenuity, especially on the typical slow days, that makes the paper so compelling, so indispensable. . . ."

Curiosity often begets creativity.

"I was an inquisitive child and was constantly reprimanded for prying into the personal lives of visitors who stopped at our home," recalls Helen Thomas, senior White House correspondent for the United Press International. Thomas once asked what flavor Jell-O Ronald Reagan had eaten during his hospitalization after he was shot.

"I've never wanted to do anything but write," Thomas says. As a youngster, she worked for her school newspaper. At Wayne State University, she majored in English and continued to write.

This creative urge, the desire to tell others what he or she has learned, marks the journalist.

In journalism, we say that the reporter who is creative and who shows ingenuity is an enterprising reporter, a self-starter. This reporter does not have to wait for assignments but generates ideas on his or her own. The reporter who sees stories on her way to work, while chatting with a secretary on his beat, or on the chance encounters in elevators, on the street and in lunchrooms—that reporter has a future.

Jim Dwyer found stories while riding the New York City subway. He found so many he became *Newsday*'s underground correspondent. He interviews a subway platform guitarist, who tells Dwyer: "People say, 'You got a million dollar voice; what you doing in the subway?' I got a wife and daughter, and I can put food on the table. I'm not rich. I know I been blessed, and I put my best foot forward." Dwyer catches the small scenes—a 4-year-old waves to a transit police officer, who salutes the child in return. Little boys still wave at police officers, Martin Robinson says. "It happens a lot. I like it. Something different."

Spotting Trends

One of the ways in which journalists show their ingenuity is to spot trends, the strong undercurrents that carry people along and that create the news events we cover as routine. Take for example the growing interest in religion. The generation of baby boomers—those born between 1946 and 1964—is taking an interest in religion that is more intense than that of their parents. Why? How is it manifesting itself—in membership in the standard denominations, or are the baby boomers flocking to the charismatic and pentacostal sects?

Trends can be spotted wherever people gather. What's the subject of the petition? Are people excited about it? Does it seem to point to a problem on campus, in the community? What are the ministers, priests and rabbis discussing in their sermons? Is there a common subject?

Why are students suddenly majoring in business and deserting the sciences and languages? Leg warmers, country rock, bran for breakfast, sexual puritanism, consumerism, junk food, junk bonds— all these excited people at one time. Why?

Look at what concerns people. Develop stories from trends. Here are some areas for stories:

Health care—Costs have skyrocketed; people want personal attention but can afford only mass medicine; people live longer and consequently need attention for geriatric diseases; the fear of AIDS is pervasive, and the fear of other sexually transmitted diseases has changed lifestyles.

Money—Everyone worries about it; no one seems to have quite enough, and some have none. How do the rich live? What taxes do people who make $100,000 a year, or $500,000 a year pay? A fifth of all children grow up in poverty; teen-age pregnancy and out-of-wedlock births are common among some segments of society, the result, it is said, of the culture of poverty.

On a larger scale, the U.S. economy is moving from manufacturing to services, from blue to white collar. Every community and many families are affected.

Localizing trends is not difficult. For example: A debate has been ongoing over whether to release those arrested but not convicted or to jail them through high bail. The law-and-order advocates stand behind preventive detention, detaining the accused as long as possible to prevent their committing further crimes. The civil rights supporters contend such an action is unconstitutional. The *St. Petersburg Times* examined arrest and crime records for one county and found that the criminal justice system is so overburdened that "accused felons by the thousands are being freed from jail. By the hundreds they commit new crimes."

Education—The way up in most societies has been through education, but people believe something has gone awry with the country's educational system: High schools graduate semi-literates; few students study foreign languages, mathematics, science. Increasingly, the middle class sends its children to private schools with the subsequent loss of interest in public schools by the people traditionally most concerned with it. Teen-agers are said to make up a subculture without feelings, morals or values. Is this the fault/responsibility of the educational system? The family?

Family life—How is it changing? Some say it is collapsing as divorce rates remain high, as parents have concerns that do not center on the home. Some contend the pressure of the young peer group is so powerful that parents no longer can influence their children. If so, what does this mean?

Racism—Despite the civil rights movement, despite laws, despite education, racism against blacks, Hispanics, Asians is pervasive and may be increasing. Why, and what are the consequences?

These seem to be enormous issues, too complicated for the journalist with a two-minute spot on the evening news, or 750 words in the newspaper. Actually, it is not difficult to turn these issues and trends into human terms. Once the idea is clear, the reporter does some research to firm up the overall situation. Then the reporter finds individuals and groups that illustrate the theme.

Every community, for example, has health clinics, a psychological and family counseling service. They help single mothers, give advice to teen-agers and try to help the elderly.

For a story about poverty, find a family trying to get through the month on a working mother's slim paycheck or a welfare payment. What do they eat? What is the children's clothing like? Sometimes, there are surprises. A poor family may spend too much on junk food or entertainment. How common is this, and what is the community doing about it?

Some of these stories require extended reporting. One of the most extensive reporting projects in recent years was carried out by *The Commercial Appeal* of Memphis. The newspaper sent two reporters and a photographer to Tunica, Miss., to examine the cycle of poverty. The three lived in Tunica for two months, often as unwelcome guests.

Two are white: Jeff McAdory, the 28-year-old photographer who was born in Mississippi, and Kevin Kittredge, 30, who had been covering Tunica as part of his northwest Mississippi beat. The other reporter was Celeste Williams, 28, a black, who was born in New York City, graduated from high school in Detroit and from Ball State University in Muncie, Ind.

In 1984, Jesse Jackson had visited Tunica and declared it "America's Ethiopia." Tunica County came to be a symbol of poverty in the United States. Later that year, the three moved to Tunica to examine it first-hand.

Tunica

Arrived in Tunica. Felt a strange sensation in my gut, resembling what I feel when stepping into a darkened room—a strange sense of the unknown, maybe dread. Another strange feeling—leaving Memphis only 30 or so miles behind, yet feeling I have been planted in a foreign country. While unloading the car, three young folks—one young man, two young women—stopped in the street next to the house we were renting.

The young man—I think Derrick was his name—sucked on a straw dipped into his soft drink cup and grinned openly and warmly, while the girls stood to one side and smiled more shyly. Derrick said he was a senior at Rosa Fort. He said he wanted to get a good job, maybe start a construction company and rebuild houses in Tunica. I looked at the houses around him. I remembered Sugar Ditch. I wished him well.

This was Williams' first entry in the diary she kept. It is dated Sunday, Sept. 8.

The reporters looked at all the indicators of community life in the poorest county in the United States:

Income—The leading source of income is government assistance, welfare for most. Median household income, $6,620. U.S. median household income, $17,710.

Education—Still segregated, not by law but by residence.

Health—The infant mortality rate among blacks was 31 deaths per 1,000 livebirths, among whites 11. The reasons—poverty and ignorance. Teen-age pregnancy is common.

"Teen-agers who get pregnant here are overwhelmingly black, poor and unmarried; they do not seek out available family planning information, and they wait months for prenatal care," writes Williams. " 'I've seen and heard everything,' says a health worker, but admits, 'Twelve-year-olds delivering babies still throws me.' "

Employment—"Forty-five of every 100 families are officially in poverty. Almost all the poor people are black."

Politics—In a county with a 73 percent black population, whites are in the majority in all city and county boards but the county election commission. One article quotes a professor of history at the University of Mississippi: "As long as you've got an economically dependent population, then you're always vulnerable to at least informal, unspoken or unrecognized pressures if you start to exercise your political rights."

Live In. A photographer and two reporters from *The Commercial Appeal* spent two months in one of the poorest communities in the country, Tunica, Miss. The team found residents living near an open ditch that carried off human waste, in homes that lacked electricity and plumbing. Teen-age pregnancy ran high, as did infant mortality. The infant mortality rate for blacks was 31; for whites nearby it was 11. Income was a third the national median, and most people relied on welfare and other government assistance. The reporter-photographer team found blacks warmed up to them, but whites were reserved, fearing bad publicity.

Photos by Jeff McAdory, The Commercial Appeal. Used with permission.

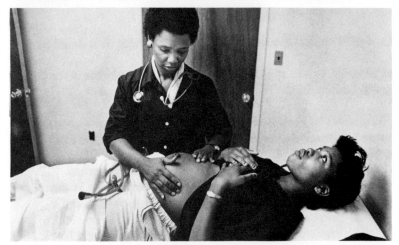

The news team found that most blacks were glad to see them, but whites in official positions declined to be interviewed. The officials complained that previous news reports had stirred up trouble.

Nevertheless, the reporters were able to dig deeply into the separate worlds of white and black. They interviewed well-to-do whites, teen-agers with two and three children, and they went to church:

Let us pray.

The Rev. Holmes looks familiar: short, mustache, receding hairline, brow furrowed in perpetual concern. Still, I can't place him. I interrupt his Sunday school lesson at the African Methodist Episcopal Church, slipping in the back door about 10:45; at the front of the room are Rev. Holmes and Brother Peace—a plump black man with a sonorous voice. Rev. Holmes smiles a greeting nervously, smelling reporter.

I take a seat by Jeff and Celeste in the second row. The first two or three pews are half-filled with small children and a few adults—mostly female. The girl's choir, The Sunbeams, is already seated behind the pulpit for 11 o'clock service.

We are asked to introduce ourselves—Celeste warned me this would happen.

Jeff stands up, smiling.

"Good morning. My name is Jeff McAdory, I'm visiting in Tunica and I'm happy to be able to worship with you here on this fine Lord's Day."

That's a tough act to follow. When my turn comes I just say my name.

Services start. They sing a lot—three songs right off the bat. The church is still only half full, but the singers aren't timid and the songs come off good and strong. An enormous woman in front of me sings a low harmony, while Mrs. Grant, the funeral director's wife, adds a fine soprano.

During Rev. Holmes' sermon he adopts a sing-song style of speaking I've never heard before, though Celeste says it's common in black churches. A sentence begins on a relatively high note, then drops a third at the final syllable—gaining resonance throughout and trembling with vibrato. It is like an impromptu song.

At the end of the service nearly everyone there seeks us out to shake hands and say "hello."

I leave feeling fine.

—Kevin Kittredge

Press attention helped. The shacks that many blacks lived in were replaced. The open ditch that carried off human waste along Sugar Ditch Alley cleared:

TUNICA, Miss.—Christine Bell's struggle to keep enough wood burning in a stove to warm her and her three children ended yesterday when the door opened to her new apartment at a housing project here. . . .

For some families, such as Andrew Jones and his wife, the new apartment means running water for the first time in 12 years. For others, such as Doris Moore and her 10-year-old son Adrian, it means the first living quarters they can call their own. . . .

Other Characteristics of the Journalist

Commitment

Some of those who become journalists do so because they have a strong urge to reveal injustices. Clearly, this was the motivation of *The Commercial Appeal*. A.M. Rosenthal, former executive editor of *The New York Times*, says most reporters are reformers. They have a deep sense of compassion. Unlike most people who are frustrated by their inability to do something about injustice, the journalist can. In this sense, journalism is a profession—like law or medicine—because it seeks to render public service.

Patricia McCormick and Herb Jackson of *The Home News* in New Brunswick, N.J., found a state parole system that was seriously flawed. They began their exposure with a lead based on a case study:

George Booker "seemed happy" according to the Sept. 3, 1985, entry in his parole officer's log book. He talked enthusiastically about the warehouse job he was due to start that week.

Two weeks later, he reportedly went on a rape, robbery and murder rampage.

Police say Booker, a convicted murderer, killed two young women, raped two other women—one of whom was 93—and ran over a man with a stolen car.

Only three months earlier, his parole officer had written a letter recommending that Booker's parole be revoked. Booker had been arrested for one assault and convicted in connection with another; his parole officer thought Booker was showing signs of a return to violence.

But because there was no typist in the New Brunswick parole office, the letter sat in a cardboard box for three months.

Even if the report had found its way to the proper authorities, it is likely that Booker would have remained free. In New Jersey, parolees can go back to crime and not go back to prison. If they do go astray, their parole officers are powerless to put them back behind bars.

No one knows how many George Bookers there are in New Jersey because no one keeps track of the crimes committed by people on parole. Moreover, when parolees go back to crime, no one can be held accountable.

The stories stirred state legislators to action. They decided to overhaul the state's criminal code and parole laws, and they re-examined a plan to give early release to 250 prisoners because of crowded prison conditions.

Listen to Mary Ann Giordano of the *Daily News* talk about the stories she wrote for her newspaper about a family caught in the coils of poverty and helplessness:

"It was cold in the eighth-floor office of the *Daily News* Brooklyn bureau. It was Sunday and the landlord doesn't usually give heat on the weekends. It was a bitter cold day—all the more painful because it was late in the winter and the freezing temperatures had been unexpected.

"As we tried to warm ourselves, my editor in Brooklyn suggested we do a story about a family without heat. Problem one was how to find one—not a very great problem since in Brooklyn that day there were untold numbers of people living without heat and hot water through the cold spell." Giordano obtained the name of a woman who called the city to complain she was without heat and hot water.

"Bedford-Stuyvesant was virtually deserted in the freeze. The stairway up to the Walker home was dark and creaky. But when I reached the Walker apartment, there was a startling warmth in the back kitchen where Marie Walker sat, water bubbling steadily around her and the stove door propped open.

"The Walkers were lively, cheerful, friendly people. Despite their hardships, they were able to joke about it. The children were well behaved, the apartment spotlessly clean.

"Through interviews with the family members and a quick check through some of their records, I was able to piece together an account of just how such nice people wound up living in an abandoned building with no heat, no hot water, no toilets, no locks on the doors—with rats and junkies as neighbors and fear an ever-present companion."

Giordano spent about two hours with the Walker family. They all sat bundled up in their coats in the front room, where a few rays of sunlight warmed the floor at their feet.

"I could now understand how they had fallen into this situation. And I had come to like the Walkers very much."

Giordano next had to think about a story. "Heading back to the office, I tried to organize my thoughts," she recalled. "I knew that describing the cold in the apartment was important, and showing how the Walkers coped with it was an essential ingredient of the story.

"I also knew that people would want to know why the Walkers were living that way, and I had to explain that, too.

"I had about 45 minutes to write the story when I returned to the office. The *News* ran the story as I wrote it, word for word."

Here is how Giordano's story began:

It is warm and bright in Marie Walker's kitchen. Four flames glow on the aging stove as a pot of water boils steadily. The door of the oven is open, and she sits in front of it, her sock-covered feet propped on the door as the gas heat warms her toes.

It is the only hot spot in the apartment, the only place in the entire building where warm breath does not send puffs of vapor into the air.

A thermometer in a front room, where the sun shines through a window, registers 52 degrees. That is warm, the Walker family says. Saturday it reached a high of 39 degrees inside.

It is so cold, the pipes burst in the four-story apartment building at 587 Gates Ave. in Bedford-Stuyvesant and the seven members of the Walker family must take turns drawing water from a hydrant on the street.

City officials responded to the Walkers' plight and promised to find public housing for them. Knowing how slowly the city wheels can turn, Giordano kept checking, and three weeks later wrote a second story that began:

> The plumbing is still broken, the heat is still out, the junkies and rats still roam freely through the lower floors, and the Walker family of Bedford-Stuyvesant is still looking for decent housing.
>
> Three weeks after an article appeared in the *Daily News* detailing the plight of the seven members of the Walker family, they are still trekking through the maze of housing regulations—cruel realities that confront New Yorkers searching for livable housing.

The second article brought action. "Within a short time, the Walkers were in better housing," Giordano said. "They faced last winter without fear of the cold and live today as safely as anyone does in New York."

This sense of accomplishment, the opportunity to be of service, is the greatest of all journalism's rewards.

Journalists are committed to fair play and equal treatment for all. For some, George Orwell, the British writer who sought to set things right-side-up in a crazily spinning world, is the perfect journalist. Orwell's journalism was on the side of decency, and his commitment made his writing vivid and forceful. He knew that to reach people, he had to make his writing clear and simple, though he often wrote about complex issues.

Orwell, who wrote *Animal Farm* and *1984*—novels that describe the horror of totalitarian governments—stressed independent thinking. He believed the journalist must never accept unquestioningly a line formulated by a party or an authority. The journalist must work things out for himself or herself.

Integrity

Journalists are faithful to the facts, whatever the consequences. When he was covering the Nixon administration for CBS television, Dan Rather was under enormous pressure to let up on his dogged coverage of the president.

He said later that the White House had a "journalistic goon squad" that pressured reporters who did not accept at face value the pronouncements from the president's office.

"If a truck runs over me tomorrow," he said once, "what I really would love to have someone tell my kids is that their father wouldn't buckle—not under Lyndon Johnson, not under Richard Nixon."

Toward the end of Ronald Reagan's presidency, when he was being pressed by reporters for details about sales of arms to Iran and funneling of money to Nicaraguan rebel soldiers, Reagan described reporters as "sons of bitches," and as "sharks" who sensed "blood in the water."

We live in a world of exaggeration and lies. A movie reviewer writes that a new motion picture is "spectacular." We pay $6 and find it no better than last month's so-so movie. A president says he knows nothing about a break-in, and a vice president swears he never received payoffs in office. Lies. The television comedies we watch have laughter fed into the sound track by machine. The producers do not trust us to find the humor and manufacture laughter when there is nothing funny. Advertisers praise their products, and we find the two-man rubber raft seats only two 5-year-olds comfortably, and the four-man raft is really suitable for two. The braking mechanism on the expensive new car is faulty and the model has to be recalled.

Honesty for the journalist extends to the use of language. News stories should be accurate, and no more exciting—through the manipulation of words—than the event itself.

The journalist is expected to tell truths, which requires digging beneath the surface to find the real story and then choosing appropriate words to describe it.

The journalist matches language to the event. If the meeting of the city council was routine, the news writer does not try to dramatize it with hyperactive prose.

In interviews with editors and reporters and in observations of them at work, dependability continually surfaces as an essential characteristic of the journalist. Dependability encompasses a number of traits:

Dependability, Initiative

Sent out on a story, the journalist works at it until it is fit for broadcast or print.The public depends on the journalist, as it does on all professionals, to do his or her best.

The journalist shows initiative in generating story ideas and is relentless and enterprising in pursuing a story. A few months after his graduation from Notre Dame, Phil Cackley was hired by *The Albuquerque Tribune* and given the University of New Mexico beat.

"When I got the beat, I didn't expect any major stories to result from it," Cackley said. "My first story was about a student who hatched a duck from an orphan egg."

But Cackley was a self-starter and digger. Within a few months, he had unearthed an academic scandal involving the athletic department. Cackley found that grades were being faked on the transcripts of certain athletes to maintain their eligibility to play.

In his reporting, Cackley had to be absolutely accurate. Editors depend on their reporters never to guess, to assume nothing, to verify as much as possible. Whether it is the spelling of a word, the address of someone in a story, or the charge filed against a person arrested in connection with a traffic death, the journalist checks, and checks again.

Unsafe Terrain

Courage is a trait journalists are called upon to muster, even though they don't talk about it much. When reporters were sent to the South to cover the civil rights protests, many were abused, and for some it was unsafe territory. Bill Minor, who covered Mississippi for more than 40 years, recalled what happened in 1961 when a bus terminal in McComb was desegregated under a federal court order.

Black freedom riders were on their way to town and as arrival time drew near "tension was thick as the Dixie dew," Minor said. In the July/August 1987 *Quill* he describes the incident in his piece "Mississippi Dateline":

I had gone into the office of the local newspaper, the McComb *Enterprise-Journal*, with three guys from *Time* and *Life* who were friends of mine. As we stepped out on the sidewalk to leave, four young toughs jumped us. They had apparently fingered the three *Life* and *Time* fellows and went after them, leaving me alone.

The toughest of the lot, whom I later learned was something of an amateur fighter, went after Simmons Fentress, then an Atlanta-based correspondent for *Time*, hitting him with full fist on the side of the head with a resounding smack. Fentress, somewhat amazingly, did not go down.

Meanwhile, two of the other hoodlums rammed Don Urbrock, a stocky writer for *Life* out of Miami, into a plate glass storefront with such force that the glass cracked and came sliding down like a guillotine blade. Urbrock managed to pull himself away just in time to avoid the pane of glass as it came crashing down; it would have sliced him in two if he had been a little slower.

As the four toughs ran away, I shouted to the storekeeper whose plate glass window had been smashed, asking him if he knew who they were. He shook his head and said, "I've never seen them before in my life." That was a lie, of course. The leader of the gang, at least, was well known around town.

(There's a poetic postscript to that incident: Two years later, I learned, the storekeeper was shot to death at a roadside tavern by the same tough guy he could not recognize as the one who slugged Simmons Fentress.)

Advice from the Consummate Comic

W. C. Fields, one of the greatest film comedians ever, seemed to be a natural comic.

Actually, he labored at his craft.

"Show me a comic who isn't a perfectionist and I'll show you a starving man," he said. "You have to sweat and toil and practice indefinitely. A comic should suffer as much over a single line as a man with a hernia would in picking up a heavy barbell."

The ability to work steadily at a task until it meets the highest level of a person's capabilities is another trait common to all who work creatively—writers, musicians, painters, designers, builders, dancers, actors, teachers. Ernest Hemingway labored over his sentences and paragraphs until he was satisfied. He would rewrite a paragraph time after time until it did his bidding.

Discipline

John McPhee, a *New Yorker* writer who describes himself as a "working journalist," walks into his office at 8:30 in the morning and leaves at 8:30 in the evening. He takes only a 90-minute break each day.

McPhee, considered one of the finest journalists in the country, disciplines himself to write.

"People want to be writers without writing," he says. Impossible. After he graduated from college he tried to write television plays. He was learning and so the task was arduous. The temptation to leave the typewriter was so great that he resorted to tying himself to a chair with his bathrobe sash.

Dan Rather enjoys hunting and fishing, but he has little time for recreation. "I work about 110 hours a week," he says. "It will eat you up, but if it doesn't you have a difficult time being good at it. I think you have to care that much."

In his autobiography, Anthony Trollope, the English novelist, says he wrote every day, although he held a full-time job for many years. Once, on his way to Egypt to help set up postal service between the Middle East and England, he became violently seasick. Between bouts of nausea, he managed to write more than a thousand words a day.

Skepticism

When Gerald Ford found himself in the presidency as the aftermath of the Watergate scandals, Washington reporters were concerned that he was not intellectually fit for the position. When their concern became manifest, Ford denied that he was too dumb to be president. He said he had finished in the upper third of his class. Whereupon reporters asked that he show them his college transcript.

Reporters learn early that sources sometimes shade the truth, can be misleading, and that now and then they intentionally lie. In the best of worlds, everyone would be forthright, honest, aboveboard. But the stakes are so high, the prizes so great in politics and the marketplace that deception and lying are sometimes standard procedure for those in business and in public office.

When Chrysler was accused of selling as new, automobiles that its executives had been driving, the president of the corporation, Lee Iacocca, denied the charge. Newspapers and broadcast stations carried his vehement denial, only—a few days later—to carry Chrysler's admission that it had been turning back the odometers on these cars.

Reporters learn to have faith in physical sources—their observations and in the documents and records they dig up. They learn to be wary of human sources—claims and assertions. Yet they must rely on their sources, for usually there is little time to check everything in the rush to print or to broadcast. They protect themselves by attributing material, but reporters know that readers and listeners tend to accept what they read and hear without making distinctions between what is attributed and what the reporter knows to be true.

As a result, reporters have a mental handbook of those who cannot be trusted. During the Vietnam War, reporters knew that the government was making claims of success that were untrue. Veteran hands at the front treated these news releases carefully. One day, the tale has it, a young reporter for a wire service sent out a story based on a government release about an engagement that was played on page one of *The New York Times,* to the dismay of the *Times'* regular war correspondent, Homer Bigart.

Bigart had seen the actual situation and knew the truth. He took the young reporter to the front. The handout had been dead wrong. Bigart told him: "That's what I wanted you to see—it isn't here."

Generally, reporters ignore material they know to be untrue, or they hold it until they can verify the information. Some material can never be checked. Records are sealed or do not exist; the people involved will not comment. Then the reporter's feel for news takes over.

Come On, Lynn

Sometimes a reporter's skepticism sees print. *People* magazine ran a piece about Lynn Armandt, who was the companion of a young woman who was Sen. Gary Hart's special friend on weekend yacht trips and at his Washington, D.C., townhouse. The relationship led to leading questions about Hart's sex life away from home and the collapse of his presidential candidacy.

People said Ms. Armandt felt she had to speak out. She was quoted by *People* as saying that her life "would never return to normal until I made a statement." Her declaration appeared in *People's* cover story, "Chronicle of a Ruinous Affair."

The Wall Street Journal wasn't buying Ms. Armandt's story about her reasons for telling all, or as much as she knew. Says the *Journal:*

> Her article fails to mention, however, another *small* reason she may have broken her silence—and why she chose *People* as the forum in which to do it. That is: *People* paid her $125,000 for the interview on which the story was based, according to *People* staffers. . . .
>
> Elizabeth Wagner, a spokeswoman for *People,* declined to comment on whether Ms. Armandt had been paid at all. Ms. Armandt, the proprietor of a bikini boutique near Miami, couldn't be reached for comment.

Skepticism is an ingredient of what reporters describe as their news sense or street smarts. They talk about a *feeling* that something is wrong, unsound, incorrect; they have a gut reaction or a sixth sense that tells them to check, to ask some questions, to look again at the material.

When confronted by information he or she senses is questionable, the standard procedure for the reporter is to ask the source for proof. If none is forthcoming, the reporter says so in his or her story.

Involvement

In their openness to new ideas, journalists become involved with people of all kinds. This is not accidental. Journalists are committed to involvement in the affairs of all people.

The news is where people are. News is found in factories and service stations, supermarkets and laundromats, unemployment offices and executive suites, schoolrooms and homes. By seeking out people with varied backgrounds, journalists can hear the heartbeat of their communities.

When Christopher Scanlan and Mark Patinkin of the *Journal-Bulletin* in Providence wanted to know about the black communities in Rhode Island, they set out on a series of interviews that took them into the offices of black lawyers and to the homes of welfare mothers. They spoke to merchants and hookers. They went to housing projects—monuments of despair to some of the tenants, models of hope to others.

All Kinds. The journalist finds news in classrooms, at the workplace and in homes. The reporter seeks out those who toil in the fields and factories, talks to young and old, the well-to-do and the poor. In this way, the journalist is able to give readers and viewers an insight into the community, to tell people how policies and programs affect human beings.

Bottom right, Joseph Noble, The Stuart (Fla.) News. All other photos by Ken Elkins, The Anniston (Ala.) Star.

Objectivity in news stories allows the reader to have the facts without the interference of the reporter's opinions, feelings, conclusions and guesswork. Despite their involvement in the affairs of other people, journalists must be able to distance themselves from the people and the events they are observing. This distance allows for better understanding and objectivity.

Garry Trudeau, the creator of the comic strip "Doonesbury," says that he is able to develop ideas for his work by being an outsider rather than by fraternizing with important people. Like the journalist, Trudeau says he wants his work to represent the outsider looking at the activities of people.

The journalist must be close enough—physically and emotionally—to his or her subject to understand what is being observed. At the same time, the journalist must maintain a certain distance to keep things in perspective.

Complete detachment is sometimes impossible. When 6-year-old Adam Walsh disappeared from the Sears department store in Hollywood, Fla., reporter Charlie Brennan of the *Sun-Tattler* decided to stay with the story, and his newspaper agreed.

Every day for two weeks Brennan's stories appeared on page one. In his stories, the 26-year-old reporter described the concern of the entire community and its attempts to find the child. Brennan kept in close touch with the parents, and each day he felt their grief and desperation increase.

Brennan accompanied the parents to New York for their appearance on a television show that discussed the disappearance of children throughout the country.

Three hours after the program, the telephone rang in the couple's hotel room. John Walsh took the call. It was from Florida. The search was over.

The remains of a child had been found floating in a canal, and the head was that of Adam Walsh.

Brennan was with Walsh when the news came.

"Oh Christ, Oh Christ, who could do this to my little boy?" the father cried. "Who could cut his head off?"

Brennan mourned with Walsh.

"It was absolutely the worst thing I've ever been associated with," Brennan said. "The parents will never be the same. I don't know if I'll ever be the same."

Of his involvement with the family and its tragedy, Brennan said, "Getting deeply involved was the only way to cover the story. To remain detached would have been inhuman."

Satisfaction . . .

In a study of reporters on Iowa daily newspapers, these sentiments emerged as the joys of the job:

We're beholden to nobody. This place has integrity.

I'm involved in what's going on in the community.

The camaraderie of the news staff.

Independence for creative writing.

Being where the action is.

Good discipline, effective on-the-job training.

Opportunity to express opinions on the editorial page.

The freedom of adventure a small newspaper affords.

The responsibility given to me and to each reporter by management.

. . . and Frustration

Charles M. Young is a worrier. He sweats and strains over his stories, never really happy about them. But his stories for *Rolling Stone* and other publications about rock groups and entertainers seem to flow like maple syrup over a short stack.

Despite his pain, Young enjoys writing. It is his affliction and his joy. His delight in language and his subjects is evident in his piece "Carly Simon, Life, Liberty and the Pursuit of Roast Beef Hash" that begins:

Most rock writers, it has been observed, would rather be the people they write about; that is, trade in their typewriters to scream nonsense at 20,000 rioting lude freaks while Keith Richard powerchords their brains into Cool Whip. Not me. I don't want to be Mick Jagger. Nor do I want to be Carly Simon and have millions of college students think dirty thoughts about my album covers. I don't even want to be James Taylor, who is married to Carly Simon.

I would trade it all to be Benjamin Taylor. Here is someone with a good deal in life; all Benjamin Taylor has to do is cry and Carly Simon sticks her breast in his mouth. The other 4 billion of us on earth could cry for the rest of our lives and Carly Simon would not stick her breast in our mouths.

Greater injustices have marred human history, I suppose, but I can't think of them right now, because Carly Simon has just placed her breast in Benjamin Taylor's mouth. He is having a good time. I am breaking into a cold sweat, wondering if it is obvious from ten feet away that my eyes are dropping from Carly Simon's face to her uplifted blouse every three seconds.

"This is beginning to look obscene," says Carly Simon in the living room of her huge ten-room Central Park West apartment. Benjamin, a cuter-than-hell miniature of James Taylor, is gymnastically curled around his dinner, which he is clutching with both hands and both feet, as well as his mouth.

For every upbeat, enjoyable event, the journalist encounters a situation that is offensive, embarrassing, gloomy, or heartbreaking.

Sarah Booth Conroy of *The Washington Post* remembers a particularly sad story she covered as a reporter in Tennessee for *The Knoxville News-Sentinel*. She was sent out to interview a young mother who had been stricken with polio just before Christmas. The woman had been placed in an iron lung to aid her breathing. Conroy's city editor wanted a story and pictures of her three small children wishing their mother a Merry Christmas.

"I was getting along fine," Conroy recalls, "until the children, all below table height, one by one mounted steps to kiss her face, all that was left outside the iron lung."

The city editor is king of his domain, the city staff, and Conroy recalls being told by her editor in the early 1950s, when she was starting out as a reporter, to interview the young wife of Vice President Alben Barkley, who was in his 70s. The Barkleys were visiting Knoxville a few months after their wedding.

"Find out if she's pregnant," the city editor instructed Conroy.

"I went with fear and trembling," Conroy says. "But I was more afraid of Mr. Levitt (the city editor) than Mrs. Barkley."

"She looked appalled by my question," Conroy says. Mrs. Barkley asked her, "Why do you ask?"

"Because my city editor told me to," she replied.

"Go back and tell him," Mrs. Barkley said softly, "I think he must be a horrid man to send a nice little girl like you to ask a question like that."

In Liberia to do stories about the work of missionaries from the Southwestern Baptist Theological Seminary, the reporter-photographer team for the *Fort Worth Star-Telegram* was suddenly thrust into history's cauldron.

Liberia had erupted with savage violence. A young soldier, Master Sergeant Samuel K. Doe, had led his troops in a military coup. Under Doe's command, soldiers had assassinated the president and then set about eliminating the country's leaders.

The executions were to be carried out on a hot afternoon on a Liberian beach, and the press was invited.

Larry C. Price, the photographer, and Paul Rowan, the reporter, made their way to the beach where thick, sturdy posts 10 feet high were being placed in the white sand. As the posts were being adjusted, Price broke away from the knot of newsmen gathered 100 yards from the beach. Alone, he walked toward the posts anchored in the sand. As he walked, he snapped pictures. The heavily armed soldiers watched him but did nothing.

Rowan edged closer and took notes. The number of posts grew, Rowan noted on his pad, from four to five, from five to seven, seven to nine. In the middle of the work stood the 27-year-old photographer, snapping pictures.

The men were then brought out.

© Larry C. Price/Fort Worth Star-Telegram

© Larry C. Price/Fort Worth Star-Telegram

© Larry C. Price/Fort Worth Star-Telegram

Witness To History

Photographer Larry C. Price stood so close to soldiers in the firing squad on a Liberian beach that an ejected shell casing struck his cheek. "The central thing in photojournalism is that you have to get it when it happens," he said. "There are no second chances. If you miss the shot, it's gone forever." These photos won Price the first of two Pulitzer Prizes for his photography.

Journalists in Action

© Larry C. Price/Fort Worth Star-Telegram

© Larry C. Price/Fort Worth Star-Telegram

"They tied nine men, old-looking men, paunchy, gray-haired men, to the posts," Rowan wrote.

Then the shots rang out, and the bodies began to crumple into the sand. Price was so close an ejected shell casing struck him.

He continued to take pictures.

Price's photographs of the deaths of the old rulers won the 1981 Pulitzer Prize for spot news photography. The pictures are horrifying, a grim record of men calculating the death of fellow men, and the moment of death.

Price and Rowan were appalled by what they saw. But their job was to record for their readers, and for history, the momentous event.

"I'm certainly not coldhearted," Price said later. "Taking pictures of tragedy does affect me."

Journalists are witnesses to life's tragedies—sudden death in the afternoon, a youngster mangled beneath the wreckage of his motorcycle, a young mother immobilized by crippling disease and confined to an iron lung.

But the journalist endures. Journalism has been called history in a hurry. Though they laugh off such descriptions, journalists know theirs is an important and serious task that demands self-control and self-discipline.

Some Realities

"When my office sued a car dealer who had violated our state's advertising laws—clearly a news story of interest to the state's consumers—one Connecticut radio station spiked the story for fear of alienating one of its major advertisers, the car dealership in question."— Joseph Lieberman, former attorney general of Connecticut.

For all the excitement and its dedication to the values of a free and open society, there is a basic restraint in journalism—it is a commercial enterprise. It survives through the sale of space and time to advertisers. The consequence is that many publishers and some editors pay more attention to the ledger than to the news. Increasingly, as newspapers and broadcast networks and stations become part of big business, the pressure from investors tilts news coverage. Stockholders want larger and larger dividends.

Rarely is there direct pressure to include or exclude certain news. There is, though, pressure to reduce news staffs, to rely on press releases rather than staff reporters, to give advertisers more space and time, cutting into news space and time, and to emphasize entertainment at the expense of news.

The student thinking of a career in journalism should understand this and more: Much of the journalism of conscience is not rewarded by change. People often ignore what to the journalist is an obvious wrong. They return incompetents, sometimes convicted criminals, to office. They tolerate an educational or criminal justice system that does not work.

Despite newsroom politics—which can be bloody—publisher greed and public indifference, journalism can do good, as we have seen, and it continues to attract young men and women of conscience and ability.

One of the realities of preparing for a profession is the job market. For the well-trained person, there is always a job—not at the top of the heap at once, but with a small or medium-sized station or newspaper. Employers are always looking out for the young man or woman who has basic competences and is willing to work at a variety of tasks.

Starting small is the best preparation for ending big. That's the advice of editors and veteran journalists. In a good small organization, the beginner has an opportunity to learn all aspects of the job.

"Working on a smaller paper and covering the police, the board of education and the council is invaluable experience," says Clyde Haberman, a foreign correspondent for *The New York Times*. "At one time or another there will be a fire in Tokyo, or there will be an earthquake, and what is needed out of me then is not someone who is a student of history or language, but someone who has covered a fire in his day, and someone who knows how to cover people in situations having to deal with tragedy. It doesn't make a difference if it's happening in Tokyo or Newark."

Each year, about 10,000 college graduates are hired by newspapers, broadcast stations, advertising agencies and public relations firms. About three-fourths of the jobs go to journalism graduates.

Of those hired by newspapers and wire services, 60 percent were news-editorial majors, 12 percent advertising majors, 7 percent public relations majors.

For every job offer, there were 1.5 news-editorial graduates; for broadcast, one job for two graduates.

Median starting salaries:

Daily newspapers—$13,900

Radio and television—$12,600

With experience, salaries go up and up. Reporters on large metropolitan newspapers that have contracts with the Newspaper Guild receive salaries upwards of $700 a week. The pay is similar at broadcast stations in the major markets.

Editors of large newspapers and managers of large stations are paid $75,000–100,000 a year. Executives of all these organizations earn $250,000–500,000 a year, and we all know of the million-dollar contracts of network anchors.

Over the past 10 years the number of journalism graduates who found jobs in print journalism has stayed about the same, whereas the number who took jobs in public relations and advertising nearly doubled. Enrollment in journalism schools and departments reflects these job opportunities.

Women

Women are majoring in these fields in increasing numbers, and employment follows the same pattern. A majority of all journalism school majors are women, with public relations showing 70 percent of majors as women. For the other fields, the figure is about 60 percent.

Women are heavily represented on the smaller newspapers. The number of women on the larger newspapers is significantly smaller. Only 10 of every 100 editors and news executives are women, most of them on newspapers with circulations under 25,000. The same is true of radio and television stations. The situation is gradually improving, partly as a result of lawsuits brought by female journalists who charged they were discriminated against in promotions and salaries. *The New York Times* and *The Washington Post,* for example, agreed in out-of-court settlements to put more women in managerial positions.

Minorities

The Associated Press Managing Editors organization surveyed 600 newspapers and found that 13 percent of the new reporters hired in 1985 were members of minority groups. The APME found that the large newspapers—newspapers with circulations of more than 150,000—are hiring minority entry-level journalists at a 40 percent rate.

"The route of entry of minority journalists differs from that of others," the APME says. "The majority of whites who get into the newsroom start at smaller newspapers. Minorities tend to get to larger papers more quickly."

The Dow Jones Newspaper Fund study of 1986 hiring found that 13.4 percent of those hired by daily newspapers were members of minority groups. Public relations firms hired 10.3 percent and advertising agencies 3.1 percent. The figure for television was 7.2 percent. The percentages continued at these levels in the late 1980's.

The effort to hire black, Hispanic and Asian journalists began in the 1960s in reponse to the civil rights movement. Over the next decade, minority employment increased by 35 percent. In the 1960s, minority employment in newspaper editorial positions was estimated at 1 percent of the total. The figure stands at about 6 percent today, still too low to suit many in journalism. Almost two-thirds of the nation's newspapers employ no members of minority groups, and 90 percent have none in executive news positions.

Newspaper Chains

Most newspapers and many radio and television stations are owned by companies that have several media properties. Of the 1,675 daily newspapers, almost 1,200 are owned by chains, newspaper groups that own more than one newspaper.

The chains sell 50 million papers every day, which is 80 percent of total daily paid circulation. The chains with the largest circulations are Knight-Ridder, 3.8 million, and the Gannett Company, which has 4.7 million circulation of its more than 120 daily, semi-weekly and weekly newspapers.

(Don't confuse buyers and readers. The circulation of a newspaper indicates buyers. For every buyer, though, one to two others read the newspaper that was purchased.)

The chains are aggressive buyers of newspapers, and some press critics contend that should the trend of group ownership continue, absentee ownership will mean less sensitivity to local affairs and greater concern with profits.

A Job Tryout

Graduates who have tried out for jobs say that the best preparation is to master the kind of writing the field demands. Most employers give applicants a writing test. They look for accuracy, clarity, brevity and focus. The piece must be well organized also.

Let's look at the experience of a young man who got over the first hurdle of the newspaper's test and was put on the job on probation. We focus on a luncheonette in Gloucester, Mass., where a young man is eating a sandwich. His name is Nicholas Trowbridge and he is recalling for a friend his first few days on the local daily, *The Gloucester Times.* He had just graduated from college, where he had worked on his college weekly.

"I had a three-day tryout for the job," he recalls. "The editor had told me it would be two days, and by the third day the one suit I had needed cleaning.

"The first day had been a disaster. I was told to condense five stories to capsule length. After two hours, I had five two-page stories.

"The boss looked at them and said, 'When I said brief I meant two grafs, not two pages.'

"When the third day came and the paper's veteran reporter suggested I do a sidebar to go along with his story on a mayoral election debate at the local Legion Hall, I knew this was it.

"My assignment was to talk to people in the bar downstairs and ask them why they weren't upstairs listening to the debate. The reporter introduced me to the bartender and went upstairs.

The Wise Guys

"I talked to a few of the regulars at the bar and had the beginnings of a story. Then I ran into the wise guys.

"They were playing pool in one of the rooms off the bar, and after I identified myself, one turned to me and said, 'You're new, aren't you?'

"When I told him I hadn't even been hired yet, that I was on trial, he said, 'Well if you want the job, the big story's in the bar. Jack's his name and he set a record last week.'

"The record, they told me with complete sincerity and honesty, was for not going to the toilet. It was going to be published in the *Guinness Book of World Records,* they said.

" 'Come on, you're kidding me,' I laughed.

"They assured me it was no lie. Jack had survived on water, vitamins and beer during the long wait.

"I went into the bar and asked if Jack was in.

" 'Why do you want Jack?' one woman asked as she cradled a Seven-and-Seven between her forearms.

" 'I hear he set a record, he's the one who didn't go . . . uh, forget it,' I stammered. 'Why aren't you upstairs, listening to the politicians at the debate?'

" 'One's an idiot and one's retarded,' she answered." "No, that's not it, they're both retarded.'

"I put the quote high in my story and the editor ran it on page one. The next day he told me I had the job and said I could thank the woman in the bar for it. A few days later the paper received an angry letter on my story from one of the two mayoral aspirants who claimed the story was derogatory to those with mental handicaps.

"But it's lucky my story wasn't about a mythical Jack who avoided the call of nature for a record number of days. Had it been, I'd probably still be wandering through the South in search of a job, hitching with truckers through an endless succession of roadside truck stops and interviews."

Lost in the Crowd

A few weeks later, a wiser and tougher reporter—he thought—he was assigned to go to Boston with a busload of parishioners who were going to see the Pope during his U.S. tour. He met the people at 7 a.m. in front of a local church and a short time later in Boston they split into four groups to walk to Boston Common, where the Pope was to celebrate Mass.

"I decided to stick with the largest group for the day, listen to their comments, watch their reaction to the Pope.

"On the way to the park, I ducked out for a cup of coffee. When I got out of the coffee shop, the group was gone.

"I raced to the Common. They were lost in a sea of people. After a two-hour search, I realized I was wasting my time.

"I went to a pay phone and called the boss, collect.

" 'I've lost them,' I said.

" 'Lost who, Nick?'

" 'The parishioners from St. Ann's. I went into this place to get some coffee, and when I came out they were gone, vanished,' I told him, thinking that his advice would be to head south to look for another job.

" 'Nick lost the parishioners and he's looking for them on Boston Common,' I could hear him telling the staff.

"I could hear laughter in the newsroom.

" 'Don't worry,' he told me. 'Just get some good quotes on the bus on the way back.

" 'And don't miss the bus.'

" 'No problem,' I told him. 'I've got it under control.' "

The young reporter's self-assurance may seem to have been built on a foundation of toothpicks. But he managed to hold his job and to do well.

We are now ready to take up the job of writing the news and to look at some specific areas of coverage for journalists.

Some tips: The AP advises new reporters to be on time, to dress properly and to stay in touch with the desk while on assignment. When answering the telephone, give the name of the paper or station, your name, and add: "May I help you?"

Berkow, Ira. *Red: A Biography of Red Smith*. New York: Times Books, 1986.

Chancellor, John and Walter R. Mears. *The News Business*. New York: Harper and Row, 1983.

Crouse, Timothy. *The Boys on the Bus*. New York: Random House, 1973.

Mills, Kay. *A Place in the News: Women's Pages to the Front Page*. New York: Dodd, Mead, 1988.

Scanlan, Christopher. *How I Wrote the Story*. Providence, R.I.: Providence Journal Co., 1986.

Sheean, Vincent. *Personal History*. Boston: Houghton Mifflin Co., 1969.

Steffens, Lincoln. *The Autobiography of Lincoln Steffens*. New York: Harcourt, Brace and Co., Inc., 1931.

Suggested Reading

Part Two
Writing

3

Making of the Story

News has been defined as a break in the normal flow of events, an action or statement so important or unusual that it is worth sharing with others. Airplane crashes, annual budgets, election results, fires and floods make news. This picture of California flooding and the accompanying story was page 1 news in *The San Francisco Examiner*.
Photo by Craig Lee of The San Francisco Examiner. Used with permission.

Looking Ahead

Before we can write a story we need to know what is newsworthy, what makes an event worth writing about, and what aspects of the event should be emphasized. In brief, we have to develop something called news sense.

Reporters agree that the news value of an event can be judged by its **impact** or **consequences,** whether the event is **unusual** and whether the people involved in the event are well-known or **prominent.**

Other factors can increase or diminish the news value of the event—**conflict,** the **proximity** of the event to those we are writing for, **timeliness** and **currency,** whether people are still interested in the event even though it may not be new.

We will see how a story is written, the decisions that are made about how to begin it and whether the story is to be a straight news account or a feature. Finally, we'll look at the rudiments of well-written, reliable writing.

Our examination of the news story begins in a stately old building, the county courthouse. On the second floor, in a large room filled with metal file cabinets, a young woman is standing at a long counter looking over some documents. She is the county courthouse reporter for the local newspaper.

The reporter has two piles of paper in front of her. One, much larger than the other, consists of court documents that she has looked through for news and has rejected. The other pile includes material she has set aside to take notes from for news stories.

She is going through the day's records at a rapid pace, but the drawer in which the damage suits, pleadings and other documents are filed contains still more papers. At one sheaf of papers, she hesitates, then studies the pages closely. She tosses the document on her newsworthy pile. A co-worker, a new reporter learning the beat, asks her why she decided to take a second look at the document.

"It seems to be important," she answers. "On this beat, you have to make decisions quickly or you'll be snowed under and never have time to write.

"I have two guides I use to separate material. Either the material is important or it's so unusual that it will make an interesting story.

"This one is important because it is a request by a big developer to have the court force the county to issue a building permit for a shopping mall north of town."

She picks up two pages stapled together from her pile of possible news stories.

"Here's one that isn't important at all. But it will make a good little story. It's wild."

The papers describe a suit for damages of several thousand dollars by a woman who accused a department store Santa Claus of slapping her 6-year-old son.

"Whoever heard of someone suing Santa Claus?" she says. "This is the kind of story readers enjoy."

That evening, the novice reporter thought about what the courthouse reporter told him. He had recently graduated from college and was being given a tryout by the newspaper. He realized that all his training in how to write would not amount to much unless he could distinguish between what is newsworthy and what isn't.

He wrote down two definitions:

1. News is material that the public must have because it's important.
2. News is material that is entertaining, that is fun to read.

He recalled reading something that illustrated his first definition of news:
News is information that helps people solve their problems intelligently.

But what about the second category of news, entertainment? Well, as his grandfather used to say, man does not live by bread alone—he has to have an occasional delicacy.

What Is News?

A rule of thumb for determining what is newsworthy: The smaller the community or the audience, the greater the amount of personal news. Local radio stations in small towns broadcast all births, and newspapers in small cities publish not only all births but also all deaths, hospital admissions, court cases, marriages, divorces, club meetings and the names of all who graduate from high school.

The courthouse reporter's guidelines are helpful in figuring out what makes news. Another way to determine what makes news is to examine newspapers and the transcripts of newscasts. If we were to do this, we would find that news falls into three general categories.

Three Basic Determinants of News

Most news stories (1) are about events that have an **impact** on many people, (2) describe **unusual** or exceptional situations or events, or (3) are about widely known or **prominent** people. The length of a news story is usually determined by the number of people affected by the event and/or the number of people interested in the event.

Impact/ Consequence

By impact, we mean importance or significance. One way to judge impact is to figure out what the results or consequences of a news story about the event might be. If many people will be affected, then the reporter knows that the event is important enough for a news story.

Impact. The battleship *USS Arizona* burns after being struck by Japanese bombers on Dec. 7, 1941. The surprise attack caught the Pacific fleet at its base in Pearl Harbor. More than 1,100 men were entombed in the ship.
U.S. Navy Photograph.

One of the oldest definitions of news says that when a dog bites a man, it isn't news, but when a man bites a dog, it's news. The interruption in the expected, the different, makes news. If something makes a reporter stop and stare, wonder, exclaim, then the reporter knows that what he or she is looking at is newsworthy.

News Is. . .

"News is what interests a good newspaperman."—Gerald Johnson, *The Sun,* Baltimore.

"News is anything that will make people talk."—Charles A. Dana, editor, *New York Sun,* 1869–97.

"News is anything that makes the reader say, 'Gee whiz.' "—Arthur McEwen, longtime editor.

Journalists, like historians, prefer dramatic events to the "great constants of the human condition—birth, childhood, marriage, old age and death."—Robert Darnton, professor of history, Princeton University.

Unusual events, actions or statements that make us stop and shake our heads in wonder or puzzlement are newsworthy. All news is a deviation from the expected, a shift from what we consider the usual, the average, the ordinary. But when the event is so unexpected, when it deviates so far from the possible—then we have the bizarre. And the bizarre makes good features.
Joel Librizzi, The Berkshire Eagle.

The prominent are newsworthy. We like to read about the famous and the well known. Here, Patti Hayden congratulates her husband, Mike, who has just been elected governor of Kansas.
Photo by Charlie Riedel of The Hays Daily News. Used with permission.

Prominence

People who are widely known or who have positions of authority are said to be prominent. These are the newsmakers of our community and country. They may be politicians or car dealers, priests or labor leaders, entertainers or cabinet members. If you recognize the name and think your readers will, chances are that the person is prominent. What prominent people do, even if unimportant, is often newsworthy. Names make news.

A Yale historian, Peter Gay, says that the "fundamental building blocks of the human experience" are "love, aggression and conflict."

People like to read about those in the spotlight, whatever they might do. When the president has a cold, the governor spends a week in Wyoming fishing, a television talk show host has an argument in a night club—all this becomes news. People are inquisitive and enjoy reading about the personal lives of the famous.

More Determinants

We need to examine four other factors that heighten the news value of an event: **conflict, proximity, timeliness** and **currency.**

Conflict

Conflict underlies our lives. There are internal conflicts we are all familiar with. The student must master a list of Spanish verbs for a test the following day, but his friends are leaving for a movie. Conflict. The car owner notices that his car is slow to start. The battery is running down. A new battery will cost $75. He has the money, but he had planned to use it for a special set of tools he saw advertised. Conflict.

Almost every meeting of the city council, state legislature or Congress involves conflicts. The U.S. Constitution purposely sets governmental powers in conflict so that no one branch of government can dominate the others.

56   Writing

Conflict. People battle each other, and they fight the elements. Conflict is a constant in life. After the U.S. Supreme Court declared school segregation unconstitutional, violence erupted in some cities in the South. When black youngsters tried to enter Central High School in Little Rock, whites attacked the parents and friends who accompanied black children to school (top).

Man's battle against an inhospitable nature is symbolized in this famous photograph of a farm family in Cimarron County, Okla., during the 1930s when drought ravaged the land and created the Dust Bowl. *Top, Wilmer Counts, The Arkansas Democrat; bottom, Arthur Rothstein, courtesy of the Library of Congress.*

Probably because we are so familiar with strife we overlook its drama except for the most obvious confrontations: strikes, political campaigns, wrongdoers and police, wars.

Less-evident conflicts are newsworthy too: the struggles of individuals against adversity, the woman trying to hold a family together on $100 a week, the historian with a view of Thomas Jefferson that conflicts with the established perception, the handicapped youngster trying to play baseball. Some of the best stories a reporter can dig up are the attempts by groups, organizations or individuals to contest prevailing attitudes. When women first banded together to protest what they called a sexist society, few reporters paid attention. In fact, the women were ridiculed as "bra burners." The few reporters who recognized the movement became acquainted at the outset with what was to become a massive and effective drive for sexual equality.

Proximity. We feel close to people we know and to events with which we are familiar. In the farm country of western Kansas, the wheat harvest is big news. Everywhere, money is a familar subject, and it is the topic of two of the front-page stories in *The Hays Daily News.*

Front page from The Hays Daily News. Used with permission.

"Anything that is close to my readers or listeners is more important than something remote." This is how one reporter defines proximity. When sociology students at the local college stage mock marriages for a class project, that's news in a local newspaper. It's of no interest to newspaper readers in a neighboring state, unless one of the couples decides to elope there.

Proximity usually refers to something physically or geographically close. A fatal accident at an intersection near town interests local readers, but is of no interest to people 100 miles away.

Proximity has another meaning. People feel attached to those like themselves and to those with whom they share common interests. Catholics want to read about the activities of the Pope, and many Jews are interested in events in Israel. When a plane crashes in Cyprus, people in the United States wonder whether any Americans were aboard. They have an attachment to fellow cit-

---

Prominence and Proximity—Willie Nelson and Distant Death

The United Press International ran these two stories on its major news wire on the same day.

```
     LOUISVILLE, KY. (UPI)--Country music
singer Willie Nelson canceled his scheduled
appearance Saturday night at the Kentucky
State Fair's closing concert because he is
hospitalized with a lung ailment.
     Julie Shaw, Manager of the 10-day fair,
said Sunday that Nelson--the top drawing card
at last year's fair--had been hospitalized in
another state for a serious respiratory
ailment.
     Mrs. Shaw said she hoped to announce
today a replacement for Nelson.
     10:21 AED
```

The story above is not important, but Nelson's **prominence** led the UPI to give it this much space on its wire.

The following story is certainly more important than the illness of a country music singer, but its impact is diminished by its lack of **proximity** to readers in the United States. UPI gave it half the length of the Willie Nelson story.

```
     NEW DELHI, INDIA (UPI)--A bus fell into
a canal today in the northern state of
Kashmir killing 22 people, the Press Trust of
India reported.
     The accident occurred near Pahalgaon,
about 400 miles northwest of New Delhi.
```

Timeliness. Readers and listeners want to know the latest from Washington and Moscow, and they want to have the details about the boating accident on a nearby lake this morning. The more timely the news, the greater its news value.
Photo by Greg Lovett. Used with permission.

Loneliness is one of the continuing themes of modern life. People feel distant from neighbors, even their families. Loneliness is a theme that never loses its currency.
Photo copyright by Joel Strasser. Used with permission.

izens, even though the event was thousands of miles away. In carrying the event, newspapers and broadcast stations will tell readers and listeners whether any Americans were aboard. The fewer the number of Americans, the less important the story will be in the United States.

Timeliness

We always want to know the latest. We march to the minute hand on the clock. Our all-news radio stations, our newspapers and our television stations rattle out a drumfire of news for us. We awake to the morning news, and we eat lunch to news and music. Driving to and from school or work, the news is with us in our cars.

News has a short lifespan in this barrage. What occurs today has greater impact than an event that occurred a week ago, even if that event was not reported at that time. To impress their readers with the timeliness of their stories, news writers usually put the word *today* in their leads.

Some situations are always interesting, though. We have a continuing interest in matters that affect us, and reporters know this. This takes us to the last of our news determinants.

> **"When people wake** up in the morning, they want to know who died last night and whether it's going to rain. It's always been that way."—Reuven Frank, television news pioneer.

Currency

The care and education of children is one of these continuing concerns of people. The efforts to make schools more demanding, for example, have been the subject of stories for a decade. Injustice, health, money—stories that relate to these timeless themes are usually newsworthy.

What people talk about makes news. Reporters who are good listeners and who frequent the places where people gather are likely to discover news that fits into the category of currency. A reporter for a California newspaper who was taking a break from a political convention sat in the hotel lobby and overheard delegates chatting. They were not talking about any of the items on the agenda; nor were they exchanging political gossip. What concerned them was the rising property tax.

The reporter kept the discussion in the back of his mind and the following week when he had time he looked into it. He was able to gather information from a number of cities and wrote a series that predicted what later became known as the taxpayers' revolt in California.

Generally, important stories use the straight news form. That is, the story begins with the most important fact or facts, the information that the reporter considers to be the crux of the event.

The ability to write straight news stories is essential to the beginning reporter. No editor will hire the beginner whose only ability is feature writing. Look at the newspaper; listen to the newscast. For every feature story, there are five or more straight news stories.

We have now sketched out the seven determinants of news: impact, the unusual, prominence, conflict, proximity, timeliness and currency. As we have pointed out, the first three are the most important. The other four extend or diminish the news value of an event by their presence or absence.

The Guide: Importance

The single most important guide to whether something is worth a news story is its importance to the public. The writer might ask: Does it meet the "primary purpose" of journalism? This purpose is described by the American Society of Newspaper Editors in "A Statement of Principles" this way:

> The primary purpose of gathering and distributing news and opinion
> is to serve the general welfare by informing the people and enabling them
> to make judgments on the issues of the time.

Obviously, not everything in newspapers or on newscasts is about a matter of great consequence. Newspapers, radio and television stations and newsmagazines try to reach a large audience of different needs and tastes. Still, if a study were to be made of the newspapers, stations and magazines we consider the best, we would find most of their articles to be about important issues.

A bit of advice at this point: Learning to differentiate the important from the inconsequential, the unusual from the ordinary, and the prominent from the little-known comes with experience. Reporters learn from reading newspapers, listening to newscasts and seeing how the professionals handle news. Every reporter sooner or later develops what is called news sense. Without this news sense, a journalist cannot function.

Writing the Story

We are now ready to use these news determinants or news values to write news stories. But first, let's stop in at a newsroom in California where the city editor is striding past the desks of reporters and editors like the captain walking the deck of a man-of-war. Although he holds no lash, only some papers, George's steely eyes and rasping voice make all hands squirm. George is one of the last of the old-fashioned city editors who believe that might is right.

The final edition has been put to bed and reporters are looking it over. George spots one reporter, a new man, who is sitting at his desk and staring at the ceiling.

"What do you think you're doing?" George snarls.

"Thinking, George," the reporter answers calmly.

"You're paid to write, not think," George shoots back.

"George, you can't write if you can't think," says the reporter, and he resumes his communion with the ceiling.

For the first time in the memory of the oldest reporter on the staff, George is speechless. His mouth opens, shuts. Opens. Shuts. George walks back to his desk, sits down, stares out a window.

They say in that newsroom that on that fateful day George had come across something so true, so profound—for him—that he ceased his thunderous newsroom wanderings thereafter.

The reporter knew what he was talking about. Clear thinking underlies clear writing.

Before a reporter can write, he or she must have some kind of plan. Before writing, the reporter must ask:

1. What's the main point or focus of the story? What's the event about?

2. Does this event make for a straight news story or a feature story?

3. What kind of lead should I put on the story, a direct or a delayed lead?

4. If this is a straight news story and I put a direct lead on it, what major fact should I place in the lead?

5. If this is a feature story and I use a delayed lead, what anecdote or illustration will I use at the beginning to lure the reader into the story?

6. How do I structure the piece? What goes where?

This may look as intricate as the preparations a surgeon makes before complicated brain surgery. Far from it. In fact, with practice the steps become automatic. And some stories seem to write themselves, even for the most inexperienced writer. But for now, keep this process in mind before writing.

Finding the Focus

What's this all about? the writer asks. It may come as a surprise to the beginner to be told that this question is asked even before the reporter goes out on the assignment, as soon as he or she is told about the event. The reason is that the reporter wants a jump on the story, what reporters call a *handle* on the event. The sooner the reporter has some idea of what's going on, what to expect, the better.

Boiled down to its essentials, every story is about either:

1. A **person** who has said or done something important or interesting, or a **person** to whom something important or interesting has happened.

2. An **event** of importance or interest to many people.

The beginning of the news story, or **lead,** usually summarizes the main theme of the story. Look at a batch of news stories. Almost all of them will begin with a lead that answers one of these two questions:

1. **Who** said or did what? What was it that happened to the **person**?

2. **What** happened?

This takes us to the heart of news writing. When a reporter sits down to write, there are almost always two choices:

1. If a person is central to the event, the writer answers the question: **What did the person say or do; what happened to the person?**

2. When the event is important or unusual, the writer answers the question: **What happened of significance or was exceptional or unusual?**

Look closely at the numbered items and you will see that they embody the three key news determinants—impact or consequence; the unusual, and prominence.

"When I was in college I believed that inspiration sat on your shoulder. I think that a lot less now. The most important thing in the story is finding the central idea. It's one thing to be given a topic, but you have to find the idea or the concept within that topic. Once you find that idea or thread, all the other anecdotes, illustrations and quotes are pearls that you hang on this thread. The thread may seem very humble, the pearls may seem very flashy, but it's still the thread that makes the necklace."—Thomas Boswell, *The Washington Post*.

Focus on Person. When the news event involves a prominent person, the news story focuses on that person's statements or actions. A routine event that would not be newsworthy becomes newsworthy if a well-known person, like Prince, is involved. But the event is newsworthy only in newspapers and magazines or on programs whose audience knows who the person is.
Jeff Katz, Warner Bros. Photograph of Prince used with permission.

When the event involves an individual saying or doing something, or when the individual has something happen to him or her, the writer first must decide whether readers and listeners recognize the name.

Focusing on the Person

Is the singer Michael Jackson or Ralph Martin? If it is Jackson, most people will recognize the name, and "Jackson" will go into the lead. If it is Martin, few will know that name, and some kind of **identifying label** will have to be used: "A 26-year-old rock singer," for example.

Here are some leads using the **name** of the person involved in the news event:

Who? (name) **did what?**

MALDEN, Mass. (AP)— *Malden Police Commissioner William A. Davidson* yesterday *ordered two police officers fired* after they arrested him for drunk driving.

Who? (name) **said what?**

SPRINGFIELD—*Chancellor William E. Barnes told* entering freshmen today *the way to academic success is through "unstinting effort."*

If the person central to the event is not well known to the news writer's audience, a label must be used that allows the reader or listener to quickly visualize the person. Sometimes, the label is **age** and **address** or **home town:**

Who? (label) **had something happen to him?**

A 39-year-old Kansas City, Kansas, man was charged Monday in Wyandotte County District Court *with the fatal shooting* early Saturday *of a patron* at a tavern in that city.

—*Kansas City Times*

The label can also be the **occupation** of the person:

Who? (label) **had something happen to him?**

A Kentucky State Police detective was *shot to death* yesterday afternoon while searching for marijuana in a field in rural Edmonson County.

—*Lexington* (Ky.) *Herald*

A person's **title** may be used as the identifying label. This is common on radio and television news:

Who? (label) **did what?**

The administrator of a defunct Brooklyn health-care corporation was indicted yesterday *on charges of failing to file state income tax returns* from 1984 to 1987.

—*The New York Times*

When the person's **connection to the event** identifies him or her, that relationship can be used as the identifying label:

Who? (label) **had something happen to him?**

HOUSTON (UPI)—*A Rolling Stones fan was stabbed to death* during the British rock group's near-sellout show at the Astrodome, police said Thursday.

Focusing on the Event

When **the event** is the most important aspect of the story, the writer uses the lead to describe what occurred in the briefest way possible:

What happened?

A supply ship was blown to bits today when it hit a mine in the Gulf of Oman.
—"NBC Nightly News"

What happened?

THROOP, Pa. (AP)—*Eight teenage party-goers were crushed to death* when their car swerved into a guard rail, plunged some 190 feet through the air and crashed on its roof, officials said Friday.

What happened?

CHICAGO (AP)—*DePaul University's student newspaper was shut down* Friday after printing a story about a rape on campus, in defiance of orders from the director of student publications, the editor said.

Notice that these are all straight news leads. This is the type of story the reporter most frequently writes, and its mastery is important. Sometimes, though, the event is unusual, perhaps freakish. In such cases the reporter writes another type of story.

A story takes its form from its purpose. If the purpose is to tell people quickly about an important event, then the reporter writes a spot news story. If the purpose is to entertain, the reporter writes a feature story. Each type of story has a different kind of lead and structure.

Feature or News Story?

Let's imagine that you have been told about a fire that damaged a student hangout, the Pork Parlor, located near the campus. You are to write a story for class. You gather information from the fire department and the owner. Here is the story you write:

```
    A favorite student dining spot, the Pork Parlor, at
150 College Lane, was damaged today by a fire that
started in the kitchen.
    The fire destroyed the kitchen and caused some
damage in the dining area. Fire department officials
said fat in a frying pan caught fire at around 6:30
a.m.
    The fire was under control in about 15 minutes, an
official said. No one was hurt.
    Damage was estimated at $25,000. The owner, Steve
Poulton, said insurance covered the loss. He said he
plans to reopen in three weeks.
```

This is a straightforward news story. But suppose you also heard that one of the part-time employees, a college student, lost something valuable in the fire. A fire department official says he recalls her looking through some charred equipment in the kitchen. He thinks he heard her ask about a manuscript she had left there. You call Poulton and learn her name, Karen Yount.

You manage to reach her and she says that she had just finished a term paper for her English class and had put it with her books in a cabinet in a corner of the kitchen when she went to work. The paper was to be the basis of her grade in the course. She is an English major and needs the course credit to graduate. But now. . . . Her voice trails off.

What would you do? You might still write a straight news story and add Karen's loss to the piece with this paragraph at the end:

> But Karen Yount, a college senior, has no insurance for her loss. Her term paper for an English class was destroyed by the fire. She had put it in the kitchen when she went to work this morning at the Pork Parlor.

That's not a bad ending to the story. But would it have made a better beginning? Should Karen's misfortune have been put into the lead of a straight news story? No, that would have been overplaying her loss, which obviously has less impact on the community than the damage to the restaurant.

On the other hand, the fire was not serious. No one was hurt and $25,000 in damage is not large. As fires go, it is routine. What makes it different from other fires is Yount's loss.

All this reasoning could lead you to conclude that the fire might make a better news-feature story than a straight news account. You call Yount and obtain more information, and you write:

> For three months, Karen Yount spent most of her evenings in the library and over a typewriter.
> A college senior, she was writing a term paper on the novelist George Eliot. It was to be the basis of her grade in the class and, she hoped, strong enough to impress the admissions committee at the University of Michigan, where she hopes to do graduate work.
> But her paper, and perhaps her grade and her hopes, went up in flames this morning.
> A fire at the Pork Parlor at 150 College Lane, where Yount works, destroyed the kitchen. Yount had put her term paper and books in a corner of the kitchen. She had not made a copy of her paper.
> The fire broke out at. . . .

Most editors would prefer this approach to the straight news account.

Burnout. Two people were injured and their hiking gear and personal belongings were destroyed in this fire on the freeway after their car was struck from behind.
Alex Robertson, Pepperdine University.

Feature or Straight News Story?

Coming Event. A former tennis star, Guillermo Vilas, will be visiting your city next month for a workshop. The local sponsor gives you a photo and a press release.
Karen Leff.

Trailer Park. A real estate developer announces that his firm has started construction of a large trailer park outside town. Water lines are being laid. The developer says he bought the range land for $100,000 and plans ''a large-scale park.'' Environmental groups in the city are protesting the plans. They say that the area has some unusual and rare plants and that development will endanger the species. They also contend that since the area is outside the city, zoning laws will not apply.
Mike McClure.

Washing Up. A student organization has collected $450 for a Toys for Tots fund drive in a one-day car-washing operation on campus. *Pepperdine University.*

Exhibition. A photography show of small-town America will be mounted next month in the local art museum. Some of the nation's prominent photographers will be represented in the exhibition with pictures taken in the past and present, a press release states. This photograph, taken in March 1942, is of Judith Gap, Mont. The photographer is John Vachon of the Farm Security Administration staff of photographers. *John Vachon, Courtesy of the Library of Congress.*

Before we move on, let's look a little closer at the lead. Students are forever amazed when they find out how important the lead is. The lead organizes the story, as we will see when we turn in the next chapter to structuring the story. The right lead sets the writer on the right track.

The lead is important to the reader and listener as well. It's hard to resist reading a book that begins: "Mom and pop were just a couple of kids when they got married. He was eighteen, she was sixteen and I was three."

This is how jazz singer Billie Holiday starts her book of recollections.

People whose job it is to communicate information, ideas and feelings know that the beginning is the most important part of the work—whether it be a poem, play, novel, news story, song or symphony. Not only does an interesting beginning grab the attention of the reader, viewer or listener, it also helps the writer or composer keep the theme or focus clearly in view.

Robert Schumann, the composer, advised a fellow composer, Johannes Brahms, to study the "beginning of the Beethoven symphonies . . . to try to make something like them.

"The beginning is the main thing; if only one makes the beginning, then the end comes of itself."

Donald M. Murray, a University of New Hampshire professor of writing who coaches news writers for several newspapers, says the writer must engage the reader at once. "Three seconds and the reader decides to read or turn to the next story," he says.

When we see a lead like the following we want to know more about this con artist:

A 73-year-old man was sentenced Tuesday to 10 years in prison for using the mails and telephone lines to cheat 30 people, including a Kansas City widow and a San Francisco physician, out of more than $500,000.

Newly minted writers are surprised at how important lead writing is on the job. Editors often toss back stories after glancing at the lead only, but when they handle a good lead the lines around their mouths relax and they settle back for a good read. The fastest way up is through the lead.

Direct and Delayed Leads

There are few rules of the road about leads. Generally, we say they should be short, less than 35 words if possible. From here, the rules depend on whether the story is a straight news piece or a feature.

The news story forces the writer to fashion a lead that moves directly to the news point or focus of the event. If the writer decides to tell a feature story, the pace can be leisurely, as when a storyteller relates a tale. The feature writer need not get right to the point; the lead may be delayed.

There we have the two types of leads, the only two you need think about. All other types fall into these two categories, direct and delayed. Don't fret about the long lists of lead types you will sometimes see—contrast, narrative, staccato, direct address, etc. No one in the newsroom talks this way. You may hear the terms *hard* and *soft*. These terms are synonymous with direct and delayed.

The courthouse reporter we have been watching covers a lot of important stories. The Santa Claus suit would be a change of pace for readers, she felt. It was a soft story, so she began it with a delayed lead:

Santa Claus is a child's best friend.

The kindly old gent pats little boys on the head and little girls on the cheek.

But two weeks ago, says Carolyn Elliott, a Zale's Department store Santa whacked her 6-year-old son, Dennis.

When she had written about a $1 million damage suit that involved fatal burns in an office building fire, her story had a direct lead and began:

An elderly couple filed suit today for $1 million against the Franklin Realty Co. in whose downtown offices the couple's daughter was fatally burned last August.

Mr. and Mrs. Grant Foster, 22 Eastern Ave., claimed the company was negligent in. . . .

The rule of thumb for leads:

When the event is important or significant, the story stresses the theme at once. The lead is **direct.** When the story is about an unusual, odd or strange event, the story does not need to describe what happened or what was said at once. The lead can be **delayed.**

Use these guidelines:

Direct leads are used for important, breaking news events.

Delayed leads are used on feature and news feature stories.

Let's presume you know what you want to say, you have decided whether the piece is a news story or feature, whether you want a direct or delayed lead, and you have some idea of how long the piece will be. Now you're ready to write.

First, you should know that most sentences in the news story—certainly at least three-fourths of them—are simple, declarative sentences. They begin with a subject, which is closely followed by a verb, and then an object. To put it another way, these sentences describe someone doing or saying something, or they show something happening:

Chancellor Robert Hartmann asked the legislature to approve a $50 million university building program to meet the demands of increased enrollment.

The state legislature last night defeated by a vote of 67–73 the $50 million university building bill.

Let's apply the subject-verb-object (S-V-O) structure to these leads.

Who said or did what
S—Chancellor Robert Hartmann
V—asked
O—the legislature

What happened
S—The state legislature
V—defeated
O—building bill

Now that you can see the structure of the lead, it follows that to write a lead you look at the theme or focus and break it into its S-V-O components. You then build the lead on this foundation.

Another approach is the time-tested "Five W's and an H." Some beginners list these and answer the questions:

Who—Chancellor Robert Hartmann
What—asked the legislature to approve program
When—today
Where—(Not in lead)
Why—to meet demands
How—(Not in lead)

Lead Guideline

Sometimes, the lead just won't come. Gladwin Hill, for many years with *The New York Times,* suggests that if the lead does not pop into mind quickly, "skip over it and jump right into the body of the piece. By the time you get to the end, a workable introduction will have occurred to you."

Here are 10 brief statements or notes that you might have on your notepad. Try to write leads from them. Then read on and we will see what reporters have done with these notes.

1. A Trans-American jetliner on a flight from Los Angeles to Miami runs out of fuel and must put down in Tampa.

2. Disturbances occur in Worcester, Mass., when it is revealed that the Cockroaches, a rock group giving a concert at a local night spot, are actually the Rolling Stones practicing for their first American tour in three years.

3. A group of women block the approach to a nuclear reactor in Diablo Canyon, Calif.

4. A company makes a wage offer to striking steel workers.

5. More city jobs will be eliminated Friday to balance the budget.

6. An 18-year-old high school student in Wisconsin devises a program to teach youngsters about the dangers of alcohol.

7. A New York City radio station switches music formats and becomes the most-listened-to station in the nation.

8. A new state law sends youngsters into the adult court system.

9. A figure skating champion is superstitious.

10. A blind man sails a 35-foot sailboat.

We are now ready for the last and most important step, writing the lead.

Writing the 10 Leads

The writer doing a straight news story knows he or she must get to the point at once. Since the lead will revolve about someone saying or doing something, or something happening, the writer begins with the person or the event—Who or What.

If the writer is working from the S-V-O summary, the **Subject** will begin the lead. If the Five W's and an H are being used, **Who** or **What** will start the lead.

The S-V-O of number 1 of our list is:

> S—Jet
> V—makes
> O—emergency landing

The Five W's and an H give us a more complete set of facts to work from:

> Who—Jetliner
> What—made emergency landing
> When—today
> Where—in Tampa
> Why—ran out of fuel
> How—unknown

From either the S-V-O skeleton or the answers to the Five W's and an H, the lead is built. First, the **Who** or **Subject** of the sentence is written:

```
A Trans-American jetliner on a flight from Los
Angeles to Miami
```

Notice that we say as much about the jetliner as possible to identify it, to separate this jetliner from the thousands that were flying on this day. We do the same thing when the **Who** or the **Subject** is a person. We don't say a man or a woman. We say a 29-year-old steel worker or Mildred Sherman, 69, of 166 Chapel St.

Next, we move to the **What** or the Verb and the Object:

```
made an emergency landing in Tampa today
```

Notice that we added the **Where** and the **When** here. Place and time are usually placed near the verb or the object.

We could stop here, but the lead would leave people wondering about the cause of the emergency, the **Why.** So we add:

```
when it ran out of fuel.
```

Now we have:

```
A Trans-American jetliner on a flight from Los
Angeles to Miami made an emergency landing in Tampa
today when it ran out of fuel.
```

This is almost a word-for-word duplicate of the wire service leads on the story.

Our presumption in number 1 was that this was a news story that required a direct lead. But what about number 2?

Our first reaction is that this could be serious business—news story, direct lead. For those with some knowledge of the music scene, it was a disturbance at a Rolling Stones concert in Altamont, Calif., that led to the knifing death of a spectator. But the Cockroaches? There's something funny about that. Maybe a feature would be better.

When in doubt, play it straight. That is, if the choice is not obvious, the best way to write the story is with a news approach and a direct lead. This is the safe way. To make light of a serious matter could be offensive.

Number 2 was played straight by most newspapers. There were no serious injuries and some minor damage.

Number 3: Straight news story. Direct lead.

Number 4: Straight news story. Direct lead.

Number 5: At first glance, this seems like a straight news story. But is it?

A tipoff to the nature of number 5 is the word *more*. This means the layoffs are part of a series of layoffs. Words like *again, still, continued* indicate there is not much new. Thus we lose the news determinant of immediacy.

Bob Rose of *The Blade* in Toledo made the event into a news feature with some enterprising reporting. In his story, he used a delayed lead. The theme does not come until the sixth paragraph:

Delayed lead: Use of incidents to begin the story

One night this week, some Mabel Street residents went hunting for rats that had moved into their North Toledo neighborhood.

"I called rodent control, and they're closed up," Tom Munger said. "I talked to the mayor's office and the woman who answered the phone said she didn't know what I could do about it. She said I should have voted."

Mr. Munger, who admitted he did not cast a ballot on the payroll-income tax increase issue last month, said he and a neighbor took the problem into their own hands. "I think we got one," he said of the pests.

Delayed lead (continued)

One night later, L. Michael Duckworth, assistant city manager, got a telephone call at home from someone asking when the city's swimming pools would open.

Transition to theme

City officials know it, but some citizens apparently do not: With 846 layoffs in the last two years, Toledo cannot control rats and it cannot open the pools. It cannot do a lot of things it used to do.

Theme: News point

When 262 more city jobs are eliminated Friday, the city will have taken another step toward balancing its budget by bringing the work force down to 2,875. But the list of what it cannot do will grow longer.

Number 6: This story obviously does not require a *today* in the lead. It is a news feature, so the AP put a delayed lead on it:

```
     FOND DU LAC, WIS. (AP)--Sometimes the
best help a junior high school student can
receive comes not from a teacher or parent but
from a senior high school student.
```

That theory, ``Kids Helping Kids,'' is the
idea behind a new alcohol awareness program
developed by a St. Mary's Springs High School
student for elementary and junior high school
students.

The program was developed by Jeff
Weinshrott, an 18-year-old Springs
senior. . . .

The lead idea is: High school student develops program to combat alcoholism. The AP writer realized that the unique or unusual aspect of it was a student teaching students about the dangers of alcohol. The writer emphasized the unique aspect by using that general idea to begin the story. The lead follows quickly in the second and third paragraphs.

Number 7: What happened here? An FM station switched from mellow music to disco and its ratings jumped. Significant or entertaining? For a magazine devoted to reporting broadcast news, this is significant and a direct lead is in order. Something like this:

By switching to disco, New York radio station WKTU-
FM has become the most-listened-to station in the
country.

But for a general audience, the reaction to that lead may well be: So what? For Geoff Walden, a student who wrote this story on assignment for a journalism class, this was an entertaining story, and so he put a delayed lead on the piece. He dramatized the switch this way:

NEW YORK—Last July 24th, at 5:59 p.m., WKTU-FM "Mellow 92," was playing Neil Young's soft-rock song, "It's Over."

At 6 p.m., WKTU-FM, "The new Disco 92," was playing Donna Summer's "The Last Dance."

For Donna Summer, the song went on to win this year's Oscar for the Best Original Song, for the movie "Thank God It's Friday." For the radio station, the song was the start of an all-disco format that has made WKTU the most-listened-to station in America, with an average of 275,000 people tuning in every quarter hour.

The direct lead tells readers: Here comes something important. Walden's beginning tells them: Relax, I'm going to entertain you. But notice that the theme or lead idea is exactly the same for both:

S—Format change
V—makes
O—station most-listened-to

Number 8: This story falls into the category editors call an update. This type of story brings the reader or listener up to date on something that has happened. An update usually is not a straight news story and does not require a direct lead. In this example, we have a law that was passed a while back. How should the story be approached?

Richard Higgins, another journalism student, reasoned that his story should describe the law in action. So he began his story by portraying two young offenders in the new courtroom setting.

NEW YORK—Rafael Torres and Hector Valdez sat at the brown wooden table, playing with Superman coloring books, combing their hair, waving and occasionally shouting to friends in the room.

It could have been a scene out of the South Bronx junior high school where they are enrolled in the eighth grade. But it was the beginning of an arson and multiple murder trial in the Bronx Criminal Courthouse and the two skinny, squirming boys were not there to learn; they were the defendants.

In the next paragraph Higgins introduces the lead that tells the reader that these youngsters are in court because of a new law and that other youngsters are being tried in the adult courts. He makes a news feature out of his material.

Number 9: For this kind of feature story, Linda Kramer, an AP reporter, says she gathers "piles of material for a story." When she writes, she tries to "weed out the non-essential copy. I want to choose the anecdote that best reflects and highlights what I want to say."

This is a precise description of how the writer must use the anecdote or incident chosen to begin the feature or news feature story. The material must feed directly into the theme or lead.

"In writing about figure-skating champion Linda Fratianne, I led with a description of a lucky charm she pins to her costume during competition. To me, this little touch of superstitiousness illustrated the 17-year-old behind the star," Kramer says. This, then, was her theme: Although Fratianne's magnificent presence on the ice makes her seem almost regal, the real Linda Fratianne is a youngster with a girl's feelings. Here is Kramer's first paragraph in her delayed lead:

Tucked in a tiny blue pouch pinned to Linda Fratianne's sequinned skating costume are two four-leaf clovers, a piece of gold foil, and a snip of green yarn.

Number 10: The news writer takes the reader aboard the blind man's sailboat:

Keeping a grip on the sheet, Albert Adams draws the maximum amount of speed from his 35-foot sailboat.

The yellow-hulled boat responds to Adams' touch and picks up speed. Adams turns to his crew—his wife and two teen-age sons—and asks them to lend a hand.

Adams has been blind since birth. The 33-year-old accountant sails regularly. He can tell from which direction the wind is coming by ear. . . .

Like the beginning of many features, this one **shows** the subject doing something.

Basic Decisions

Study the picture on this page and the pictures on the two pages that follow. Decide whether the story (1) is about a person or event, (2) should be a straight news story or a feature story, and (3) should be given a direct or delayed lead.

Blaze. A fire of undetermined origin at an oceanfront apartment building causes $175,000 in damage to an apartment. A 61-year-old woman who lived alone in the apartment is critically injured. Adjacent apartment has smoke and water damage, and a pet cat died from the smoke in the apartment.
Mona Oxford, Pepperdine University.

Official. A city official says she will run for mayor. She is the first woman to run for mayor in 40 years. She makes the announcement at a news conference outside city hall.
Leslie Jean-Bart.

Shark. A shark-fishing contest began today, and one angler landed this 725-pound, 12½-foot-long tiger shark. The fisherman had never caught a shark before.
The St. Petersburg Times.

Race. A 100-1 shot, Kayellen, won today's Juvenile Stakes. The two-year-old filly had never finished better than sixth in four previous races, and not even her owner, Norman Pearlstein, had wagered on her to win. Kayellen, No. 4, took the lead around the final turn and won by a neck.
Susan Plageman, The Berkshire Eagle.

Farm. Children and their parents from farms nearby protest foreclosures of farms whose owners have been unable to meet mortgage payments. Some of the children express fear of having to leave their homes for unknown places.
Photo by Charlie Riedel of The Hays (Kan.) Daily News. Used with permission.

Straight News Lead

Let's look further at the spot news story, which is also called the straight news story, or simply the news story.

In Chapter 1 we watched a reporter begin to write the obituary of Rose Harriet Allen. The event contains one major news determinant, prominence. There is some impact in that a fund drive will be launched that will involve the public. The reporter decided to make this a straight news story, as most obituaries are.

When we ask the two questions that give a story its focus, we have two replies that might be elements in the lead for the Allen story:

1. What was it that happened to the person?
    Rose Harriet Allen died.
2. What happened?
    A scholarship fund is being set up.

Which should be the lead? One or the other, or both? Let's listen in on the writer's thinking:

"Everyone in town knows Allen, so I'll start with that and immediately go to the fund drive. The lead will include both elements." Here is her lead:

```
    Rose Harriet Allen, 71, of 33 Fulton Ave., who
taught school here for 30 years and was a school
principal for 13 years before her retirement, died
yesterday in the Community Hospital. A fund drive
will be. . . .
```

"No, that won't do. The first paragraph will be a blockbuster, much too long. Maybe the better lead is the fund drive since that has lasting significance. Obviously, with that as a beginning Allen's name will be worked into the story since the drive is in her memory."

```
A college scholarship fund is being set up in
memory of Rose Harriet Allen, 71, who died yesterday
after a career of 43 years in the local public
schools.
```

"That's better. It's shorter and it combines the two elements."

She continues to write, and in the middle of the fourth paragraph she suddenly stops and slowly reads what she has written.

"This is becoming a story about a fund drive, not the death of a well-known teacher who probably has thousands of friends in town. The impact, the real significance, is not the fund drive but her death. Allen's death will affect many of our readers.

"The lead should concentrate on Allen's death and the fund drive should go lower in the story." She starts over.

```
Rose Harriet Allen, whose teaching and
administrative career spanned 43 years in local
public schools, died here yesterday at the age of 71.
     Allen died in the Community Hospital where she had
been since suffering a heart attack last week in her
home at 33 Fulton Ave.
     For 30 years, Allen taught in several of the city's
elementary schools. For the next 13 years of her
education career, she was the principal of the
Lincoln School. She retired six years ago.
     She is remembered as a friendly, outgoing teacher.
As a principal, she delighted in taking a class for a
teacher who was ill.
     "She was strict," recalled Albert Green, a local
lawyer. "If you didn't do your homework, she wanted
to see your parents in school the next day."
     Green and some of Allen's other former students
said they are planning to establish a college
scholarship fund in her memory.
     "Miss Allen came from a poor farm family," Green
said. "She used to tell us how hard it was for her to
stay in school at State Teachers College, how she
worked for a family for her room and board and did
chores six hours a day, went to class, and
studied.". . . .
```

This version satisfies her. It balances both important elements of the story, Allen's death and the fund drive. She has good quotes that tell something of Allen's personality. The personal details about Allen help the reader to visualize the kind of person she was.

Presidential Assassinations

The direct lead tells the reader or listener what happened in as few words as possible. This has always been the reporter's purpose in covering breaking news stories, as these leads about two presidential assassinations illustrate:

```
     TO THE ASSOCIATED PRESS
     THE PRESIDENT WAS SHOT
IN A THEATRE TONIGHT AND
PERHAPS MORTALLY WOUNDED.
        --Lawrence A.
          Gobright,
          April 14, 1865.
        _____

UPI A7N DA
     PRECEDE KENNEDY
DALLAS, NOV. 22
     (UPI)--THREE SHOTS WERE
FIRED AT PRESIDENT KENNEDY'S
MOTORCADE IN DOWNTOWN
DALLAS.
               JT1234PCS . .


UPI ASN DA
          URGENT
1ST ADD SHOTS, DALLAS (A7N)
     XXX DOWNTOWN DALLAS
     NO CASUALTIES WERE
REPORTED
     THE INCIDENT OCCURRED
NEAR THE COUNTY SHERIFF'S
OFFICE ON MAIN STREET, JUST
EAST OF AN UNDERPASS LEADING
TOWARD THE TRADE MART WHERE
THE PRESIDENT WAS TO MA


FLASH
     KENNEDY SERIOUSLY
WOUNDED
PERHAPS SERIOUSLY
PERHAPS FATALLY SHOT BY
ASSASSINS BULLET
          JT1239PCS
--Merriam Smith,
Nov. 22, 1963.
```

Feature Lead

When David Stacks was sent to cover an arm-wrestling tournament, he knew that his story for *The Anniston Star* probably would not be the most important story in the newspaper the next day. He also knew that he would be writing a feature story, which meant he would need to watch for a good incident to begin his story:

"Brevity (in leads) is not the primary goal. Clarity is. The old rule holds that the shorter the lead, the better. That's old enough to be forgotten. There are limits, but a 25- or 30-word lead is not necessarily better than one 35 or 40 words long. It needs to be simple and understandable, not necessarily short."—Walter Mears, AP.

Sweat beaded on Bruce Jernigan's forehead. His biceps swelled as blood rushed through his strong chest and into his right arm. His face grimaced with exertion.

Bruce's opponent, Claude Bradford, smiled in seeming defiance as the two boys' fists—locked in an arm-wrestler's grip—teetered slowly back and forth over the tabletop.

Then, with a burst of energy, 14-year-old Claude overcame his opponent's balanced show of strength. Both boys fell from near exhaustion as the referee declared the match concluded.

Theirs was a test of strength, endurance and will. In the end, Claude managed to wear down his friend and adversary Bruce, 14, in the Anniston Park and Recreation Department's first arm-wrestling tournament Saturday morning at Carver Community Center on West 14th Street.

"It's all in the way you move," Claude said afterwards.

Arm-wrestling is an ancient contest of power in which two opponents grasp each other's hands with their elbows resting on a flat surface. The one who forces the other's arm down to the surface wins.

Ancient people of the world regarded arm-wrestling as a nonviolent test of strength where one adversary could defeat the other.

The contest Saturday was staged for a different reason, said Zebedee Murphy, the city recreation leader who coordinated the event and acted as referee.

"We're trying to get them (the boys) interested in something new," he said. Murphy said he used to arm-wrestle with other kids on the block when he was growing up, but this was the first time the city had ever sponsored such a tournament.

"We'll probably do it again next year," Murphy said.

About 20 boys from the Carver area of Anniston participated in the contest Saturday. Officials divided them into three age groups and pitted contestants against each other arbitrarily, Murphy said. . . .

Gotcha. An arm-wrestling tournament was made into a feature story with a delayed lead.
Ken Elkins. The Anniston Star.

Let's look closer at how the courthouse reporter settled on her lead for the story about the suit involving a department store Santa Claus. When she came across the suit in the courthouse, she knew at once that she would write a short feature story. Her problem was how to write an entertaining lead. She had a few ideas. The best, she thought, was that although most of us visualize Santa as a kindly old man, here he is accused of a cruel act. She decided to put this idea of contrasts into her lead:

Santa Claus

> Santa Claus, that paragon of kindness, is being
> sued for cruelty to a child.

As with most first efforts, this wasn't exactly right. The idea was sound, she still felt, but not the way she had put it. Writers should use simple language, but here she was using the word *paragon,* which some people might not understand. She tried again:

> Kindly Santa Claus is being sued for being cruel to
> a youngster.

The lead was still too close to a straight news lead. The tone was wrong. The beginning of a feature should be relaxed. It should beckon the reader and say to him or her: Slow down a minute—I've got something funny I want to tell you.

Suddenly she realized there was a more serious problem than her choice of words and tone. In her effort to be entertaining, she had neglected to be scrupulously careful about the facts. Her lead mistakenly identified the party the suit was brought against, the defendant. It was not Santa Claus, as both drafts of her lead had stated. It was the department store.

She knew she did not have much space, so she could not spin out the tale for more than five or six paragraphs. After her leisurely beginning, she would have to get to the facts—name and address of mother, description of the incident, damages sought. She wrote:

Santa Claus is a child's best friend.

The kindly old gent pats little boys on the head and little girls on the cheek.

But two weeks ago, says Carolyn Elliott, a Zale's Department Store Santa whacked her 6-year-old son, Dennis.

Mrs. Elliott, of 49 East End Ave., wants $10,000 for her "humiliation and embarrassment" and her son's "nervous reaction." She filed suit against the store in the Grant County District Court yesterday.

The department store had no comment.

Now that we have talked about how news stories begin, we need to look at how to build up the body of the story. But before we turn to structuring the story, we have to glance at the essentials of stories, some guidelines to writing.

Suggested Reading

Broder, David S. *Behind the Front Page, a Candid Look at How the News is Made.* New York: Simon and Schuster, 1987.

Gans, Herbert J. *Deciding What's News.* New York: Pantheon Books, 1974.

Westin, Av. *Newswatch: How TV Decides the News.* New York: Simon & Schuster, 1983.

4
Rudiments
of the Story

News is etched more deeply when the reporter puts events in human terms. In this picture, the news event—thousands made homeless by floods in Northern California—can be seen and felt through the plight of a young mother and child in an evacuation center. *Photo by Mary Carroll Jones of The Press Democrat. Used with permission.*

Looking Ahead

Just as the basketball player must abide by the rules of the game, so the news writer must adhere to a set of guidelines. These guidelines, the rudiments of the news story, are: accuracy, attribution of statements, background, balance, brevity, clarity, human interest, identification of those named in the story, focus on the news point, objectivity and verification of information.

The news writer who follows these guidelines will write stories that are accurate, thorough, fair and readable.

The list of the rudiments for a news story begins with accuracy—words spelled correctly, the correct middle initial in names and the exact addresses of people in stories.

In their lectures on libel law, journalism instructors often reach into their bag of stories to find the one about the wrong initial. In one case, a courthouse reporter hastily wrote a *T* instead of an *F* when he was taking notes on a divorce action. In checking the address of the divorcing couple in the telephone book, he looked up their name under *T* instead of *F*.

A couple of days after the story ran, the newspaper received notice from a lawyer for the non-divorcing couple. A libel suit was on the way.

Check—Double Check. The telephone directory is used to check street addresses and to verify the spelling of names. Reporters are presumed never to make errors because, editors never tire of telling them, there is always a source to check.
Jean Pierre Rivest, The (Montreal) Gazette.

The story brings forth the desired shudders among students, for a minute or two, and then they shrug it off as just another of those scare stories they have been hearing all semester. Shrug away. These stories are based on fact. Most libel suits begin with a little mistake, a foolish error, a lapse in accuracy.

Accuracy begins with the reporter's painstaking attention to every detail when gathering facts and information. Names, ages, addresses—check. The precise number of fire trucks that answered the alarm. The exact language of the speaker. Check and double check.

Should there be an error, the reporter writes a correction. Most newspapers have a permanent location for corrections or will place them in the section or on the page where the error occurred. Broadcast stations, too, correct on-the-air-mistakes.

"Good reporters get the facts right. They seek comment from all sides. They check. They don't cut corners."—AP.

But the writer's task is not to make the mistake in the first place. Look at what *Newsweek* did in one issue—and these are only the errors that were caught by the people who were directly involved and saw the issue: Misspelled the name of a professor of political science at the University of Arizona whose work it had referred to in a piece on the Bill of Rights; attributed personal bankruptcy to a man whose corporation, not him personally, was bankrupt; confused a former Air Force pilot with a shadowy character in the Iran-Contra scandal who has the same last name.

Next time you are too rushed to double-check an initial or name or are too lazy to look up something in a reference work, remember this correction:

> Mai Thai Finn is one of the students in the program and was in the center of the photo. We incorrectly listed her as one of the items on the menu.

Mercifully, no mention will be made of the reporter who committed this blunder.

Attribution

All information and statements, except the most obvious, must be attributed to the source of the material:

> The police reported two people were killed when. . . .

> Mayor Sam Walker today urged. . . .

> Childhood diseases are declining, the state health department said. . . .

> "College grades are meaningless," Professor Alvin Goodman told. . . .

However, no attribution is necessary for assertions that are obvious and events the reporter has seen:

July 4th falls on Tuesday.

Lincoln was loved and hated in his day.

The cost of living has steadily increased.

The Tigers defeated the White Sox 3–2 last night.

By the "obvious" we mean any statement, idea or situation that is commonly accepted as true. When there is no absolute proof or common acceptance, there must be attribution.

Notice the use of attribution in the following lead:

> Police said today they expect major roads out of the city to be heavily traveled beginning Friday at midafternoon. The holiday weekend will run from Saturday through Monday.

The first statement is attributed to a source. The second is stated as fact because it is obvious.

Actions are attributed to the person or group committing or performing them:

> Mayor George Albritton ordered all city offices closed next Monday in memory of the city's first mayor, Richard Beatty, who died last week at 104 years of age.

> The state Republican Party yesterday took the first steps toward holding its November state convention. The party. . . .

Generally, when we speak of attribution, we refer to what is called "sourcing" a quote or statement. That is, reponsibility for the material is placed with the source. When there is no attribution, the reporter, newspaper or station is considered the source.

Attribution to a source does not guarantee to the reader or viewer the truth of the statement. But it does place responsibility for the assertion. When reporters doubt the accuracy or truth of a statement, they try to verify it.

In an interview, Jeff Klinkenberg of the *St. Petersburg Times,* was asked how he handled some of the information in a story he had written about a shark fisherman.

The interviewer asked: "I notice at various points in the story you are careful to attribute statements he had made about what he can do with the sharks once he has caught them. Fishermen are notorious BS artists. . . . Do you often encounter problems of credibility in the people you interview?"

Klinkenberg replied, "No, but in this instance, some of the stuff he was telling me was so remarkable I had to protect myself a little bit. Many of the things he told me I double-checked and found to be true. Things I couldn't check I went with an attribution."

With the name and the title or occupation of the source given in the story, the reader or listener can place responsibility. After a while, the public learns just how trustworthy the source is. This is important in writing about

Attribution. When the reporter is sent to the scene of a car accident, the reporter can describe the way divers pulled the woman from her submerged car. No attribution is needed for what the reporter sees or hears on the scene. The reporter who is not present when a slaying occurs must reconstruct the event from the comments and reports of investigators and attribute the account of the event to them. The reporter can describe, without attribution, what the scene looks like.

Top, Joseph Noble, The Stuart (Fla.) News; bottom, Marc Ascher, The Home News, New Brunswick, N.J.

those in public life. They must be held accountable for their actions and their statements. A reporter who spots a distortion or a lie in a statement may well run it and alongside the inaccuracy give the accurate or truthful account. That way the source is on record, as is the truth.

Placement Within the Story   Some news writers say that attribution in the lead sometimes makes it too long or spoils the intended effect. They prefer to cite the source in the second or third paragraph.

This works, but only if the material is from an official record or document or is not controversial. No source is necessary in this lead because the event is obviously on record with the police:

> Three dead men were found afloat—in two Dade canals and a lake—at midday Sunday by a fisherman, golfers and a scavenger in search of scrap metal.

Attribution is essential in any lead that contains accusations and charges:

> G. Arthur Levy today charged the state liquor authority with "capricious decisions" in denying liquor licenses to two of his clients.

Now and then a reporter will try to make the lead to a story like this more exciting by writing:

> ```
> The state liquor authority today stands accused of
> "capricious decisions" in denying two liquor
> licenses.
> ```

This kind of lead is unfair to the reader, who may conclude that the charge has been made in the courts or by some official body. When the source is finally revealed, the reader may feel cheated.

The most frequently used verb of attribution is *said*. It is an invisible word in a sentence, not calling attention to itself as do *charged, whispered, shouted, pointed out*.

When a candidate says his opponent is "incapable of sober judgment," the reporter can write, "The candidate *charged* his opponent is. . . ." And when someone does whisper or shout, we say so. But most of the time, the verb for attribution is *said*.

According to presents special problems. For some reason, beginners love to use it. Some writers approach it with caution, contending that *according to* hints at the writer's doubts about the truth of the source's statement. Yet at *The New York Times,* the phrase can be used only when it introduces a fact.

"Japan's unemployment rate rose in January to 3 percent of the labor force, the highest level since monthly reporting began in 1953, the Government announced today."—*The New York Times.*

Commented the in-house critique "Winners & Sinners," the lead "could have stood nicely on its own, without the attribution. . . . Since the matter is uncontested, a less cluttered lead would have been a better lead."

Broadcast news writer Mervin Block uses this guideline: Attribution precedes assertion. Placing the source of the information up front is essential for radio and television writing. Newspaper writers also will often begin their leads with the attribution, though the standard approach is to give the action or assertion first, then the source.

Anonymous Sources

Sources sometimes seek anonymity. They will offer information only if their identity is not disclosed. Newspapers are reluctant to run this kind of material because it absolves the source of responsibility for his or her statements.

When anonymity is promised to a source, the reporter may not use the name under any circumstances. Some editors demand to be told the source of such material, and if this is the case, the source must be informed that his or her name will be given to the editor. The AP says its "basic rule is attribute and attribute by name. Anonymity is reserved for those cases in which the information is newsworthy, factual and not available from any source on the record. We use anonymous sources only on matters of fact, not on matters of opinion or judgment."

Background

The additional material that a reporter digs up on his or her own that helps the reader or listener get closer to the truth often takes the form of background. Most often, background material comes from the reporter's knowledge and from checking references and clips.

For example:

• When the cardinal who heads the New York Roman Catholic archdiocese refused to go along with other prelates in suggesting use of condoms to combat AIDS, reporters recalled that the Catholic Church in New York had lobbied successfully for years in the state legislature against the display of condoms in drug stores.

• When the federal education department released an AIDS handbook that emphasized the avoidance of premarital sex and illegal drugs as "the smartest way to avoid infection," *The Wall Street Journal* story added:

The publication reflects Bennett's (secretary of education) criticism of government reports that point out the protection that condoms provide, without encouraging abstinence.

• When President Reagan vainly sought the help of Republican senators to sustain his veto of an $88 billion highway and mass transit bill, Steven V. Roberts of *The New York Times* quoted several senators. Then at the end of his piece he cut to the heart of the issue with this paragraph:

Many conservative Republicans who have voted with the President when he wanted to cut welfare or food stamps were less eager to go along when the issue was roads and bridges used by middle class voters.

This single sentence, brought up from Roberts' knowledge of politics, tells us a great many truths—who has political clout, how politicians are influenced, and why certain bills become laws while others die of neglect. Roberts' paragraph is also an example of interpretative reporting, which experienced and trusted reporters are allowed to do.

Background material gives readers explanations, traces the development of the event and adds facts that sources may not have provided. Reporters spend much time backgrounding their stories.

In the past, it was not unusual for newspaper publishers and editors to use their newspapers to attack ideas, groups, individuals and officials. These attacks were made in news columns, which are supposedly free of opinion.

In his book *The Powers That Be* (New York: Alfred A. Knopf, 1979), David Halberstam describes a visit a *New York Times* reporter made to California in 1934 to cover the campaign for governor. Upton Sinclair, the author of many books and a supporter of social and political change, was running against Frank Merriam, the Republican candidate. The campaign had attracted national attention because of its intensity. Sinclair was considered a wild-eyed socialist by his opponents.

On his arrival in Los Angeles, the New York reporter picked up a copy of the *Los Angeles Times* to look for news about the campaign, especially to learn something about Sinclair, who was a national figure. The only story he could find about Sinclair was one saying that he was un-Christian.

That night, the reporter went to dinner with the chief political correspondent of the *Los Angeles Times*. The reporter asked where Sinclair would be speaking so that he could cover some of his rallies.

As *The New York Times* reporter recalls, he was told, "Forget it. We don't go in for that kind of crap you have back in New York of being obliged to print both sides. We're going to beat this son of a bitch Sinclair any way we can. We're going to kill him." And Halberstam adds: "Which they did."

A quarter of a century later, in 1958, another New York reporter went to California to cover the turbulent political scene. The same Los Angeles correspondent was directing political coverage. He helped his eastern colleague with background about the Republicans. "What about the Democrats?" asked his visitor. "Oh, we don't bother with them," was the answer.

Those days of outrageous favoritism in the news are gone, except in some isolated instances. Today, the *Los Angeles Times* is among the best newspapers in the country. Although newspapers have recognized their responsibility to be fair, unfairness and imbalance do creep into stories now and then, usually because of carelessness.

By balance we mean that both sides in a controversy are given their say. In a political campaign, all candidates should be given enough space and time to present their major points. In debates, each speaker is entitled to reach the reader or listener.

By fairness, we mean that all parties involved in the news are treated without favoritism. If someone makes a charge against another person and the newspaper or station carries this allegation, it is obliged to obtain the response. Fairness requires that the reporter tie the charge and the answer together whenever possible.

The reporter is not a Ping-Pong ball, bouncing from charge to rebuttal as the sources volley away. The reporter must check the truth or accuracy of a charge when he or she believes misstatements are being made.

When a lawyer said his clients had been mistreated by the state liquor authority the reporter sought the response of the authority and put the response high in the story:

G. Arthur Levy today charged the state liquor authority with "capricious decisions" in denying liquor licenses to two of his clients.

Levy, a local attorney, said the authority had no reason to turn down Fred P. Schmidt and Alice Long, both of whom sought licenses for outlets in shopping centers north of the city.

The executive director of the authority, Theodore Landau, denied that the state agency had acted without reason. He said the applicants had failed to satisfy the authority about their backgrounds. . . .

Fairness also involves the honest use of words. Look at these statements:

Jones admitted he had seen the documents.
Jones said he had seen the documents.

What's the difference? The first sentence implies that Jones is under attack for having done something wrong, whereas the second sentence is neutral. There are appropriate occasions when *admit, refuse, complain* and other words that imply an attitude or behavior can be used. But these are loaded words. They signal caution.

Get the Other Side

Fairness in copy is essential, says the AP. Here is its guideline for stories in which charges are made:

We make every reasonable effort to get comment from someone who has a stake in a story we're reporting—especially if the person is the target of an attack or allegations. It makes no difference whether the target is an individual or a company or an institution.

This may mean awakening someone in the middle of the night or asking questions of people who are hostile and abusive. But it must be done.

If someone declines comment, we say so.

If we can't get comment from someone whose side of a story should be told, we spell out in our copy the steps we took to get that comment. In any case, it's never enough for AP to say only that no comment was available.

And in such cases, whenever possible, we also check our files to see what, if anything the person has said in the past relating to the allegations. Including past comment may provide needed balance and context.

Balance. Both sides of an argument or controversy are presented in a news story. When a charge is made against a person, the accused is sought out and the response is placed in the story close to the charge. If the accused cannot be found or refuses to comment, the news writer says so in the story.
Rafael Trias, The San Juan (Puerto Rico) Star.

Brevity

News writing is the art of knowing what to leave out and condensing the rest. Donald M. Murray, a University of New Hampshire professor and newspaper writing coach, says the most effective stories make one dominant point.

But news writers are born storytellers and tend to be long-winded. It is possible, however, to include a lot of solid information and still be brief. There are some tricks of the trade.

One way to make a little go a long way is to make one word do the work of three. By choosing a concrete noun, a noun that refers to an actual person, place or thing, the news writer can avoid adjectives. By using action verbs that whisper, sing and shout, the news writer can avoid adverbs. Good writers try to make their verbs and nouns work for them. They consider the overuse of adverbs and adjectives an admission of weak writing.

When George Eliot, the English novelist, was writing *Daniel Deronda,* she wrote this sentence: "She began to sob hysterically." Eliot's manuscript shows that she crossed off the adverb *hysterically,* realizing that the verb *sob* was strong enough to carry the meaning she intended.

Look at these sentences. The weak ones are the wordy sentences. The strong sentences make their points succinctly by using action verbs:

Weak: He was hardly able to walk.
Strong: He staggered. (He stumbled. He faltered.)
Weak: He left the room as quickly as possible.
Strong: He ran out. (He rushed out. He dashed out.)

Concrete nouns are words that stand for something we can point to as real: table, desk, chalk, crayon, basket, Ted Kennedy, Prince Charles.

Abstract nouns have no physical reference: patriotism, perception, motherhood, freedom, values, hope. These words have different meanings to different people. The news writer should avoid using abstract nouns, except in direct quotes.

Whole clusters of words can be cut out with a little thinking. Most of the extra baggage is unnecessary. The approach to making copy concise is to ask: Are these words or ideas essential?

Here are some changes the AP suggested to its reporters:

Original: A national homosexual rights law group said Wednesday it is suing several federal agencies for failing to make more AIDS treatment drugs available to victims of the fatal disease.

Thinking: Period needed after "available." They wouldn't be complaining about non-victims.

Original: A man whose eight-year reign as chief of the state Department of Natural Resources ended in scandal pleaded innocent Wednesday to extortion charges and said he had no doubt he would be cleared.

"I rewrite paragraphs over and over. There is one paragraph in that Sirhan story that I rewrote more than any other paragraph I've ever rewritten. . . . I talked it out, wrote it out, and wrote it over and over. I crumpled up pages and threw them away. It was a process of just paring down and paring down and just trying to make it clear and as short and as strong as I could."—Cynthia Gorney, *The Washington Post.*

After Calvin Coolidge returned from a church service, a friend asked the president what the sermon had been about.

"Sin," replied Coolidge. The friend asked what the clergyman had said. Coolidge replied: "He said he was against it."

Gunfight at the O.K. Corral: A Lead of 100 Years Ago

Here is the lead to the story about a famous western gunfight. It appeared under the headline:

YESTERDAY'S TRAGEDY
Three Men Hurled into
Eternity in the Dura-
tion of a Moment

Stormy as were the early days of Tombstone, nothing ever occurred equal to the event of yesterday. Since the retirement of Ben Sippy as marshal and the appointment of V. W. Earp to fill the vacancy, the town has been noted for its quietness and good order. The fractitious and formerly much dreaded cow-boys when they came to town were upon their good behavior, and no unseemly brawls were indulged in, and it was hoped by our citizens that no more such deeds would occur as led to the killing of Marshal White, one year ago. It seems that this quiet state of affairs was but the calm that precedes the storm that burst in all its fury yesterday, with the difference in results, that the lightning's bolt struck in a different quarter than the one that fell a year ago. This time it struck with its full and awful force upon those who, heretofore, have made the good name of this country a byword and a reproach, instead of upon some officer in the discharge of his duty or a peaceable and unoffending citizen.

Some time Tuesday Ike Clanton came into town and during the evening had some little talk with Doc Holliday and Marshal Earp, but nothing that caused either to suspect, further than their general knowledge of the man and the threats that had been previously conveyed to the Marshal that the gang intended to clean out the Earps, that he was thirsting for blood at this time. . . .

—*The Tombstone Epitaph.,*
Oct. 27, 1881.

Thinking: Period needed after "charges." What else would he say? Guilty as charged?

Original: The American Medical Association has called for a ban on smoking on all commercial U.S. aircraft, citing the dangers of second-hand smoke and accidental fire inside a sealed cabin.

Thinking: Too wordy. Make it: The American Medical Association wants smoking banned on U.S. commercial flights because of health and fire hazards.

When Jackie Robinson became the first black in major league baseball, many players refused to talk to him. Jimmy Cannon, a sportswriter for a New York newspaper, captured the situation with this brief sentence about Robinson: "He is the loneliest man in sports."

Relevance

A major cause of unwanted length is the piling on of irrelevant themes and details. As we have stressed, the average news story has one, two or sometimes three themes. It's up to the reporter to pick the most important. Some reporters want to include everything that happened. The news story will sag out of shape with that overload, bulging like a fullback who has trained on beer.

After the theme(s) has been selected, the reporter must pick the best quotes, anecdotes and illustrations for the supporting detail. A few quotes and a single pertinent illustration are all that are necessary to prove the point.

If an event is loaded with interesting and relevant material, the writer can use a device to summarize the secondary material:

The city council also:

1. Approved an expenditure of $5,000 for paving Grant Street between Arrow and Baltic Avenues.

2. Appointed Frank C. Barnes of 103 Elm Ave. assistant to the sanitary engineer.

3. Put off until next month consideration of a proposal to adopt an anti-litter ordinance.

The reporter did not believe these items were worth any more than a brief mention. This technique also can be used in an interview by selecting choice quotations:

Nelson ranged widely over the field of music in his remarks:

"Country western will be around as long as people are romantics. . . .

"The mainstream singers give people what they think people want. They're wrong. People want authenticity. . . .

"Travel is no way to make a living, but it's our only way. We are today's minstrels. . . .

"Country music appeals to grandpa and his granddaughter."

Clarity

Ask editors or readers what they want most from the people who write and the response will be almost unanimous—clear stories. There are several ways the reporter achieves clarity. The common starting point is clear thinking. Badly written stories—written material that does not communicate clearly—are the result of muddy thinking.

"There is only one trick to writing clearly," says an editor. "The writer must understand the event before writing." If the writer has the information under control, then he or she can put it into understandable language.

George Orwell said the key to clear writing is clear thinking. If the thinking is uncertain and confused, so is the writing. He criticized writers who hide their ignorance of the subject with "purple passages, sentences without meaning, decorative adjectives and humbug generally."

"Literature is not read and journalism is unreadable."—Oscar Wilde.

Clarity, says AP writer Saul Pett, "is the newspaper writer's first obligation." At Notre Dame, Red Smith, one of the great sports writers, studied under a teacher who would begin class by saying, "Let us pray for sense." Smith's teacher said he liked to see a sentence "so definite it would cast a shadow." *Joseph Noble, The Stuart (Fla.) News.*

Clear thinking extends to the writing as well as to the subject matter. The reporter has to find the lead that will best summarize the event and arrange all the supporting material in a logical and organized fashion. News writers see themselves as guides leading the reader through the thicket of events. Inept guides lead their followers in circles or into a swamp of confusion.

Short, crisp, to-the-point leads and logical story structure are the basic guides to clarity. We can add another essential guideline: the S-V-O sentence structure (Subject-Verb-Object). The sentence that has someone saying or doing something is usually clear.

Some tips:

Avoid excess punctuation. Too many commas confuse readers.

Stay away from adjectives and adverbs if possible. They usually are unnecessary.

Watch out for long sentences linked with the words *and, but, for* and other conjunctions. Usually, long sentences can be broken into two sentences with a period in place of the connecting words.

Human Interest

A California newspaper carried an interview with a family therapist about single parenthood. The reporter described the therapist as "a single mother." This was the sole reference to the woman's personal life.

The reporter failed to realize that she had in front of her an example of what the story was describing in the abstract. She should have told the reader whether the therapist was widowed, divorced. . . .

The campus correspondent for a local newspaper showed the city editor a story he had written for his college newspaper. He wanted to know whether it would interest the editor. The story began this way:

College students face problems ranging from alcohol abuse to loneliness, but the difficulties can be handled with a little friendly assistance, say members of the Campus Ministerial Association.

The organization's members, composed of ministers representing six denominations, say that students here are like other young people.

"Students are not that different from anyone else," the Rev. . . .

The city editor looked up after reading the story. The piece has possibilities, he told the student. "You've done a lot of work. You quote the director of the Wesley Foundation, the director of the Baptist Student Center, a Catholic priest and an Episcopal vicar.

"They have interesting things to say about students experimenting with drugs, sex and alcohol and then feeling guilty or lost.

Human Interest Adds Life

Lifeless. A story that lacks people is as lifeless as a photograph without a human form. Most events affect people, which is why editors instruct reporters to tell their stories in human terms.

Lively. When readers see people in news stories they identify with them, sharing their problems, successes and defeats. The presence of people in stories also makes the stories clearer.

"But the story is missing a key element. It's about the problems of students, but there are no students in it. You haven't talked to any students.

"The story lacks human interest. It moves all around the subject but never shows us the people who are directly involved."

He suggested the student reporter return to his sources and ask for some typical cases. The reporter could promise not to use names if necessary.

Readers and listeners want to see, hear and read about the way people are affected by events. Since the human element catches the reader's interest, it should be put high in the story. Tell the story in human terms.

We all want to get behind the walls and fences people construct around themselves, and we want to pierce the anonymity of the city. We want to know what went on inside a room down the hall last night when someone screamed. Or whose 10-speed bike was left chained to a post and stripped of every part but the frame. Or what happened to the family whose home burned last night. Who took them in? Have they any clothing?

We want to know what people do under stress, what they think about when they have problems. We wonder why the striking postal worker cannot make it on his salary, what people do when their homes are flooded. What, we ask ourselves, does the unemployed teen-ager want—a job or a handout? The church page has the usual sermons, but nothing about what the 7-year-old child or the old woman in the black shawl are praying for. The newlyweds are honeymooning at the Lake of the Ozarks, but the wedding story says nothing about why they chose this particular place.

Good stories answer our questions. They give us the information we need and want.

After high waters flooded three Kentucky counties, R.G. Dunlop of *The Courier-Journal* talked to some of the people in the area. He began his account with a human interest detail.

SALYERSVILLE, KY.—For the second time in less than three years, Anita Frazier will be shopping for new carpet.

The old rugs in her home on East Maple Street didn't wear out—they were soaked useless by flood waters.

December 1978 was the first time the water had ever crept into the house where Mrs. Frazier has lived since 1920.

Monday morning was the second time.

Residents in Magoffin, Morgan and Bath counties continued to clean up yesterday in the wake of flooding that damaged many roads and bridges and an estimated 300 homes, and that laid waste to countless acres of tobacco, corn and family gardens. . . .

Beyond the Statistics

"I notice that it is always the seemingly inconsequential stories that retain their life. The front-page news about treaties signed and generals traveling to China has been superseded by other treaties and other journeys of state; most of the editorial opinion has been proved wrong, and the melodramatic generalization turns out to have missed the point. But the stories toward the back of the paper, about a lost child or a woman paying alimony or the New York City police catching stray madmen in nets, lose nothing with the passage of time.

"The press makes sculptures in snow; its truth dwells in the concrete fact and the fleeting sound of the human voice."—Lewis H. Lapham, editor, *Harper's.*

What's bothering you?
Put that question to people.
What they say could tip
you off to story ideas. Polls
have shown that people are
worried about drunken
driving, drug abuse,
schooling, crime and fatal
diseases such as AIDS.

When postal workers went on strike, Marcia Chambers, then with *The News Tribune* in Perth Amboy, N.J., dug beneath the union and government statements to look into the life of a striking worker. Here is how her story began:

This March Joe Capik will have worked as a mail carrier in Perth Amboy for 20 years. He takes care of his wife and four children on $110 a week.

Mostly he and his four children, who live at 56 Maplewood Ave. in a Cape Cod bungalow in Keasbey, eat dinners of stews and soups and spaghetti. Things were bad enough last year, he said, that he applied for food stamps. But the county turned him down.

As a mail carrier, he cannot afford much more than stews and spaghetti.

Last week Joe Capik went out on strike for the first time in his life. He joined 49 letter carriers who were on strike for the first time in the 195-year history of the postal system.

"I don't feel right about striking. I really don't," he said outside the deserted post office in Perth Amboy.

"But it's a question of desperation. The situation has been forced upon us," he said. . . .

Human interest takes the reader to the heart of the event. A strike involves people seeking to change their circumstances. Joe Capik represents that human desire.

Sharp Observations

As the dean listened to students presenting a student council study of dormitory regulations, he drummed his fingers on the desk in front of him. He frequently looked at the clock on the wall above the door, and now and then he stared out the window for half a minute or more.

What do you think the dean thought of the student presentation? Whatever he might have said about the study, his actions reveal impatience and boredom. A story that includes these observations would capture the full dimension, the human dimension, of the event.

We can tell the reader or listener a great deal by including these human interest details. The house whose lawn is littered with beer cans says more about the people living there than quotations from the residents themselves.

Human interest can also be put into a story by the use of personal pronouns and concrete nouns:

1. Johnson put **his** pencil down and closed **his** book.
2. Johnson put the pencil down and closed the book.
3. For a textbook, he thought, it was as lively as one of **Professor Albrecht's** good lectures.
4. For a textbook, he thought, it was as lively as a good lecture.

Sentences 1 and 3 have human interest: 1 contains a personal pronoun, and 3 has the name of a teacher, a concrete noun. Compare the following sentences and indicate which have human interest:

5. It had a bad odor.
6. It smelled like burned rubber.
7. His back ached.
8. His back felt like the football team had practiced on it.

Sentences 6 and 8 introduce the human senses. Reporters should ask their sources what it smelled like, just how bad it felt, what the noise reminded them of, and so on.

Identification

Writers identify the people they are writing about so that readers and listeners can visualize, locate and identify these people. The standard identifying material is **name, age, address** and **occupation.**

Another kind of identification is essential in stories that quote a source as an authority. In this situation, the source must be identified by title or background to give the person the authority to speak on the subject on which he or she is being quoted:

> "Freedom of the press is guaranteed only to those who own one," A.J. Liebling wrote. Liebling, a newspaper reporter who turned to magazine and book writing, was a staunch critic of the press. For years he wrote a column called "Wayward Press" for *The New Yorker* magazine.

Identification is the journalist's way of drawing a quick portrait of the people about whom he or she writes.

Name The best source for the proper spelling of a person's name is the individual. The telephone book and city directory are usually accurate. If a person uses a middle initial, include that in the story. Nicknames are rarely used except in sports stories or features.

Identify titles and names in a story with which the reader is unfamiliar. "When a faculty member at George Mason University won the Nobel Memorial Prize in Economic Science, we ran a 1,000-word profile of the institution (Dec. 31). Not one word revealed the identity of George Mason. (He was a lifelong friend of George Washington and co-author of the Bill of Rights, among many distinctions)," said *The New York Times* staff critique, "Winners & Sinners."

Age A person's age should be used only when it bears directly on the story. It is always used in obituaries and in stories about the victims of accidents and fires. It is also used when it helps to make the point of the story. The youth of John Kennedy and the age of Ronald Reagan were relevant in their presidential campaigns.

The older that people become in this youth-conscious culture, the more reticent they are about their age. When it is relevant, the reporter is obligated to put it in. This can be done with taste:

> She graduated from high school in 1932.

> He was 30 when the United States entered World War II, and he immediately volunteered.

Address Where a person lives can tell the reader a great deal. An address in a high-income neighborhood sends one kind of message, an address in a poor neighborhood another. The address also helps the reader to put the person in a setting—large lawns and single residence homes or low-income city projects. The address can indicate a lifestyle.

Occupation Work defines many people. That is, the jobs that people hold often describe their character and personality. Think of the images that you build from the following job titles: hotel maid, film producer, grocer, commercial fisherman, teacher, actor. Obviously, those pictures are general and we cannot push them too far or we will stereotype individuals.

We can use still more visual detail. Height, weight, hair color, distinguishing physical characteristics. How a person speaks, his or her posture and mannerisms. All these help us see a person. They are used in profiles and feature stories when the writer is trying to draw a full portrait of the subject.

Race, religion and national origin are sometimes essential to a story but too often they are injected when they have no bearing on the story.

The New York Times Manual of Style and Usage cautions writers:

> Race should be specified only if it is truly pertinent. The same stricture applies to ethnic and religious identifications.

When the Roman Catholic Church appointed an archbishop in France, news stories pointed out that he was born a Jew. To keep him from death in the Nazi concentration camps, his parents turned him over to a Catholic family, which reared him in the Catholic faith. His parents died in the Holocaust. Obviously, religion was pertinent in this story.

Every story has a theme, the point the writer is trying to make. This is also the focus of the piece. As we've seen, this usually is placed at the beginning of the story. Newspapers and magazines that use the delayed lead often place the news point in what they call the **nut graph.** This paragraph sums up the key points of the story.

Reporters determine the news point or lead as soon as possible so that they can gather supporting and buttressing material for the lead while reporting. Writers who discover the news point while writing often find they lack the supporting facts and quotations for the body of the story.

Experienced reporters usually have a good idea of the story early in their reporting, though they are alert to the possibility of contradicting material. When their reporting reveals information that contradicts their idea about the story, reporters develop a new idea that is consistent with their observations. Reporters are aware of the danger of seeing and hearing only what they set out to see and hear.

No reporter should start to write the story without a sure grasp of what his or her point is.

News Point. Every story has a theme, a central idea. It can be firemen successfully battling an oil tank blaze or the mayor losing his bid for reelection. The theme usually is stated in the lead so that readers know the point of the story. The lead may state that it took 35 firefighters four hours to bring the fire under control or that the mayor lost the election by fewer than 100 votes, or was buried in a landslide of votes for his opponent.
Photo by Charlie Riedel of The Hays (Kan.) Daily News. Used with permission.

Objectivity

The great strength of journalism in the United States, Canada and a number of western European countries is its objectivity. Newspaper readers and listeners and viewers know that the news is written by journalists who are impartial and independent. That is, the journalists' loyalty is to the public, not to a political party, an organization or a sect.

Objectivity has two meanings:

The work itself: A story is objective when it is balanced and impersonal; the reporter does not include his or her opinions, feelings, biases. Information is verified through the reporter's direct observation of the event or by documents and records to which the reporter can point as proof of his or her account. The objective writer subordinates feelings to the facts.

The tradition: Journalism in the so-called free world represents "an impartial third party, the one that speaks for the general interest," says James Boylan, a member of the journalism faculty at the University of Massachusetts at Amherst. Walter Lippmann, the philosopher of journalistic objectivity, "depicted journalism as an institution apart, charged with supplying society with reliable, impartial information," says Boylan.

The reader of a newspaper in Boston and the viewer of a morning news program in Muncie take it for granted that what they are reading and viewing is accurate, reliable information and not propaganda. The material has been examined by a reporter for errors, misstatements, vagueness. In other words, the reporter is not a transmission belt but acts as a filter to ensure the reader and viewer that the information is balanced, fair and accurate.

Beginners have a difficult time keeping their enthusiasms, their feelings and opinions out of stories.

How do these sentences differ?

1. The city council last night gave city workers an extravagant wage increase of 15 percent.

2. The city council last night gave city workers a wage increase of only 15 percent.

3. The city council last night gave city workers a 15 percent wage increase.

If your answer is that sentences 1 and 2 express opinions, you are right. Neither belongs in a news story, unless attributed to a source. The writer cannot make these statements.

The opinion in the first sentence is obvious. The use of the word *extravagant* reveals that the news writer believes the workers should not have been given such an increase. Opinions of this sort belong on the editorial page of the newspaper.

The second sentence implies that the workers deserve more than the 15 percent increase granted to them: They received an increase of *only* 15 percent. The third sentence is acceptable because it states the fact without opinion. The reader can draw whatever conclusion he or she wishes.

Objectivity requires that the reporter keep to himself or herself feelings and opinions. A reporter may believe it is tragic and unnecessary that children suffer from poverty. But in his or her story the reporter is confined to the facts about poverty. By presenting the facts, by showing a child in poverty, the reporter communicates information that leads the reader to feel compassion, perhaps anger at the child's plight. Also, when a reader draws his or her own conclusion, the message is more intensely felt than when the reader is hammered with a message.
Photo copyright by Joel Strasser. Used with permission.

Opinion is the writer's injection of his or her feelings about the subject. Usually, it is an expression that indicates the writer's approval or disapproval. Sentences 1 and 2 imply the writer's disapproval. A lead like the following expresses approval, which is common in sports copy when the reporter becomes a fan instead of an unbiased observer:

```
The Spartans lost in overtime 58-53 last night to
the LaGrange Wildcats, but the state champion
visitors knew that they had met their match in the
courageous Spartans.
```

At first glance, this may not seem to be opinion, and that's the trouble with opinions in copy. Nine times out of 10, the writer is unaware that they are there. Usually, opinions insinuate themselves into the story when the writer gets too close to the subject. No question that the sports writer who wrote this lead was carried away by the home team's valiant effort. By putting in the adjective *courageous* the writer shows he or she approves of the team's effort. That's something the reader should be allowed to conclude from the facts the writer presents.

"... **reporters can't** afford to remain in awe of those they cover. People expect the press to hold the mayor's feet to the fire and to bore in on the city council and to make sure the governor doesn't get away with a thing."—Sam Donaldson, ABC White House correspondent.

Good advice for writers: Keep cool. This is especially sound advice for sports writers. They have no business rooting for any team. Unlike radio and television sports announcers who are hired by local teams, the sports reporter should be as non-partisan as the political reporter.

Now, look over these sentences and try to spot where the reporter has intruded.

A

The women's fencing team won its first match of the year under its outstanding new coach, Alice Meyers.

B

His reluctance to speak about the incident indicated fear of being trapped by the police.

C

The building was the fourth in the area to report fire damage, and, like the three others, was probably the handiwork of an arsonist.

D

The Democratic candidate, like others of his party, favors spending on social issues, which invariably leads to an unbalanced budget.

Here is how an editor analyzed these sentences:

A. "Be careful of adjectives. Every time you use one make sure it is justified, that you can prove it. The first sentence says the coach is 'outstanding.' Also that she is 'new.' Clearly, if this is her first year, she is new, and the reader presumes that you can prove that. But 'outstanding'? What's that mean? That she is good? If she's new, she still has to show that she is outstanding. No, here we have the reporter's enthusiasm—or his or her bias toward the new coach—taking over. You could quote the athletic director if he says Alice Meyers is outstanding, but you cannot say it yourself."

B. "All we know is that he didn't answer police questions. How does the reporter know what was on the guy's mind? Has the reporter 20–20 X-ray eyes that can bore into the guy's head? Maybe he was afraid. Maybe he was taking his lawyer's advice to be mum. Who knows? Of course, if a police officer says to you, 'The guy wouldn't talk—afraid of getting himself in a bind,' then you can quote that. You have someone to pin that conclusion or inference on. The question, though, is whether it's fair to use the officer's quote. I wouldn't. After all, how does he know? And he is implying guilt. Only a jury can determine that."

C. "We don't guess or deal in probabilities. Even if this were the hundredth building to burn and 99 had been torched by an arsonist, we can't make the inference about the hundredth. When we talk about inferences we mean that the person who makes an inference jumps from what is known to the unknown. In this case, we know there was a fourth fire and we know that three others in the same area involved arson. But we do not know that the fourth was caused by arson. It's possible, but until an authority says he has proof of arson, it's not our job to say so. If the reader wants to jump to the conclusion— make the inference—that the fourth fire was arson, that's fine with us."

D. "No opinions, please. There are two in the sentence. The reporter says, 'like others of his party.' Well, it is true that Democrats in general have been more willing than Republicans to have the government support the poor, the handicapped and others. But not all Democrats follow this philosophy, as is obvious from reading the papers. The second opinion is that spending for social purposes leads to an unbalanced budget. There are many causes of an unbalanced budget—huge defense spending, low taxes, for example."

Before we let the editor persuade us that the journalist can be as detached as the engineer measuring a girder, we have to point out that journalists do have ideas of their own. They have strong opinions, and they jump to conclusions as rapidly as a fan leaps to his feet when the hometown team scores a basket. Like everyone else, journalists have convictions, a sense of right and wrong.

Total Objectivity Impossible

Shades of Opinion

"We are proud not of our objectivity but of our independence. Readers know the views of the reporter and expect them to be reflected in their stories."—an editor of *Le Monde*.

"Why should freedom of speech be allowed? Why should a government which is doing what it believes to be right allow itself to be criticized?" Journalists should be "agitators, propagandists and agents of the state."—Lenin.

"We shut them [the newspaper *Ayendegan*] up because we knew who they were and what they were after. And this is not contrary to freedom. This is done everywhere. . . ."—Ayatollah Khomeini.

"The press is the chief democratic instrument of freedom."—Alexis de Tocqueville.

"The theory of a free press is that the truth will emerge from free reporting and free discussion, not that it will be presented perfectly and instantly in any one account."—Walter Lippmann.

"The majority of the countries in the world have no free press. In only a fourth are newspapers and broadcast stations free to carry what journalists write. In countries where journalists challenge censorship, they are arrested, tortured and murdered."—Freedom House.

These convictions, beliefs and opinions can direct the reporter's journalism to rewarding stories. But they cannot be inserted into the story.

"Every good journalist I know has convictions," says Thomas Griffith, a veteran reporter and editor with *Time*. "But it is in his capacity to separate his beliefs from his reporting that a journalist should be judged."

Verification

When a reporter checks his or her information against some kind of objective source, we say that the material has been verified.

The New York Times has a rule: "Don't trust anybody on anything that is checkable." This rule applies even to the most trustworthy sources. They can make mistakes, such as the press release from an artists' representative who reported a show at a gallery on East 66th Street. The reporter given the release made a routine check in the phone book. The gallery was on East 61st Street. A press release carried an attractive photograph and an interesting text. But it was marred by the mispelling of the word *embarrassed*.

Verification requires checking spellings and meanings in the dictionary, addresses in the telephone directory, background in clippings and reference works. It also requires that the reporter ask sources for proof of their important assertions. Reporters are not megaphones for sources.

First and *record* are sometimes claimed by sources. Be careful, advises the AP. They often turn out "to be a lot less than someone claimed. Try to check such claims with an agency or reference who might know whether the superlatives apply. If you can't confirm a claim is valid, qualify it in your story—if you decide to use it. For example, if a bank says it's the first to give rifles to depositors, say in your copy that the bank believes it's first."

Mary Hargrove, special-projects editor of *The Tulsa Tribune,* describes what happens when a source has his way with a reporter—chagrin and embarrassment result. She interviewed officials of the Penn Square Bank of Oklahoma City after the bank was reported to be in trouble.

No problems, bank officials told her. "I go on my way, fat, dumb, and happy," she said. She wrote a page-one story about the soundness of the bank. That was on the July 4th weekend.

"After the holiday, the bank is closed," she said.

Hargrove did not take it lying down. "I was mad. Those guys lied to me. I wanted to know what happened." She and three other reporters spent a month gathering information and disclosed the activities of the officers of the bank whose failure sent shudders through the country's banking system. (A profile of Hargrove, "Best in the West," by Alan Prendergast was published in the July/August 1987 *Washington Journalism Review.*)

Hoaxes

Although reporters often are warned about shooting from the hip, about going with what they've got before verification, even the most sophisticated are taken in now and then. One day, a messenger showed up in the New York UPI newsroom with a death announcement from a law firm. The obituary was on the firm's letterhead, and the packet included a biographical sketch of the deceased and a photograph. The dead man was L. Dennis Plunkett, aged 31, editor-in-chief of *National Lampoon,* according to the statement. Plunkett died, the note said, after addressing about 300 students at Cornell University the previous evening. Cause of death was undetermined.

The UPI desk moved the obituary on the wires, and within a short time the UPI's Chicago bureau called New York and said the obituary sounded fishy. New York killed the story and checked with the magazine, which informed the UPI it had no one named Plunkett on its staff and no such title as editor-in-chief. At the New York AP bureau, the staff was trying to verify the obituary when it was called by the UPI to warn the agency about the hoax.

UPI tightened its procedures to require verification of all obituaries.

The point of verifying or confirming material is to try to guarantee its truth for the reader or listener. Accuracy is important, but it is not enough.

"The fact without the truth is futile; indeed, the fact without the truth is false." The source is G.K. Chesterton, an English writer who lanced shams and charlatans. This same idea was taken up in the 1950s by Elmer Davis, a radio journalist who was one of the few journalists who sought to determine the truth of the charges of treason and subversion being made by Sen. Joseph McCarthy of Wisconsin.

While it was a fact that McCarthy said many people prominent in government were members or sympathizers of the Communist Party, which the press dutifully reported, Davis asked: Is it true? He asked further: Does the press have an obligation to tell people the truth of the fact?

Attribution does take the responsibility of assertions, charges and declarations from the shoulders of the press. But in serious matters, shouldn't the press try to dig out the truth on its own?

Davis said yes, and the press through the years has come to agree with him. Reporters have made independent verification of charges, statements, accusations, even of convictions in court.

Paul Henderson of *The Seattle Times* took seriously the protestations of innocence of a man convicted of first-degree rape. Henderson dug into the story and five days before the man was to be sentenced, he presented evidence that set the man free.

Next, we turn to story building. Bad story structure is one of the three most common faults of newswriting. The others are the wrong lead, and vague or unclear writing.

When we say a story is badly put together or structured, we usually mean that the newswriter is jumping here and there, from one topic to another so that the reader or listener is left on the corner as the story goes whizzing by in six different directions. Read on and we'll see how to make that driver follow the rules of the road.

Sad, very sad, the journalism instructor said to himself as he read a student's story about a homeless and penniless young man who said he was a graduate of West Point. The instructor was even sadder when a week after the piece had been distributed to newspaper subscribers of the student service, the West Point public information officer called to say no person by that name had ever attended West Point. The moral: People make all sorts of assertions. Check them out.

Bernstein, Theodore. *Watch Your Language*. Great Neck, N.Y.: Channel Press, 1958.

White, E.B. *Essays of E.B. White*. New York: Harper & Row, 1977.

Suggested Reading

5

Structuring the Story

Building the news story begins with the lead as the foundation. Once the news writer knows what he or she wants to emphasize the story begins to form a shape or pattern.
Photo by Jim Peppler of Newsday. Used with permission.

Looking Ahead

The news story is put together or structured according to the number of main elements or themes the writer decides to use in the lead.

The single-element story is the most common. The body of the news story includes the facts, quotes and incidents that explain, buttress and support the element used in the lead. Less important material is included in the body of the story after the lead element has been adequately explained.

Some stories have two or three important elements. Leads for these stories include all the elements or a summary of the elements. The body of the story explains each element in order, supplying the reader with the supporting material to buttress the elements stated in the lead. Any secondary material follows.

The news writer is a builder. From notes, background and personal knowledge he or she constructs a logical and complete structure. Like any builder, the news writer works from plans. Just as the builder has one set of plans for an office structure, another for an apartment building and a third for a three-bedroom home, so the news writer has different plans for different types of stories.

If one idea, action or event clearly stands out as the most important or unusual aspect of what was said or done, then the writer has a single-theme story. All other ideas, actions and occurrences are secondary. A single-theme story requires a single-element lead. When two or three aspects stand out, the writer has a two-element or three-element story. The lead will include these elements. Once the writer selects the main theme or themes and decides whether the event requires a straight news story or feature, he or she begins to structure the story.

Let's first examine the organization of the straight news story. The starting point is deciding how many major elements or themes the story will include.

Organizing the Straight News Story

When we talk about themes or elements we don't mean individual facts. A story may contain many facts but only one, two or three major themes or elements. You might say that a theme or element of a story is the summary of a set of facts.

The city council votes 4–3 in favor of a major street paving program. That becomes the major element for the lead. The arguments for and against the program, the present condition of city streets, the city engineer's statement that twice the proposed amount is needed to fix the streets—all these are facts that go into the body of the story to support the major element in the lead.

The city council also considered other items that the news writer will include in the story: hiring a new director for the city recreation department, a city-county garbage disposal plan and the suggestion that holidays be scheduled so that city employees can have three-day weekends.

These themes are secondary in importance to the street-paving program and are included in the story after the news writer has given ample attention in the body of the story to the street-paving program, which is the major theme.

If the city council had voted to spend $500,000 on the garbage disposal plan, that would have been a major element also. Approval of the paving program and the garbage disposal plan could be included in the lead. After these two elements are explained in the body of the story, the writer goes on to the secondary material.

Donald M. Murray, a news writing coach, says the lead can be thought of as the promise and the body what makes good on that promise. The lead says to the reader or listener: Hey, look at what I found out. The body says: Let me explain it to you.

No news story should try to say so much that the reader or listener will turn away in confusion. This is why the news story must confine itself to only the most important or interesting elements of the event.

Single-Element Story. The score in this soccer game is the major element of the story and usually goes into the lead. The names of the players who scored, the key offensive and defensive plays, the changes in the standings and the home team's next game are additional facts that are placed in the body of the story.
Susan Plageman, The Berkshire Eagle.

Single-Element News Story

A plane crash kills three people. A local clothing store is swept by fire. The president flies to Mexico for a conference. A former school principal dies. The Rangers beat the Red Sox.

These are spot news stories, and like most spot news stories, they make for single-element news stories. All single-element news stories take the basic structure shown in figure 5.1.

The first paragraph contains the lead. The second paragraph either elaborates on the lead or provides the necessary background. The story continues with additional supporting and buttressing information about the lead. When the writer has finished with all the relevant material to support the main element of the story, secondary themes are then added.

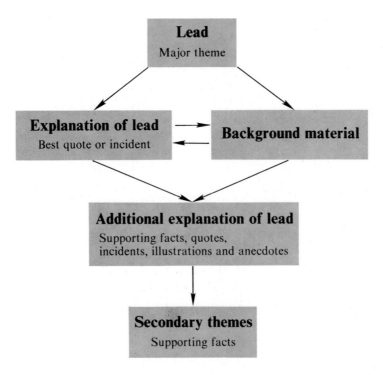

Figure 5.1 Single-element story structure.

Forest Fire   The following is an example of a spot news story with a single major theme, a one-element story:

Lead: Fire may spread

A fire in the Daniel Boone National Forest that has destroyed 500 acres of woodland is threatening to spread to private lands.

Explanation of the lead: High winds causing fire to spread

The Kentucky Division of Forestry reported today that high winds have made control of the blaze difficult. The winds are pushing the fire toward timberlands to the northeast, agency officials said.

Background: When started, cause, weather conditions

The fire broke out Thursday. The cause is undetermined. Forest fires are common during periods of dry, warm weather such as the area is now experiencing, an official said.

Additional explanation of the lead	The forestry division has sent 40 firefighters to the area to try to contain the fire. But they have been hampered by the lack of access roads.
More explanation of the lead	No inhabited areas are threatened by the fire, the official said. But there are valuable timberlands to the northeast owned by private growers.
Secondary theme	The forestry division is trying a new form of forest-fire spray that was developed by the state's engineers. In addition to digging trenches and felling trees in the path of the fire, the firefighters are using a spray that temporarily causes leaves and needles to drop, thus making it more difficult for the fire to spread.

Two-Element News Story

The governor announces that because of financial problems he must take drastic action on two educational matters. He is ordering an immediate halt in the $25 million construction program on college and university campuses. He also says he will recommend to the state board of education that all salaries for public school teachers in the state be frozen for next year.

As a reporter on your college newspaper, you want to know whether construction will be halted on your campus. You discover that the order eliminates a plan for a $3 million dormitory to be built with state funds. This gives you a good single-element story. The freezing of salaries for public school teachers does not directly affect your readers, so it becomes secondary material.

Press association reporters and state capital bureau reporters from large daily newspapers realize that both announcements will interest their readers. Because the reporters consider the items of equal importance, they will construct their stories on a two-element lead.

There are three ways to structure the two-element story:

1. If the two elements conveniently fit into a single sentence, the writer can put them both in the first paragraph.

2. If combining both elements into a single sentence requires more than 35 or 40 words, the writer will have to give each element a sentence of its own. This option allows the writer to place both sentences in the first paragraph or to make each sentence into a separate paragraph.

3. If the two elements cannot be squeezed into a sentence (option one) and the writer does not want to write a two-sentence or two-paragraph lead (option two) because it would be too long and cumbersome, a third option is available—the summary lead. A summary lead is just what its name implies: It sums up the two elements by using an introductory statement.

"Go through all your notes and sort them in some kind of order. Recheck anything you're not certain of. Make an outline for the story or series. Decide what information *not* to include (oh, the pain). Talk it over with your editor. Argue. Write the first draft. Write it again. And again, if necessary."—Roberta Heiman, special assignments editor of *The Evansville* (Ind.) *Courier*.

Money Troubles   Let's see what a news writer for a daily in the state capital does with the governor's announcement about financial cutbacks. He takes the options in order. He would prefer a lead that can handle both elements in fewer than 35 words (the first option). He writes:

```
    Gov. Mark Acosta said today that financial problems
necessitate an immediate halt to a $25 million state
college construction program, and he also said he
will recommend a freeze in salaries for public school
teachers.
```

The lead just makes it by word count, but it has a jammed-up feel to it. He decides to try the second option, two sentences:

```
    Gov. Mark Acosta said today financial problems
necessitate an immediate halt to a $25 million state
college construction program. He also said he will
recommend a freeze in salaries for public school
teachers.
```

No. Still jammed-up. What's more, he suddenly sees he has the lead turned around. He should put the wage freeze first since more people are affected by the freeze than by the college construction program.

Even if he does reverse the elements, he still has a bulky lead. As for making each sentence into a paragraph, he does not like two-paragraph leads unless he is forced to use them.

Can he cut down on the number of words? Yes, he can put the reason for the governor's drastic actions in the second paragraph:

```
    Gov. Mark Acosta said today he will recommend a
freeze in salaries for public school teachers next
year, and he ordered an immediate halt to a $25
million state college construction program.
    The governor said financial problems necessitated
his actions. He said that cutbacks in federal aid for
education had not been anticipated when the
construction program was adopted.
```

That's better, he thinks. He has also managed to insert background material into the second paragraph. But the city editor is a short-lead advocate. He likes leads under 25 words, so the reporter now must try a summary lead, the third option. In writing a summary lead, the trick is to find something common to both elements. The state's financial troubles ties in both elements here.

The reporter also notes that the actions were described by the governor as "drastic" and so he decides to use that as the basis of his summary lead:

> Gov. Mark Acosta said today financial problems have
> forced him to take "drastic" action on teacher
> salaries and the state college construction program.
> The governor said he will recommend a freeze on the
> salaries of public school teachers. And he ordered an
> immediate halt to the $25 million college
> construction program.
> The governor said unforeseen federal cutbacks
> necessitated his actions. . . .

Trouble at the Dump   Here is a two-paragraph lead (the second option) that a reporter wrote about a city countil meeting because he decided the two major elements could not be squeezed into a lead sentence:

> The city council last night voted to postpone a
> decision on the purchase of acreage north of the city
> for a garbage dump after angry residents in the area
> disrupted the council meeting.
> In another action, the council voted 4-3 to end
> financing of the city's summer educational programs
> despite protests from parent groups.

Too much action for the reader to grasp, the writer thinks. He decides on a summary lead (the third option). He has to find a common idea that links the two elements. Obviously, one common idea is that the two actions were taken by the city council. But that's so broad it says next to nothing. Another idea is that the actions are important, but that's too broad also. There is another common idea, the protesting groups. He tries to make something of this:

> One group of residents had their way with the city
> council last night, but a second group of angry
> protesters lost out.

Not too bad. Let's accept this, then see what comes next. The writer must immediately elaborate on the two actions in order:

> The successful protest was aimed at the council's
> consideration of the purchase of acreage north of the
> city for a garbage dump. Residents from the area
> disrupted the council meeting with their protest.
> The council postponed a decision.
> In the other action, the council voted 4-3 to end
> financing of the city's summer educational programs
> despite the protests of parent groups.

Two-Element Story. A story about a flood that takes several lives and causes considerable property damage has these two elements in the lead. Rescue efforts, loss of power and telephone service, the weather forecast for the rest of the week and closed highways are secondary facts that are placed in the story after the deaths and the property loss are explained.
Photo by Stewart Bowman of The Courier-Journal. Used with permission.

Although the summary lead takes a while to get the reader to the heart of the story, it is preferred by many newspapers and is the way broadcast leads for complex stories are written. It does not overwhelm the reader or listener. The summary lead beckons the reader to come into the story.

Organize Supporting Material   We saw in the single-element story that the body of the piece consists of background information and the explanation or elaboration of the lead. Additional or secondary material is included deep in the story. The two-element story follows the same general outline with one major difference.

The important principle to remember in writing multiple-element stories is not to jump around. The writer should not write a paragraph with material that supports lead element A and then jump to a paragraph of supporting material for lead element B, and then back to A, and so forth. The result would be a confused reader or listener.

The guideline is to put similar material together. Put all the supporting material about lead element A together before you begin to elaborate on element B. In the city council meeting story, the body includes material about the garbage dump first since that was the first element mentioned in the lead. After the key supporting material about the dump is used in the body, the reporter writes a transition or swing paragraph introducing the summer program, and then the buttressing material for the vote on the summer program is used.

To jump from element A to element B would be too abrupt. We need a transition from one element to the other. By this we mean a paragraph, a sentence, one or two words that will swing the reader from one topic to another. The move must be made in a graceful sweep.

Here is a possible transition in the council meeting story after the explanation of element A (successful protest against the garbage dump) to element B (vote to end the city's summer programs):

```
While the garbage-dump protesters were pleased by
the council action, the parents hoping to retain the
summer programs were disappointed.
```

A good transition tells readers where they have been (action on dump) and then informs them where they are being taken (action on summer program).

Notice the word *while* in the sentence that serves as a transition. *While* is a conjunction, a word or phrase that serves as a connector. Connectors join the different elements in a story and make the piece have the structure of a linked chain. Here are some other conjunctions:

and	next
but	before
however	after
on the other hand	in addition to
meanwhile	moreover
although	later
then	furthermore
now	nevertheless

You can see that these words are two-directional, taking the reader back and then projecting the reader forward. Notice their use in these transitional sentences:

The Hawks had no trouble with tonight's opponents, **but** tomorrow's game should be another story.

In addition to commenting on the high price of fuel she discussed the need for home insulation.

Next in his list of objections was the department's action on street repairs.

No reporter should be a slave to a formula. Sometimes, a news writer handling a two-element story will amplify A and B with a paragraph or two for each before moving into the fairly rigid compartmentalizing of the supporting material for each.

Some news writers will bring up secondary material before they have finished with all the supporting material for the lead elements. They do this when they consider the secondary material to be important but not important enough for the lead.

We are now ready to turn to the three-element story. There are no surprises. Our basic approach is the same.

For a roundup of college basketball games, the wire service sports writer found three important contests and put them all in the lead this way:

Three-Element
News Story

```
     UCLA, Georgia and Ohio State won key basketball
games last night against conference rivals.
```

Then the writer gave the score and important plays or strategy of each game in order.

Teen-agers and Dope The city editor has just finished reading a story in the Sunday *New York Times* about youngsters and marijuana. He calls over a reporter and tells her, "Boil this down and give the *Times* full credit. We're going to have a series on the local drug scene among youngsters and I want to show our readers that we are not sensationalizing the local scene."

The reporter reads through the story and sees that there are three elements: Teen-agers can find pot easily, don't feel guilty about using it and have no fear of using it.

The reporter takes three sheets of paper and puts one element at the top of each sheet. Under each element, she lists the supporting data. (Saul Pett of AP Newsfeatures and other professionals often make outlines for their features.)

On her first sheet, for example, under the heading "Find easily," she writes:

```
     Buy from classmates.
     Buy from street salesmen.
     Even pushers at famous Public Library.
     Cocaine and heroin also sold here.
```

She makes similar lists on the other two sheets. On a fourth sheet she lists the secondary material, such as the increase in drinking among teen-agers.

She is now ready to write. She would like to put all three elements in the lead for emphasis, to show the scope of the situation:

```
New York teen-agers who smoke marijuana can find it
easily, do not feel guilty about using it and have
little fear of being arrested.
    These are the findings of a survey of 1,000 high
school students as reported in "The New York Times"
Sunday. . . .
```

Now, all she need do is go to her first sheet and elaborate on the availability of pot. When that is finished, she will write a transition and go to the second sheet about lack of guilt, and so on until she has completed the secondary material.

The 1, 2, 3 Approach Reporters occasionally use a variation of the summary lead for a story with three elements. The 1, 2, 3 approach (the fourth option) looks something like this:

"The writer," Samuel Johnson is supposed to have said, "is a person for whom the act of writing is more difficult than it is for other people."

```
    The city council took three far-reaching actions at
its meeting last night.
    The council voted to:
    1. Open bids on the controversial community center
that had been stalled in court.
    2. Buy three parcels of land for a new downtown
mass transit center.
    3. Construct a pedestrian overpass over Highway 28
where the Arden Hills Shopping Center will be built.
```

The three items can also be listed right at the outset as Margaret Sullivan does in a story for the *Buffalo News* that begins this way:

• If a woman is really smart and aggressive in business, she's good at hiding the fact that she's smart and aggressive.

• The sexual thing just doesn't go away in business situations.

• Nightmares, depression and stress are the price women pay as they make their way through a male-dominated corporate superstructure.

Those statements—the words of a Buffalo businessman, a local woman accountant and a Stanford University study—just begin to tell the story about women in business, a story that doesn't show up on any company's balance sheet.

Suddenly, without warning, women have become a presence in Buffalo business, and not as glorified secretaries—not by a long shot.

There are a couple of partners in national accounting firms, a bank president and several vice presidents, some owners of mid-sized businesses and a big group of up-and-comers.

So far the sailing hasn't all been smooth, and as women head into the 1980s—a decade that should see them growing in numbers and prominence—they'll face problems most businessmen never even think about.

In the fourth paragraph, Sullivan summarizes her points by saying that the three items are part of the story on women in business. The fifth and sixth paragraphs give background.

Sullivan is then ready to tackle the supporting material to back up her major themes. She uses a transition to swing into the body in the seventh paragraph.

Now to the supporting material. To buttress her first theme, she quotes the dean of the School of Management at the State University at Buffalo, Joseph Alutto:

> "Businesswomen are often very aggressive and need to be, but it's a trait that people accept better in a man than in a woman."

She also quotes a woman shopowner in Buffalo:

> "Women walk a thin line in deciding how forward to be."

To buttress her second theme, sexual relationships in business, she writes:

> "The sexual issue does create problems," says Rand Capital Corp. president Donald Ross. "There are lots of liaisons, and they complicate and obscure the real issues."
>
> Romantic involvements are nothing new, these business people note, but they add that it's different now that some women are men's equals on the job.

> "No one cared when women were only secretaries and could be replaced like disposable parts," says Susan Jacoby.
>
> "It's always a two-way street, but usually there's a poor, misguided female involved who thinks that's the way to get to the top," observes stockbroker Rosemary Ligotti.

To support her third theme, the price women pay for going into business, she begins with a quick transition and then goes into the subject:

> The problems may lie deeper—taking a toll on a woman's emotional well-being.
>
> "Women may not realize the kinds of sacrifices they have to make to forge a successful career," says Miss Ptak.
>
> "They have to realize that it means taking things home, making business calls at night," she continues. "It's not 9-to-5. And it's stressful. They may have to sacrifice their social lives."

> Women who try to do it all—manage a family as well as an executive position—are far more likely to become depressed, anxious, and suffer nightmares. They also are four times more likely than men to seek psychological help, according to a Stanford University study of business school graduates.
>
> "These women are very hard on themselves. They feel they constantly have to be proving themselves," says co-author Harvey Weinstein.

Caution: Leads with two and three elements can be the lazy writer's way out of making tough decisions, and editors know this. Most events have one important element, not two or three, and it's up to the news writer to figure out which element stands out. The two- and three-element lead is used only when that struggle for the single-element lead fails to fix on the one element.

Experienced reporters have a way of handling complex stories within the single-element story structure. After a single-element lead and a couple of paragraphs that elaborate on the lead, this paragraph is written:

```
The mayor also:
• Asked for more parking garages downtown.
• Authorized the welfare director to create a
special agency to "cope with the homeless."
```

The writer then will develop the parking garage and homeless elements.

The Chronological Approach

Now that we have outlined the basic structure of the straight news story, we will look at a technique that is often used for the dramatic news story.

Ever since humans sat around a fire in a prehistoric cave and listened to the storyteller, people have liked a tale. No matter how often it is told, people will listen. Even when they know the outcome, they will hear the speaker out.

This is the reasoning behind the chronological approach to the breaking news story. Essentially, the story is told twice.

The lead tells the reader what happens, and a few paragraphs of buttressing and supporting material amplify the lead. Then there is a transition and the writer turns back to give an account of how the situation occurred—the day the crime was committed, the excitement of two couples as they set out for a wedding party, the first play of the dramatic last two minutes of the game.

Here is how the story of a frightening ride on a school bus began in *The Advocate* in Stamford, Conn.:

Forty junior high school students on school bus 10 were terrified Friday afternoon.

Their normal 15-minute ride home from Cloonan Middle School to the Westover and Long Ridge sections took more than an hour. The students said they spent the hour watching the bus career around curves and listening to drivers of oncoming cars honk warnings to slow down.

Some believed they were being kidnapped by their driver, but the school bus company said the man was merely lost.

"All the kids were screaming and some of the kids were crying," said Karen Seren, a seventh-grader, "We screamed to a policeman out the window, but he didn't believe us."

In their fear, eight students jumped out the rear door when the bus stopped at Rippowam High School, and they flagged down a police car for help. All the students eventually were returned home, late but safe.

Allen Graften, assistant superintendent of schools, said he will look into the incident and have some answers by Monday.

In these six paragraphs of this spot news story, Rita Jensen and Kevin Flynn have described the climax and the essentials of the event. The account could stop here. But there is so much local interest in an event of this kind, the writers knew, that they decided to go on. They wrote a transition paragraph and then picked up the chronological account that appeared this way:

> From accounts of the parents and children who called "The Advocate" and from the manager of ARA bus operations here, the ride of terror and confusion began when. . . .

Notice the word *began*. This tells the reader to sit back while the writer spins out the tale.

Inverted Pyramid If you noticed, these stories do not end with a climax. The climax is at the beginning, in the lead. The writer gives the major material, then the secondary information. It's the traditional story structure, the inverted pyramid.

This is a perfectly good overall guide to the straight news story. For important events, readers and listeners want to know what happened—now.

However, its use does limit the storytelling abilities of the writer. The chronological approach is one way out, but this approach can be overused.

For a long time writers struggled with the bonds of the inverted pyramid. In fact, they made it the symbol of the limitations of journalistic writing. It became fashionable for gifted writers to scoff at the inverted pyramid.

Their protests were valid—to a point. Actually, news writers who had mastered the basic style had for years been able to transcend the inverted pyramid and the traditional structures of the news story—when the occasion permitted it. The last clause bears repeating—when the occasion permitted it.

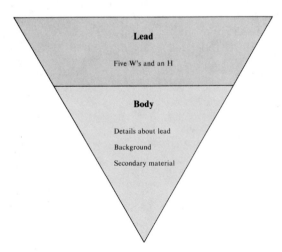

Figure 5.2 The inverted pyramid is so named because the major information is clustered at the top of the story. As the drawing illustrates, this leads to a top-heavy story. Some writers prefer to develop their stories gradually. However, straight news stories almost always do begin with the most important material high up.

Long before the New Journalists burst onto the scene, A.J. Liebling was writing brilliant, non-traditional stories, as were other journalists. One former newspaperman recalls covering the appearance of Miss America in California with an approach that predated the New Journalists.

Enter: Miss America "I was sent out to a motel where Miss America was to hold a news conference," the former reporter-turned-journalism teacher recalls. "She had just been crowned and she was making a national tour. That was news in those days, the 1950s, in small and medium-size towns."

The two print reporters and a television camera crew and reporter were sent to her suite, and they awaited her arrival in one of the rooms. In a corner was Miss America's mother, ironing a dress. They waited. After a five- or 10-minute delay, Miss America entered.

"She was holding a Pepsi, as I recall. Clutching it to her bosom, unopened. On one of the bureaus was a cardboard poster advertising another sponsor of the Miss America pageant," he said. "The whole business seemed arranged, staged."

At that point, he had the idea for his story about Miss America's visit. It would be in the form of a stage play.

He began his story with stage directions:

Stage right: Mother ironing blue evening gown. Advertising poster on bureau to left. Opened luggage on low racks. Reporters and camera crew sitting, chatting quietly.

Enter from rear of center stage: Miss America. She enters slowly, holding a soda bottle to her breast, unopened. There is a moment of silence. She speaks.

Miss America: "Thank you for coming. I have something to say and then I will answer questions. . . .

The former reporter says that when he handed in his story, the city editor laughed, started to hand it back, then decided to run it. "It was a one-day stand. I never wrote another play, but not because the idea was bad. I never had the opportunity. But it fitted the occasion."

At that time, such editors were rare. Most stayed with formula writing: Five W's and an H, even when the lead ran 50 or 60 words; inverted pyramid structure on most stories. These days, most editors want imagination and color in the writing, and when the event will allow it, they urge their reporters to use the techniques of the feature writer, even on straight news stories. Enter the news feature.

Before we examine the news feature in detail, let's look at the other parent that produced the hybrid we call the news feature—the feature.

The feature is journalism's grab bag. It can be about anything under the sun—even the sun itself. The feature can be as light and fluffy as a cream puff, or as solid and substantial as a rib roast. It can make us cry or laugh. One difference between the straight news story and the feature is that while the news story informs us by involving our reason and logic, the feature informs or entertains us by engaging our feelings.

Another distinctive mark of the feature is its style. The straight news story is just that, a straightforward account of an event. The feature is . . . well, there is no telling what form the feature may take. And this may well be its trademark. Some are humorous, some somber. And some cannot be catalogued, like this one:

> Six-year-old Brian Waters spotted a fence down the street from school yesterday and made a detour from his usual way home.
>
> He stared at the iron fence: IIIIIII.
>
> Then he decided to look into the yard through the fence: IIIoIII. But when Brian had seen enough he couldn't pull his head back.
>
> A passer-by called the fire department and a fireman approached the fence with a sledgehammer: /
>
> In short order, he had pried apart a couple of the bars: II(o)II. Brian wiped his tears and went on home.

The style of the feature is, as we can see, simple and relaxed. In a feature by Mike Stanton that moved over the AP wires, the story roams around almost as much as its subject—a college student who rode the rails to gather information for a term paper. Despite the rolling, informal style, Stanton gives us enough information by the end of the sixth paragraph that we have a solid picture of the person and what he did.

Here is the beginning of the story:

> AMHERST, MASS. (AP)— Ted Conover's classroom was a rolling boxcar, his first big test a fight with a drunken hobo. He fell off a train, foraged through garbage cans for food and got lice in his hair.
>
> The Amherst College student rode the rails for 3½ months, living the life of a railroad tramp, to research his senior thesis.
>
> He found that it wasn't all bad.
>
> "There's something about jumping on a freight train that just feels right," said Conover, a 23-year-old anthropology major from Denver.
>
> "It's the feeling of the wind in your face and the train pulling you along. I think there's some truth to the saying that every red-blooded American boy should hop a train."
>
> Conover rode the rails for 10,000 miles last fall, criss-crossing the American West to study what author John Steinbeck called "the last free men."
>
> Conover said he didn't want to "suffer in the library" researching his thesis, so he spent a semester observing or interviewing 460 tramps. He estimates there are at least 10,000 hobos living in the United States today.

"They're invisible to most of us," he noted. "But there's a romance about tramps. They've found something valuable that the rest of us have missed."

But Conover also discovered some unpleasant realities about the life of a tramp.

"I went 2½ weeks without a shower once," he said. "My friends thought it sounded romantic to get really dirty. But when I got lice it took away a lot of the romance."

Writing the Feature

Style: Relaxed, informal. Let the people in the story do things; let them talk. Underwrite. Keep the story moving with quotes and incidents. If possible, use dialogue. That is, have people talking to each other; have them interacting by watching them at work or play. Tom Wolfe, master of the profile, said "realistic dialogue" fascinates readers. Use verbs that make pictures for the reader. When possible, use the present tense to give the reader a sense of continuing action or of being present at the scene.

Lead: Delayed leads are preferred. An anecdote or incident can be used to begin. Stress human interest in the lead by using someone directly involved in the situation. Make sure the lead fits into the main theme of the feature.

Body: Avoid overwhelming the reader with detail. A few well-chosen quotes and incidents will tell the story. Selection is the essence of the feature. What is left out is as important as what is put into the piece. A Zen saying makes the point: "To make a vase, you need both clay and the absence of clay." You are not obligated to use everything a source has given you. Remember: One good quote, one telling incident is all the reader needs to put the paper down and say: "That's interesting. I never knew that."

Focus on a Theme

Because the feature has a relaxed, leisurely approach and contains many quotes and several interesting incidents, beginners think all that is necessary to write one is to pile on quotes and anecdotes and then glue them together with a few transitions.

Tom Wolfe says that too many feature writers think "that somehow if you get in enough details, enough random fact—somehow this *trenchant portrait* is going to rise up off the pages."

Yes, he agrees, detail and dialogue are essential, but the good feature writer "piles it all up *very carefully,* building up toward a single point. . . ."

Wolfe's "single point" is the theme or point of the article.

The writer must give the reader only those quotes, facts and anecdotes that illustrate and buttress the point the writer intends to make.

In this respect, a feature is no different from any news story. It must have a main theme that is clear from the beginning, certainly by the fourth or fifth paragraph of the feature.

The main theme is always the spine of the story. Everything else branches from it. Most feature writers have a general idea of what they want to say even before they conduct their interviews. At least they have an idea that guides their questions.

If a better theme comes along, they pursue it. The reporter who interviews a rock singer who has just been released from a clinic for alcoholics and drug addicts has a good idea of the questions she needs answered for her feature. So does the sports writer who wants to do a piece about the 38-year-old pitcher who has been named Comeback Player of the Year.

The rock singer may surprise the reporter and say, "I'm through with music. With music, I am going to be back on the habit. Without it, I'll be poor, but alive." The pitcher may be petulant and angry. Instead of being happy about his award, he may take off about his salary, fellow players, and the baseball commissioner. The unexpected material becomes the main theme of the story.

The Wall Street Journal Formula

Here is a structure that *The Wall Street Journal* has used successfully for many years:

Beginning—Start with an anecdote or illustration of the theme.

Theme—Shortly after the beginning, state the point of the piece. Don't drop this lower than the sixth paragraph.

Body—Provide details that elaborate on the theme. Tell the reader what is happening, why and what's being done about the situation.

The Ending

Most features have a strong ending. Rather than end on a secondary piece of information, the feature may have what is called a kicker, a punch at the end. It can be an exciting quotation or a significant anecdote or incident. The ending usually drives home the theme of the feature.

In a story about a woman who visits prisoners in the Dade County Jail to help them with their problems, *Miami Herald* reporter Shula Beyer describes Georgia Jones Ayers as "53, an activist in the black community with a degree of access to the criminal justice system that is unique."

Ayers is shown to be sympathetic to prisoners she believes unjustly accused and imprisoned, but she is no bleeding heart. She does not tolerate crime. To make this point about Ayers, Beyer ends her story with this dramatic incident and quote:

> One of the stories people tell about Georgia Ayers is that she turned over a drug pusher to the police. He was sentenced to eight years. The pusher was her son, Cecil.
>
> "When my own children do wrong, I don't uphold them. The law is the law. He respects me for what I did. I couldn't afford to see him destroy himself.
>
> "I would rather see him behind bars than for someone to call me to identify his body in a morgue."

The News Feature

Early one cold Saturday morning, as Bob Rose was at home preparing to go to work at *The Blade* in Toledo, the telephone rang. It was the police reporter. A house a few blocks from Rose's apartment on Parkwood Avenue had caught fire. Could he get over there? Yes, he could.

Rose started out in minutes. He tried to drive, but the frost on his car window was unyielding. After a few blocks, he hopped out of the car and ran the rest of the way.

"I arrived in time to see the fireman carry a child out of the house," he said. He spent about an hour at the scene gathering information from fire department officials and from the people who had been driven out of their home.

At the office, he checked the hospital where the injured had been taken, and by early afternoon he had finished his story. But he was not happy with it.

"Somehow it didn't seem right," Rose recalled. He asked the assistant city editor what she thought of the story, and she told him she thought it lacked drama. He worked on it some more and left the office feeling somewhat satisfied.

Soon, he had another call. Ed Whipple, an assistant managing editor, had made a change. "He wanted to bring the reader right into the story. My lead ended up being the third graph, and the scene of a tearful firefighter with the dead girl went first," Rose said. The story was put on page one.

In the past, most editors would have wanted Rose's straight news lead. But Whipple wanted a news feature. Rose's story as it appeared in *The Blade* is on the next page.

Girl, 4, Dies In Fire; 8 In House Rescued

By BOB ROSE
Blade Staff Writer

It was 7:50 a.m. Saturday when fireman Jack Rynn carried 4-year-old Quanous Russell out of a burning house at 2346 Lawrence Ave.

"She's gone," he said minutes later of the bundle in the blue baby blanket, his eyes welling with tears.

Fighting zero-degree weather and their own emotions, Toledo firemen — aided by alert neighbors — helped save eight other family members in the house.

Timmy Hicks, 2, was rescued by fireman Fred White, who, like Mr. Rynn, struggled through thick smoke and flames to take the child from an upstairs bedroom.

Timmy had stopped breathing, but paramedic Larry LaVigne revived him en route to St. Vincent Hospital, where he was in serious condition Saturday.

Neighbors Help

Before firemen arrived, neighbors had helped others from the home.

Paula Russell, 26, the mother of the dead girl, jumped from a second-floor window into the arms of Bruce Ethridge, who heard her screams from a block away. She was in fair condition at St. Vincent Saturday.

Johnny Hicks, 4, was found on steps in the house by Eron Villanveva, who lives next door. He had summoned firemen after hearing screams and breaking glass.

Others escaped through the front door or were pulled from the roof of the house by firemen who arrived at 7:33 a.m., two minutes after the alarm sounded.

Curtain Was Burning

Kevin Russell, 19, said he was the first to be wakened by the blaze. "Something told me to wake up," he said at a neighbor's house after other family members were taken to the hospital. "When I woke up, my curtain was burning down the side."

An electric space heater in his room had ignited the curtain. He struggled to put the fire out, first by stamping on the curtain and then by running for buckets of water, but the fire was winning.

"It happened so quick, I couldn't even get everybody woke," he said.

His father, Clinton Russell, 72, wearing a tattered coat zipped over his pajama top, shivered as he watched firemen work on the white frame house he has owned since the 1960s. He was the only family member sleeping on the first floor.

"I can't think," he finally said after trying to name other family members who had gone to sleep in the house the night before.

All But 2 Released

They were identified by hospital and fire officials as his daughter, Elizabeth Hicks, 23, who was visiting from Cincinnati with sons Timmy and Johnny. Others were Clinton's wife, Lois, 52, and son, Quincy, 16.

All but Timmy Hicks and Paula Russell were released after treatment.

Toledo Fire Chief William Winkle arrived soon after he was called at home by firemen. "Those guys did a hell of a job," he said of the men who were directed in the freezing weather by acting deputy chief Ron Sturgill.

Chief Sturgill, who estimated damage at $18,000, said the two closest fire hydrants were frozen and water from pumper trucks had to be used while another hydrant was hooked up.

"The first guys there ran into the house without masks (for air) and got to the top of the stairs," Chief Winkle said. "But they couldn't go farther. Guys with masks had to go in to get the kids."

Chief Winkle kicked a snow bank when he talked about the year's first fatal fire. "Damn," he said.

Structuring the Story 133

The news feature takes its content and structure from the feature. In content, it emphasizes human interest and drama. It uses the dramatic quote and the telling incident to point up the major theme. In structure, it may use the delayed lead to lure the reader into the story, and then get to the point of the piece after several paragraphs, or it may put the lead theme in a kicker at the end.

Rose's story puts the reader on the scene at once. We visualize this large man in his dark cold-weather clothing holding tight to a small figure.

The second paragraph stuns the reader with that brief quote. The summary paragraph, which in a straight news account would be part of a first-paragraph lead, comes in the third paragraph. The way the story is told reflects the poignancy of the event more closely than would a straight news story with this direct lead:

```
A 4-year-old child died and two other family
members were hospitalized when their home at 2346
Lawrence Ave. was damaged by a fire this morning.
```

This straight lead is satisfactory, but the point of this fire is the tragedy of a child's death. Why not show the reader this and let the reader share the grief. The lead on the published story fits the event.

Many news features use the delayed lead to set a mood or establish a scene. Look back to Berkley Hudson's lead on his story about Chester Jefferds. The lead is delayed seven paragraphs, and finally, in the eighth, we are told: Jefferds is not sick; he does not belong in the state institution.

Volunteers to the Dying   The news feature is usually built around incidents, examples, anecdotes and quotes that involve people. Human interest is a major factor in the news feature.

Rick Sluder, a reporter for *The News and Observer* in Raleigh, N.C., built his story about a hospice around the people involved. A hospice is an organization that serves the needs of the dying and their families.

The story originated in a press release from the recently formed Hospice of Wake County. "My editor felt this was a worthwhile organization and that I should look into it," Sluder said. "Getting the lowdown on how the organization worked was the easy part. Volunteers and officials were eager to meet with me."

Sluder decided that this kind of information was only part of the story. He knew he needed the human element. The story should be about the people the hospice volunteers worked with, the dying. He wanted to **show** the hospice at work, not **tell** about it through the words of officials.

"This caused officials to rub their hands for a moment," he said. "Their concern was understandable. Relationships in situations like this are confidential." They did agree to reach some families to ask whether Sluder could talk to them.

"A day or two later, I got the names of the Silvers and the Voelkers. And that's when it became a bit sticky for me. I found myself phoning these people to ask if they would talk to me, a stranger, about the deaths of their loved ones."

Sluder learned what many young reporters find surprising. Despite the tragedies that afflict some people, they are willing to talk to reporters if they believe the reporters are sincere and want to perform a service by writing the story.

Notice how Sluder structures the beginning of his story. He uses an illustration, with quotations, of the point he will be making—that the dedicated volunteers ease the pain of the dying:

Three-year-old Bethany Voelker was sick, and she didn't want any visitors. When Elizabeth Hernandez appeared, she said so.

"Would it be all right if I came to visit you?" Ms. Hernandez asked.

"No," Bethany said. "I'll throw you out."

"I'm going to come anyway."

"Well, I'll throw you out again."

Undaunted, Ms. Hernandez came—and she visited again and again. As days passed, Bethany's uneasiness gave way to tolerance. Friendship followed, and finally, surely, love.

One day the two were together and Bethany was feeling worse than usual. They talked little. As Ms. Hernandez bent to kiss her, Bethany whispered with childhood's sincerity: "I'll be your friend forever."

The bond was sealed. And though Bethany died of leukemia a few weeks ago, it remains strong. Loved ones are not forgotten.

Bethany's parents, Robert and Darlene Voelker of Raleigh, are certain the friendship brightened their daughter's last days of life, just as Ms. Hernandez says she is richer for having known Bethany.

It's a sentiment shared by most of the volunteers with Hospice of Wake County, an organization intended to minister to the needs—physical and emotional—of the dying and their families.

But it's hard to think of Hospice as an organization, with budgets and letterheads and articles of incorporation. Instead, Hospice is people, caring people, who celebrate each second of life by meeting moments of death, accepting death for what it is, refusing to turn away. It is, by any reckoning, in the major leagues of human interaction.

Hospice of Wake County began accepting clients in April. So far it is serving six families; deaths have occurred in five of them.

Its mission is simple, said Dr. William R. Berry, medical director. "We provide medical care for terminally ill patients in the home setting," he said. "We help them and their families any way we can to meet their needs."

In the first nine paragraphs, Sluder shows us how a hospice works, though he never uses that word. It is not until the 10th paragraph that he introduces the hospice, and this and the next three paragraphs provide the lead and background. No question that this is the more effective way to begin the story.

The ending of the news feature and feature must be carefully crafted as well. Unlike the straight news story, which stops when the writer runs out of secondary material, the endings of feature stories must leave the reader or listener with a reminder of the point of the piece. Sluder does this with a vivid combination of incidents and quotations about the two families in which deaths occurred. Here is the end of his story:

Bethany turned 4 shortly before she died. She got a birthday party her little friends are still talking about. Uncle Paul from TV and Guppy the clown were there. So were many of the Hospice workers, who with some others helped arrange it.

James Silver had a birthday party, too, the Friday before his death on Monday. He had planned it and left instructions it was to be held even if he couldn't attend. "He wanted his friends, the ones who had done so much for him, to have a good time," Mrs. Silver said. The Hospice people were there.

They were there at the two funerals, too. And they're still there, the families said, calling, dropping by, sharing lunch and memories and hopes for the future.

"Sometimes you forget how wonderful people can be," Mrs. Silver said, "but I guess it's like James always said. It isn't how long you're on Earth, it's what you do while you're here."

Finding the Theme. Some feature writers develop themes for their stories by choosing a word that best describes the event. A piece about a riding school for youngsters might develop from the word *excitement* because of the reporter's recollection of the youngsters' thrill at seeing their mounts for the first time. Or if the day's lesson was in making the horse go left and right, *turn* might make the writer recall the trouble some children had with the maneuver.
Joe Luper.

Overcoming Writer's Block

Getting started is the most difficult part of writing. Here are some suggestions:

Ritual: Ernest Hemingway sharpened 20 pencils. Some writers glance through a favorite book or story. Some take a slow walk to the water fountain, drink, walk back.

Summary: Jotting down a few sentences that highlight the event helps focus the mind and put it in a writing mood.

Excerpt: Start with anything that you think will be part of the story. This is like warming up the engine. When you are hot, put the excerpt aside and tackle the lead.

Cloudy Crystal Ball One way to end the news feature or feature is to put the lead at the end of the piece.

A writer for *The Wall Street Journal* decided to have a little fun with a market analyst whose predictions are taken seriously by many people—so seriously that when he told his clients to sell stock, the stock market industrial average fell 23.8 points. The *Journal* sent Alan Bayless to cover a talk by the analyst, and this is how his story began:

> VANCOUVER—Market prophet Joseph Granville made news again Tuesday night, predicting a 16-point selloff of shares in the Dow Jones industrial average on Wednesday . . .

The story then describes some other predictions Granville made, including a Los Angeles earthquake, and then, in the 11th and final paragraph of the story, Bayless writes:

> His prediction for Wednesday was, presumably, a minor matter. Instead of falling the 16 points or so that it was supposed to, the industrial average rose by more than eight points.

So much for the prophet. Notice that Bayless **shows** the reader that Granville failed. By giving Granville's forecast in the lead and then noting the actual market performance at the end, Bayless lets readers draw their own conclusions.

Structuring the Feature and News Feature

The feature and news feature are built around the examples, anecdotes and quotations that the writer uses to illustrate the story. The writer is trying to unfold a tale, and the structure depends on whether the writer chooses to get to the point immediately or to hold the reader in suspense. Sometimes the lead will be up high, in the first paragraph or two. This is the first option for the news feature and feature. Often, the lead comes after an introductory section, as in Sluder's piece about the hospice (second option), or it may be placed at the end, as Bayless did with the market prophet (third option).

These alternatives are diagrammed in figure 5.3.

Some writers think that they can select any exciting incident, any interesting anecdote or startling quotation and use this as the human interest material at the top of the story. It does not work that way. The most common error made in writing features is the careless selection of anecdotes, illustrations, incidents and quotations for the beginning.

The material selected for the beginning must lead directly to the major theme. Look at how this *Wall Street Journal* story begins:

> It was 1940 when Elmer Novak walked out of his sophomore year in high school and into the coal mines, just as his brothers had before him and his father before them.

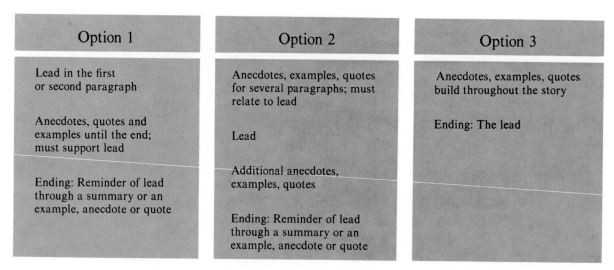

Figure 5.3 Alternate story structures for features and news feature stories.

Immediately, the reader has a picture of the treadmill life of this family. The reporter follows this beginning with such pieces of information as, "Novak has a mortgage, 10 kids, and black lung." From the present, the reporter looks back: "He quit the mine once, in 1947, after his brother was crushed to death by a coal car, but in a few months he was back, for the money."

The article was part of a series on jobs that are physically draining and mentally numbing. For this piece on coal mining, the incidents and quotes used were selected to make this point.

Now that we have examined the basic elements of writing the story, you are ready to move up a notch, to fine tune your newswriting. In the next chapter, we will see how professionals make words work for them.

Suggested Reading

Clark, Roy Peter, ed. *Improving Newswriting*. St. Petersburg, Fla.: Poynter Institute for Media Studies, 1982.

Murray, Donald. *Writing for Your Readers*. Chester, Conn.: The Globe Pequot Press, 1983.

6

Fine Tuning
the Story

The writer's task is to find the words and the form that allow the reader to see, hear and understand what the writer has experienced. *Pepperdine University.*

Looking Ahead

Articles are written so people can understand them quickly and effortlessly. The news writer uses everyday words in short sentences and paragraphs, structures the story so that it moves logically from beginning to end and includes quotations, incidents and specific details that make the story interesting and convincing.

Writers select a style for each story that reflects the nature of the event. A story about a game decided in the last minute may contain unusually short sentences to give a sense of the quick movement of the game, whereas a story about a teacher retiring after many years will have longer sentences and a relaxed pace.

Writers are scrupulously careful to keep errors out of their copy—incorrect grammar, misspellings, improper word use. Copy is edited by the writer before turning it in.

When he was a young reporter struggling to make a name for himself during the rough-and-tumble days of New York tabloid journalism, Jim Bishop was taken aside by a famous columnist and given some advice.

"If you want to write," Mark Hellinger told him, "you are going to have to learn to pound out terse sentences composed of small words."

Bishop took the advice and applied it to all he wrote. He became a successful reporter, then a syndicated columnist and the author of such books as *The Day Lincoln Died* and *A Day in the Life of President Kennedy.* In his stories, columns and books, Bishop wrote short sentences and he used everyday language.

Short sentences and ordinary words lead to clarity, one of the most important ingredients of the news story. The news story must be understandable. If it is not, it is words cast to the wind.

The good news story has two other ingredients. It is convincing, and it is natural. By this, we mean that the story can be believed and that the style suits the nature of the event.

Easy to Understand

Clarity is achieved through familiar language and logical structure. Sentences are short and follow the S-V-O pattern. The story moves in a linear progression. A theme is stated in the lead and immediately developed. If there is more than one theme, the themes are developed in the order stated in the lead. When a delayed lead is used, the incidents and quotes used in the first few paragraphs move directly to the theme.

William J. Storm uses a two-paragraph delayed lead to move the reader into his story. Notice the use of quotations and short sentences:

Delayed lead

OLD FORGE, PA.—Until Wednesday night, no one in this Scranton suburb complained much about Joseph Aulisio.

The teen-ager rode a noisy motorcycle up and down the street, one neighbor said. He overturned garbage cans, another claimed—"mostly kid stuff."

Lead

But now Aulisio, 15, is accused of the shotgun slaying of two neighborhood children, Cheryl Ziemba, 8, and her brother Christopher, 4. The neighbors were shocked.

Aulisio, son of a former Old Forge school board member, is being held without bail in Lackawanna County Jail, charged with criminal homicide, kidnapping, hindering an investigation and arrest.

Quotations

"We never expected anything like this," said Joan Lilli, the mother of a 4½-year-old girl.

"We're all really worried around here," Ms. Lilli said. "We just don't know what's going to happen."

"I was never afraid in my life," said Ceil McGarry, 62, who lives next door to the Ziemba family. "We never had to be afraid in this area, and now I'm numb."

Chronology

About 500 searchers, including Aulisio and his brother and father, began hunting for Cheryl and Christopher shortly after they were reported missing early Sunday evening. They were last seen in the 18-unit trailer park where Aulisio lives.

Early Monday morning, three bloody sandals and two pieces of rug containing human bone fragments and brain tissue were found at the top of an overgrown, 100-foot-long abandoned strip mine where a neighbor said Aulisio used to ride his motorcycle.

The bodies were discovered shortly after noon Tuesday in a nearby abandoned strip mine pit. . . .

Not every sentence in this story is short. A parade of 10- and 12-word sentences would be tedious. The trick is to set a rhythm by balancing long sentences with short, concise sentences.

Frederick C. Othman, a master reporter for the UPI, was asked to give advice to colleagues about the art of writing. He said: "I shall not repeat any warnings about the need for keeping sentences simple, but I do urge you count words. If you've got a long sentence, make the next one short. Like this.

"The idea is to produce variety, but if your average is more than 25 words per sentence, your reader will desert you. That's been proven scientifically."

Later, we will look at the evidence. Now, you can use the work of good writers as proof. Look at the first three sentences in this story from *The Washington Post*:

Edgar Allan Poe sums up the writer's goal: "In the whole composition there should be no word written, of which the tendency . . . is not to the pre-established design. . . . Undue length is . . . to be avoided."

In other words, make the story conform to the idea in the lead, and cut extra words. Or, as Ernest Hemingway said, don't write one word more than you absolutely need to.

They came in darkness before the dawn of Dec. 11, 1978. There were six or seven of them, with ski masks over their heads and guns in their hands, and they knew what was supposed to be in the Lufthansa cargo terminal that morning.

Millions.

The sentence lengths are 11, 33, 1. That's 45 words in three sentences, average length 15 words. Just as important, there is a balance—short, long, very short.

Verbs Provide Action

The power of sentences comes from their verbs. Action verbs propel the sentences. They move the subject to the object.

Stanley Walker, a legendary city editor in New York, advised young reporters "to avoid adjectives and to swear by the little verbs that bounce and leap and swim and cut."

The Youngest Mothers

Teen-age pregnancy is a grim subject, and the news feature by Sharon Cohen that begins below reflects the stark nature of what seems to have become an insoluble problem in the United States. Cohen uses a delayed lead to put the reader into the human side of this problem:

CHICAGO (AP)—For Kim, the last blush of girlhood—the whir of jump ropes, playground flirtations and slumber parties—faded and went cold at age 13. Kim got pregnant.

Today Kim is a high school freshman. She has a 10-month-old daughter and a stoic streak. "I just have to take it as it comes," she says with a shrug. "Suffer the consequences—whatever good or bad comes."

Kim is a child mother. She is one of almost 10,000 girls in the United States each year who, at 14 years and younger, are wrested from the cocoon of childhood and thrust, bewildered, into motherhood.

For teen mothers, the road is tough enough.

For child mothers, the path is tougher, and longer.

Physically, emotionally, socially, America's youngest mothers are disadvantaged at every turn.

Their risks of problem pregnancies and of delivering small, sickly babies are higher than normal. They're so immature that they often treat their babies as dolls to dress up or, at best, brothers and sisters.

Unlike older teens, it will be years before child mothers have high school diplomas, jobs or homes of their own—in short, years before they themselves will be grown up.

"Almost every (negative) consequence associated with teen pregnancy is accentuated for the younger girl. The repercussions go on and on and on," said Shelby Miller, a research associate in Atlanta for the Child Welfare League in New York and author of "Children As Parents."

Many child mothers have second babies while still in their teens, further miring themselves in a swamp of poverty, ignorance and despair where they create new generations of child mothers. Studies indicate 15 percent to 25 percent of children who bear children get pregnant again within two years.

"It's a social and cultural catastrophe for everyone concerned," said Dr. Richard Naeye, who studies disorders of newborns and is chairman of the department of pathology at the Pennsylvania State University College of Medicine. . . .

Carl Sandburg, the poet, said at age 75, "I'm still studying verbs and the mystery of how they connect nouns. I am more suspicious of adjectives than at any time in all my born days."

Beginners try to reach their readers by injecting their stories with adjectives and adverbs. Shoving the adjectives *dramatic, spectacular, terrifying, exciting* and others like these into stories is not writing. Nor is the use of adverbs to prop up verbs: *walked quickly, ran awkwardly, collided noisily.* This is hitting the reader over the head with words. It's also lazy thinking.

Less Is More

As a rewriteman, Robert Peck's job was to make cloudy stories clear. One of the major problems was the long sentence, which was a result, he said, of writers trying to include too much information in the sentence. Peck, acknowledged to have been one of the finest rewritemen ever to work in New York, said he would cut the sentences "to little more than subject, verb, and object."

The result, he said, was a story that gained "grace and speed." There, in those few words, is the essence of the good story.

Peck pared—words, sentences, paragraphs. The result was stories that were well told, and move quickly and gracefully from beginning to end.

Writers gather large amounts of information in their reporting, and they are reluctant to discard any of it, even though some of it may not bear on the point of the piece.

But if the story is about a speaker discussing the need to return to science and mathematics as requirements for college graduation, then his remarks about the beauty of the campus and the bracing spring weather are irrelevant, no matter how clever.

Know Your Audience

Simplicity and clarity are important because of the different kinds of people who read and listen to news. Most journalists are aware that the public is diverse, and that they must direct their writing at a wide range of readers and listeners.

At one end are those with minimal reading ability. A study of 23,000 recruits at the San Diego Naval Base showed that 37 percent of them could not read at the 10th grade level. At the Walter Reed Army Hospital in Washington, signs were rewritten to the third-grade level because many enlisted men could not understand them.

At the other end are college graduates and others who would resent being written down to.

Some journalists have a specific type of reader in mind. Martin Nolan, of the *Boston Globe,* has "a sort of image of the guy who works with his hands but retains a lively interest in what's going on and doesn't need to be given clichés and comfortable slogans in the copy."

Dan Rather of CBS News thinks back to his youth in Texas.

"I know people who work with their back and hands in Texas. A number of them are in my family. And I ask myself, will they understand this story? They're the people I know best . . . good, decent, intelligent people."

Readability

Studies of written material find sentence length to be a key factor in readability. Some studies also conclude that paragraph length and word length are factors. This table is given to wire service reporters:

Average Sentence Length	Readability
8 words or less	Very easy to read
11 words	Easy to read
14 words	Fairly easy to read
17 words	Standard
21 words	Fairly difficult to read
25 words	Difficult to read
29 words or more	Very difficult to read

If the sentences are long, one way out of the trouble is to remember the advice of the English author George Orwell, "If it is possible to cut a word out, always cut it out." A good place to start cutting is with adjectives and adverbs. A sentence that repeats a previous idea should be cut. An old rule for journalists helps to cut sentence length: one idea to a sentence. Watch for the words *and* and *but*. These words sometimes introduce a second idea. Try putting a period before the *and* or *but*.

Paragraphs should not be long. A long paragraph can discourage a reader. By dividing the number of words in the article by the number of paragraphs, an average paragraph length is obtained. Some editors say they prefer no more than 50 to 70 words to a paragraph. One way to keep paragraph length down is to limit paragraphs to no more than three or four sentences.

Big words, by which we mean words with three or more syllables, are difficult for readers to understand. The fewer big words, the better. One long word in 10 at most. Orwell put it simply: "Never use a long word where a short one will do."

Muddy writing can be made clearer with these techniques. But no one can learn to write by using a formula. The formula is a thermometer to find hot spots. If you write simply, clearly and directly, if you use quotes and anecdotes and illustrations, and if you write with a firm idea of what you want to say, then your writing will be easily understood, which is the writer's goal.

Not only does the reporter have to write each story simply and clearly, he or she must also prove the case, must convince the reader that the story is true.

To test the readability of a story look at:

1. *Sentence pattern*— Average number of words per sentence. An average of 20+ means the story is hard to read.

2. *Fog index*—Abstract or complex words per sentence. Simple words are understood easily. Replace "rendezvous" with "meeting," "compelled" with "forced," and so on.

3. *Human interest*— People are interested in people. Name people; show them talking and acting.

Convincing

A reporter, on assignment in a Central American country that had been ruled by three generations of dictators—beginning with the grandfather of the present head of state—wanted to learn what the people thought of the grandson. The grandfather had been ruthless. One of his favorite methods of torturing opponents was to dip them head down in a well. The grandson supposedly was enlightened.

The reporter went into the countryside to find out what the peasants thought of the three presidents. In one of his interviews, he asked an elderly farmer whether there was any difference among them.

Unsafe bridges in Tulsa was the subject of *The Tulsa Tribune* reporter's study. Some of them were used by school buses. Mary Hargrove, the special projects editor of the newspaper, suggested that the reporter ride on a school bus before filing the story. "Put me on that bus," she said. "Make me care."

"Un arbol no puede dar tres clases de frutas," the peasant replied, and the reporter wrote this in his story, along with the English translation, "One tree cannot give three kinds of fruits."

Despite the president's elaborate and expensive public relations apparatus in the United States, directed at painting him as democratic, the reporter's story had the ring of truth. The homespun saying of the peasant carried more weight than the press releases of propagandists.

The combination of on-the-scene reporting and persuasive writing carries conviction. By convincing writing we mean stories that illustrate with examples (show, don't tell), that quote people involved in the event and that contain specific details.

Convincing. Writers usually are most convincing when they have witnessed the event they are describing. Watching people act, listening to them speak, the reporter is able to catch the flavor of the event. Here, Dan Rather interviews an Afghan guerrilla fighter.
CBS News photo. Used with permission.

When Jeff Klinkenberg of the *St. Petersburg Times* interviewed A.J. McClane, a world-famous fisherman, he wanted his readers to draw some conclusions about McClane. He could have said that McClane is world-famous. Instead, he **showed** the reader with the following incident:

> Inside ritzy Capriccio's Restaurant where luncheon guests include ITT's board chairman, waiters hover about A.J. McClane like pilotfish around a shark. A waiter lights his cigarette while another pours his drink. The maître d'—and then the owner—stop and ask him if his meal is satisfactory.

We might have taken Klinkenberg's word for it if he had told us McClane was famous. Or we might not have. But after reading this incident, we know. We are convinced.

Klinkenberg wants to make a point about the democracy of fishing. On a stream, in a river, at the ocean, all are equal. Klinkenberg lets McClane provide the incident to make this point:

> I went fishing once with King Zahir of Afghanistan, but do you know what I remember most about the day? I remember him reaching deep into his wallet and producing a little snapshot of him holding a five-pound trout. Here was this king, and all he wanted was to show me a fish he was proud of. Remarkable! The point is this: Fishing is a universal thing. When people are fishing, it does not matter who they are. They're all the same.

Klinkenberg spent five hours with McClane, read some of his writings and interviewed several people who knew him. The result was a notebook filled with material. From these notes, he wrote for nine hours. He revised the story 17 times.

In one Klinkenberg story about a shark fisherman, he **shows** us the man on the bridge. The story begins this way:

> Ron Swint moaned in the dark about the shark called Old Hitler, the largest shark in Tampa Bay, as traffic roared by on the Skyway Bridge. Somebody in a car shouted and Swint automatically winced. . . .

The reader is put on the bridge with Swint, in the dark, in the middle of traffic, hearing Swint moan, seeing the traffic roar past.

Telling this would have led to something like this:

```
Ron Swint is after the largest shark in Tampa Bay,
Old Hitler, and he fishes from the Skyway Bridge in
the dark, as traffic roars by.
```

That's not the worst lead that can be written, but it pales beside Klinkenberg's.

Klinkenberg likes to organize his stories around quotations. When he organizes his story, he underlines his "best quotes," he said, and he breaks his story "into anecdotes.

"When I have the time, I'll type them (quotes) out, and then I'll assign different values to different quotes. My best quotes I'll try to get high in the story and then proceed in a kind of descending order.

"I'll try to save a couple of good ones for the end. I think it's a good way to organize a story."

The guideline: Good quotes up high.

Showing lets the reader see, feel, smell and even taste:

The food at political picnics in Vadonia County starts with chowder, large bowls of it with the clams so thick you can hardly see the broth. Then there are the vegetables—green beans, long and slender; zucchini, sliced lengthwise and chopped and—take your pick—fried or boiled; corn, heaped in bowls, a large gob of butter slowly melting into the kernels; beets, red and succulent, sweet as candy. . . .

Simply **telling** the reader takes away the joy of feeling, tasting, smelling:

The food at political picnics in Vadonia County is plentiful. There are various vegetables, clam chowder and several kinds of meat to choose from.

Might as well write menus for the fried chicken outfit down the street with a touch like that.

Sometimes, the showing can be done quickly. The reader can see a great deal with one shaft of light. When Red Smith, the great sports writer, wanted to tell his readers about the power of the owner of the Los Angeles Dodgers baseball team, he did not say that the owner, Walter O'Malley, was more powerful than Bowie Kuhn, the commissioner of baseball. Smith showed the reader by writing:

When O'Malley sends out for coffee, Kuhn asks, "One lump or two?"

Red Smith wrote a column and columnists are given plenty of freedom. However, the point is still valid: Show the reader or listener and conviction follows.

Ten Keys to Good Writing

Begin to write only after you know what you want to say.

Write the way you talk.

Use the S-V-O sentence structure for most sentences.

Use action verbs.

Avoid adjectives and adverbs.

Keep sentences short.

Show, don't tell.

Good quotes up high.

Use words you're familiar with.

Never turn in a story you think you can improve.

Show, Don't Tell

From a story by Homer Bigart, 1943, with the 5th Army in Italy:

> On the far side of the field sprawled some dead. One boy lay crumpled in a shallow slit trench beneath a rock. Another, still grasping his rifle, peered from behind a tree, staring with sightless eyes toward the Liri plain. A third lay prone where he had fallen. He had heard the warning scream of a German shell. He had dropped flat on his stomach but on level ground affording no cover. Evidently some fragment had killed him instantly, for there had been no struggle.

In a profile in the *Boston Globe* about Bigart, who had then retired, the author ended his piece this way:

> He wanted to rise from his chair to escort the visitor to the door, but his back hurt and he couldn't, so he said goodbye from his chair, and turned his eyes back to the fireplace. And there he was, a reporter, a war correspondent. He believed in the singular beauty of doing one thing in life and doing it well, of beating the deadlines.

The first sentence of the section from the profile **shows** us the once-active Bigart in retirement. The final two sentences are unnecessary—they **tell** us what the writer had already shown us.

Quotes Convince

Quotes carry conviction. Mervin Block, a newspaper and television writer, was assigned to do a magazine piece about the newspaper war between the *Daily News* and *The New York Post*.

He quotes the *Post's* metropolitan editor:

> "What competition?" snaps the Post's metropolitan editor, Steve Dunleavy. "If it's war, it's a massacre—by the Post. We're gaining two to every one they lose . . . we're so confident we walk around the trenches with our helmets off."

We can visualize the colorful, confident, cocky editor.

Handling quotes can be an art—the art of knowing when to use direct quotes and when to paraphrase. Not everything a person says should be quoted directly. Use a direct quotation when:

• It's important to put a person on the record with his or her own words.

• The quotation sums up what the person is saying.

• The quotation lets the reader or listener visualize the person or situation.

• The quotations are essential in question and answer stories such as those about meetings, trials, and confrontations.

Studs Terkel interviewed a telephone solicitor for a Chicago newspaper. Enid Du Bois' job was to call people to ask them to subscribe. She talks to Terkel:

At first I liked the idea of talking to people. But pretty soon, knowing the area I was calling—they couldn't afford to eat, let alone buy a newspaper—my job was getting me down. They'd say, "Lady, I have nine to feed or I would help you." What can you say? One woman I had called early in the morning, she had just gotten out of the hospital. She had to get up and answer the phone.

They would tell me their problems. Some of them couldn't read, honest to God. They weren't educated enough to read a newspaper. Know what I would say? "If you don't read anything but the comic strips . . ." "If you got kids, they have to learn how to read the paper." I'm so ashamed thinking of it.

In the middle-class area, the people were busy and they couldn't talk. But in the poor area, the people really wanted to help the charity I talked about. They said I sounded so nice, they would take it anyway. A lot of them were so happy that someone actually called. They could talk all day long to me. They told me all their problems and I'd listen.

They were so elated to hear someone nice, someone just to listen a few minutes to something that had happened to them. Somehow to show concern about them. I didn't care if there was no order. So I'd listen. I heard a lot of their life stories on the phone. I didn't care if the supervisor clicked in.

In these quotes, so much is revealed: the compassion of Du Bois, her disgust with her job, the generosity of the poor, the terrible solitude and loneliness of people. All of this in just four paragraphs.

Fixing Quotes

Bad grammar, factual errors, sentences that make no sense. These occur frequently in interviews. Should the reporter clean up the quote? Reporters have been doing just that for a long time—when the object of the story is to communicate information. President Eisenhower's syntax was often jumbled, but reporters—and Eisenhower's press secretary—managed to make sense of his sentences for readers and listeners. Some journalists insist that it is unethical to tamper with quotes. They paraphrase.

It seems senseless, and at times cruel, to quote someone's grammatical mistake or factual error. *The New York Times* advises its reporters to steer around such spoken lapses and to get at the point the source is making.

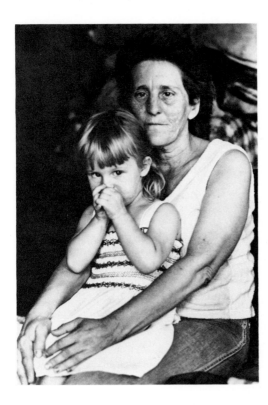

Quotes Convince. In the heart of the Appalachian Mountains in East Tennessee, the mines and the jobs have mostly gone. In his story and photographs of life in Still House Hollow, Robert E. Kollar describes a poor but proud and resourceful people, and he lets them tell their stories. Daisy Pierce, shown here with her granddaughter, maintains a garden: "Why, I share with them, you know, and then if they have got something that I am out of, well, then they share with me. We just share back and forth. If we didn't, people up on this hill just couldn't make it."
Photo by Robert E. Kollar, Tennessee Valley Authority.

Terkel is a master interviewer. Many of his taped interviews have been collected in books. His interviews with working people are included in *Working: People Talk About What They Do All Day and What They Think of While They Do It* (New York: Pantheon Books, 1972). *The Good War, An Oral History of World War II* (New York: Pantheon Books, 1984) relates stories told by the fighting men.

Quotes are not only convincing but also memorable. An international economist has never forgotten an incident in a restaurant where he was seated next to a family of three, father, mother, and a boy of 8 or 10. The waitress brought the menus and waited.

The boy decided. "I want liver and bacon," he said. The mother said she wanted a steak. Father turned to the waitress. "Three steaks," he said. The waitress nodded and replied as she wrote, "Two steaks, one liver and bacon."

The boy turned to his mother. "Mommy," he said, "she thinks I'm real."

No wonder the economist remembered this story. The boy's exclamation sums up the refusal of some parents to take their children seriously.

Reporters always listen for the quote and watch for the incident that penetrates to the heart of the matter.

Be Specific

Finally, conviction is achieved through specifics. The writer who writes, "There were about a dozen people in the courtroom" is not taken as seriously as the writer who writes, "There were 11 people in the courtroom."

We know that the writer who wrote "11" was there.

If the book stolen from the library was 4 inches by 6 inches, don't say it was a "small book." Say, "The book was 4 inches by 6 inches, small enough to fit into a coat pocket."

Readers love details, specific details. Readers can visualize the event if they are told that the suspect was five-foot-four, thin, wore blue jogging shoes, had a close-cropped haircut and used a small handgun that fit in the palm of his hand.

The reporter notes sizes, weights, numbers of things, colors, smells. Was it as large as a baseball or a basketball, as heavy as a letter or a book? Did it smell like onions, garlic or newly cut grass? Was it a deep blue, almost black, or the light blue of a sky after a rainstorm? Did it sound like the snap of a firecracker or the bang of a backfire?

Notice that in these questions, the specifics have been linked to particular things that can be seen, touched, smelled, heard. Writers use images that appeal to the senses to make their specifics spring to life and to give them the exactitude of reality.

Words as well as observations can be abstract. Just as we avoid saying *around a dozen* or *small,* we do not use abstractions, such as *patriotism, equality, affection,* unless they are tied directly to a specific event or situation or we are quoting someone.

Abstractions have no agreed-upon meaning. What is obscenity? As a federal judge observed, "One man's lyric is another man's obscenity."

Words must be anchored to real things in nature. Should the source talk of the rights of the unborn, the meaning of the Constitution, the immorality of the young, the reporter is immediately alert. The reporter knows that these words mean different things to different people. Their meanings are elusive. The reporter has to grab the slippery words and tie them down, anchor them to real things.

The reporter will ask the source, "Can you give me an example of what you mean by a fair and decent wage?" As one reporter put it, "I always ask anyone who speaks in generalities for a for-instance."

Our third component of the well-written story is an appropriate writing style. **Natural Style**
By this, we mean that the style of the story fits the subject. Words, sentence
patterns, even the paragraph lengths are chosen to be consistent with the subject matter.

The profile of a young woman who has just won a beauty contest will
not be written with the same somber style as the obituary of a local resident.
The profile will be breezy:

Evelyn Marie Welton woke up yesterday morning with a head-ache.

Last night she went to bed with a head full of dreams.

The 19-year-old Mason City college sophomore was crowned Miss Douglas County at the Civic Auditorium last night. Next month, she goes to the state finals.

"I felt terrible, just terrible all day," Welton said after her victory. "But as soon as I walked into the auditorium, something happened. Like, you know, it snapped."

The lights, the excitement of competition, the possibility of going all the way to the top had its effect.

"I just knew I could do it," she said. . . .

On the other hand the obituary will be somber and reserved:

Albert Funnel, 78, of 45 East Alpine Ave., who served as city clerk for 46 years before retiring, died yesterday after a long illness.

Funnel had been hospitalized a week ago with lung cancer.

The former city worker was known throughout the state for his innovations in the office of city clerk. He instituted a new system of. . . .

Listen to Your Words

"When you write, you make a sound in the reader's head. It can be
a dull mumble—that's why so much government prose makes you sleepy—
or it can be a joyful noise, a sly whisper, a throb of passion.

"Listen to a voice trembling in a haunted room:

" 'And the silken, sad, uncertain rustling of each purple curtain thrilled
me—filled me with fantastic terrors never felt before. . . .'

"That's Edgar Allan Poe, a master. Few of us can make paper speak
as vividly as Poe could, but even beginners will write better once they start
listening to the sound their writing makes."—Russsel Baker, columnist.

A Grim Story

Mitch Mendelson had a tragic story to cover, a house fire in which five people died. His style is simple and direct. He lets the facts show the tragedy. He gives them no adornment. Here is the beginning of his understated story, which appeared in the *Birmingham Post-Herald:*

The use of a delayed lead puts reader on the scene.

A coroner stood in the rain yesterday afternoon and poked through the smoldering rubble of what had been a house. She was looking for the bodies of four young children and their great-grandmother.

A helper standing nearby shivered.

One by one, the tiny, charred figures were carefully zipped into black vinyl body bags and carried away.

A chilling quote sums up the tragic event.

As the coroner, Dale Cunningham, was leaving, a passer-by asked if there were any bodies left in the ruins. "Five is all," she said. "Five is too many."

Reginald, 4, Stephanie, 2, Roderick, 2, and Amanda Gardner, 6 months, and Fannie Harvell, 88, were killed by a fire that destroyed their Dolomite home yesterday morning.

The essential facts of the story

The children's mother, Sandra Gardner, 23, was reportedly visiting neighbors when the fire started. Her 19-year-old brother escaped the house. Ms. Gardner was treated for shock at Lloyd Nolan Hospital in Fairfield.

All four children were in the same room. One body was found in a corner, another under a bed.

Mrs. Harvell died near the back door.

Mendelson says that he wanted to get behind the tragedy "to find reasons and aggravating circumstances." Once they have been discovered, he says, "the task is to weave the reasons and the message into the dramatic fabric, supporting the themes with facts and vivid descriptions."

In covering the fire, Mendelson learned that there were three possible reasons for the deaths. The burglar bars on the windows may have hampered escape. The community of Dolomite has no firehouse. And, third, the area has no fire hydrants.

Matching the Event. The verbs, sentence length and the style of the story about firefighters battling a blaze reflect the urgency of the event. Action verbs and short sentences move the reader with the same quick pace as the firefighters fought the fire. *Photo by Stewart Bowman of The Courier-Journal. Used with permission.*

Here is the rest of the story. Watch how Mendelson weaves these three possible causes for the tragedy into the account:

Burglar bars

Preston Countryman, a fire medic from the Hueytown Fire Department, stood in the front yard and picked up one of the steel "burglar bars" that had been on a front window. "Death traps," he said. Every window on the house had burglar bars. "They're good for keeping people out . . . plus keeping people in," he said.

No fire protection

And Dolomite, an unincorporated area of Jefferson County sandwiched between Hueytown, Pleasant Grove and Midfield, has no fire protection. By the time Hueytown firefighters arrived on the scene about 9:40 a.m., the one-story, wood-frame house at 669 Washington Ave. was, according to firemen, "heavily involved."

No hydrants

Add a third chilling fact: The area, which is heavily residential with many one-family homes, has no hydrants. Fire companies from Hueytown and Brighton had to shuttle water to the scene.

Elaboration of possible causes of the deaths

"The county should furnish protection, but they don't," said Hueytown firefighter Dale Roberts yesterday afternoon as the men cleaned up in the firehouse. "And one thing that hampers firefighting is having to shuttle water." One question that should be asked is, "Why is the Center Point area furnished with fire protection but other unincorporated areas aren't?"

The Hueytown men made it clear they are not required to answer calls outside the city. "We go provided we can get our auxiliary (volunteers) in. We can't send everyone outside of the city," said Roberts.

"It's an awkward situation."

Possible dangers for the future (Mendelson's "message")

Added volunteer firefighter Luther Brown: "I'm glad that we had enough help that we could go out. It might not happen the next time."

While the two companies had the blaze under control in about 30 minutes, Brown pointed out there was valuable time lost in finding teams to respond. "Five minutes makes a lot of difference," he said.

Description of the scene

The rain poured down on the charred ruins yesterday afternoon, and steam rose from the rooms that had been torn apart by the blaze and from the men who came on a mission of mercy to fight it. The rain made pools in the front yard where Countryman stood and talked about the burglar bars. It turned to thick mud the yards around the house and the garden in the back.

At the house next door, family, neighbors and friends gathered to console the living and mourn the dead.

Description of the scene (continued)

The rain fell on the twisted pipes that had been a kitchen set and on a scorched refrigerator and on the children's toys in the front yard.

The neighbors stood on their porches and looked out at the dismal scene. A sheriff's officer splashed through the yard and said, "mess," and shook his head.

At the house next door, Shirley Williams, Ms. Gardner's sister, slumped next to a window and looked out at the place where her grandmother and four of her nieces and nephews had died.

Steve Mahan, another Hueytown fire medic, said at the scene, "Half of our fire department is here and the city is unprotected. But it's hard to say 'No, we can't come.' "

Driving home the message

A recent report by the National Fire Data Center said Alabama and other southeastern states have the highest fire death rate in the industrialized world. Birmingham ranks second to Newark, N.J., in fire death rates among large American cities.

Supplemental heaters, such as space heaters, are considered the biggest cause of fatal fires in the South, the report said.

Driving home the message (continued)

The cause of yesterday's fire will be investigated by the state fire marshal's office, Roberts said.

Some editors would move this paragraph higher since readers want to know the cause of the fire.

As much as Mendelson wants to get his message across, he does not lecture or preach. The message is made by the people he interviews. He lets his sources do the talking.

The story won a writing award from the Scripps-Howard organization, of which the *Birmingham Post-Herald* is a member newspaper. The judges praised Mendelson for his "great sensitivity" and for "superbly organizing his facts so that readers when they had finished knew they had read something special."

The Right Word

Look at the pictures on these facing pages and find the one word or two that best describe the scene or emotion that each picture projects.
a) Joseph Noble, The Stuart (Fla.) News. b) Author's photo. c and d) Photo by Joel Sartore of The Wichita Eagle-Beacon. Used with permission. e) Matthew Brady, Courtesy of the Library of Congress. f) Arthur Rothstein, Courtesy of the Library of Congress

b

a

c

d

e

f

20 Tips for Good Writing

This list was put together by the Gannett newspapers. Most of the tips were supplied by Jim Bishop.

1. Be fair. Presenting all sides of a story is not copping out.
2. Observe good taste.
3. Make the lead provocative, clear and simple.
4. Sentences should be short.
5. Quotes improve a story. Use them.
6. An important story need not be long.
7. Select adjectives carefully. Too many are dangerous.
8. Don't be impressed with an important assignment.
9. Go directly to the source on every story when possible.
10. Leave no reasonable question unanswered. Do not assume readers know the background. And don't be afraid to write a good story you think readers already know.
11. Be polite, but don't be servile.
12. Get details. If your congressman wears high-top shoes, scratches his ears and uses a spittoon, you've created a word picture.
13. Don't be afraid to try something that isn't in the book.
14. Even if you have mastered the language, use short, easy words.
15. Stories are improved by the injection of the time element.
16. After the lead, blend the story from paragraph to paragraph.
17. Don't insult a race, an ethnic group, a minority group or other separate entity. Identify when it adds information. The distinction is thin at times.
18. Don't abuse your privileges or the weapons of your industry.
19. Admit errors quickly and fully.
20. Name the source of your story when possible. If it is an exposé from a confidential source, protect that source.

The Shift to Storytelling

Generations of student journalists were given two writing rules:

1. Structure all stories in the form of an inverted pyramid. This means that all important material is placed high in the story, preferably in the lead.
2. Leads should answer the questions:

Where	Who
Why	What
How	When

The rules work well enough, as we can see in these leads:

Gov. Bernard Carberry will speak tomorrow at 7:30 p.m. in the Civic Auditorium on methods of reducing the number of violent crimes in the state, which increased 22 percent last year over the previous year.

John Whitticomb, 22, of Hampton, a college senior, was seriously injured last night when the motorcycle he was driving struck a tree after he lost control of the vehicle on a section of Highway 28 that had recently been damaged by a washout.

These leads hold so much information that they can just about stand alone as the entire story. For brief items, such as these, the principle of the Five W's and an H works well. On longer or more complex stories, the length of the lead repels rather than attracts readers, many writers believe.

Vonnegut on Style—Respect for the Reader

Kurt Vonnegut, the author of *Slaughterhouse Five, Cat's Cradle* and other novels, says that when an author works on his or her writing style it is "a mark of respect" to the reader.

"If you scribble your thoughts any which way," he says, "your readers will surely feel that you care nothing about them. They will mark you down as an egomaniac or a chowderhead—or worse, they will stop reading you."

Vonnegut says that writers must care about the subjects they write about. "It is this genuine caring, and not your games with language, which will be the most compelling and seductive element in your style."

He adds this advice:

Do not ramble.

Keep it simple. He points out that the Bible opens "with a sentence well within the writing skills of a lively 14-year-old: 'In the beginning God created the heaven and the earth.'"

Have the guts to cut. Every sentence, he says, has to "illuminate your subject."

Sound like yourself. Write the way you speak.

Say what you mean to say.

The formulas have been found to be helpful for beginners, but stifling for professionals. They lead to cumbersome, often stilted writing. The spot news story relies on them, most of the time. But even here, good writers manage to be creative and informative.

When the city of Miami was unable to find enough lifeguards to guard its pools, it announced that pools would close at 5 p.m. instead of at 8 o'clock for the summer. Which lead do you prefer for the story?

Straight News Lead

City officials said today Miami's public pools will close at 5 p.m. this summer instead of at 8 p.m. because of a shortage of lifeguards.

News Feature Lead

Miamians seeking cool, wet relief on hot summer evenings won't find it this year at the city's public pools. For the first time in years, they are closing at 5 p.m.

It isn't a tight budget that is forcing the pools, traditionally open until 8 p.m., to close early in this summer of high inner-city unemployment. It's precisely the opposite.

The city can't hire enough certified lifeguards to staff them, said Brian Finnicum. . . .

The second lead was used by *The Miami Herald*.

Fresh and Free

"There are no rules today in writing stories for a newspaper. The ancient idea of putting 'who, how, what, when and where' in the 'lead,' or start of a story, is thoroughly ignored today. The best writers in the country are telling their stories in their own way, and readers have become educated to reading stories in many different ways.

"Newspapers today strive for individuality; strive for newness, in both the composition of the stories and the layout of the newspaper. Newspapers today look different and they are different.

"That's why editors are always looking for talent of a new kind—talent that is not bound to rules; talent that is fresh and free. . . ."—Elliott Arnold, New York newspaperman; 1941.

Clutter. One of the enemies of clear writing is the cluttered sentence, the sentence that bumps and grinds its way from capital letter to period without regard to meaning, structure and coherence. A sentence makes a single point. Each word is chosen to make that point. The useless words are tossed out. Concrete nouns—the names of specific things—are used instead of vague nouns propped up with adjectives. Action verbs help to move the sentence. Adverbs are unnecessary. Avoid clutter.
Mike McClure.

Tell It Simply and Directly

Whatever the length, whether the lead is delayed or direct, and however you may want to structure the story, there are some essentials no writer can or wants to avoid in writing the story. Basically, the story should be told in declarative sentences that pull the reader along. Subject, verb, object, period. "A more complicated sentence can lead you into trouble," says Relman Morin, an AP correspondent who won two Pulitzer Prizes.

Look at this section of the story that won Morin his second Pulitzer. He was in a telephone booth outside Little Rock Central High School in 1957, dictating the dramatic story that was unfolding before him:

> At that instant, the eight Negroes—the three boys and five girls—were crossing the school-yard toward a side door at the south end of the school. The girls were in bobby sox and the boys were dressed in shirts open at the neck.
>
> They were not running, not even walking fast. They simply strolled toward the steps, went up and were inside before all but a few of the 200 people at the end of the street knew it.
>
> "They've gone in," a man roared. "Oh, God, the niggers are in the school."

Clear Writing	**Muddy Prose**
Simple language	Flowery language
Active verbs	Passive verbs
Straightforward sentences	Complex sentences
Tight writing	Loose writing
Easily understood	Difficult to follow

Rewriting

Young writers should not be discouraged by the realization that writing requires work. Everyone who writes for a living—poets, novelists, advertising copywriters, public relations practitioners, magazine writers—knows the joy of making ideas come to life on paper. And the agony—especially the pain of rereading and, invariably, rewriting.

"Good writing is rewriting," says Fred Zimmerman, Editor of *The Chapel Hill* (N.C.) *Newspaper.*

"Even on deadline, a good writer will take at least 20 or 30 seconds to glance over a piece of copy, not really editing it, but simply because it is the writer's habit to reflect on what he or she has written before letting go of it," Zimmerman says. The more time the writer has, the more attention he or she will give to the copy.

"Rewrite, rewrite and edit," says Zimmerman.

The original manuscript of the American classic *Walden* by Henry David Thoreau shows how hard Thoreau worked. He produced seven versions in the six years he worked on the book. Behind the beautiful and clear story of his two years alone by a Concord pond are years of toil.

Caskie Stinnett, an essayist and critic, says Thoreau "stopped and started, tinkered and rearranged, selected and discarded, chose and reconsidered, and fought with the English language until he forced it to come to terms with him."

Here are some checkpoints for the writer as he or she re-reads copy:

1. Is the lead on target or buried? What is most of the body of the story about? If it is not about the theme selected as the lead, the lead is wrong.

2. If a delayed lead is used, does the quote or incident move directly into the main theme?

3. Is the story organized properly, or does it jump from one topic to another and back? Is secondary information placed above primary material in the body?

4. Does the story move? Do the nouns and verbs carry it forward with an internal momentum? Do the facts that are chosen give movement to the piece?

5. Do quotes, incidents, details support the lead?

"Make Me See"

"My first editor in the newspaper business was blind. . . . His name was Henry Belk. He was the editor of the Goldsboro (N.C.) *News Argus,* which then had a circulation of 9,000. He was a tall man, six foot seven, I believe, and he walked with a stretch aluminum cane. He wore a battered fedora, which must have been bought at a time when he had his vision and saw movies like "The Front Page." . . . Lucille, his wife, and a succession of high school students read to him every word of every issue of both the *News Argus* and the *Raleigh News and Observer.* And many, many days— I still wince at the thought of how many times—he would summon me into his cubicle after having heard my stories word by word and say, 'You aren't making me see. Make me see.'

"It took me years to realize it, but no one ever handed down the prescription for good writing more succinctly or better than Henry Belk in those three words, 'Make me see.'

"There is not much left to say. That is, after all, what good writing is all about—good reporting, too, for that matter. It is putting the reader on the scene, making him see, making him hear, making him understand. The task, of course, of every editor who wants to improve the quality of newspaper writing is to make reporters see that what they have to do is to make the reader see. It is that simple and, alas, that complex."—Gene Roberts, executive editor, *The Philadelphia Inquirer.*

Rewriting Press Releases

One of the first discoveries new journalists make is their sudden popularity. They are sought out and courted. Most of these new-found friends, it turns out, have something they want to see in print or hear on the 7 o'clock news. The friends call and write, and the organized ones among them have material sent by press agents and public relations firms.

Some of this material makes good news stories. These sources supply information about the fund drive that is soliciting money to send needy youngsters to summer camp, and they tell the press when the governor will be in town to speak.

The proud mother calls to tell the social news or lifestyle reporter about her daughter's engagement, and the bank's information officer announces the hiring of an executive assistant to the president. The local college sends out a press release about an award given to a professor of chemistry.

One of the most frequently performed tasks in the newsroom is rewriting releases. Publicity and press releases are essential to the news operation because they provide information no news staff is large enough to gather. As much as half to three-fourths of all news can be traced to a press release, also known as a handout.

Whatever the source, however perfect the material may seem, the reporter always checks before using the release. Nothing is accepted at face value. The first check is with the newspaper files. The governor might be making his first visit locally since elected; the press release did not mention that. The professor of chemistry may have recently been denied tenure; the college press office neglected to mention that. And the mother may have forgotten to tell the newspaper her daughter is a former Rhodes Scholar.

Because other news outlets in the community will also be using the news release as the basis for stories, the writer seeks to find an aspect or angle of the story that he or she considers unique. It may be lurking in the fifth paragraph of the release, or it may be something that turns up during the checking.

Many small, local organizations send out news releases, usually written by volunteers whose copy may start this way:

```
The local chapter of the League of Women Voters met
last night at the home of Mrs. Albert Morrison. The
invited guest was Rep. Frances Gilmore of Ardmore.
    Rep. Gilmore spoke about impending legislation in
Congress. She is on a two-week tour of her district
to. . . .
```

Avoiding a gradual drowsiness, the news writer plows through the next two paragraphs and, yes, there in the fifth paragraph is the lead: Rep. Gilmore said she intends to vote against protective tariffs of any kind. The writer knows that because some local industry benefits from such tariffs, the lead and story are here. The writer knows he has to do some more reporting at once—question Rep. Gilmore, talk to heads of affected companies, check to see what is going on in Congress on this issue.

No matter how searching the reporting and checking may be, however interesting the writing, all this work can be undone by a small slip, an error in spelling or incorrect grammar. Errors are like mosquitoes at a campsite. No matter how careful the camper, they manage to infiltrate the tent. There are just too many of them, and their determination exceeds our precautions. They surround us—incorrect and inappropriate word use, misspellings, clichés, poor grammar, misdirected apostrophes and periods.

Let's sashay around the states and see what we find.

The sign on the canopy over the pumps at an Exxon service station in Batavia, N.Y., reads:

CLEARENCE   12′ 9″

A sign at the entrance to the Publix Supermarket in Homestead, Fla., warns customers:

> According to our license, alcoholic beverages may not be drank in this store or on the parking lot.

A poster in Roosevelt Hospital in New York City invites patients and visitors to a nutrition clinic with this sign:

Want to loose weight?

The AAA Tour Book for Georgia, North Carolina and South Carolina contains an advertisement for the Swamp Fox Motor Inn in Myrtle Beach, S.C., that boasts of a "**seperate** meeting room."

A sign on U.S. 90 invites travelers to visit a "**Tradeing** Post" in Uvalde, Tex.

An article describing the Copper Queen Hotel, built around the turn of the century when Bisbee, Ariz., was the largest copper mining town in the world, says that the town "remains architecturally as it stood in **it's** heyday."

Some Bizarre Language

Bizarre, bazaar? Which is it?

The conductor "found enough strength to stop at a Christmas **bizarre.**"—*Eugene Register-Guard*.

"Despite the **bazaar** delay, the 'Brigadoon' was the first boat past the finish line."—*The Beaufort* (S.C.) *Gazette*.

"Bazaar circumstances" were reported in Shreveport, La.—Gannett News Service.

And:

In 1983, at the St. Patrick's Day Parade, the *Savannah Morning News* recalled, 86 of the 87 females in the parade "stripped to the **waste.**"

A columnist wrote that Jesse Jackson may find Louis Farrakhan "is his **Ulysses'** heel."

Editor & Publisher said that the faculty of Boston University's School of Public Communication found "the Pakistan environment **teaming** with secret agents. . . ."

New York University's School of Continuing Education sent out a brochure advertising its writing courses: "NYU has something for every**one** who wants to insure that words never fail **them.**"

In its brochures, the Stihl company warns users of its chainsaws about the "**occurance** called 'kickback.' "

The wrap in the freezer unit of the Safeway market in McKinleyville, Calif., indicates that the packages contain **"sordfish."**

A radio commercial for a resort hotel in Pennsylvania suggests to listeners:

Why not get out this weekend and lay under a tree?

The people whose job it is to write or to broadcast the news do little better.

The story in *The Miami Herald* about the death of actor William Holden said that after a drinking bout, he fell, gashed his head and "went to **lay** on his bed."

The network sports announcer commented that Notre Dame was completing many passes because the pass defenders **"have overran** the receivers."

A headline writer for *The San Francisco Examiner* contributes this one:

Climber peaks inside volcano

The Washington Post, The New York Times, The Boston Globe, The Milwaukee Journal and other usually well-edited newspapers have also contributed to the pollution of the written language:

The *Post* described attempts to keep Northern Virginia's **principle** reservoir from drying up. It mentioned a company that **has became** the first to put a new machine in use.

The *Times* contained this quote: "But I have **alot** of respect for the people. . . ." The *Times* described a character in a movie "struggling to wrap a skimpy towel around his **waste.**"

The *Globe* referred to a man who had been arraigned on a charge of **"negligible homicide."**

The *Journal* ran a story about tourists who **"pour** over English lessons."

The Des Moines Register ran a headline, "Insurance agent **please** guilty of theft."

The wire services contribute their share to the mess:

A UPI story from Peking begins—"China's official media **is**. . . ." It describes an attack by nationalists on a U.S. air base that **"totally destroyed"** eight airplanes.

The AP wrote of the **"first annual** International Congress." From Jackson, Miss., it reported FBI agents "are **pouring** over thousands of pictures. . . ."

The *Surfside News,* a magazine for visitors to the Outer Banks off the coast of North Carolina, reports that a college student "plans to **persue**" his study of geology.

"To read almost any American daily today is to conclude that copy editors have vanished as completely from our city rooms as the ivory-billed woodpecker has vanished from the southern woodlands. We appear to have reared a generation of young reporters whose mastery of spelling, to put the matter mildly, is something less than nil. In today's hushed and antiseptic newsrooms, the path from the video display terminal seems to run straight to the waiting press. Once there was a white-haired geezer in an eye shade to intercept a reporter's copy, and to explain gently but firmly to the author that *phase* and *faze* are different words, and that *affect* and *effect* ought not to be confused. The old geezer has gone, and literacy with him."— James J. Kilpatrick, columnist.

James Reston, the respected columnist for *The New York Times,* told his readers of a **"serious crisis"** abroad.

If a carpenter treated his tools the way some journalists treat the language, the carpenter's walls would sag and his floors would slope. He would be on the unemployment line before long.

Granted, language does change. But some things never change. Periods will always be used to end sentences, and the verb will always have to agree with the subject. The spelling of *grammar* will always have *ar* at the end, not *er,* and *sophomore* will undoubtedly always be spelled that way and never *sophmore.*

David Shaw, the media writer for the *Los Angeles Times,* interviewed editors around the country about the problems they were facing. Shaw found:

"Bad grammar. Misspellings. Incorrect punctuations. Poorly constructed sentences. Misused words. Mixed metaphors. Non sequiturs. Clichés. Redundancies. Circumlocutions. Imprecision. Jargon."

An important point needs to be made about why these mistakes occur. Much of the time they are the result of poor thinking, or no thinking at all.

Every person who works with tools knows just what each tool can do. The auto mechanic would not think of using an air pressure gauge to measure the gap of a spark plug. It makes no sense. Writers sometimes fling words around with that kind of abandon. They reach into their word kit and haul out something that looks or sounds as though it can do the job.

Muddy Thinking = Mistakes

```
    TWO SOVIET COSMONAUTS SUCCESSFULLY DOCKED
THEIR SOYUZ 35 SPACE CAPSULE. . . .

    GOSSIPOL WAS FIRST DISCOVERED IN 1971 AFTER
PEASANTS IN. . . .

    ARMED GUNMEN SUNDAY KIDNAPPED THE OWNER AND
EDITOR OF THE WORLD'S LARGEST
CIRCULATION. . . .
```

These are from wire service stories.

The fact that the capsule was docked indicates it was a successful venture. The modifier *successfully* is a wasted word.

The second excerpt has another unnecessary modifying word, *first.* When something is discovered, it is obviously for the first time. It's as though we were to write: Columbus first discovered America in 1492 . . . and then discovered it again a few years later on another voyage.

As for the third sentence, ask your friends if they have ever heard of an *unarmed* gunman.

These three sentences are examples of redundancies, needlessly repetitive words.

Another common error is the misused word: *effect* for *affect, imply* for *infer, disinterested* for *uninterested.*

"Recent reports have said a number of graduates cannot even read or **right**," said an editorial in a college newspaper in Kentucky. The editorial writer could not have been thinking when that was written.

"Albert Henry, the **disposed** former premier of the Cook Islands, has died. . . ." This is from a UPI story. How could the writer confuse disposed with deposed? Obviously, he was not thinking as he wrote.

Word Usage

Writers can sometimes profit from their mistakes and the mistakes of others. Mervin Block, who writes news for network television, watched the news wires for the most frequent errors, bloopers and blunders. In a few days he came up with a two-inch pile of redundancies, poor grammar and improper use of words.

What was remarkable about the errors he collected was not that the mistakes were made by professionals but that the same errors occurred time and time again.

Among Block's findings were:

A pair of small earthquakes about an hour apart. . . .

A trio of bandits held up a. . . .

Some might argue that technically these sentences are acceptable. But not to the journalist, who uses common sense along with the dictionary. To the journalist, shoes come in pairs and trios form singing groups. When writers push too hard they distort language, as in this lead:

A Frankie Valli and the Four Seasons concert—part of Philadelphia's Fourth of July Freedom Festival—ended in tragedy Saturday night when high winds sent 40 spotlights crashing onto a bandstand.

Watch Your Language

A little girl fell from a window onto a bread box which broke her fall, and the child walked away uninjured. The story had the makings of a good feature, and the cub reporter began his lead:

Providence and a bread box intervened to save the life of. . . .

The city editor beckoned to the reporter and advised him: "About words, it's not too soon for you to learn that the *Post-Dispatch* uses them in their exact meaning and only in their exact meaning. As far as *Post-Dispatch* readers are concerned, Providence is only a town in Rhode Island."

The city editor was the legendary O.K. Bovard, and the incident occurred in 1900. The advice holds good today.

Tragedy is a strong word. Familiar with accounts of people being trampled at rock concerts, the reader expects the worst. What actually happened: A pianist suffered a broken hand and others had cuts and bruises.

When thieves tunneled into a bank vault in Massachusetts and made off with the contents of 700 safety deposit boxes, the AP described the theft as a robbery. Robbery involves taking by force and is a crime of violence. Burglary is theft of property, which was the case here.

The most frequent misuse of language in Block's collection was the cliché.

Clichés

If at first you don't succeed, try, try again. Hit the nail on the head. Cool as a cucumber. Out of the frying pan into the fire. Sadder but wiser. Make hay while the sun shines. Love makes the world go 'round.

At one time these were original and picturesque expressions. But their novelty was their undoing. Writers picked them up and used them, and overused them. They have been ground down to the humdrum and dull, so that today phrases like these are known as clichés. No writer who is proud of his or her writing will resort to using these stale and tired expressions.

Because these sentences and phrases are heard everywhere, all the time, writers have them imprinted in their memory banks, and in the struggle to find an apt expression they pop out. Shove them back in again.

George Orwell advised writers to be wary of using any phrase they are accustomed to seeing in print.

Here is a list of clichés Block put together from the wires of the press services. Block says these are a small portion of those he gathered in a few days:

```
    CHICAGO--THIS IS THE UNKINDEST CUT OF
ALL. . . .
    KHARTOUM, SUDAN--THE SOVIET MILITARY
INTERVENTION IN AFGHANISTAN AND THE IRANIAN
CRISIS RANG BELLS OF ALARM. . . .
    NEW YORK--THE FIGHT FOR THE NOMINATIONS
SEEMS TO BE ALL OVER SAVE THE SHOUTING.
    NEW YORK--ALEX KARRAS CONTINUES TO BE THE
EXCEPTION THAT PROVES THE RULE. . . .
    FORT WAYNE, IND.--MARTHA COLEMAN . . .
MET WITH FEDERAL AGENTS BEHIND CLOSED
DOORS. . . .
    NEW YORK--ABC AND NBC BELIEVE COMEDY IS
THE WAY TO KEEP LAUGHING ALL THE WAY TO THE
BANK.
    UNIONDALE, L.I.--THE NEW YORK ISLANDERS
COMPLETE A RAGS-TO-RICHES CLIMB TO. . . .
```

Block says the most breathtaking set of clichés he heard came from the typewriter of a radio news writer describing the entry of a reluctant candidate into a race: "Jones dropped the other shoe, threw his hat in the ring and now it's a whole new ball game."

Redundancies

In the early part of this chapter we quoted wire service stories that described planes that were "totally destroyed" and a meeting that was the "first annual" Congress. When something is destroyed, that's it. It's gone, a pile of scrap. It cannot be partially destroyed. If a meeting is the first of its kind, it cannot be annual, which means something that has happened yearly. It may be "the first of what its sponsors plan to make an annual. . . ." These needless repetitions are called redundancies.

David Shaw says that the redundancy "seems to be an occupational hazard for journalists—as witness 'planning ahead' (*Boston Globe*), 'apparent heir apparent' (*UPI*), and 'ominous portent' (*Los Angeles Times*)." A moment's thought and the absurdity of some of these pairings would be obvious. One way to avoid redundancies and other mistakes is to train yourself to be wary of adjectives and adverbs:

totally destroyed—adverb
first annual—adjective
serious crisis—adjective
successfully docked—adverb

Nouns and verbs do the work in journalistic writing, and all good writing for that matter. Look at this sentence:

```
The workers trudged slowly past the factory in the
rain.
```

The verb *trudged* was picked precisely because it means to walk wearily. It does not need any propping up with the adverb *slowly*.

The student wrote of a professor who "carefully scrutinized" all student papers. "Have you ever heard of anyone carelessly scrutinizing papers?" the student was asked in a marginal comment. Puzzled, the student went to the dictionary and looked up the word *scrutinize*. He learned it meant to examine closely, minutely, critically, in detail—all of which certainly implied that the papers were carefully read. His word *carefully* was a waste.

Beware these Redundancies

Here is a list of the most common redundancies seen in newspaper copy. It was compiled by the Minnesota Newspaper Association. You may want to add some of your own.

absolutely necessary	enclosed you will find	reasonable and fair
advance planning	exactly identical	redo again
ask the question	fair and just	refer back
assemble together	fall down	refuse and decline
at a later day	first and foremost	revert back
attached hereto	friend of mine	right and proper
at the present time	gathered together	rise up
canceled out	honest truth	rules and regulations
city of Chicago	important essentials	send in
close proximity	necessary requirements	small in size
consensus of opinion	open up	still remain
carbon copy	other alternative	temporarily suspended
continue on	patently obvious	totally unnecessary
cooperate together	plain and simple	true facts
each and every	postpone until later	various and sundry

Journalese

The dictionary defines journalese as the language style characteristic of newspaper writing. That's the sanitized version. Among journalists, journalese is known as the combination of clichés, hack writing, overwriting, exhausted phrases and supercharged prose that are the signs of the hopeful beginner or the hopeless veteran.

In journalese, costs and the crime rate are always *skyrocketing,* and officials who worry about speedy solutions to problems often *raise the red flag.*

When a group meets for any period longer than an hour, the meeting is said to last *long hours.* The facts raised in meetings are *cold facts,* sometimes *hard facts.*

Close elections are always *cliff-hangers,* and when someone is elected he or she may *kick off* the term with an inaugural speech. An official who does something unusual is said to have *written a page in the political history books.*

When someone is pleased by something, the person often *hails* the action or statement.

The AP once polled its correspondents to determine the most overworked word or phrase in reporting. They chose the verb *to hail.* Or, as journalese would have it, *to hail took the honors.*

Watch Out—Trouble Here

Coke This word, like Kleenex, Stetson, Styrofoam and others, is a trademark. Such words are registered by the manufacturer and protected by law to keep others from using the words. These words must be capitalized.

finalize, prioritize Watch out for invented words, especially those that arise from the unintelligible jargon of government agencies.

irregardless No such word. The word is *regardless.*

minorities Do not use when you mean members of minority groups:
Wrong: "When women and minorities are selected to open. . . ."
Right: "When women and members of minority groups are selected to open. . . .

The same caution applies to faculty, as in: "Five faculty served with the president." It should be: "Five faculty members served with the president."

miracle Much overused, as in, "Jones miraculously escaped death when. . . ." Leave miracles to the spiritual world.

most unique Delete *most.* Unique means one of a kind. Same for very unique, and quite unique.

presently The word means soon. It does not mean now, although usage may alter the meaning some day.

Another strong entry was the variety of synonyms for the word *said*. For some reason, writers prefer *declared, stated, asserted; whispered, shouted, declaimed; repeated, recalled, remembered; inquired, asked; pronounced, related* and *announced*.

The reluctance to use the word *said* has at least two causes. One is a fear of using the same word twice in a news story. If a news writer is doing a piece about Expo '88, it's perfectly all right to use synonyms—exposition, event, exhibition, display, presentation. But *said* catches no one's attention, no matter how often it is used, and substitutes for it usually exaggerate the nature of the statement and mislead the reader.

The other cause is the inherent desire of the writer to strut his or her stuff. Anyone can use the verb *said*. "Look at how many words I can think of to dazzle you," says the writer. In its extreme state, this self-intoxication leads to the refusal to use simple words. A person does not repeat something he or she has heard. He *echoes* it. A project is not completed but *finalized*. An event is not set or scheduled to begin but *slated*. Future events are *upcoming*.

Writers know that attribution is necessary, but they find a barrage of *police said, he said, she said,* unappealing. To make their stories move faster, careful writers will use a phrase that avoids this repetition: *Police gave this account, he offered these suggestions, she made these points.* This is followed by the points the source made, or the information offered.

Journalese is contagious. A word or phrase that is unusual is quickly picked up. President Nixon was mocked for using "at this point in time" for *now* and "at that point in time" for *then*. Nevertheless, these cumbersome phrases began to work their way into speech and then into news copy.

"She was credited with the murder of her son." This sentence is from a wire service story. The phrase "credited with" makes the sentence grotesque. Even so, some reporters use it to express causation. A similar phrase is "thanks to," as in this one from a southern newspaper: "Thanks to the recent storm, 600 people were left homeless in the delta area." Soon we may expect to see sports writers writing: "Thanks to Johnson's tackle, Simms suffered three broken ribs and a fractured nose." Simms' mother will have to send Johnson a thank-you note.

Thanks. A last-minute basket gave the home team's opponents the game, and a student journalist wrote: "Thanks to a closing-seconds basket, the Waves lost a West Coast Athletic Conference game they needed."
Joe Luper.

First the Formula, then Mastery

One of Elvis Presley's songwriters said that after five years of writing successful songs for Presley, he realized he was repeating himself. The songs were successful, but they were ground out to a formula, the writer said. There was no reason for Presley to change his style since it had proved to be a huge financial success.

However, the writer felt he was not being challenged, so he decided to move on to new forms of music.

Much of what has been said may seem as much a formula as the ingredients of Presley's hits. Granted. But there is nothing wrong with a formula if it guides the inexperienced writer to successful work. Once the formula is mastered, the writer can move on, like Presley's songwriter, to more ambitious undertakings.

Now, we move on to a closer examination of how writers gather information. In the next section we will go along with some reporters to see how they work.

Summary

A news editor for a newspaper in New York was asked to list some of the most frequent problems he sees in the copy that moves past him. Here's his list:

1. **Not enough self-editing.** Reporters fight so hard to put their words on paper, they have a vested interest in them and are reluctant to change them. No story is perfect on first writing. Don't cherish every word you write. Always ask: Does this word, this sentence, this paragraph move the story forward? Have I edited the story carefully, thoughtfully?

2. **Wrong lead.** The writer has used a secondary theme for the main point of the story. The writer has to keep asking: What made this event different from all others like it? The answer is the lead.

3. **Poor organization.** This is often a result of not locating the main theme and getting it high in the story. The reader should not be forced to go beyond the first four paragraphs to have a good idea of the thrust of the piece.

4. **Misuse of the delayed lead.** Too many hard news stories are given a soft news approach.

5. **Overwriting.** You don't have to use every quotation, every observation. In journalism, quantity does not count—the quality of the quote and the observation do.

6. **Dullness.** This can be the result of overwriting. It also stems from poorly selected verbs, long sentences, lack of quotes.

7. **Holes in the story.** Unanswered questions.

Capon, Rene J. *The Word.* New York. Associated Press, 1982.

Clark, Roy Peter, ed. *Best Newspaper Writing for (year).* St. Petersburg, Fla.: Poynter Institute for Media Studies (year). (Annual anthology.)

Howarth, W. L. *The John McPhee Reader.* New York: Vintage Books, 1977.

Strunk, William Jr. and E. B. White. *The Elements of Style.* New York: The Macmillan Co., 3rd Edition, 1979.

Suggested Reading

Part Three
Reporting

7

Finding Information and Gathering Facts

Reporting first hand is the best building block for the news story. The observed event, the individual personally interviewed, the original document examined . . . these make for the best stories. *Perry Werner, The Hays Daily News.*

Looking Ahead

News is developed from the journalist's observation of events, from interviews with the people involved and by research in records, files and reference material. This material is supplemented by the journalist's general knowledge, primarily of how things work—how city government functions, how the school system operates, how the local criminal justice system is structured. To enrich background knowledge, the journalist seeks a wide range of experiences, reads widely and knows how to use a variety of reference materials.

The news story stands on facts, and the facts that are most convincing are those that the reporter gathers by direct observation.

Penny Lernoux, who covers Latin America for a number of newspapers and magazines, was doing a story on tin miners in Bolivia who work under difficult conditions high in the Andes. Lernoux was determined to see the miners at work, although she had heard that the miners sometimes threw dynamite at visitors and were especially suspicious of women, whom they believed brought them bad luck.

She disguised herself as a man and went along with an engineer who had volunteered to show her the inside of a mine.

She was deep inside the Siglo Veinte mine, she recalled, "when a miner approached, a smile on his face and a stick of dynamite in his hand."

"Don't panic," the engineer shouted. "Just run."

Fortunately, there was a sharp bend in the corridor, which they scrambled around just as the dynamite exploded. Lernoux survived, and she had her story.

In Philadelphia, newspapers carried stories of crime, delays, fires and accidents in the city's subways. One story reported the case of a widely known Philadelphia lawyer who was beaten, raped and left for dead in the darkened track area. She was discovered 18 hours after the attack.

Mike Mallowe of *Philadelphia* magazine decided to look into the subway system. He interviewed crime victims, patrolled with the police, worked with the subway motormen and rode the subway for months as a commuter. His piece, "Tunnel of Terror," included his findings:

> . . . a trunk line to hell . . . 40 miles of dark, deadly terror . . . 40 miles of drunks collapsed in their own vomit; of howling teenage punks pissing in public; of hulking panhandlers, not asking, but demanding money; it's 40 miles of old people too terrified to look around them; of women alone, too scared to speak. . . .

Only direct observation could generate the tension and terror in these lines.

Pushing to the front of a crowd, asking questions that embarrass sources, refusing to be put off by an uncooperative official—this can be the daily routine for reporters. Some newcomers to journalism find this behavior aggressive and discourteous. No reporter should be impolite, but the reporter's job is to gather information for people who want to know and who need to know, and so beginners must overcome their timidity.

A Fish Story

On a skyway over Tampa Bay, a couple of fishermen are trying their luck. Jeff Klinkenberg, an outdoors reporter for the *St. Petersburg Times,* and another reporter are "catching nothing," as Klinkenberg puts it, when a fisherman walks by with what seems to be about 60 pounds of equipment.

He looks at Klinkenberg and his companion and laughs. "You'll never catch anything with that," he says to them, pointing to their equipment.

Then he begins talking about a shark he is determined to catch, name of "Old Hitler." Klinkenberg manages to get in a few questions before the fisherman goes his way. The reporters resume fishing, but Klinkenberg is distracted. He is thinking, this guy is worth a story.

Two weeks later, Klinkenberg called the shark fisherman and made arrangements to meet him on the skyway.

"I went back out there with him. We went to the bridge about 6 p.m. and stayed until 2 a.m., fooling around with sharks and ladyfish," Klinkenberg says.

Klinkenberg returned to the newspaper and typed up three pages of single-spaced notes for his story. Then he wrote:

Ron Swint moaned in the dark about the shark called Old Hitler, the largest shark in Tampa Bay, as traffic roared by on the Skyway Bridge. Somebody in a car shouted and Swint automatically winced. He has been hit by beer cans thrown from passing cars. A huge truck rumbled by so fast the bridge shook. Diesel fumes hung in the air.

The first shark to come along was not Old Hitler, but it was a big one, a shark Swint later estimated at 500 pounds, a shark that swallowed a three-pound live ladyfish bait and swam toward the lights of Tampa. The shark almost killed Swint.

Again, we see that the reporter who has observed the event is able to make the story come alive for readers.

It is not always possible to witness the event. A bank is robbed, a truck slams into a car, a flash flood rips out a bridge. These happen so quickly, only sheer luck would have the reporter there at the moment the news breaks. In these situations, the reporter turns to sources for information—eyewitnesses and authorities.

When Bonnie Van Gilder was assigned to do a story about street gangs for her journalism class, she hoped to observe a gang on the prowl. She was unable to do so, and so she had to settle for other sources.

Van Gilder could have relied on the police alone for information. She did interview police officers. She also examined police documents, along with news clippings. But she wanted more direct contact with a gang. She managed to locate a Times Square gang, the Crazy Bishops, and she was able to interview some members.

Here is her story:

NEW YORK—"China," a female member of a Times Square teen gang called the Crazy Bishops, narrowed her black eyes and declared, "If you want to be a Bishop, you got to mug people and beat them up and take whatever you can."

Like most of the other Crazy Bishops, China, 15, comes from a broken home, is a runaway and has an extensive arrest record. Police have identified 60 Bishops, but suspect as many as 200 Hispanic boys and girls, ranging in age from 14 to 19, are associated with the gang.

Detective John McNamee knew where to find China. When the 42nd Street policemen change shifts at 7:30 a.m., the Bishops come out of a nearby park where they sleep. They go to a local coffee shop or sit on the stoops of pornography and peep show businesses that line 42nd Street.

At night they work the streets and vast network of area subway tunnels. The gang has rampaged through the theater district, looting stores, mugging tourists and harassing transients.

"When you're a Bishop, you don't have no pity for people," China said, "You got to hustle to survive."

Area merchants complain about the gang. But police say they can arrest the Bishops only for disorderly conduct unless they are caught committing a more serious crime.

Louis Corbo, head of the Youth Gang Information Unit of the New York City Police, said, "We think this gang grew out of the film 'The Warriors.' It may just be coincidence, but there was never a gang around Times Square before."

Corbo said the Crazy Bishops are unlike any other youth gang he has investigated. Usually gangs are made up of neighborhood kids, living within the same 10-block residential area. But the Crazy Bishops operate in a commercial district and recruit members from gangs in the Bronx, Brooklyn or New Jersey. Also they recruit runaways at the New York Port Authority and outside "Under 21"—a church-operated organization that houses and feeds runaways.

The Crazy Bishops

Direct observation allowed AP correspondent Nancy Shulins to capture poignant moments in the life of an 8-year-old boy who is brain damaged but whose pluck has helped him overcome enormous obstacles. Shulins interviewed some of the neighbors who volunteer to help with Matthew's rehabilitation; she watched the youngster struggle to use his arms, his legs. As she was leaving, the youngster, "strapped into his braces" was "hard at work practicing creeping." Just as she reached the door, Shulins wrote, she saw Matthew "flailing one arm back and forth in front of his face. 'He's blowing you kisses,' his mother explained."

To become a member of the Crazy Bishops, a boy must hand over $50 from robberies and allow a high-ranking gang officer to cut a one-inch gash in his arm. The initiation is different for the girls. To become a full-fledged Queen Bishop, a girl must sleep with several gang members.

"You got to prove you're hard," one gang member said, "They put you to the test when the godfather—the top man—cuts you."

The gang has an elaborate hierarchy. "Dice," 19, is the "pres," or top man, because he is older and shrewd. "Sinbad" is the war chancellor in charge of rip-offs and fights, and is said to be one of the most violent gang members. The group also has a vice president and an intelligence officer, who keeps track of treaties with rival gangs and arrest records for the Crazy Bishops.

"They aren't angels," said McNamee. "They usually don't carry guns. But they have makeshift weapons—sticks, belts with sharpened buckles or homemade blackjacks."

China admitted the gang carries chains and knives, but "stashes them" when the "heat is on." She said female gang members usually carry the weapons because they can't be searched by police officers.

"We do most of our stuff at night," China said. "We put a knife to a white boy's side and tell him to walk. When you get him to the park, you slice him up or beat the ---- out of him."

The Crazy Bishops are what the police call a horizontal gang because there are other divisions in other boroughs. Members of the Times Square Bishops—the third division—wear a rabbit's foot around their necks or a bandana around their legs for identification. There are no rumbles between Bishop divisions, but sometimes there are turf wars with rival gangs.

"When gang members 'fly their colors' (wear jackets with the gang's name emblazoned on the back), that usually means a turf war," Corbo said.

Recently the Crazy Homicides—a Coney Island deaf-mute gang—flew their colors in Bishop territory. About 60 Bishops and Homicides fought with chains in 42nd Street subway tunnels. The police, however, were tipped off in advance. They stopped the fighting and arrested nine Bishops.

Van Gilder's vivid story stands out because she went beyond official sources to those directly involved in the event, the gang members themselves.

Talk to Participants

The reporter covering a flood will try to reach those on the scene, someone who saw the water's surge carry off the bridge. If he or she cannot find an eyewitness, the reporter will settle for quotes from someone who can attest to the storm's fury.

The reporter covering a fatal accident will try to talk to a passenger or the driver, if the accident is worth a detailed story. If this is not possible, the reporter will try to reconstruct the event from the investigating officers' written report.

A bank robbery story will be given the detail and color necessary through interviews with bank employees and customers who were in the bank at the time. The teller who was held up will be interviewed in detail.

Getting the Story

Information Gathering

Reporters have three major sources of information: direct observation (bottom left); interviews (top left); and references, records, documents and clippings (top right). These sources provide the material for the news story or feature. Reporters also look for the candidate's gesture of impatience, and they listen to the conversations of the tornado's victims as they console their children. Stories are made as often by these little items as they are by formal aspects of the event— the speech, the list of survivors and damages.

Top left, The Evening and Sunday Bulletin; top right, author's photo; lower left, photo by Keith Warren of The Commercial Dispatch, Columbus, Miss. Used with permission.

Three Basic Sources of Information

We have sketched the three basic sources of information for news stories:

1. Direct observation.
2. Human sources. People who have witnessed the event; authorities and experts who know about the subject, and people who are involved in the event.
3. Reports, documents, reference material. This includes newspaper clippings; film and tape from broadcast station libraries; minutes of meetings; tape recordings; court, police and legislative records; budgets; tax records.

Most stories combine all three types of sources. Lernoux used her observations from her trip into the bowels of the Bolivian mine. She collected detailed material about the production of these mines, the salaries of miners, the profits of the mining companies from records and documents. And she gathered information from interviews with engineers, mining officials and others connected with the mines.

Mallowe rode the subways, talked to passengers, motormen, transit officials, and read all the newspaper clips he could dig up about the subway system.

A vast amount of information is filed daily—in the courthouse, in legislatures, in newspapers and magazines. It's all there. The only problems for the journalist are knowing what's available and knowing how to locate it.

What's there: There is no easy way to learn this. But the journalists who know how systems work can put their hands on records and documents because they know what has to be filed, when it is filed and where it is.

Getting it: All information—with a few exceptions—in departments and agencies that are tax supported is available to the public. All city, county, state and federal reports, documents, studies and the like are open to the reporter. The beat reporter who befriends the people who keep records is likely to have access to them. Another treasure trove of material lies in the vast array of publications. Getting at them has been made simpler with the computerized data base.

> **"Make use of all** available resources. Always look in the newspaper library to see what's already been written about the topic, and talk with older reporters on the staff. They know a lot. Local university professors are great interpreters for technical things. If experts aren't available locally, call them wherever they are. Librarians and historians are invaluable sources. So are good photographers, who see or think of things you might miss."—Roberta Heiman, *The Evansville* (Ind.) *Courier.*

Data Bases

A computerized data base is a machine-readable storehouse of information. Dozens of newspapers put their contents into computers, as do magazines and research publications. For that matter, many government documents are also computerized, along with court opinions, thesis topics and dissertations, and government statistics such as Census reports.

A data base saves the reporter time, provides the most recent information and allows access to information usually not available anywhere else, or available only through expensive travel and telephone calls. Some newspapers subscribe to a few data bases. Most university libraries have many. The law school, for example, will subscribe to a data base, Lexis, for legal opinions, and the medical school may have Medline.

An important source of information is the federal government. Studies, reports, even FBI files are available to reporters through the Freedom of Information Act, which Congress passed in 1966.

The Act states that the public has the right to examine any document the executive branch of government has in its possession, with nine exceptions: income tax returns, intra-agency letters, and secret documents relating to foreign policy and national defense. The government has a time limit that it must abide by after a request is made. All federal agencies have Freedom of Information offices, and requests for information should be sent to these offices. No reason need be given for asking for the material, though a specific request helps the agency answer faster. Charges are reasonable.

Appendix C contains the request procedure and a sample letter.

Public opinion polls are a major source of information for news stories. Polls are a systematic way of finding out what people say they are thinking about at a given time. They are used to determine how people feel about a wide variety of issues, from legalized abortion and prayer in schools to the construction of a civic auditorium. Polls are conducted by hundreds of organizations, including newspaper and broadcast stations.

The results of polls can be used to predict how people will act in the immediate future. But since people change their minds, long-range forecasts are dangerous. Also, times change and new circumstances influence people. For example:

High school seniors in 1975 ranked the country's colleges and universities, churches and religious organizations, and the national news media first, second and third, respectively, as doing a good job for the country. Ten years later, seniors still ranked colleges and universities first. But the U.S. military had taken second place.

High school seniors were also asked about the dishonesty and immorality of certain institutions. Here are the percentages of those who said there was "considerable" or "great" dishonesty and immorality in the leadership of the following institutions:

Institution	Percent responding immoral or dishonest		Rank	
	'75	'85	'75	'85
Presidency and administration	49.7	27.8	1	2
Large corporations	45.9	27.4	2	4
Congress	44.8	27.7	3	3
Churches and religious organizations	21.4	27.7	12	3
National news media (TV, magazines, news services)	40.0	34.0	4	1

—Institute for Social Research, University of Michigan

(Twelve institutions were listed.)

FOIA

When Janet Wilson of *The Hudson Dispatch* (Union City, N.J.) heard rumors about the head of a city anti-drug agency, she used the FOIA and learned that the man had been arrested 33 times for rape, atrocious assault, drug use and sale, burglary and assaulting a police officer.

Polls

Social scientists say that today's high school and college students are more conservative, more traditional than their predecessors of a decade ago. Polls confirm this. Asked about marijuana use, 30.5 percent of high school seniors in 1975 said it should be a crime. A decade later, 40.8 percent said pot smoking should be a crime.

Polls can tell us what people in various age groups prefer; what ethnic and racial groups favor. They can identify groups by income, education, occupation, religion, politics and tell us what these subgroups favor.

A 1986 Gallup Poll asked people about their attitudes toward the Supreme Court ruling on abortion: "The U.S. Supreme Court has ruled that a woman may go to a doctor to end pregnancy at any time during the first three months of pregnancy. Do you favor or oppose this ruling?"

Some of the findings were:

	Favor	Oppose	No opinion
Sex			
Male	45	43	12
Female	45	46	9
Age			
18–24	50	39	11
25–29	48	45	7
30–49	49	44	7
50–64	38	48	14
65 and older	40	49	11
Race, ethnicity			
White	44	45	11
Nonwhite	55	39	6
Black	53	41	6
Hispanic	24	53	23
Education			
College graduate	59	35	6
College incomplete	47	42	11
High school graduate	43	47	10
Less than high school graduate	36	50	14
Politics			
Republican	42	49	9
Democrat	48	44	8
Independent	45	42	13
Occupation			
Professional and business	53	40	7
Clerical and sales	51	43	6
Manual worker	42	47	11
Skilled worker	46	47	7
Unskilled worker	39	48	13

	Favor	Oppose	No opinion
Income			
$50,000 and over	52	43	5
$35,000–$49,999	51	41	8
$25,000–$34,999	50	43	7
$15,000–$24,999	40	47	13
$10,000–$14,999	43	45	12
Under $10,000	38	51	11
Religion			
Protestant	42	50	8
Catholic	41	48	11
National	45	45	10

Caution: Reporters have to approach polls with care, lest they swallow a line the pollster is peddling. Generally, the major polling organizations, Roper, Harris and Gallup, are careful about the questions they ask, the people they poll and the interpretations they make of the results.

Here are some suggestions for reporting poll results:

1. Ask to see the questions. Examine the wording to determine whether the questions are clear and unbiased.

2. When was the poll taken? On controversial issues, people change their minds with new developments.

3. How was the poll conducted: coupon, call-in, man-in-the-street? These techniques are suspect since they use what is known as a "non-probability" sample, a sample that is not representative of the population at large. Usually, reliable pollsters select telephone numbers at random and call or—better still—make household interviews. Ask to see how the sample was selected and who is in it.

4. Who sponsored the poll?

5. Is the margin of error stated, and is it accurate? A 51–49 percent Smith over Jones result means nothing with a three percentage point margin of error. Jones could have been on top 52–48.

We should add another source of material essential to the content of the news story. This is the reporter's background knowledge, the information he or she has about the subject.

Background Is Essential

The first step a reporter takes on a new job or beat is to learn how the systems in that city, on this beat work. What's the form of local government? Does the school board exercise much control over the curriculum? How does the city purchase goods and services?

As an outdoors reporter, Klinkenberg knows fishing. He was able to add material to his story of the shark fisherman from his wide knowledge. He was also able to ask questions more intelligently, to understand some of the points Swint was making about the difficulties in landing a 500-pound shark from a bridge far above the water.

a

Know It All

Biking and ballet . . . space, surfing and the stock market. The journalist is expected to know something about everything. A reporter may be sent to interview a ballerina one day, an astronaut the next. When the stock market plunges, the reporter will localize the story. The variety is endless and demands wide reading and the cultivation of many and varied sources.

a) Jeff Widener, The Evansville (Ind.) Press; b) Joe Luper, Pepperdine University; c) NASA; d) Joe Luper; e) The New York Stock Exchange.

The Reporter Ranges Widely

b

d

c

e

Finding Information and Gathering Facts   191

A television station carried a report that Gov. Mario Cuomo of New York had visited a hospital. Reporters who saw the broadcast immediately checked with the governor's press secretary to see whether Cuomo, a presidential possibility, was ill.

"Tell them I'm here at the mansion watching the Knicks game on television," Cuomo told his press secretary, and that was the message he gave reporters.

"Impossible," shot back a reporter. "The Knicks are on the West Coast, and the game doesn't start until 11." The governor then admitted he had been to the hospital for a CAT scan for his back pains.

When a reporter is sent out on an unfamiliar story, he or she has to take a quick course in the nature of the event. The reporter assigned to interview a country music singer will do some fast reading if all the reporter knows is rock or jazz. When the singer says he is true to the tradition of Jimmie Rodgers and that other singers are cashing in on the bland commercial sound introduced by the Nashville record producers, the reporter should know what the singer is talking about.

The short item in the *Boston Herald American* read:

> The Civic Symphony Orchestra of Boston, Max Hobart, conductor, will present the Beethoven Piano Concerto No. 4 with Stephanie Brown, soloist, in Jordan Hall, tomorrow night at 8:30. There'll also be an exhibition of pictures by Mussorgsky.

To many readers of the newspaper, the item was hilarious. Those who knew classical music realized that the reporter did not. Mussorgsky is a Russian composer who wrote a piece called "Pictures at an Exhibition." It was to be played along with the piano concerto.

A news writer whose wide range of knowledge included all kinds of music would not have made the error committed by the writer for the *Boston Herald American*.

No one is expected to know every detail of every subject. But editors do expect their writers and copy editors to consult the appropriate references. Before we examine in detail the reference works with which every journalist should be familiar, let's see what reporters are expected to know.

A Reporter's Range of Knowledge

Know the Beat

A reporter should know **how things work on his or her beat.** The police reporter knows the chain of command in the police department, why police officers sometimes throw the book at offenders and how juveniles are used by drug pushers to avoid felony arrests. The courthouse reporter knows the wheelers and dealers among the courthouse lawyers, the process from arraignment to trial, what plea bargaining is and why damage suits are settled out of court so often.

The Education Beat Let's look at what an education reporter needs to know to cover his or her beat properly. The reporter must know how a school system is organized and how it is financed, how the board sets the property tax. The reporter understands the politics of setting the property tax. The educators usually want smaller classes, more teaching aids, athletic programs, a school band, a bigger library, special classes for slow learners. All of this costs money, which is raised through taxes. Property owners want good schools for their children, but they resist higher taxes.

The board is usually caught in the middle. It is responsive to property owners since many board members are property owners themselves and may represent interests in the community with a commitment to lower taxes. At the same time the board is also responsive to the educators and understands the importance of high-grade education to the community.

In addition to knowing the system, the reporter keeps up with current affairs through visits to the classroom and by constant reading. The education reporter knows that public education is being attacked for failing to educate large numbers of youngsters. Through her reading, the reporter has established several guidelines for judging schools. She has them listed in a notebook:

Strong principal
Disciplined atmosphere
High expectations for students
Homework
Individual attention to students
Emphasis on basic skills
Systematic evaluation of pupil and teacher performance

On her visits to schools the education reporter bases her questions and observations on her list of guidelines.

City Boy on the Farm Beat Editors want a reporter who can go out on a beat and take hold quickly. They do not have time to wait while the reporter learns at his or her pace. A veteran reporter recalls the problem he had on his first beat. A city boy, he was assigned by his newspaper in the southwest to cover agriculture. His first days on the job coincided with the county fair. The editor told him to do a story on the agricultural exhibits and the judging.

The reporter took careful notes of his editor's instructions and drove to the fairgrounds. He located the exhibit area and looked at his instructions. He deciphered his handwriting carefully, but the best he could make out of one key word was "barrows." He had no idea what that meant. Must be wheelbarrows, he thought, some new kind of mechanical device for the farm.

His search for wheelbarrows got him nowhere. He asked a farm equipment salesman what kind of machinery a "barrow" is.

"Must mean harrows," the salesman replied. So the reporter took copious notes about harrows, but he had no idea how he would work that into the story since the salesman said that there hadn't been any new developments with the cultivator in a few years.

The reporter drifted over to the barns to get the results of the livestock judging. An official handed him several slips of paper with the results. At the top of the first slip was a single word, *Barrows*.

The reporter tossed away all the notes he had taken about harrows and made a beeline for the youngster whose barrows had taken the blue ribbon. (A barrow, for the edification of city folks, is a castrated hog.)

Know the Community

The reporter should also know **how things work in the community.** The reporter should know about:

The political process—how the mayor and city council are elected; who appoints the police chief; whether the mayor or the council is the source of power; how the judicial system works.

The social setting—who the influential people in town are; how people get along with each other; the racial, religious and ethnic makeup of the community.

The economics of the city—how people make a living; the major employers; who the power brokers are; the relationship of business and politics.

Press Law and History

Journalists also need to know press law, the history of the press and the special needs of their newspapers and stations. An understanding of the laws of libel and privacy helps reporters avoid troublesome legal suits and encourages them to be venturesome. (The law of the press is examined in Part 5.)

Understanding the history of the press opens the past to the journalist. Knowledge of those who helped to make the press a bastion of democracy gives the journalist courage when attacked, stamina when the routine approaches drudgery and confidence when journalism is belittled.

When Dan Rather was covering President Nixon for CBS television, the White House chief of staff accused him of inaccurate and biased reporting and tried to have him removed from the beat. Rather's tough coverage of the president antagonized Nixon and his aides. Rather's home in Washington was broken into and the only material taken was his files. Many people were convinced the theft was engineered by the same "White House plumbers" who broke into Democratic headquarters in Watergate.

Rather did not buckle. He knew what a journalist is supposed to do, and he persevered in his job.

Rather was described by one television critic as "the only person whom the network news system of journalism has produced since Edward R. Murrow who can conceivably supply the conscience missing from television news."

Murrow's name is prominent in any broadcast journalist's hall of fame. As a radio and television reporter, he took broadcast journalism from the routine reporting of official activities to the task of digging behind the pronouncements. His tradition remains powerful in broadcast journalism.

The reporter never stops learning. He or she is always replenishing the store-house of knowledge essential to the journalist.

"A good reporter is a student all his or her life," says Joseph Galloway Jr., a veteran reporter. "Each new assignment demands a crash course in the theory and practice of yet another profession or system.

"From station house to courthouse, you have to find out what the official sitting in the chair knows, and you cannot recognize the truth from a position of blind ignorance."

Trying to accumulate knowledge of all kinds may seem to spread a person so thin he or she cannot learn much about a single subject, the subject that is the basis of the reporter's beat. It doesn't work that way. Information has a way of linking, of patterning. As the journalist finds out, often to his or her amazement, knowledge comes together.

The writer can never know enough, for he or she may be given an un-familiar assignment at any time. Most news staffs are shorthanded. The police reporter often has to cover an arraignment in court, and the courthouse re-porter may double as an education reporter now and then. This is the rule on small newspapers. In radio and television, only the networks have beat re-porters. Most broadcast reporters cover fires, arrests, political speeches and city council meetings.

The journalist also knows what is happening in the community, state, nation and the world.

Technology has knitted the world closer. The people of the world now live in one neighborhood, and the journalist who knows what goes on next door is better able to serve those in his or her home. Reporters keep up by moving among all kinds of people and by seeking out diverse experiences. But expe-rience is not enough. Journalists read—they read everything from geography and history to fiction.

"To be a good reporter, you must read," says Galloway, who worked his way up from a small daily in Texas to serve as the UPI's bureau manager in Moscow after combat correspondence in Vietnam and then moved to *U.S. News & World Report*.

"If in this electronic era you are not accustomed to it, then you must train yourself to gulp down the printed word with the same thirst of someone who has covered the last 15 miles of Death Valley on his belly.

"Read for your life.

"Read every newspaper that comes under your eye for style, for content, for ideas, for pleasure. And the books, my God, the books. The world of modern publishing has a 500-year headstart on you and is pulling further ahead every year.

"Never mind your transcript or your resume. Let me see your bookshelves at home and your library card."

Ideas and information valuable to journalists can also be found in magazines. A reporter for a New Mexico newspaper wrote a prize-winning series of articles about drunk driving after reading an article in *The New Republic* about the cost of alcoholism in this country. Another reporter obtained a major local story after reading a magazine article about mining the ocean floor. His reporting revealed that a large local mining industry would be affected if international agreements were worked out to permit large-scale underwater mining.

Keeping up also involves learning what the tangled events of the nation and the world mean. This requires the journalist to seek out interpretative columns in newspapers and in magazines of opinion. Among the magazines journalists read are *The Atlantic, Commentary, Harper's, The Nation, National Review, The New Republic* and *The New Yorker.*

Favorite Authors

Books are helpful in two ways. Non-fiction books can aid the reporter in the accumulation of background information. Fiction has been an inspiration to many news writers, teaching style and the use of dialogue and description.

Some journalists find Ernest Hemingway a good model for their writing. As a young man, Hemingway was a reporter in Kansas City and the journalistic style can be seen in his fiction. The prose in his novels and short stories is cut to the bone. Hemingway was an avid reader. "Thank God for books," he wrote a friend. He most admired Mark Twain. Hemingway wrote:

"All modern American literature comes from one book by Mark Twain called Huckleberry Finn. . . . It's the best book we've had. All American writing comes from that. There was nothing before. There has been nothing as good since."

All writers have favorite authors. John McPhee of *The New Yorker* says he always reads Shakespeare with awe. There is nothing Shakespeare cannot do, he says. Dickens is a favorite of others who admire his feeling for the poor and defenseless, his powerful writing and his amazing output.

A modern essayist many journalists respect is E.B. White, for years a writer for *The New Yorker.* Other American writers that journalists like and learn from are: Eugene O'Neill, the playwright; John Steinbeck, William Faulkner and F. Scott Fitzgerald, novelists; and John O'Hara, short story writer and novelist. Among the current generation of writers, journalists have learned from Gay Talese, Tom Wolfe, Hunter S. Thompson and the fiction writers John Updike, Norman Mailer, J.D. Salinger and Saul Bellow.

Some news writers have learned how to pace their stories from the mysteries of Raymond Chandler and Dashiell Hammett.

High school seniors spend less time reading books than fourth graders.—National Assessment of Educational Progress report.

Know How to Use Basic References

City directory
Bartlett's Familiar Quotations
Reader's Guide to Periodical Literature
New York Times Index
Who's Who in America
Dictionary of American Biography
Current Biography

Journalists may go through their lives without reading Hemingway, Twain, *The Wall Street Journal* or *Harper's,* but they will be helpless without a mastery of basic references.

These references begin with the telephone directory and the dictionary. In cities where there is a city directory, this should be added to the list of essentials. The telephone directory is the authoritative reference for the spelling of names and for addresses and telephone numbers.

A number of good dictionaries are available, and some reporters carry a pocket-size dictionary when they go on assignment out of town or have to send copy from outside the office. The dictionary is the authoritative source for correct spelling.

Editors may excuse a buried lead or a story that is disorganized. Even the best writers have their bad days. Editors accept this. But they snarl at misspellings. There is no excuse for an incorrectly spelled word. Worse, editors consider the reporter who consistently misspells to be indolent, too lazy to check the dictionary. The reporter who hasn't the energy to turn the pages of a dictionary doesn't belong on the news staff, editors have told poor spellers.

The city directory (fig. 7.1) is invaluable in checking information about individuals and businesses.

Every reporter should own the following:
Dictionary
World almanac
Grammar book
Atlas and road maps

The reporter also should have a copy of the newspaper or station stylebook, a guide to consistent usage in spelling, punctuation and grammar. (A stylebook is included in Appendix B. Use it.)

Stories often require more detailed background than newspaper clips can provide. The reporter who wrote the series on drunk driving wanted to check what other work had been done on the subject.

Finding Out

Much has been made of the skimpy background knowledge of college students. Richard Anderson, a college teacher and writing coach, says he taught a class in a New York college in which only one student had heard of Grant and Lee, and "in which not one student knew there was a wall around Berlin."

A midwestern college instructor found almost 90 percent of his students thought Russia fought alongside Germany in World War II.

Editors, says Anderson, should "never assume" new reporters "know anything before the day they first walk into a newsroom."

Journalism students can do just what journalists do—use references. To locate a book on a subject for a story, for example, the card catalogue is checked for relevant subjects. A much-underutilized source of information is the dissertation, which college and university libraries catalogue. These contain original and revealing source material.

ALPHABETICAL DIRECTORY
WHITE PAGES

(h) HEAD OF HOUSE   (r) RESIDENT (ROOMER)

Figure 7.1 City Directory.
This basic reference provides the news writer with a wide variety of information. More than 20 items can be gleaned from a city directory entry. Here is a sample page from a directory published by R. L. Polk & Co. Most newsrooms have such directories.

correct full name	Landon Edw G (Charlotte D) servmn B F Goodrich h1215 Oak Dr
occupation and employer	Landon Fred M (Mary E) supvr Reliance Elec h609 Norman Av
complete street address including apartment number	Landon Kenneth A (Carol L) clk First Natl Bk h1400 E Main St Apt 14
student 18 years of age or older	Landon Kenneth A Jr studt r1400 E Main St Apt 14
	Landon Virginia E (Wid Walter J) r1641 W 4th St
cross reference of surnames	Lane See Also Layne
	Lane Allen M (Joan M) (Allen's Bakery) h1234 Grand Blvd
	Lane Avenue Restaurant (Ernest G Long) 2106 L Lane Av
out-of-town resident employed in area	Lane James M (Betty B) brkmn Penn Central r Rt 1 Jefferson O
armed force member and branch of service	Lane Marvin L USA r1234 Grand Blvd
	Lane Robt B (Margt E) retd h1402 N High St
	Lane Walter M r1234 Grand Blvd
	Layne See Also Lane
	Layne Agnes E Mrs v-pres Layne Co r2325 Eureka Rd
wife's name and initial	Layne Albert M (Minnie B) slsmn Hoover Co h1919 Bellows Av
corporation showing officers and nature of business	Layne Co Inc Thos E Layne Pres Mrs Agnes E Layne V-Pres Edw T Layne Sec-Treas bldg contrs 100 N High St
	Layne Edw T (Diane E) sec-treas Layne Co h1407 Oakwood Dr
	Layne Ralph P (Gladys M) formn Layne Co h1687 Maple Dr
	Layne Thos E (Agnes E) pres Layne Co h2325 Eureka Rd
suburban designation	Leach See Also Leech
retiree	Leach Wm E USMC r1209 Ravenscroft Rd (EF)
	Lee Alf M (Celia J) retd r2106 Oakwood Dr
business partnership showing partners in parenthesis	Lee Bros (Louis J And Harry M Lee) plmbs 1513 Abbott St
husband and wife employed	Lee Harry M (Karen L) (Lee Bros) h2023 Stone Rd
	Lee Louis J (Martha B) (Lee Bros) h1616 Fulton St
	Lee Martha B Mrs ofc sec Lee Bros r1616 Fulton St
"r" resident (roomer)	Lee Minnie M Mrs h87 Eastview Dr
"h" head of household	Lee Muriel E (Wid Fred M) r810 LaForge St
	Lee Sterling T (Nadine S) mtcemn Eastview Apts h2020 Wilson St Apt 1
	Lee Thos W (Effie M) (Tom's Men's Wear) r Rt 2
owner of business showing name of business in parenthesis bold type denotes paid listing	**LEE'S PHARMACY (Lee A Shaw) Prescriptions Carefully Compounded, Complete Line Of Toiletries And Cosmetics, Fountain Service, Greeting Cards, 1705 N High St (21505) Tel 245-3312**
business firm showing name of owner in parenthesis	Leech See Also Leach
widow indicating deceased husband's name	Leech Doris E (Wid Donald L) tchr North High Sch h1323 W McLean St
	Leech Joseph B (Lucy V) slsmn Metropolitan Dept Store h824 Wilson St
	Leech Joseph B Jr studt r824 Wilson St
	Leech Marcia M clk Community Hosp r1323 W McLean St
unmarried and unemployed resident	Lewis Anne M Mrs clk County Hwy Dept r914 Wilson Av
more than one adult in household	Lewis Ernest W studt r914 Wilson Av
	Lewis Harold G (Anne M) mgr Cooper Paint Store h914 Wilson Av
	Lewis Robt B lab County Hwy Dept r1410 Union Hwy Rt 2
church showing name of pastor	Lewistown Methodist Church Rev John R Allen Pastor 515 Maple Valley Rd

First, he looked at *The New York Times Index,* a guide to all stories that have appeared in the *Times.* The index contains a brief description of the story and the date, which is used to consult the microfilms of the newspaper. Many newspapers subscribe to the index and have the microfilms. This reporter's newspaper did not, so he used the material at the public library.

He also wanted to know whether any magazines had carried articles about the subject. He consulted the *Reader's Guide to Periodical Literature.* It contains summaries of articles from all the major magazines. Knowing the date the article appeared, the reporter can usually obtain the original article from the library. Some newspapers have access to data bases that contain stories from newspapers and magazines.

For background on living Americans, *Who's Who in America* or *Current Biography* are indispensable. The *Dictionary of American Biography* contains biographical sketches of people of prominence who have died.

Research

Journalists seem unwilling to admit that they do research. Too stuffy, too academic. They say they report. But a lot of reporting is research. The computer has helped reporters do sophisticated research. The computer, an information processing machine, can digest, sort and present vast amounts of material that would take reporters weeks to put together.

With the help of the computer, the Paddock newspapers in the Chicago area processed 1,500 drunk driving arrests. More than two-thirds of those arrested escaped conviction, the data processing revealed. Only one of 15 defendants was jailed or fined heavily.

The computer magnifies mental power as the steam engine magnified muscle power.

Localizing

Extensive reading and thorough research turn up materials that reporters can localize. By localizing a story, we mean taking some national or international development and applying it locally. For example:

Studies of family life reveal that contrary to what we had assumed, the poor are concentrated among the children, not the aged. Almost one in four under the age of 3 lives in poverty. That's a national figure. What is it in your state? In New York, it's 22.7 percent; Mississippi, 36 percent.

The studies also show that most of these poor children live in single-parent homes, usually in a household headed by a mother. Data indicate that the number of single-parent homes now being formed is about the same as those of the traditional husband-wife home.

And this leads to still another good local story, teen-age pregnancy. The national teen-age pregnancy rate is the highest in the world, and unlike other countries it is not declining. The local figures can be compared to national and state data.

Another national figure: Almost a third of American youth can expect to be on welfare by the age of 18. Welfare is second only to education in non-defense governmental expenses. What is it locally?

Sometimes an assignment is so complex or so unfamiliar to a reporter that he or she hardly knows where to begin. The clips on the subject prove to be too sketchy, and the references presume some knowledge of the subject. The reporter needs a crash course in the topic, but the assignment is due and there is no time for in-depth research.

This is what happened to Jan Wong on her second day as the marine news reporter for *The Gazette* in Montreal. She had been told to do the piece quickly because she would have another assignment the next day. She was adrift.

Wong did what reporters do in such circumstances. She turned to people who know, authoritative sources.

"I must have called 20 people," she says. "I called everyone I could find in the marine directory. People were very helpful, but I felt I was drowning."

The people she called were patient. Gradually, she learned enough from the sources to make sense of the clippings and to take advantage of other resource material in the newspaper library.

"I learned an awful lot in that one day about sources, phone books, the library and clippings," she says.

"I worked at the story until I was sure I had it right, and when I submitted it to the editor, he looked it over and approved it with minor changes.

"The very next day, I had to write a story about the acquisition of Canada's largest shipyard by Canada's largest petroleum company. That was just as hard as the previous day's story. I had no idea what was involved.

"But again, a million calls and reading the clips saved me. The story made the front page of the business section."

Wong has become more confident since her learning period, which all new reporters go through. She is a bit embarrassed by the questions she had to ask in her first days on the job though.

"I'm sure my sources thought I was asking dumb questions," she says.

For a reporter gathering information and background for a story, there are no dumb questions, and sources who have an interest in seeing that the stories about themselves and their concerns are reported accurately know this. They do, however, expect the reporter to learn the beat after a while.

No matter how wide the reporter's range of knowledge may be, no matter how assiduously he or she keeps up with the news and events in city, state and nation, all this will be wasted unless the reporter has common sense.

In his presidential campaign in 1980, Ronald Reagan was fond of telling a moving story of sacrifice. During World War II, he said, a bomber was badly damaged. The pilot refused to bail out, he said, because the belly gunner was too badly wounded to move. In a quavering voice, Reagan told his audiences that the pilot reassured the frightened young gunner, "Never mind, son, we'll ride it down together."

The story worked for a while . . . until a few reporters noted in their stories that if the two airmen had died in the crash of their plane no one would have known about their last words.

Taking Notes

". . . notes were used to trigger memory; they were cryptic and brief, but provided enough information to allow the subjects to fill in the details." This is one of the observations of Beverley J. Pitts, director of graduate studies at Ball State University, in her study "The Newswriting Process of Experienced Journalists, A Case Study in the Newsroom."

First, Find A Theme

In gathering all this information—from references, research, interviews and direct observation—reporters take notes. Few reporters have total recall, and only the suicidal would dare to trust to memory the spelling of names, exact addresses and other specific information. It's not enough to jot down notes; they must be jotted down legibly, a demanding task for journalists whose penmanship usually is at a fourth grade level.

Some reporters put their faith in the tape recorder, which is all right for the sit-down interview. But on breaking stories and with people who might freeze up at the idea they are being recorded, notes are best.

Take copious notes, advises a journalism textbook. Not really, say experienced reporters. Only the most inexperienced or hopelessly confused reporter jots down everything heard and seen. The trick in gathering information is to know what the story is while reporting—even beforehand—and to note the material relevant to the story idea. The notes—often sparse—plus a good memory are sufficient for the reporter.

Bill Blundell, an editor and reporter for *The Wall Street Journal* who holds writing clinics for *Journal* staffers, says: "I always try to have some sort of theme. . . ."

Then you gather the relevant information. Other themes "may pop up that are even more interesting and you have to have the flexibility to grab them," says Blundell.

Without a directing idea, he says, "you are asking for trouble . . . your horizon is so wide you cannot cover it all."

Homer Bigart, considered the reporter's reporter, could write his lead at any instant he was covering a story, said a colleague. "He had a complete grasp of the story at all times."

Walter Mears of the AP says, "Having too much in your notebook can be as severe a problem as having too little. So the best reporters don't write down every word. They only write down the important ones. The best reporters know which ones those are. . . ."

In other words, the reporter has to establish as soon as possible the theme and direction of the story. We already have guidelines on how to do this.

The news values indicate to us what is newsworthy. When the editor says the mayor is planning a news conference at which he's expected to announce his candidacy for re-election, we know that's the story because it will have great impact. But we also know that conflict heightens newsworthiness, and so we plan—in the office, just after being given the assignment—to call some of his political opponents and some of those who have opposed his actions in office.

We also know from the rudiments of the story that balance and fairness are important, so we not only call the mayor's opponents, we reach supporters and we look into the files to see just what he has done in his last two years in office.

Pierce confab

Uk city council csdr inc sales tax nxt mtng. No idea how he'll vote on inc. 2-3%.

City Pres mgr. Herbert Smyth (eg) plans retire next.. mo to take new job in Nashville. No replacement yet. "Has done exc job. Hard to replace."

Tdy ordered MTA to resume bus service to Freedston. Will hv to find other ways of cutting MTA expenses. "Too gt hardship on residents." 750 ppl/day used line. Will resume next Monday. Same routes, same schedule as before cut on June 15.

(lots protests city council, petitions -- background) #

Hopes to be able to buy 45 acres undvlp land for "wilderness park" in newly annexed area w town. Maint. cost will be minimal cuz leave as is. Cost $40,500 "within our budget." Will be new mgr's baby to dvlp. No specific plans.

A Reporter's Notepad

Here are some pages from a reporter's notepad. The reporter covered Mayor Pierce's news conference. The mayor made several announcements; among the items were: sales tax increase on the agenda for next council meeting; an official's retirement; resumption of bus service; plans to purchase park land. Notice the reporter's shorthand: Uk for understand; vowels are often eliminated; articles (the, a) are eliminated. As he went along he noted in the margin different themes. The check denotes the tax item. The circled X concerns the park manager. The #, which he uses when he spots a possible lead, was used for the bus item. He makes a note to himself in parentheses to put in background on the bus item; he has a # next to the note. Then the mayor talked about a plan to buy land for a park, and the reporter gave this the same circled X as he gave the retirement of the park manager because the two are related. He's not certain whether # or X will be his lead. The tax increase proposal had been introduced weeks before and is not lead material. Some reporters will use different colored markers in the office to indicate different themes if they have time to study their notes.

Already, the story is taking shape, and it is still two hours from the news conference. You have notes, a few comments from those you have called, and, best of all, you have ideas for questions to ask at the news conference about a theme you have in mind from all this work.

On the reporting scene, little is as organized as the reporter hopes. Other reporters have questions on other themes. On a breaking event, the unexpected is routine. The result: A notepad of notes with several themes.

Here is a trick to help organize the story: As soon as a theme develops that you are fairly sure will be in the story, put a mark of some kind next to it—let's say an **X**—and put this mark next to all your notes as you go along that are related to this theme.

When another theme or idea pops us, use another mark—say a circle—to identify it in the column of your notepad. Other marks: #, /, *, + or you can use letters, **A, B, C, D.**

The series of marks or letters are used to organize the piece. In the office, you group similar marks. Lo and behold, the story is structured because you are putting similar material together. The piece has logic and coherence.

On longer pieces, when the reporter has a notepad or two, perhaps some taped interviews, research notes and even a data base report, the pile can be overwhelming. Here's some good advice from Saul Pett, AP Newsfeatures writer:

> Try to picture this. I'm back at the office now. I've got several notebooks full of stuff. I've got clips. I've got maybe portions of a book, or magazine and taped interviews which I've transcribed. All that is done. It is my basic material. But it's all kind of in bunches. So I sit down, and this is just dull donkey work, and I hate it, but find it necessary, and I kind of outline my material. I don't outline the story because I don't know that yet. I'm outlining the material. I try to put it in piles. Here's stuff about his wit. (Pett was discussing a profile of New York Mayor Ed Koch.) Here's stuff about his independence. Here's stuff about how he can be tough with minorities. Here's stuff about his background. All that exists in my notebooks scattered throughout. So the advantage of the outline is that I've got it on paper in long segments. It's a lot of dull work. I spent two or three days on that.
>
> I'm getting more familiar with the material. So that when I'm ready to write, I don't have to pause and go fishing around in notebooks or in stacks of clips. By then I almost never have to consult my notebooks.

Next, let's move into the field with reporters and watch them as they go about gathering information for stories.

Suggested Reading   Hayakawa, S.I. *Language in Thought and Action.* New York: Harcourt Brace Jovanovich, 4th Edition, 1978.

Lippmann, Walter. *Public Opinion.* New York: The Free Press, 1965.

Ross, Lillian. *Reporting.* New York: Dodd Mead & Co., 1981.

8

How Reporters Work

The reporting process begins with two closely related actions— assignment by the editor and idea formation by the reporter. As soon as possible following the assignment, the reporter develops ideas for the story, and these direct the reporting.
Photo by Wayne Miller. Used with permission.

Looking Ahead

Reporters develop an idea or framework for their stories before and during their reporting. This preparation guides their observations and determines the questions they ask their sources.

If a reporter's observations or the statements of sources point in a different direction, the reporter adopts a new idea for the story. Reporters follow the facts.

When the idea or framework is supported by facts, it becomes the lead of the story and the supporting facts become the body of the story.

Fred Zimmerman knew that he had a good story for his university newspaper. He had heard that a teacher at nearby Emporia State College had been summarily fired. The teacher was young, bearded and had unconventional political and social ideas. Students were angry.

"I raced all over Emporia, interviewed everybody I could think of," Zimmerman recalls. "I filled two notebooks.

"Then I sat down at a typewriter—where I found I didn't have the foggiest notion of what I wanted my story to look like."

Early in his newspaper career, Zimmerman learned about the reporting process that underlies news writing. He discovered that reporters begin to visualize their stories as soon as they are given an assignment, even before they begin their reporting. They are able to develop ideas for their stories from the nature of their assignments, from knowledge of their beats and from their general fund of information. By the time a reporter sits down to write, he or she usually has a lead and most of the important themes for the story firmly in mind.

After his experience at the University of Kansas, Zimmerman went on to a career with *The Wall Street Journal,* which included covering the White House.

As a reporter, Zimmerman always had an idea or two in mind when he went out on a story. These initial ideas would give Zimmerman a framework from which to make his observations and to ask questions of his sources. If his observations or the answers to his questions indicated he was on the wrong track, he would ditch his original idea for one that conformed to his findings.

The reporter who is assigned to interview a local banker about the steep rise in interest rates may banter with the banker about the weather for a few minutes. But the reporter knows exactly what he is there to find out: How has this increase affected local home building? Can people afford to build when they have to borrow at record-high interest rates?

The reporter who has been told to find out the reaction of university officials to a bare-bones budget just adopted by the state legislature knows what the focus of his story will be: What cuts will have to be made by the university? Will courses or programs have to be eliminated? How will the local building trades industry be affected? What about faculty and staff salaries?

The reporting process is much like any other investigative process, whether it is conducted by a detective, a nuclear physicist or an historian. First, the investigator develops a theory. The investigator's observations will then either support or refute the theory. If the theory is not supported by the facts, the investigator develops a new theory.

In his story, "The Hound of the Baskervilles," Arthur Conan Doyle described Sherlock Holmes sitting in seclusion in his Baker Street rooms after learning of the murder of Sir Charles Baskerville. Holmes "weighed every

Give Direction to Your Reporting

Caution: Studies have shown that people who have pre-set ideas about what they are to see and hear will have those ideas reinforced, whatever the facts of the event they are observing. Selective perception and retention are dangerous for reporters, who must be alert to observations that contradict their assumptions.

particle of evidence, constructed alternative theories, balanced one against the other, and made up his mind as to which points were essential and which immaterial." Holmes needed a starting point for his inquiry, long before he visited the scene of the murder.

Unlike the master detective, the reporter cannot spend hours in seclusion mulling over particles of evidence. The reporter sometimes has only minutes to prepare. Remarkable as it may seem, reporters develop the ability to generate useful ideas under pressure.

The Sheriff Was a Criminal

Linda Kramer had done a number of spot news stories for the AP about Sheriff Richard Hongisto, who had an unusual approach to law enforcement. Now, she wanted to do a profile of the man who had once gone to jail on a contempt of court charge and was now in charge of the county jail in San Francisco.

Kramer said she first took time to "read years of clips on his doings and to interview people about him." She began to develop an idea for her story that crystallized when she spent a day walking around the county jail with him.

"His rapport with inmates and his pride in jail improvements showed the man in his element," she says. On her tour of the jail, she picked up quotations from the inmates and she made observations that buttressed the idea she had developed for her story of a new-style sheriff who was friendly with inmates and non-traditional in his approach to his work.

When she was ready to write, she knew how she wanted to begin her piece. She chose an illustration from her tour of the county jail that demonstrated his easygoing relationship with the men behind bars:

SAN FRANCISCO (AP)—At a desk, he checks the .38-caliber revolver he wears in a holster at the waist of his dapper, pin-striped suit and enters the county prison for an inspection tour.

"Hey, sheriff," an inmate sings out, "we hear you was in jail."

"Yeah," Sheriff Richard Hongisto replies, "you mind being seen with a criminal?"

Laughing, he saunters past. The inmate looks after him, admiringly. "He's different than most sheriffs," he says. "Sometimes I doubt if he's a sheriff at all."

Others have been similarly bemused since Hongisto, a former city cop, took office in 1971 and began shaking up traditional notions of how sheriffs should act.

Look again at how Berkley Hudson handled his story. When Chester Jefferds told Hudson about his lengthy confinement, Hudson developed an idea for the article: Jefferds was held without good reason.

Hudson's early reporting was directed at seeing whether this theme was accurate. His reporting substantiated his original idea and it became the backbone of his piece.

When Bob Rose of *The Blade* of Toledo, Ohio, was told to interview the former president of the American Cancer Society, he had a framework in mind. He would ask about the major kinds of cancer and their causes. When he arrived at the hotel where the doctor was staying, he picked up a copy of the day's events at the hotel desk to see if anything newsworthy was happening.

On the schedule was a room number for the R.J. Reynolds Tobacco Co. The company was using a suite to instruct workers involved in a local advertising campaign. Rose quickly changed his plans. He decided to focus on lung cancer and cigarettes. The story that emerged from his interviews is on the following page.

Rose sums up the process: You know what you want to write and how you want to write it while you are doing the reporting. But whenever there is a hitch, be prepared to change plans.

Surgeon, Tobacco Firm Salesman

2 Men Worlds Apart On Smoking

Both In Toledo
To Promote Cause

By BOB ROSE
Blade Staff Writer

Two men who have a deep interest in whether Americans smoke cigarettes were in downtown Toledo Tuesday morning.

They were a floor apart in the Commodore Perry Motor Inn, but they were a world apart in what they said.

One was the immediate past president of the American Cancer Society. The other was a representative of the R.J. Reynolds Tobacco Co.

In an interview on the second floor, Dr. Lasalle Leffall, Jr. talked about what a killer lung cancer is.

In a talk to 14 temporary workers one floor above Dr. Leffall, the R.J. Reynolds man talked about handing out free samples of his firm's products.

Dr. Leffall, who until last week was president of the American Cancer Society, was eager to talk, to warn people about the more than 100 types of cancer.

The Reynolds man was not so eager. "The media is an entity that we do not deal with," he told his group in the smoke-filled room.

Dr. Leffall told about what he does when he meets a smoker. "If someone asks me if I mind if they smoke, I say, 'Yes, I do.' In doing that, I emphasize

— Blade Photo
DR. LASALLE LEFFALL
Eager to warn of cancer

that they are doing something dangerous to my health and dangerous to their health."

The Reynolds man recommended a different routine in handing out cigarettes:

"Are you a smoker or a nonsmoker?

Regular or menthol? Full flavor or lights? Longs or regular length?"

Dr. Leffall would not like the euphemism, "full flavor." He'd say "High tar and nicotine."

And he would recommend neither high nor low tar. "The American Cancer Society believes that there is no safe cigarette, but that if you must smoke, the lower tar cigarettes cause fewer changes in your system that lead to lung cancer."

Dr. Leffall said he hopes smokers will kick the habit at least on Thursday, the date of the society's annual "great American smokeout."

Not willing to fight such an effort, the R.J. Reynolds man told his people to take the day off.

Dr. Leffall, who is chairman of the surgery department at Howard University's college of medicine in Washington, D.C., said the biggest opposition to the anti-smoking drive is the person who continues to smoke in spite of all the evidence that it can be deadly.

"We're not winning the battle," he said. "We're making progress, but we're not winning the battle."

The R.J. Reynolds man, who declined to give his name, said he has no quarrel with the American Cancer Society.

"They have their job to do," he said. "And we have our job to do."

Forming Ideas

"Let's say the mayor is going to reduce the number of policemen because the city has a budget problem. We would lose a lot of cops. Big story. My duty would be not to just take it down like a tape recorder, but to try and find out by interviewing the mayor and, more likely, other officials, and other people involved with budget or the police force and ask what does it mean in terms of: Is he serious? Is it just a bargaining ploy to get more money out of the state? How easily would he be able to do this? What would that mean in terms of patrol? What would that mean in terms of crime?"—Clyde Haberman, *The New York Times*.

The theory that Mark Patinkin had developed for the profile of a woman who had killed her husband was that of a housewife "forced to fight back after years of abuse." But after Lucy Foster told him that although her husband was hard to get along with, she loved him, Patinkin knew his theory was sour.

At first, he was angry. No story. Then *The Providence Bulletin* reporter decided to shift his focus. "The abused wife who fought back was a cliché." Patinkin tried to portray him as a "decent husband and father" who had drunken rages. "Making a villain human, I think, adds to the story. Gray beats black and white."

The County Fair

When the Hamilton County Fair opened in Carthage, Ann Marie Laskiewicz of *The Cincinnati Post* had an idea for a story about the company that furnished the amusement rides. She had heard that the firm had been sued by people who claimed they were injured on the rides.

"I wanted to do a piece on how unsafe amusement rides are," she said. Then she started her reporting. She called a state agency that regulates portable amusement rides.

"I found out this company was one of the most safety-conscious in the state and that it had never been cited for an infraction of the state's safety regulations." Her whole approach changed.

"The evidence suggested another view. Instead of the original story, I wrote a story that detailed the difficulties for owners in keeping rides safe and the regulations that make Ohio one of the strictest states in the eyes of owners of portable amusement rides."

By now, an important point should be clear. After the idea or framework is substantiated by reporting it becomes the lead of the story, and the supporting evidence—the observations, quotations and research—makes up the body of the story. This is the reason we are spending so much time on this concept. An understanding of the process of news reporting makes writing the news story easier.

Remember: The idea or framework is always tentative or experimental. It is used to get the reporting moving. It is used in the story only if the facts obtained in the reporting support the idea. The framework is only as strong as the beams and joints supplied by the reporting.

Spot News Stories

Breaking news stories might seem an exception to this approach. After all, the reporter never knows what to expect on such a story. The fact is that most spot news stories do fit a pattern, and if the reporter knows the pattern, it is much easier to report and write the story. You could call this pattern the necessities or essentials of the story.

Look back at Lindy Washburn covering a fire for the AP. As soon as she heard that the fire in Bradley Beach was a big one, ideas came to mind and a framework developed. Her first question to the fire department dispatcher in Asbury Park was, "Any deaths?"

Story Essentials

Washburn knew that an essential element of a fire story is the number of dead and injured. There are other necessities or essentials of a fire story, and if we look at Washburn's questions we can see what these essentials are. She asked the dispatcher for the address of the building, what it was being used for, when the first alarm had been received. She wanted to know the cause of the fire and what the building looked like. The answers to these questions would shape her story, Washburn knew.

The obituary writer also had a series of questions to ask because she, too, knew that the answers would be essential to her story: The name and identification of the deceased. Accomplishments. Survivors. Funeral plans.

These essentials can be established for various types of stories. Chapters 9 and 10 list the basic ingredients or necessities for many types of stories.

The essentials are the writer's starting point in all reporting. They determine the reporter's early observations and the first questions asked of sources. One of the most frequent failings of beginning reporters is that they do not cover these essentials in their stories. In the newsroom, the editor will say that the writer has left a hole in his story, or that she has failed to anticipate and answer the reader's questions.

Once the essentials are tucked away in the notebook, the reporter moves on to more specific and detailed observations and questions. The answers to the routine essential questions usually provide leads for more questions.

In preparing—whether the preparation lasts a few minutes on a breaking story or a few hours for a profile of a lawyer—the reporter reviews the essentials, and may even jot down a few questions to ask. Also, the story assignment will set up ideas for observations and questions that move beyond the essentials.

Essentials. The reporter assigned to cover a fire knows at once that the story must include casualties, property damage, cause, structure involved. If the fire breaks out in a department store Saturday afternoon, the reporter thinks of deaths and injuries and rescues. If the fire is in an area with several recent fires, the reporter prepares to ask the fire chief about the possibility of arson. These ideas direct the reporter's observations and questions.
Photo by Charlie Riedel of The Hays (Kan.) Daily News. Used with permission.

For example: Say you are assigned to interview a woman lawyer who donates considerable time to helping battered children and women and the victims of sex crimes. The essentials for this profile—as for any profile—are:

Appearance. Show us what the person looks like.

Background. Where does this person come from? Education, upbringing, interests.

Occupation. Training. Length of time in field. Reason for selecting it.

Examples. Anecdotes and illustrations to show the person at work. Personal observation, if possible.

These are the essentials. The reporter also can jot down specific questions to ask, observations to make, which spring from the nature of the particular assignment. In this case, the reporter will want to know about motivation, why the lawyer has chosen to help victims. Was she—and this will have to be handled delicately—herself a battered child or the victim of a sex crime? And so on with more specifics. All these questions may be written down and asked from notes, or they can be memorized.

Such preparations are essential. But no one can predict the twists and turns a news event will take. The idea is to have a jump on the story. Then adjustment is easier.

When the obituary writer learned that a memorial scholarship fund would be set up for Rose Harriet Allen, that was an unexpected element and it became an important part of her story. The standard questions she asked did start her on the way, and the answers provided considerable material for her story. Be Prepared for Surprises

The reporters and photographers accompanying President Reagan as he left the Hilton Hotel one afternoon were thrust suddenly into a totally unpredictable situation—an attempt on the president's life.

Though surprised, the White House reporters did have a framework for such an event. Just as Lindy Washburn knew that for a fire story she had to include in her story certain essentials—number of dead and injured, location of fire and so on—the White House correspondents with President Reagan knew that the story of an assassination attempt had to be structured around two central facts: Was the president struck by any of the shots and if so, how badly was he injured?

In fact, in their haste to answer these questions, they were at first misled into presuming the president was unhurt. Although three others were hit and sent sprawling into the street, the president continued into his car. The reporters jumped to the conclusion that the shots had missed him. The truth was quickly put on the news wires when reporters learned that the president had been taken to a hospital emergency room.

The reporter began to plan when he was told by his editor that he would have to cover an announcement by the president of the local college about the school's athletic program later that day. He checked the newspaper library for clippings about the college, and he learned that the school had been trying to build up its intercollegiate athletic program. It had recently hired a basketball coach from a Big Ten team. Another clipping described the activities of a booster club that was trying to raise money for the football team. It seemed the college was trying to go big time. Trouble on the Playing Field

The reporter covered the college as a beat, but he was not acquainted with the athletic program because the newspaper's sports department handled that. He knew he needed a lot of information in a short time, so he called people on the campus whom he considered good sources.

A psychology professor who had once served on the college athletic board told him that there had been talk among the players of special favors and under-the-table payments. Perhaps the president was going to comment on these rumors. The reporter called the college public relations office and asked the head of the office, an old friend, about his theory. He hit his friend with the key question at once.

"Tom, is the president going to talk about the rumors of payoffs to players today?"

Tom was too old a hand to become flustered, and he laughed.

"I won't confirm that," he replied. A pause. "But I won't deny it either."

This last comment indicated to the reporter that he was on the right track. At the news conference later, he was not surprised to see the college athletic director and two coaches with the president. Nor was he surprised to hear the president deny the allegations about under-the-table payments. He had expected that.

No wonder that when the reporter returned to the office, he was able to write quickly and to have a comprehensive story ready for the early edition. He had been prepared with background information, and he had a concept of what the event might be—the denial of wrongdoing.

One of his most difficult tasks was selecting what to use. The president had spoken, and so had the college athletic director and two coaches. The reporters asked questions. Thousands of words and at least a dozen ideas had swirled through the room, but the reporter was told to hold his story to about 350 to 400 words. The reporter used his judgment to select material that was relevant to his central theme of the denial of illegal activities.

Walter Lippmann, one of the great figures in American journalism, once observed that there are too many facts for the reporter to gather and that even if a reporter could gather them all, nobody would want to read all of them. The nature of journalism, he said, is selective judgment.

News stories are capsulated reality. They can hold just so much—one, two, perhaps three major themes. The job of the journalist is to select the theme or themes that best describe and summarize the event. Since events are often disorganized and time is always short, the reporter seeks to get a jump, to have a headstart on fact gathering by developing an idea of the story as quickly as possible after receiving the assignment.

Then the task is to make the observations, ask the questions and do the background research that provide the details that make up the supporting or buttressing material that is placed in the body of the story.

Details Make the Difference

"**I think** we should be walking through the jungle listening for odd noises and reporting exactly what we see and hear—and be wary and vigilant."—Mary McGrory, syndicated columnist.

It is the details that make all stories unique. No two fires are the same, and no two basketball games are alike. Solid reporting will dig up the details that make stories stand out.

Details help the reader and listener to see and understand the event. When H.D. Quigg was sent by the UPI to Austin to cover the sniper who was shooting students from the University of Texas observation tower he itemized every one of the score of unusual items that the young sniper had put in the footlocker that he had carried up with him. After reading the list, readers knew that the young man was deranged.

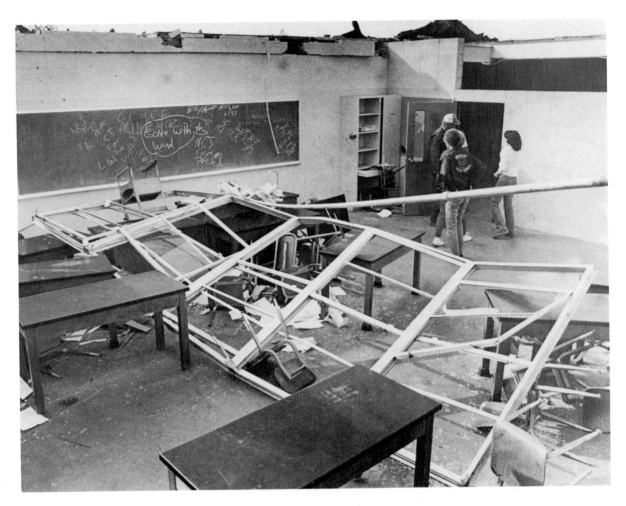

Looking and Listening

Keith Warren, a reporter-photographer for *The Commercial Dispatch* in Columbus, Miss., was sent to cover the aftermath of a tornado that tore through Jones County in southeastern Mississippi. Although there were six deaths, 100 injuries and massive damage, the residents were undaunted. Warren said he was surprised they were not overcome by the disaster.

"They even joked about the storm," he said. He caught this spirit in a photograph of the roofless Northeast Jones High School. On a blackboard someone had written: "Gone with the wind."

These are a plain-spoken, church-going people, and Warren captured this in an interview with Austin Wade and his wife Willie:

"It sounded like a train coming. It sounded awful," Mrs. Wade said, "We went in the bathroom and Austin grabbed onto the sink and I grabbed him. Then he said, 'Bill, some people call me Bill, we're gone.' And I said, 'No, we're not. The Lord is with us.' Then we started praying. And when you pray you have to pray with faith."

Photo by Keith Warren, The Commercial Dispatch, Columbus, Miss. Used with permission.

Keep Digging

This story came into the office of *Newsday* from one of its bureaus:

```
     Plainview--A 12-year-old newsboy died
Wednesday after he was struck by a car while
delivering papers by bicycle, police reported.
     Philip Goldstein, of 6 Ramsey Rd., left his
home at 5:48 AM and rode his bike to Old
Country Road, where police said he crossed the
path of a car driven by Joseph Havranck, 53, of
7 Timon Ct., Huntington. Havranck, who was
unhurt and was not charged in the incident,
told police his car skidded on wet pavement
when he attempted to stop.
     The Goldstein boy was taken to Central
General Hospital, in Plainview, and was later
transferred to Nassau County Medical Center,
East Meadow, for surgery. He was pronounced
dead at 2:40 PM.
```

An editor at the newspaper sensed there was more to the story, and he asked a reporter to dig further. Here is the story written by Jeff Sommer:

PLAINVIEW—By 9 AM Tuesday, doctors at Nassau County Medical Center told Gerald and Barbara Goldstein there was little chance that their 12½-year-old-son, Philip, injured in an auto accident, would live.

The Goldsteins thought of Philip's bar mitzvah—his ceremonial coming of age as a Jew—which was scheduled for tomorrow. And they thought of a close friend of Philip's who was to attend the bar mitzvah. The friend was confined to a Manhattan hospital, where he recently received a kidney transplant from his father.

"We decided immediately to donate his [Philip's] kidneys for transplants," Gerald Goldstein said yesterday, sitting in the sunlit yard of the family's Plainview home. "Philip was a very sensitive, compassionate boy. He was very concerned about his friend. We're sure he would've wanted it this way."

The seventh-grader, who hoped one day to attend Harvard Medical School and become a doctor, died Wednesday. And yesterday at StonyBrook University Hospital two young Suffolk residents who Philip never knew received his kidneys. Philip's parents say their son lives on, symbolically.

"I hope some day my wife and I will be able to break bread with these people," Goldstein, a Manhattan lawyer, said. "We have been told that they share our grief and we hope to be able to share their joy in this gift from our son."

The kidney recipients—Kathy Kuhl, 22, of 16 Reynolds St., Huntington Station, and Robert Tagliaferro, 23, of 15 Longacre Court, Port Jefferson—were in stable condition last night at the hospital, resting after their operations performed by a team of 30 medical personnel, headed by Dr. Felix Rapaport.

The recipients, who had been undergoing dialysis treatments because their own kidneys had failed, were chosen from among 60 people for whom the hospital is seeking kidneys, according to Winnie Mack, the hospital's transplant coordinator.

The tissues of Philip and of the recipients are so well-matched that the chance the operations will be successful is more than 75 percent—"as good as a parent-to-child transplant," Rapaport said at 4 PM yesterday, nearly 16 hours after the operations began.

Eva Kuhl, Kathy's mother, said last night she hoped the transplant would allow her daughter "to be independent . . . She's been through hell . . . If it doesn't take, she won't be any further back than when she started." Kathy has been a diabetic since age 12. She is legally blind but she "is a fighter," Mrs. Kuhl said.

The Goldsteins said they are not bitter about the accident, which occurred on Old Country Road while Philip was delivering newspapers on his bicycle. No charges were brought in the accident. "He was such a good, bright boy," Goldstein said. "But now all we can do is hope something good comes of it."

Rabbi Louis Stein had expected to see Philip bar mitzvahed tomorrow at Temple Beth Elohim in Old Bethpage. Instead, the rabbi was to officiate at the boy's funeral at 10:30 this morning at Gutterman's Funeral Home, Westbury. Burial was to be private.

"He was sure a fine, all-around boy," Stein said last night. "He was active in our congregation, in his school band, in the local soccer league. He had friends throughout the community . . . His parents have made a very thoughtful gesture—by extending life for others while their child has lost his own."

Good Reporting = Good Writing

Why is the second account so much better than the first? Only one reason—better reporting. This is what editors mean when they tell their reporters: You don't write writing; you write reporting.

No matter how proficient a news writer may become at manipulating words, there is only so much even the most gifted writer can do without good material to work with.

Listen to the latest songs; watch the television talk shows; recall the last movie you saw. When the material is ordinary and run-of-the-mill, not even the most gifted performer can make it come alive. Not every song The Rolling Stones recorded became a gold record, and Bruce Springsteen cannot turn a so-so tune into a hit. Some of Michael Jackson's performances are flat. All of David Letterman's nimble wit cannot bring a dull guest to life. Even Tom Cruise and Jane Fonda have appeared in some lemons they and their fans prefer to forget.

But given good material, the rock group, singer, talk show host, talented actor or actress can make you sit up and exclaim, "That's something." So can the news writer who makes perceptive observations and uses interesting quotations and relevant background.

Carol McCabe, an editor who was instrumental in improving the writing of staffers with *The Providence Journal* advises:

"You ask the questions: What was it like? What did it feel like? Take the reader where he cannot go. You, reporter, go in and bring back information. What was it like in those woods? What is it like on that island? What is it like in the person's dreams? And you do that by accumulating every bit of meaningful detail and using it where it seems appropriate. It's what you leave out sometimes that is as important as what you put in."

On the Beat

The heart of news gathering for the newspaper is the beat. Reporters are placed at strategic locations where news usually develops. These locations are designated as beats—the police station, the county courthouse, city hall, the federal courthouse. The reporters assigned to these locations are called beat reporters.

Some reporters have topical rather than geographical beats. While the police and the city hall reporters spend most of their time at one location (a geographical beat), the education reporter moves over a wide territory and examines a variety of topics on this subject (a topical beat). The education reporter visits grade schools, looks in on community colleges, attends school board sessions and even goes to the state capital to cover legislative sessions that deal with educational matters.

Other topical beats include medicine, science, labor, agriculture, politics and the performing arts. Sports is considered a topical beat because most sports writers handle a variety of sports events.

Because radio and television stations have fewer reporters, almost all stations make their staffers general assignment reporters. Only the networks and the largest stations have beat reporters.

Know the Subject Matter

Beat reporters are expected to have a thorough knowledge of the subject matter of their beats. This enables them to work quickly and accurately, whatever the deadline pressure. Their knowledge of how things work on their beats also enables reporters to do **enterprise** stories. These are the stories that are dug up by the reporter's own initiative. The coverage of a crime is a spot news story; the enterprising reporter delves into statistics to find that most crimes are committed between 9 p.m. and 2 a.m. by males in their teens and early twenties.

Good sources and persistence are essential. Sources provide tips and ideas, but not all of them lay out their information like merchants displaying their wares at a flea market. Some sources have to be pushed or praised and patted. Extracting information is an art. Usually, though, sources are cooperative.

A reporter cannot be everywhere on the beat. In the courthouse, where hundreds of transactions occur daily, the reporter who has good sources will be called by a lawyer who is about to file a request for an injunction. Or the court clerk will leave a call for the reporter to check with her about the injunction.

In city hall, when a developer files a plan with the planning office for a large housing project, a secretary may spot the reporter in the hall and beckon him into the office to show him the plans.

A school principal will call the education reporter to invite her to look over a new reading program intended for the fourth grade.

When Dan Rather covered the White House for CBS News, he said he survived the highly competitive race for news by relying on his personal sources. "They didn't pass me notes in invisible ink, but I made it my business to know them—secretaries, chauffeurs, elevator operators and waiters," Rather says. "They see a lot of papers and overhear conversations.

"I take them to dinner and keep them in cigars or whatever turns them on."

Courtesy, a cheerful word or two and personal interest often are enough to make friends of potential sources. People on the fringes like to be thought to be close to those in power and to feel they are a part of important activities. They do this by feeding information to journalists.

Sources also are essential for background stories. Every reporter has friends who can be counted on to explain the complexities of certain stories.

Five Keys to Covering the News Beat

Know how things work. Know the laws that guide those in charge, the regulations and rules and the processes that underlie the daily activities of the agency, department or unit.

Cultivate sources. Good sources are not always those in charge. Secretaries, elevator operators, clerks, deputies, telephone operators can provide valuable information.

Keep abreast. Know what is happening in the field you are covering by reading good newspapers and specialized journals.

Be persistent. Dig beneath the handout and the press release. Do not take "no comment" for an answer from public officials.

Anticipate developments. Follow developments on the beat closely so that you have a sense of what logically must follow the present situation.

On the Beat

Beat reporters do most of the reporting on
newspapers. The business reporter covers new
construction, local business conditions and
changes in company personnel. The sports
reporter covers participatory sports activities such
as fishing, hunting, bowling as well as the games
and the athletic activities of local schools and
professional teams. The education reporter covers
campus and school activities such as student
protests, changes in curriculum and personnel and
school budgets.

General assignment reporters cover a wide
range of news events. They are not assigned to a
specific beat. Whereas the beat reporter has a
specific geographical or topical area, the general
assignment reporter may be assigned to a speech
at the Rotary luncheon, a housing development
opening in the afternoon, and a landfill protest in
the evening.

Common to the beat and general assignment
reporters are knowledge of the subject and the
ability to write quickly and clearly under pressure.

*Photo top right by Joel Strasser. Used with permission.
Others by author.*

When Marcia Chambers covered the criminal courts for *The New York Times*, she knew a few judges who could explain to her the fine points of the law, and when she moved on to cover education she developed sources on the school board who helped her penetrate the wall of silence of the bureaucracy.

Beat reporters face two dangers in dealing with sources: writing for them and getting too close to them. Sometimes, a reporter will become too technical. The sources will understand, but the average reader will be lost. Since reporters are in frequent touch with their sources and can only visualize their readers and listeners, the tendency often is to write for the sources.

A more insidious pitfall is becoming too close to sources, so close that the reporter may be soft on his or her friends. A reporter also may not want to risk losing a good source by writing a tough story.

Checking A Source's Credibility

The credibility of a source can be checked in several ways, says Bob Greene, chief of investigative reporting for *Newsday:*

Previous reliability. Has this source proved accurate in the past?

Confirmability. Is the source able to supply material that will confirm the information he or she is giving you?

Proximity. Was the source in a position to know the facts he or she gave you?

Motive. Is the source's reason for giving you information logical?

Contextuality. Does the information fit with known facts?

Believability. Does the source appear to be stable and rational?

Investigative Reporting

Once a reporter has shown that he or she understands the way organizations, agencies and branches of government work in the community and has shown enterprise in digging up stories on a beat, the reporter may be given the go-ahead to do investigative reporting.

Investigative reporters seek to uncover material that people want to hide. Some of the activities are illegal, and some are legal but abusive. By abusive, we mean that the activities in some way hurt people or deny them their rights.

In recent years, investigative reporters have paid as much attention to the affairs of private industry and organizations as they did to governmental abuses and illegalities. *The Charlotte Observer* won a Pulitzer Prize for meritorious public service for a series on the effects of unsafe and unsanitary conditions in southern textile mills. The series was titled "Brown Lung—a Case of Deadly Neglect." It won another Pulitzer for exposing the financial misdeeds in the PTL religious organization involving Jim and Tammy Bakker. The Gannett News Service was awarded the prize for exposing the activities of a charity run by a Catholic order, the Pauline Fathers.

Investigative reporting is based on digging, the scrutiny of records, documents and files. Investigative reporters also rely on sources for tips and inside information. Good sources enabled two young reporters, Bob Woodward and Carl Bernstein, to expose the cover-up of Watergate for *The Washington Post*. These sources provided the reporters with enough information for them to reveal the fact that the so-called Watergate burglary was part of a plan by the Nixon administration to win re-election.

Although some reporters are assigned investigative reporting as a special beat, all reporters are expected to dig out information on their beats. The reporter who accepts without checking handouts and press releases and who relies on the assertions of authorities without checking them fails to inform readers and listeners of the full dimension of his or her beat. Such a reporter can never hope to do investigative reporting.

Editors also want reporters who can do interpretive reporting and writing.

Interpretive Stories

The reporter who knows his or her beat, who has good sources and who can place current events in context is often asked to write interpretive pieces. These articles, sometimes in the form of columns, sometimes called news analyses, give the **causes** and **consequences** of events.

For instance, a writer might try to show how a city ordinance came into existence—the groups that pushed for it, the organizations that opposed it and lost and the reasons for their positions. The writer will also describe the effect of the new ordinance.

The term *interpretive reporting* means that the writer seeks to find the meaning of the event. This is not editorial writing. Editorial writers tell readers or listeners that something is good or bad. That is, they make value judgments. The interpretive news writer puts the event in its context.

By placing an event in context, we mean that the interpretive writer's job is to place the news event in the stream of cause and effect. An event that is isolated for a news story is plucked from a larger cycle or stream of related events. The interpretative story shows the news event to be part of a stream of events.

A city council decision to allow a developer to build homes on a small tract near the city limits can be shown to be the consequence of population pressure, people in the inner city wanting to move out of older homes into newer houses.

"The finest reporting, short or long, is always investigative in that it digs and digs and digs. The finest writing is almost by definition explanatory in that it puts things so vividly, so compellingly, that readers see and understand."—Gene Roberts, executive editor of *The Philadelphia Inquirer.*

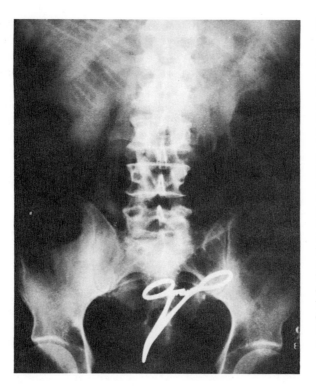

Aids and Impediments to Reporting

In our discussion of reporting, we have stressed the logical, thoughtful approach to reporting. We have talked about reporters adopting tentative ideas, then going out on the story to find supporting material. If the material is not there, the reporter adopts another idea.

All of this makes the reporter seem cool and detached, dispassionately jotting down data from his or her observations, a scientist tracking electrons. Most journalists don't work that way. Like everyone else, they have feelings, attitudes and personal values. No one is exempt from these emotions, prejudices and biases. Some are positive and can reinforce good journalism.

Moral Indignation

The persistent underlying sentiment of many investigative reporters is a sense of moral indignation. They want to make the world a better place, and they cannot abide the misuse and abuse of wealth and power that makes life painful and arduous for so many. Not content with official statements, versions or excuses, reporters blessed—or afflicted—with moral indignation get things done. Look at what radio station WIND in Chicago did.

Accidents in big cities are frequent, so frequent they are not given much attention by the media. But this accident bothered the staff of the radio station. It involved a woman and her two children.

Their car had stalled on the Dan Ryan Expressway. The three waited almost two hours as thousands of cars passed, including several police cars. No one offered to help.

Finally, the mother and her 12-year-old son went to seek assistance. They left the other son, a paraplegic, behind in the car. But they never found help. As the older son watched from the car, his mother and brother were struck by a car and were killed.

The deaths angered a staff member of WIND. The stories and editorials the station carried revealed the need for a communications system on the 125 miles of expressway around Chicago. During the campaign, people called in with horror stories of their own. One man said his son had been driving on the Eisenhower Expressway when his windshield was shot out by a passing motorist.

"The car swerved, banged into the median and threw the boy out of the car," the station quoted the father as saying. "He lay by the side of the damaged car for nearly an hour before help came."

The campaign by WIND won a Sigma Delta Chi Award for public service by a radio station.

Other prizes have gone to reporters who have exposed dangerous working conditions, the incompetence of doctors in Veterans Administration hospitals, the freeing of a man wrongly convicted of murder, the death of inmates in a county jail because of lack of medical attention, illegal burying of hazardous waste.

Although emotional involvement can lead to good stories, some feelings and attitudes can distort observations and can blind the reporter to some kinds of stories.

Personal Biases

As we have seen, news reporting and writing is the art of selection. Reporters choose what they want to observe, and then they select from those observations the elements they want to put into their stories. The reporter who believes that the poor bring about their own misery would not have recognized the story that Mary Ann Giordano of the *Daily News* saw in the plight of a family living in a tenement without heat or water.

The reporter who grew up in a home with liberal political views may be convinced that Republicans are well-to-do people whose philosophy is built on keeping taxes low so they can have more. The reporter may see all Republican candidates in this mold. The reporter who was convinced as a college freshman that conservative values are the only valid political concepts may conclude that liberals—especially the kind found in the big cities—believe in a tax-and-spend theory of government that will bankrupt the nation.

If these reporters were assigned to cover politics, their stereotyped beliefs might produce slanted stories.

Unquestionably, many reporters do have strong political views, but they hold them in check. They realize that the complexities of life cannot be reduced to the simplistic absolutes of our young liberal and conservative.

Some reporters are unaware of their biases, of the distorted pictures they carry around with them. We all grew up with images of things and people we like and dislike, of ideas we find admirable and those we consider repulsive.

Our parents, our church or synagogue, our friends, our schools, our favorite television programs—all these and more influence us to see the world in certain ways. Journalists see these images, too, and sometimes they can distort a journalist's perceptions.

The aspiring journalist should remember that no one, not even those who follow a credo that calls for an open mind, compassion and a commitment to democratic values, is exempt from the prejudices of time and place. **Useless Baggage**

Developing an open mind requires jettisoning some customs, beliefs and ideas that may go back to childhood: a parent's prejudice against Jews and Italians, a teacher's indifference to the slow learner, friends' hostility to blacks and Puerto Ricans, a church's intolerance of critics.

One of the most difficult tasks young journalists face in freeing themselves from the weight of the past is establishing a proper attitude toward authority. The youngster is taught to respect and abide by authority—parents, teachers, professionals. As children, we grew up doing what others told us to do.

Then there was the period of rebellion. If father is so smart, why can't he meet his bills? If the politicians are so wise, why couldn't they rescue the hostages in Iran and Lebanon? As for teachers, every high school and college student has a favorite tale that proves teachers are hopeless cases. As someone said, "Those who can, do. Those who can't, teach."

There is a middle road. The journalist must be skeptical of authority. An assertion is not true simply because someone in power or an expert said so. The journalist's task is to check statements, claims and declarations, no matter how authoritative the source.

Skepticism is not cynicism. It makes no sense to turn away from someone in authority merely because the person has a credential or a title. An open mind, a broad outlook, association with all kinds of people and the realization that although people have much in common they are different—these are useful to counter the pictures in our heads that can distort reality.

The beginning reporter is supposed to be able to do it all. Well, maybe not everything, but a lot. Even though the city editor may assign the beginner a beat, the editor also expects the new hand to be able to write personal items, turn out a feature about the volunteer program at a local hospital, make readers smile with clever brights and help out with obituaries and weekend traffic accidents. **Story Essentials**

On the small- or medium-sized newspaper—where most beginners start their careers—there are few specialists. Everyone has to be able to handle the basic types of stories.

The next two chapters will show you how to handle some of these basic stories by giving you the essential ingredients of a dozen different types of stories.

Every story that a reporter writes can be fitted into a type or category. There are game stories that sports writers handle, fire and arrest stories police reporters write, meeting stories that a variety of beat and general assignment reporters cover and write. There are also news conferences, meetings, obituaries, accidents, crimes, weather and personals. Each of these types of events has essential ingredients or elements that must be included in the stories.

Here is what we mean by the essential elements of the news story:

An obituary obviously must include the name of the person who died. Since the reader wants to know something about the person, every obituary must also include the person's address or home town and his or her occupation and accomplishments. There are other absolute necessities for the obituary, one of which was left out of the following wire service story. See if you can figure out what is missing.

```
AM-HOBGOOD DIES, 180<
OLDEST WAR VETERAN DIES<
     ARKADELPHIA, ARK. (AP)-Funeral services
will be held Monday for Norman Hobgood, the man
the government calls the nation's oldest war
veteran.
     Hobgood, who died Friday, enlisted in the
army in 1898, serving in the third Kentucky
Volunteer Infantry during the Spanish-American
War. The veteran's administration said he was
the oldest of 30 million veterans listed in its
records.
     Only about 250 veterans of the Spanish-
American War are living, according to the VA.
     The Kentucky Native also was Arkansas'
oldest State Legislator. He was elected to the
State House of Representatives for two terms in
1925 and 1927.
     Hobgood, who lived in an Arkadelphia
nursing home, frequently was interviewed about
his status as the oldest veteran. He also was
in the limelight in the annual Veterans Day
celebrations in Arkadelphia.
     Last year, Hobgood was awarded the Arkansas
Distinguished Service Medal in a Veterans Day
ceremony at Henderson State University.
     Hobgood was a lawyer, teacher and farmer.
He farmed until he was 99 and preached the
Sunday worship service at his church on his
100th birthday.
     AP-NR-03-02 1413EST<
```

A few minutes after this story moved on the wires, an alert editor caught the lapse and ordered a new story written with the essential information included. The new story was identical to the first except for this second paragraph:

```
    Hobgood, who died Friday at the age of 108,
enlisted in the army in 1898, serving in the
Third Kentucky Volunteer Infantry during the
Spanish-American War. The Veteran's
Administration said he was the oldest of 30
million veterans listed in its records.
```

(In case you did not catch the blooper, the news writer had forgotten to include the man's age, an essential ingredient of all obituaries.)

Journalists like to say that there are no rules for journalism. Since no event is quite like another event, there can be no rigid rules for writing stories, they say. It is true that no two basketball games are exactly alike. One may be an easy victory, another may be won in the last three seconds. Even the games won at the final buzzer differ. One may be won on a foul shot, another on a desperation-heave from midcourt. A third might be won by a guard playing his first game. Another game was not so much won by a team as lost by its opponent when the defense had a mental lapse. And so on.

Every event—game, speech, interview, obituary, arrest, accident—is different from others like it, and the good news writer handles each differently, no matter how many games he has covered, how many speeches she has had to sit through, how many interviews he has conducted.

Yes, all events are different. Each should be handled with an individual touch, with full attention to its unique characteristics. However, every basketball game story must include the score, the names of the teams, the key plays and the names of the players scoring the most points. Every speech story must include the main point of the talk, the speaker's name and his or her title or occupation, where the talk was given, the response of the audience. All accident stories tell the reader or listener the names of those injured, where the accident occurred, the names of the drivers involved and the cause.

To sum up, there are essential elements for every type of story and they must be included. They are non-negotiable. You can complain about being forced into a rigid style by these requirements all you want. But forget one of them and you will face the embarrassment of the wire service writer who neglected to put in the obituary the age of the Spanish-American War veteran.

These essentials can be placed anywhere in the story—in the lead, the middle, at the end. Placement is up to the news writer and his or her feel for the relative importance of the elements and the structure of the story.

Non-negotiable Essentials

Fire stories all seem more or less the same. Good reporters can spot the item that makes the one they cover today different from last week's. Here's a lead by Emil Venere of *The Mesa Tribune:*

```
    An 81-year-
old Mesa man
was burned
seriously in a
natural-gas
fire Wednesday
morning and a
neighbor used
slices of
white bread to
smother the
man's
smoldering
skin.
```

No list can predict the full dimensions of any story. The writer must be aware of the unique aspects of the event. Often, it is the unusual, the strange fact, that makes the story that is being written different from other fire, sports or speech stories. If the fact is unique and significant, the writer begins the story with it—the tears in the firefighter's eyes as he carries the body of the child from the smoking ruins, the mistake of the base runner in the ninth inning, the sparse attendance at a meeting of school board candidates.

Journalism is not mechanical. It cannot be carried out by the number, like a drill team automatically stepping out its patterns. Journalism is an art that requires its practitioners to look with a fresh eye at each event so that the unique aspects of the event can be captured in the story. But the eye must have a focus, a direction in which to begin looking. The essentials point the news writer in the proper direction.

To begin our examination of story types, we will look first at the interview. Editors say the ability to conduct an interview is one of the most important competences they look for in a new staff member. We will then go to other types of stories involving the spoken word—meetings, news conferences and speeches. In chapter 10, we will look at how accident and fire stories, crime and court stories, obituaries, sports stories and personals are handled.

Suggested Reading

Broder, David. *Behind the Front Page: A Candid Look at How the News Is Made*. New York: Simon & Schuster, 1987.

Liebling, A.J. *The Press*. New York: Ballantine Books, 1961.

Snyder, Louis and Richard B. Morris. *A Treasury of Great Reporting*. New York: Simon & Schuster, 1969.

Woodward Bob, and Carl Bernstein. *All the President's Men*. New York: Simon & Schuster, 1974.

9

Capturing the
Spoken Word

Interviews are at the heart of just about every news story. A reporter may seek information about the injured in a fire or automobile accident from the paramedic at the scene. Or the interview may provide background for a story about taxes. A major use of interviews is the profile.

Looking Ahead

Interviews are of two types: Spot news interviews develop information that supplements the news story; profiles and personality interviews focus on the person. The emphasis in the spot news interview is on the event; the depth interview emphasizes the individual being featured.

To carry out a successful interview, the reporter acquaints himself or herself with the nature of the event or the person being profiled, asks direct questions, listens and watches carefully.

Meeting stories focus on the decision reached if one is made; if not, the focus is on the consensus reached or the most significant issue raised in the discussion.

For **panel discussions and symposia,** the writer looks for an area of agreement or significant differences among the panelists to use as the lead. If there is no common ground, the writer may single out important points made by one or two speakers, or may use the lack of common ground as the lead.

Most **news conferences** are called for a specific purpose, and this is usually the lead.

Speech stories concentrate on the speaker's main point, audience reaction or the answers to questions asked by reporters after the speech.

These stories must contain quotes that back up and buttress the theme the writer has selected for the lead of the story.

The Interview

Most stories are based in part or wholly on an interview of some kind. It may be a few short questions asked of a police officer investigating a robbery, an extended interview for background to a piece on college tuition, or a lengthy interview for a profile of the new owner of the local professional basketball team.

Municipal budget or college basketball game. Campus rock group concert or sociology instructor with a new theory about student relationships. In every one of these stories, a reporter asks someone for information.

Since we know that the news story should reflect the nature of the event, we have a starting point for stories that contain or are based on interviews: **Use quotes**—but not just any quotes. Use the quotes that capture the meaning of the event.

Of course, we want background material and description in these stories, too. But our stories will revolve around what we hear.

Kidnapping. Mary Ann Giordano of the New York *Daily News* interviews the friend of a family whose baby was kidnapped. Giordano was assigned to the arraignment of a suspect and is seeking information to background her story. *Michael Lipak, Daily News.*

Spot News Interview

The spot news interview is used to gather material to supplement the theme of the news story. Properly interviewed—asked the right questions—the source can add information that makes the story complete.

Reporters interview police officers for information about crimes, fire marshals for possible causes of fires. Sports reporters talk to coaches and players for background material for game stories. In these spot news interviews, the reporter usually is looking for supplementary material—the facts that will illustrate or highlight the event being described.

This usually leads the news writer to play down the person being interviewed because the focus is on the event rather than on the person. This does not mean that we ignore the source's direct quotes. Often, the quotes add drama and interest as well as meaning and conviction to the story.

In the following story, a state highway patrol officer was the source of information about a fatal traffic accident:

Three people were killed in a grinding collision between a truck and an automobile last night on Highway 10, 15 miles north of Morgantown, the state highway patrol reported.

Those fatally injured were in the automobile. They were Albert Foster, 22, of 237 Western Ave.; his brother, Michael, 18, of the same address; and the driver, Bert Pierce, 21, of Tampa, Fla. The truck driver, George Allen, 48, of New Orleans, suffered minor bruises.

A state highway patrol spokesman, Robert Jackson, said the automobile apparently tried to make a U-turn off the westbound lane and moved into the path of the truck as it sped eastward.

"The car was demolished," Jackson said. "There were parts all over the road for 100 yards." Traffic was delayed on the eastbound section for 90 minutes, he said. . . .

Notice that the lead contains the major news theme—the deaths—and attribution. The next paragraph gives the names and identifications of the victims. The third paragraph describes the accident, and the fourth contains a good quotation.

This is the standard approach to the spot news story. Since we have a dramatic quote, why not use it high in the story:

```
    Three people were killed in a grinding collision
between a truck and an automobile last night on
Highway 10, 15 miles north of Morgantown.
    "The car was demolished," said Robert Jackson of
the State Highway Patrol. "There were parts all over
the road for 100 yards."
    Those fatally injured were. . . .
```

This version is an improvement because the direct quote captures the essence of the event—a horrible traffic accident.

Some Tips for Interviews

Clyde Haberman of *The New York Times* on interviewing:

Police are often very difficult to interview. Once you get going they're okay. But often they surround what they say with some bureaucratic jargon that sounds like it was made up in the police academy or something. Things like, 'As best as we can ascertain the perpetrator was a male Caucasian.' Nobody talks that way. And that makes it hard to penetrate that armor of bureaucratese which they surround themselves with. . . .

Most people are willing to grant interviews. I've never understood why, but they are. It's always very surprising. People who have no benefit to be gained by it either want to help you or are flattered that you'll be taking time out to interview them. . . . And that includes people under very adverse circumstances. People who have had terrible things happen to them, like having members of their family killed. . . .

If you have a lot of information that you want to get from a person, it really makes no sense to ask as the first question when did you stop beating your wife or when did you start. Better to get everything else you want, and then, when you're ready to get thrown out, ask that question. In questions that are clearly delicate, questions about the personal lives of people, their finances, and their feelings about things that are not necessarily your business, I find it sometimes helps to preface the question with the acknowledgement that this in truth is not a very nice question, but it has to be asked, so please forgive me. That at least takes some of the sting out of the question.

The patrol officer's description was in response to the reporter's question asking him to describe the scene. Good questions not only lead to valuable information; they also can evoke responses that provide the color and excitement that give life to a story.

The questions to ask for a spot news interview are based on the story type essentials. In this example, a fatal traffic accident, the reporter first asked the essential questions. When the officer mentioned the wreckage, the reporter asked for more details and elicited the descriptive quotation. In the next chapter we will examine the essentials for 14 types of stories.

Information from sources for spot news stories usually is summarized or paraphrased. But the reporter who listens attentively can sometimes find the quote that breathes life into the news story. A good direct quote is better than any paraphrase.

For a story about a refresher course offered by the School of Nursing at the University of North Carolina at Chapel Hill, a woman who had taken the course was interviewed. She had been a nurse, then married and had spent 20 years at home raising a family. She decided to return to nursing and took the nursing-update course. Here is a quote from the story in *The Coastline Times* of Manteo, N.C. It captures the story's theme:

"I would not have dared walk on a hospital floor without having gone back to school," she said. "There have been so many advances and so many changes."

Nothing earthshaking about the quote, but it does the job.

Theme Story Interviews

Increasingly, reporters are interviewing people for theme stories. These are stories that examine an idea or current development. For example: People have been talking about teen-agers adjusting to the pressures of modern life. How well are they adjusting, and what do they see themselves doing in 5, 10 or 20 years?

It would be possible to do a poll. But the more interesting story is one based on interviews with some of these youngsters. The AP did just that. Its reporters interviewed teen-agers around the world, and they found young people worried and tense. They also heard about the need for constant stimulation by easily bored youths.

"They are so bored and so in need of more stimulation," said a psychiatrist the AP interviewed. "It's like being a drug addict."

Generally, when an editor asks a reporter to interview someone, the editor has a personality sketch or profile in mind. Here, the individual is the center of the story. Before we turn to the profile, some points have to be made about the business of interviewing.

Interviewing Techniques

Whether the interview is for a spot news story or a profile, the key to a successful interview is knowing what you want to find out. Since the spot interview often is conducted by telephone with busy sources, the reporter has to get to the point quickly. For the profile, there is more time to report. Still, the reporter must not waste the subject's time. Also, the reporter must be knowledgeable. A firm grasp of the topic shows the subject that the reporter took time to look into the person and his or her fields and interests.

Here are some guidelines for interviews:

- **Have a good idea of what you want to learn from the source or subject.**
- **Get to the point quickly.**
- **Listen for the pertinent comments.**
- **Ask if there is anything important you did not ask about.**
- **Ask the source if he or she can be called back should you need further information.** (Some sources will not take calls at home after they leave the office. Ask for the name of another person who can be called.)

We are all curious, maybe even nosy. We want to know why the brightest young woman in the class suddenly quit school, how the elderly couple around the corner can afford a new Cadillac every year, why the couple down the street suddenly separated. We wonder what kind of person Sean Penn really is, how the 20-year-old outfielder for the Kansas City Royals spends his $1.5 million salary.

Most of our questions will never be answered, but some will—by a reporter writing a profile or personality feature. The fact that people have always been curious about the lives of others has made the profile the most frequently written feature story. Sooner or later, every reporter writes a profile.

Sometimes, the profile can be a small snapshot in a long piece. In a series on Rhode Island's jewelry manufacturing business—the state's largest industry—Bruce Butterfield of *The Providence Journal-Bulletin* tells us about Mary, a high school student who works part-time in a factory. Butterfield lets Mary talk:

. . . . Like, what I'm doing now. I stand up the entire time. I go in there for three hours and 45 minutes a day.

It's in a room and you have metal that's melted down. I think it's twelve hundred degrees.

There's people who've been working in there 25 years and they're still making less than $4 an hour.

And they deserve more 'cause they're such nice people that work in there. And they just can't do anything else. They either don't have a high school diploma or they just have a high school diploma and there aren't many jobs in our society today for these people. And they're over 40.

They deserve more.

These quotes tell us something about the factory and a lot about Mary. She works hard at an arduous job, and she is concerned about the people she works with. She is a decent young woman. Of her co-workers, she says they deserve more because they are such nice people. But she is realistic about her co-workers' lack of education. She knows there aren't many jobs for people without an education.

"They deserve more." Mary's words make the reader put down the newspaper to reflect a minute. Although we are told little about Mary, we feel we know her.

Our first requirement for the profile: It must capture the person.

That may seem to be emphasizing the obvious. Yet, many profiles are written about people in public life—politicians, entertainers, athletes, television personalities, business leaders—that never get beneath the public personality they have manufactured.

Caution: Never select an exciting or colorful quote only because it is provocative. The quote must be consistent with the personality being drawn.

"I found that most people not only hunger to talk, but also have a story to tell. They are often not heard, but they have something to say. They are desperate to escape the stereotypes into which the pollsters and the media and the politicians have packaged them."—Bill Moyers, television journalist.

Here are four guidelines for successful interviews for the profile:

1. **Prepare carefully.** Know the subject matter and the person who is to be interviewed.
2. From these preparations, **devise a theme** or two as the basis of questions.
3. **Establish a relationship** with the subject that induces him or her to talk.
4. **Listen carefully and watch attentively.** Be alert to what is said and how it is said. Look around at the room or office for clues to the subject's interests, tastes, personal life.

Preparing for the Interview

Careful preparations begin with the newspaper or broadcast station library. The library material provides background and suggests questions to ask at the interview. (Many reporters prepare lists of questions for their interviews.) The next step is a quick look at references. The new college president may be listed in *Who's Who in America*. Although *Who's Who* is brought up to date frequently, biographical material should always be checked with the subject.

If the new president is a specialist in a field, she might have written articles that are indexed in the *Reader's Guide to Periodical Literature*. Her comments about a subject in one of her articles could be the basis of the first question. Sources are flattered by a reporter's interest in them and their work.

When Mal Vincent of the *Virginian-Pilot* in Norfolk, Va., was preparing for an interview with actress Jacqueline Bisset, he went back to an interview he had with Bisset 10 years before.

Vincent had tried to interview Bisset on the set of a thriller in which she was co-starring with Alan Alda. In those days, Bisset had been cast in her movies as a sex object. She had done a nude scene in a surfing movie, "The Sweet Ride," and she had played a bedhopping jetsetter in "The Grass-hopper."

At that time, Vincent had a definite personality in mind, the kind of young actress that moviegoers glance at in minor films and forget. But Bisset had surprised him then.

She had taken over the interview. "The name is Bisset," she had said at the outset. "It rhymes with *kiss it.*"

When Vincent had tried to ask her about her relationship with an actor, Bisset bristled. Although she had been widely publicized as living with him, she refused to discuss the matter.

Vincent then tried women's liberation, a new phenomenon at that time.

"I have no intention of discussing women's rights with you," she had flared at him. "You wouldn't agree with me." She beckoned to her chauffeur and departed.

Bisset was a prickly subject for an interview, Vincent knew. In his preparations for his current interview he found that she was financing a movie in an attempt to convince critics she could act. As the co-producer, she had a stake in good publicity for the new film. Therefore, Vincent knew, she had to be patient with interviewers. He also remembered she had a mind of her own—as she proved in the new interview.

"I don't want to be a pinup," she told Vincent curtly. "I want to be something more than just an attractive woman. The public makes a mistake in labeling people that way."

Still bristling Bisset—but she stayed through the interview this time. Vincent knew how to approach her because of his preparations.

Devising a Theme

Vincent's preparations for his interview with Bisset point out the importance of figuring out some lines of questioning by having a tentative theme or idea for the story before the interview.

Sometimes, the theme is the news peg, the reason the individual is newsworthy. For example: A local merchant is recognized by the city's United Way organization for his charity work. A profile of the businessman will focus on the activities that earned him the award. Bisset's new film was the news peg. Often, though, the news peg is not the theme. In a profile of the new college president, the news peg was the appointment, but the theme of the profile was the appointee's ideas for reorganizing the college curriculum.

The news peg tells the reader: Here is a newsworthy person. The theme says: Here's something interesting or revealing that you ought to know about this person.

The depth interview is a confrontation between reporter-with-theme and subject-with-idea. By this, we mean that both interviewer and interviewee have points of their own they want to make. In Vincent's second interview with Bisset, she was trying to tell readers and moviegoers, through Vincent, that she is a serious actress, that they should forget her roles as a sex object, which had been stamped on the minds of the public by her scene in the movie "The Deep" in which she appeared in a wet, clinging, transparent T-shirt.

Vincent's new theme was the change from young starlet in grade B films to mature woman of 37 making serious movies. The interview went well because both themes, Bisset's and Vincent's, were parallel and not on a collision course.

Sometimes collisions are unavoidable—as were interviews with Gary Hart after *The Miami Herald* revealed details of his sex life that raised questions about his fitness for the presidency.

The reporter sent to interview a gubernatorial candidate for a profile knows that the candidate is a political novice, a person who has never sought public office. The reporter's theme is: What makes this man think he can handle the complexities of state government with no political experience whatsoever? The candidate's campaign theme is: A new broom sweeps clean.

The reporter is too experienced in politics to buy that cliché without lots of proof. So the reporter will be pressing and probing the candidate to prove that he has the ability to clean up the statehouse. Friction looms, unless the reporter can make the candidate relax and talk freely.

The reporter devises a theme from checking the background of the subject and from knowledge of the situation in which the subject is involved.

The theme or themes are launching pads for the reporter's questions. If nothing comes of the questions, the reporter works up new themes. A profile or personality sketch cannot be a shapeless biography. The story must have an interesting point to make about the subject.

Inducing the Subject to Talk

Reporters use many tactics to induce their subjects to talk freely and to act naturally. Gene Miller of *The Miami Herald* says he tries to make himself as agreeable as possible during interviews.

"I nod a lot," he says, to appear to be agreeing with what the subject is saying and to encourage him or her to keep talking. "No tape recorder and no notetaking if I suspect I'll turn off my man. The unpleasant questions always come last, often apologetically."

Miller's technique is the opposite of the confrontation tactics used by some television interviewers. After a while, a reporter learns the technique best suited to him or her. Of course, the nature of the interview will often determine the technique used. An interview with a manufacturer whose factory has been polluting the city's air and a nearby river cannot be much else but a confrontation.

The story is told of how Truman Capote, on an assignment from *The New Yorker* magazine, induced Marlon Brando to talk about his mother's alcoholism.

Capote flew to Japan where Brando was on the set of "Sayonara." They got together in the evening.

In his story for the magazine, Capote quoted Brando as saying of his mother: "I didn't care any more. She was there. In a room. Holding on to me. And I let her fall. Because I couldn't take it any more . . . breaking apart, like a piece of porcelain. I stepped right over her. I walked right out. I was indifferent. Since then, I've been indifferent."

Later, Brando was asked why he had been so open with Capote about such a personal matter.

"Well," said Brando, "the little bastard spent half the night telling me about all his problems. I figured the least I could do was to tell him a few of mine."

Interviewing Victims

All reporters sooner or later interview the victim of an accident, fire, crime, disaster, even of a disease. Such interviews require sensitivity. In some cases, the situations have a built-in sensational aspect, such as the interview with a victim of a sex crime, or the family of a person who has died in an unusual or gruesome way.

The first decision, sometimes made by an editor and not the reporter, is whether to talk to the victim. "You have to ask yourself why you are doing the story," says Helen Benedict, who has written extensively about victims. "You should have a reason that goes beyond merely doing what your editor told you to do. You should be able to find a moral or a conclusion in the story that justifies it."

Benedict says there are good reasons for covering even a sordid sex crime. "The public has to know these things happen; we have to know how devastating they are to victims, how commonly they happen, what little is done about them, the types of people who commit them."

Kathy Seligman of the *San Francisco Examiner* advises:

• Talk to the victims right after the event. Wait too long and the victim may become too grief-stricken to talk.

• Be human. Console them. Express your sympathy any way you can. You've got to take some responsibility for the emotions that are going on. I've cried a lot at these interviews.

• Sometimes it's not necessary to talk to the victim or grieving relatives. You can often get better material from an eyewitness police officer who not only saw what happened but might know something about possible motivations for the crime or other circumstances that surrounded the tragedy. Sometimes you have to realize that calling a relative or victim is a hideous invasion of privacy. So look for a way to avoid it.

In summary: Be human, gain the trust of those you interview, be polite, be gentle.

Grief. Although the reporters must work quickly when covering a breaking news story, they try to be sympathetic, even consoling to those involved in tragedies. *Joseph Noble, The Stuart (Fla.) News.*

Ralph Ellison, the author of *Invisible Man,* the classic about the lives of black Americans, interviewed many people during the 1930s for the Federal Writers Project. Those were the days of the Depression, and few had jobs. Writers had a particularly hard time, and the government hired some of them to obtain first-person accounts of Americans of all kinds.

Ellison's technique for making people talk was similar to Capote's.

"I would tell stories to get people going, and then I'd sit back and get it down as accurately as I could."

A gentle nudge is all some people need. But for many, the reporter has to ask questions, a lot of questions.

Asking Questions

The first questions asked in an interview for a profile may be throw-away questions designed to put the subject at ease if the source is not accustomed to being interviewed. The first meaningful questions will reflect the theme that the reporter has in mind for the story.

"What I ask gives me my story," says Jane Brazes, a reporter for the *Cincinnati Post.* "What I don't ask I won't find out."

Answers to questions suggest additional themes. "When you think you have found an answer, you'll have found another question," Brazes says. The key to interviewing, she says, is to "find questions and never stop asking them."

Questions should be simple and direct. Larry King, whose radio talk program, "The Larry King Show," is carried by more than 200 stations around the country, is a skilled interviewer. He says that "if it takes you more than three sentences to ask a question, it's a bad question." The point of the question is to induce the subject to talk. Complicated questions overwhelm the source.

King recalls an interview Sandy Koufax did with the winning pitcher of a baseball game. Koufax, one of the greatest pitchers in the history of the game, was an inexperienced interviewer. He asked:

"In the game tonight, I noticed that in the fourth inning you took a little off your fast ball—you still had it in reserve because you had a 4–0 lead. Then, in the seventh inning, you used your curve ball. And in the ninth inning you went back to your fast ball and you still had it left."

King recalled, "All that the pitcher could answer was, 'Right.' "

King says the best question for the interviewer is "Why?" Questions like, "Why," "How," "Give me an example of what you mean," induce people to talk.

"The wording of a question is very important. If you say to a president, 'Would you care to comment on X?,' he can always answer, 'No thanks,' or he can say anything he wants to and call it a comment. . . . To be effective, questions must be specific and, preferably, short. They should invite a direct answer."—Sam Donaldson, ABC White House correspondent.

Sometimes, silence can lead a person to talk. David M. McCullough, who interviews authors for the *Book-of-the-Month Club News,* says, "I found that a little silence often gets a better response than a pointed question."

Some experienced interviewers remain silent after a source or subject has made an unusual assertion. Except for a raised eyebrow, the reporter will not move. The interviewee has the feeling that the assertion isn't going down well, and usually he or she will feel obligated to fill the silence with an explanation that clarifies the matter or that moves closer to the truth.

Generally, the tactics used and the questions asked in an interview depend on the source and the kind of information sought. A source may prefer to say little or remain silent. But a public official cannot be silent about public business, and reminding the source of this may be necessary to pry information from him or her.

The subject is not the only person a reporter should interview for a profile. Friends, relatives, employees, employers, teachers—the list of those who can provide interesting information about the subject is endless. Sometimes, these sources may have a perception of the subject that gives the reporter a fresh insight, material for a theme the reporter had not thought about.

By asking good questions and by listening carefully, the reporter usually can find the one quote that best sums up the person or the event. When Wayne King was sent by *The New York Times* to cover a coal mine disaster in Colorado, King interviewed the brother of one of the 15 miners who had died. The man looked toward the western slope of the Colorado Rockies where the Dutch Creek mine is located and said, "That big mountain ate my brother."

King put the quote high in his story. It symbolized the life and death of the miner.

Gestures can speak. The narrowing of a person's eyes as he or she is talking can emphasize a statement as emphatically as boldface type in a written sentence. And if the source turns away as he or she says something, this may signal that the person is uncomfortable about what he or she is saying. This is the area of nonverbal communication, and good reporters are alert to the actions as well as the words of the source.

When the interview is conducted in the subject's home or office, notes are made of the furnishings, pictures on the wall, magazines on the coffee table or desk. These sometimes reveal a person's interests, tastes and concerns.

A well-known journalism professor covered his office walls with pictures of himself with famous people. Noticing this during an interview, a reporter concluded that the man's ego was monumental, that he needed to parade his fame to visitors. More than this, the reporter concluded that the professor— as famous as he was—had a sense of inferiority. The reporter filed away his observations for later use. Reporters often do this. Some save observations, anecdotes and stories they hear for a year or more, until the right moment.

"Experts appreciate that you've done your homework and can ask intelligent questions, but they don't want to hear you talk. Don't try to impress them. Let them impress you. Remind yourself to listen."—Bruce Selcraig, special contributor to *Sports Illustrated.*

Listening and Watching

"I listen. I ask questions and I listen. I'm constantly overwhelmed at the number of first-rate reporters who spend their time telling the source what they think."— Hugh Sidey, *Time.*

Howell Raines of *The New York Times* saved an anecdote a source gave him about a rising young politician. "I saved that quote because I knew that some day I would need it," Raines said. A year later he used it as the concluding anecdote in a profile of the young politician.

Taking Notes

Many reporters use tape recorders for profiles, but some prefer the note pad, finding it less obtrusive.

Raines told Roy Peter Clark, who interviewed him about interview techniques, "If I'm working with a notebook, I bring it out early, and I take a pen out early. I do a lot of business with them. People then lose interest in your taking notes.

"If someone really gets cooking on something and I feel taking notes will be obtrusive, I won't take notes. Then, when the person is finished on that point—I've got a good memory—I'll take out my pad and write down what he said.

"But I try to be open about taking notes for two reasons. One, it establishes your authority. No one is going to come back to you and question a quote that he's seen you write down as it came out of his mouth. And two, these are people that are used to seeing reporters."

On and Off the Record

The reporter's job is to write stories. Most experienced reporters are reluctant to go off the record, and they almost never bring up the possibility with a source.

"I never suggest putting anything off the record," Raines says. Most of those he interviews are experienced sources, usually public or political figures. They know that what they say is going to be used.

"I never put anything off the record retroactively," Raines says. "If they say to me, 'What I just told you is off the record,' they can say that all they want to, but I'm not bound by it. I'll usually tell them that, but I don't feel compelled to tell them that."

Raines does accept off-the-record information. When he does, he scrupulously follows certain ground rules: Off-the-record material may be used only on the grounds the source stipulates. Here are some ground rules sources may set:

Quotes are not to be attributed to the source but to "an official," or some such vague source.

The statement is to be paraphrased and used without attribution.

Material is to be used only if it is obtained from someone else and then not attributed to the original source.

For background use only—not for publication in any circumstance.

"**As soon** as another human being permits you to write about him, he is opening his life to you and you must be constantly aware that you have a responsibility . . . to that person. Even if that person encourages you to be careless about how you use your intimate knowledge of him, or if he is indiscreet . . . it is up to you to use your own judgment in deciding what to write."—Lillian Ross, *New Yorker* writer.

To Tape or Not to Tape

"I tape, therefore I am."—Studs Terkel, radio interviewer.

"Interviewers today . . . rely too much on the tape. They don't listen. They don't carry on a conversation. . . . They, especially the younger generation, are apt to treat words that come of the machine as gospel and feel they can't touch them when they transpose them to paper."—George Plimpton, author.

"The moment you introduce a mechanical device into the interview . . . you are creating an atmosphere in which the person isn't going to feel really relaxed, because they're watching themselves."—Truman Capote, author.

Master of the Interview

Her interviews have led to international conflicts, caused months of embarrassment to a U.S. secretary of state and are the envy of reporters. Oriana Fallaci has interviewed kings and presidents, tyrants and spies. For each, she had different tactics, but the underlying technique is the same: She prepares thoroughly—she reads books, articles, other interviews, everything she can put her hands on. She has a firm idea of her approach, the questions she will ask, and she is alert to the need to shift her approach and questions as the interview progresses.

In her preparations, she figures out the interviewee's vulnerabilities and moves in.

"Dr. Kissinger," she asked the then secretary of state, "how do you explain the incredible movie-star status you enjoy; how do you explain the fact that you're almost more famous and popular than a president?" Fallaci flattered Kissinger because she had decided that by appealing to his vanity and what she had concluded was his vast ego he would open up, as he did, to his everlasting regret.

Yes, he admitted that he had been a great success. Because, he said, "I've always acted alone. Americans like that immensely. Americans like the cowboy who leads the wagon train by riding ahead alone into the town, the village, with his horse and nothing else. Maybe even without a pistol, since he doesn't shoot. He acts, that's all, by being in the right place at the right time. In short, a Western."

This image of the urbane and learned Kissinger as a cowpoke-hero made headlines around the world.

Fallaci, who works for Italian publications, gets to the point quickly in her interviewing. She asked the Ayatollah Khomeini, "Are you a fanatic?" When he told her she need not wear the chador, the garment that women use to cover their bodies, since it was appropriate only for young women, Fallaci ripped it off. "This is what I do with your stupid medieval rag." That drove the Ayatollah out of the room, and Fallaci shouted after him, "Where do you go? Do you go to make pee-pee?" She then staged a sit-in, refusing to move until he continued the interview, which he promised to do. Fallaci had simply overwhelmed him.

Not many reporters can use these tactics. Fallaci is a personality, and she is allowed to inject it into her interviewing and her stories.

Fallaci's starting point is that those in power must be answerable for their actions. She confronts them with their deeds and demands explanations.

She once interrupted the Libyan dictator, Muammar Qaddafi, as he was extolling his infallability: "Do you believe in God?" she asked.

"Of course, why do you ask?"

"Because I thought you were God," she responded.

Fallaci tells many of these stories in her book, *Interview with History,* and in interviews with Lucinda Franks ("Behind the Fallaci Image," *Saturday Review,* Jan. 1981); David Sanford ("The Lady of the Tapes," *Esquire,* June 1975); Robert Scheer ("Oriana Fallaci," *Playboy,* Nov. 1981), and others.

Writing the Profile

We are now ready to look over the essential elements of the profile or personality sketch.

Profile Essentials

- Name and identification of the subject of the profile
- Theme of profile
- Reason for profile (This is called the **news peg.**)
- Background of person
- Incidents and anecdotes from the subject and from friends and associates of the subject
- Physical description
- Direct quotes from the subject and sources
- Observations of the subject at work, home or play: mannerisms, gestures
- Strong ending

Most profiles are feature stories, and as such they must move quickly. Story movement is accomplished through the use of quotes, description, anecdotes and incidents.

Observation. For profiles the reporter watches the subject at work and play. For a story about fishermen, the reporter followed a muskellunge fisherman as he trolled for the large pike in the chilly morning hours.

The news peg for Vincent's story about actress Bisset was her new film, "Rich and Famous":

Delayed lead for first two paragraphs

Hollywood—Don't call Jacqueline Bisset beautiful. Not if you want to get along with her.

"I don't want to be a pinup," she says curtly, the famous gray-green eyes flashing. "I want to be something more than just an attractive woman. The public makes a mistake in labeling people that way."

News peg at the beginning of the third paragraph

Currently, Bisset is chairman of the board—even if she is the only person on the board—of Jacquet Productions. As such, she is co producer of "Rich and Famous," the plush, expensively mounted new soap opera movie that stars her as a respected novelist who has affairs, sometimes casually, with younger men. The film, currently showing at the Lynnhaven and Circle 6 Theaters, gives

Theme at the end of the paragraph

Bisset what she calls "a chance to prove, once and for all, that I am capable of being a serious actress."

The last sentence of the third paragraph also serves as a transition or swing sentence. It takes the reader to a fuller explanation of the major theme of Vincent's piece—Bisset's attempts to prove she is more than a pinup. Notice that the news peg is not the theme of this profile. In his fourth paragraph, Vincent picks up the theme mentioned at the end of the third paragraph, Bisset's desire to be a serious actress:

> Although she thinks she has proved herself previously, she is aware that some critics haven't observed as much. "For some reason, critics like to take pot shots at me," she said. "In that way, my career has been similar to that of Candy Bergen, my co-star. We've both had our knocks from the critics."

For a profile or personality sketch, the news peg need not be momentous. It may be as simple as the one used in a profile about Sonny Greer, a famous jazz drummer playing in New York City.

The story by Timothy Weiner begins with a brief incident in Greer's life and shifts in the second paragraph to background. The third paragraph states the news peg or theme—that Sonny Greer at 83 is still playing the drums and enjoying life. It continues with quotes from Greer and the pianist who plays with him.

Greer is described at the drums. We can see his "cannonball serve," the drumsticks doing a "tapdance on the high-hat cymbal."

The ending reinforces the theme with a good quote from Duke Ellington, with whom Greer played for 32 years.

All the elements of the profile are here. Notice that Weiner does not try to tell Greer's life story. No profile can be any more than a brief glimpse into a person's life. Here is Weiner's profile:

The story should be written as soon after the interview as possible, say experienced writers. In fact, all writing should be done quickly following the event, while impressions and recollections are still fresh.

NEW YORK—When jazz great Sonny Greer was a kid, back in 1910, he had a single driving ambition: to be the world's greatest pool hustler.

Had Sonny not traded in his pool stick for drumsticks, he might never have teamed up with a young piano player named Duke Ellington in 1919. He couldn't have brought the Duke Ellington Orchestra to New York in the 1920s, where it gained fame as a worldwide paragon of jazz. And he might have spent most of his 83 years behind the eight-ball instead of behind his battery of drums and cymbals.

At an age when the rhythms of most people's lives have slowed to a crawl, Sonny Greer hasn't missed a beat.

Every Monday night at 8 o'clock, an impeccably dressed Greer sets up his drums onstage at the West End Cafe in New York City. Young admirers sit at the old gentleman's feet as he spins out stories of Harlem speakeasies and the halcyon days of jazz.

"My favorite place to play," Sonny said with a smile and a faraway gaze in his eyes, "was the old Kentucky Club. Fats Waller and me used to play duets there and sing risqué songs. We'd play all night and come walking out of the club in the morning, the sun shining and all of us walking down Broadway laughing, feeling no pain. Those were good days, baby, oh yeah."

For 32 years' worth of good days, Sonny Greer's percussion was the beating heart of the Duke Ellington Orchestra. For thousands of nights he sat like a king on his throne, elevated above the rest of the band at center stage, surrounded by chimes, gourds, tympani, vibraphone and kettle drums, a great brass gong shining behind him like a halo.

In the 1930s and '40s, the Duke Ellington Orchestra was the closest thing to royalty the jazz world has ever known. But the band's fame didn't dampen the members' creative fires.

"While we were onstage," Sonny said, "as the evening progressed, we would experiment. If Duke liked it, he would keep it in. If he didn't, well, it cost nothing—throw it out, forget it.

"The guys in the band were amazing. They always had ideas, a million ideas. They were very creative. They created."

Sonny Greer is now the sole survivor of the original orchestra. He is probably the oldest jazzman active today. What keeps him going?

"Look, the drums are my life," he said, lighting a cigarette and cradling an Old-Fashioned glass of whisky. "I get a great pleasure out of playing and making the people happy."

Brooks Kerr, the 27-year-old blind pianist and Ellington scholar who plays with Sonny, said, "One thing that Sonny has that so few people of any age have is that desire to play. I think he lives to work and works to live."

At showtime, Sonny leads Brooks to the piano and seats himself at his drums. The drums, encrusted with tiny mirrors, sparkle in the spotlights. Brooks hits the first chords of "Take the 'A' Train" and shouts, "Sonny Greer, ladies and gentlemen!"

Sonny swats his snare drum with a flick of his wrist, the sound of a cannonball serve. His drumsticks tapdance on the high-hat cymbal. His bass drum pulses. Everyone in the audience is keeping time, their fingertips and feet following the drummer's beat, their bodies swaying slowly in unison.

Sonny's drums are talking. His drumming is musical syntax, giving structure to flowing musical language. And something more: echoes of Harlem, a conjuring of the past.

He's telling his life's story on the drums, distilling all those years of remembered rhythms into fluid syncopation. Listening to Sonny Greer is a trip back in time to the golden age of jazz. To hear him solo on the drums is to briefly recapture a classic style.

Sonny Greer's drum solo won't go on forever. But, as Duke Ellington once wrote, "Sonny Greer is an endless story."

Weiner turned from features to investigative reporting and won a Pulitzer Prize for his work with *The Philadelphia Inquirer.*

Ending the Profile

A good idea in writing the profile is to use an incident or anecdote at the end of the piece that reinforces the major theme.

In his profile of Bruce A. Smathers, the son of a powerful political figure in Florida, Raines makes the point early in the story that Smathers' political future is dubious because he lacks the steely determination of his father, who, Raines writes, "never hestitated to backstab a friend for political advantage."

Raines writes of young Smathers high in his piece:

Bambi in the Jungle.
Bruce Smathers, the subject of a profile by Howell Raines, and his wife at the time Smathers was a candidate for secretary of state for Florida.
The St. Petersburg Times.

. . . .With his fawn eyes and unlined face, he has more in common with Bambi than with the rapacious roebucks normally encountered in the political forests of Tallahassee.

Yes, Bruce Smathers says, smiling, he knows about those jokes that he is indecisive, that he would starve to death in a cafeteria line trying to choose between the Salisbury steak and the Spanish mackerel.

That rap, as Smathers tells it, is the price he must pay for having a trained mind and introspective nature.

"I have almost a repulsion of the easy answer," he says, and one hears in the scholarly tone echoes of Yale, where he won honors in economics. . . .

The picture Raines draws is clear. Young Smathers is an intelligent, decent person, perhaps unfit for the raw political infighting of southern politics. For his ending, Raines drives home his theme. The last two paragraphs read:

Perhaps Smathers' political gifts are that great, but many who know politics as it is played at the top question whether this young man loves it enough or is hard enough. Most people who make it as high as governor or U.S. senator have something—a hunger, a fire in the gut, a toughness—that one can sense. It is not necessarily a good thing to have, but it is essential to winning and surviving in office.

This is not the picture of Bruce Smathers that emerges from a story once leaked from his office—an intimate of Smathers was quoted as saying, "Somebody offered him some money for a vote and Smathers got up and went out of the room and threw up."

This is the anecdote Raines says he had heard a year before and saved for the time when he would need it.

Much of the public's business is conducted in meetings. Important as they may be, few people attend them. It is the journalist's job to write clear, complete stories so the people know what their appointed and elected officials are doing. Reporters are entitled to attend these meetings.

There are, of course, all kinds of meetings in addition to those of official bodies. The parent-teacher association holds monthly meetings. College political clubs meet every so often. Church, civic and professional organizations meet regularly. Reporters are invited to attend these meetings.

The meetings of groups that are not financed with tax funds can be closed to the public and the press. A political club can call a closed meeting if it wishes. The board of the Kiwanis Club is not obligated to allow reporters to enter.

Once admitted to a meeting, a reporter can report anything that is said, unless the reporter is allowed to attend a meeting of a private organization that sets limits on coverage. When meetings are closed, the reporter can use anything he or she obtains by interviewing those who attended the meeting.

Meetings

Meetings usually have a purpose, and often the matter at hand is resolved by agreement or vote. Sometimes, there is only general discussion. Each type of meeting is handled differently.

The story of a meeting that results in an action emphasizes the action taken:

Two Types of Meetings

> A bill to change West Virginia's 10.5-cents-per-gallon liquor tax to a percentage of the wholesale price was soundly rejected by a joint House-Senate finance subcommittee yesterday by a vote of 9–2.

The meeting that does not result in any decisive action usually stresses the most significant part of the discussion:

> A student petition for more parking spaces on campus received sympathy but not much more from the trustees at yesterday's monthly meeting of the Board of Trustees.
>
> "We know it's a problem," said Alfred Breit, Board chairman. "But it is so complicated. . . ."

Meeting (Action Taken) Essentials

- Vote, decision, agreement
- Summary of the issue
- Reason(s) for action taken
- Arguments for and against issue
- Names of those for and against, if important issue
- Consequences of decision
- Discussion leading to vote or action
- Background of the issue
- Significant additional issues discussed
- Purpose, time and location of meeting
- Additional agenda items
- Makeup of audience and number attending
- Statements, comments from audience
- Significant departures from agenda
- Agenda for next meeting

Any one of these essentials can be the basis of the lead, and the story need not follow the order outlined in the list of essentials.

Here are some leads that are based on meetings in which a decision was reached. The leads stress the vote, agreement or decision.

Vote lead

The city commission voted unanimously last night to increase the property tax rate by $5 for each $1,000 in assessed value.

Agreement lead

The County Bar Association agreed yesterday to allow Grant County lawyers to advertise certain legal services.

Decision lead

Parents today warned the city school board they will fight the proposed closing of the Donald Vogt Elementary School "by every possible means."

Another type of lead can be used when an action is taken. Readers usually want to know the consequences of an action, or what it means. The reporter who wrote the agreement lead above asked lawyers what the action would mean and was told the advertised legal services, such as divorce actions and drawing up wills, would probably cost less. With this information in mind, the writer decided to rewrite the agreement lead:

Consequence lead

It may be cheaper to draw up a will or file for a divorce in Grant County soon.

When the Alabama Public Service Commission granted permission to a bus company to run bus lines from a suburb into Birmingham, the reporter had two choices, a decision lead or a consequence lead. Judge for yourself which is better:

Decision lead

The Public Service Commission yesterday granted B&B Transport and Limousine Co. permission to run bus service from Alabaster to Birmingham.

Consequence lead

People who don't want to fight commuter traffic between Shelby County and Birmingham may soon have a new way to get to work.

Let's examine a meeting story in which an action was taken:

Decision lead

The Oldham County Planning and Zoning Commission yesterday recommended a denial of new zoning for a 68-unit townhouse and apartment complex in La Grange.

Next step

The recommendation goes to the La Grange City Council, which will make the final decision.

Summary of the issue

Terry and Donna Powell want a change from low-density residential to high-density residential zoning on 7.28 acres near Russell Avenue and Madison Street in a section of La Grange known as The Courts.

Audience, time of meeting; transition to discussion

About 50 people attended a planning commission hearing on the request yesterday. Charles Brown, county zoning administrator, said the commission cited these factors in voting against the rezoning:

✔ The area contains suitable land already zoned for apartments.

✔ Two other apartment complexes have been approved in the past year in or near La Grange.

Reasons for vote

✔ The property is not close to such services as shopping areas.

✔ The proposal conflicts with La Grange's comprehensive land-use and zoning plan.

Argument against proposal

Opponents from the neighborhood argued that the development would compound traffic problems. They also expressed concern that dynamite to be used during construction might damage their homes.

Argument for proposal

James Williamson, attorney for the applicants, contended that the apartments are needed. Some of them would have been reserved for the elderly and handicapped. The developers proposed building five townhouses and six apartment buildings.

—Louisville Courier-Journal

Meeting (Discussion) Essentials

- Most important aspect of discussion: consensus (stated or implied); significant statement; strong disagreement
  - Arguments for and against issue(s)
  - Names and identifications of those for and against
  - Background of major issue(s)
  - Purpose, time and location of meeting
  - Additional matters discussed
  - Makeup of audience, number attending
  - Statements, comments from audience
  - Significant departures from agenda
  - Agenda for next meeting

When the meeting does not lead to a decision, vote or action, the writer's task is more difficult. In this situation, the writer may want to focus on what seems to be the consensus of the participants, a conflict, or on some important statement made during the meeting:

Consensus

City council members last night displayed impatience with local residents who protested a proposed increase in the property tax rate.

Conflict

City Councilman Garth Maguire last night told a delegation protesting a proposed property tax rate hike their opposition was "too strident, too narrow and too late."

Significant statement

Mayor Sam Georges last night told the city council he opposes the proposed property tax increase.

Sometimes, what emerges is a strong disagreement:

Strong disagreement

> City council members last night failed to take action on the property tax rate increase City Manager Kelly Simmons proposed last week.

Look at the beginning of this story about a meeting of candidates for the school board. What do you think of the lead?

Burying the Lead

```
    Mt. Pleasant's magnet schools, education for the
handicapped, and the quality of schooling were the
focus of debate Saturday as the six candidates for
at-large seats on the school board answered questions
posed by area black leaders.
    The election for the three posts will be held May
15.
    The candidates appeared before the Mt. Pleasant
Black Civic Organization at a meeting at the First
Methodist Church at 609 Claremont Ave. last night.
    Among the charges by the black leaders were
assertions that magnet schools and special-education
classes were being used to defeat integration, that
the quality of education is poor, and that the system
allows inferior teachers to remain in the classroom.
    Although they differed in their responses, in
general the board members, Beatrice A. Florentine,
Kyle Smith and Linda Stern, defended the school
system. . . .
```

The story has an agenda lead. That is, it tells the reader the subjects that were discussed. But it does not state what was said about these items, the conclusions reached, the consensus. The reporter did not write a specific lead.

We could make a lead out of the fourth paragraph:

```
    Black leaders told school board candidates last
night that local schools are failing to educate and
that special classes and magnet schools work against
school integration.
```

Or we could make the fifth paragraph the subject of a lead:

```
    School Board members defended the school system
last night against charges by community black leaders
that the board is not doing its job.
```

You may have even better leads than these two. Notice that the point of the rewritten leads is to pull the reader right into the meeting where there were charges and defending statements. Try your hand at writing four or five paragraphs and see whether you can put life into this important story.

Panel Discussions and Symposia

A panel or symposium is actually a meeting, but usually there is no intention to reach a decision. A consensus may emerge, however. If so, that should be the basis of the lead.

Most of the time panelists insist on going their own way, each person giving his or her opinions or findings. This puts the writer in a bind. Three, four or five people each merrily piping his or her own tune does not make for a smoothly written story.

Sometimes, the statements of one speaker are more newsworthy than those of the other speakers, and this becomes the lead, as in the story on the opposite page by Ray Cohn from *The Lexington Herald.*

No other speaker but Welch is quoted until two-thirds down the story. The third speaker isn't even mentioned until the end of the story. The writer may have decided to give Welch top billing because of his experience as an FBI agent and his authoritative position as the state's top official in the justice system.

When it is possible, an area of agreement should be used as the basis of the lead. It may be that the speakers' only agreement is to disagree. If so, the subject of their disagreement can be the basis of the lead.

It may not be easy to find a common theme, but the reporter should try. Editors know that singling out a single speaker for the lead is the easiest way to write a lead. They value the reporter who has the ability to put the statements and ideas of different speakers together, to pattern his or her observations. The ability to extract a meaningful theme from separate ideas is a competence that every writer tries to cultivate.

Here is the beginning of a story for which the writer found a common theme:

High schools are not attracting the best teachers, panelists agreed last night in a discussion on the future of the public schools.

The panelists were not of one mind about most of the issues facing public education. But they did agree that a series of factors has made high school teaching unattractive.

The panel, which met in the Community College Auditorium, was sponsored by the college's department of education.

High school teaching has suffered from the following, the panelists said:

• Women are no longer forced to go into teaching because of limited opportunities in other fields.

"Whole areas of professional life and business have opened to women," said Professor Esther Josephs, associate professor of education at the College.

• The public has "little or no confidence in high schools, and morale is at the lowest point in years," said Raymond Peterson, principal of Lima High School. "No one wants to go into a profession in which the public lacks confidence."

• Salaries are lower for high school teachers on the average than for any other field but social work, said Harry Metzger, an official of the state office of the National Education Association. . . .

Justice Secretary Says System Losing War Against White Collar Criminals

By Ray Cohn
Of The Herald Staff

White collar crime costs the country about $200 billion a year and the criminal justice system is losing the war against it, state Justice Secretary Neil J. Welch told a University of Kentucky symposium on crime and punishment last night.

Welch, a top FBI official before he came to Kentucky last year, said there has been an overwhelming increase in this type of crime.

"Profit is the motive," he said.

To illustrate the magnitude of the problem, Welch said that tax officials estimate $16 billion a year in taxes should be collected on interest income, but that only $2 billion is actually collected.

"We have won some battles," Welch said, "but we are losing the war."

He said that a conference was held about two years ago at University of California — Los Angeles on how to fight organized crime.

"You would think in 1980 we would have a strategy against organized crime, but we don't," he said.

Welch is credited as one of the masterminds of the FBI's Abscam investigation. In that probe, FBI agents posed as representatives of Arab sheiks and accepted bribes from congressmen and other public officials. The scandal resulted in the conviction of several congressman and Sen. Harrison Williams of New Jersey.

Neil J. Welch

Since becoming head of the state Justice Department in 1980, Welch has placed a heavy emphasis on combating white collar crime — and has come under fire for it.

At last night's forum he said "new leadership" is need to combat crime effectively.

He said in the past the emphasis in the United States has been "too oriented toward the legal system." The criminal justice system must now draw "on the finest business brains" to help fight white collar crime, he said, and greater use must be made of modern technology.

But Welch's approach was opposed by another member of the symposium panel, Dr. Ernest Yanarella, UK associate professor of political science. He said law enforcement officials must avoid the "nice lure" of technology as instruments of social control.

There was sharp **disagreement** among some panelists on a proposal made by a task force for U.S. Attorney General William French Smith to modify the exclusionary rule. Under that rule, evidence that police obtain illegally may not be admitted in court.

The national panel wants to permit the intoduction of such evidence if the police officer can show he made good faith effort to obtain it legally.

Yanarella said the position of civil libertarians is "that one has to make a difficult choice." But he insisted it is better to permit some guilty people to go free than "to permit great excesses."

Welch, on the other hand, said it doesn't make sense to exclude evidence because the police "may make a slight error."

Dr. Robert Granacher, a Lexington forensic psychiatrist, illustrated how difficult the issue can be.

He said "the killings in Atlanta stopped when that man was incarcerated." Yet, Granacher said, the suspect, Wayne Williams, will probably have to be released if a court rules that the fiber evidence the police seized from his home was obtained illegally

Sometimes what is said is secondary to an incident in the audience, or even what is not said, as when speakers tiptoe around a controversial issue.

In the following story by Karen Ellsworth of *The Providence Journal-Bulletin,* who did and did not show up for a political meeting became the basis of the lead. Had any of the candidates said anything of significance, that would have been the lead. But Ellsworth concluded that most of what was said was not new. Instead, she decided on what her eyes, and not her ears, told her. Her theme was apathy. Notice how her lead **shows** the reader there was public apathy.

PROVIDENCE—About half of the candidates for state general office and Congress attended a "Meet the Candidates" night at Rhode Island College last night, and they almost outnumbered the audience.

Every Republican candidate attended except James G. Reynolds, the Senate candidate. According to Doris McGarry, president of the Rhode Island League of Women Voters, his press secretary said he was ill. The league sponsored the event.

The only Democrats who attended were Robert Burns, the incumbent secretary of state, Dennis Roberts, candidate for attorney general, and Sen. Claiborne Pell. Neither independent candidate showed up.

About 30 persons, many of them students, attended the 2½-hour session in the lounge of Browne Hall. Mrs. McGarry said she didn't know whether to blame the low turnout on "illness or general apathy."

The format consisted of two-minute statements and questions from the audience, with the candidates each giving an answer and sometimes rebutting another's answer.

Only two candidates got to meet their incumbent opponents face-to-face. The livelier of those exchanges occurred between Burns and his opponent, Michael Murray, a Warwick city councilman. The Republican and Democratic candidates for attorney general, William A. Dimitri and Roberts, had just come from a live television debate on Channel 36 and they appeared a bit talked-out.

Reynolds' absence was particularly noted because of his charge last week that Pell had refused to face him head-on. At that time, Pell said he planned only two such confrontations, and one of them was last night's.

Burns said the first thing he will do when he is re-elected is to work to reform recently passed election laws.

The absentee and shut-in ballot law, which allows voters to have their ballots sent to the headquarters of a candidate who delivers it to their homes, is "wrong, wrong, wrong," Burns said.

The news conference has two scenes. Scene 1, the curtain-raiser, consists of the statement by the person calling the conference. The press politely hears out the message. Then Scene 2 begins, the questioning of the subject. News can be made during both scenes.

The potential candidate for his party's nomination for governor announces he is pulling out of the race:

State Sen. Jack Felton said today he is withdrawing from the race for the Republican nomination for governor.

He pulled himself out of the contest at a press conference at the Simcoe Hotel.

"My plans now are to seek re-election to the legislature," he said. Felton's withdrawal clears the way for Ben Appleman, the only remaining announced candidate for the GOP nomination. . . .

Most often, the news comes out of the question-and-answer period. At a presidential press conference, Ronald Reagan discussed general issues in an opening statement. The big news was made in answer to a reporter who asked how the United States could be sure a super-secret airplane Reagan wanted to sell to Saudi Arabia might not fall into the hands of unfriendly countries if the Saudi government were toppled.

Reagan replied there was "no way" the United States would stand by and let that government be overthrown.

The president's remark seemed casual, almost an aside, and the reporters went on to other issues. As the importance of his remark struck one reporter, he asked another question, and the president's reply was, again, brief.

Announcement. People in public life—and those who seek publicity—call news conferences to achieve maximum exposure to newspaper readers and on television and radio. When the source and the announcement are newsworthy the press does turn out, as it did when Gary Hart announced his withdrawal and then his re-entry in the Democratic presidential primary. *Photo by Ken Papaleo of the Rocky Mountain News, Denver, Colo. Used with permission.*

All told, Reagan's comments on this issue occupied about a twentieth of the time of the news conference. Yet because of its importance—the United States implicitly warning all nations not to step into Saudi Arabia—it became the lead of the story. Because the reporters had only seven sentences from the president to back up their lead, they called a White House spokesman for comments and checked with a variety of sources. They also included considerable background.

The Boston Globe led its account this way:

President Ronald Reagan said yesterday that the United States would defend Saudi Arabia against any threat to take over the kingdom and cut off the flow of oil to the West.

Reagan's remark, which his aides acknowledged afterward constituted a major foreign policy pronouncement, was delivered as an aside to a question. . . .

News Conference Essentials

- Major point of speaker
- Name and identification of speaker
- Purpose, time, location and length of conference
- Background of major point
- Major point in statement; major points in question-and-answer period
- Consequences of announcement

Speeches

The speech story is almost always based on the answer to the question: Who said what?

Who: The speaker

What: The major theme of the speech

The key to writing speech stories is to isolate the major point the speaker is trying to make and then to select direct quotes that amplify this point. The major point goes into the lead, in the writer's own words. The quotes go into the body of the story.

Since speeches are often long and may include several themes, the reporter has to be choosy. A speech story should not include more than three or four of the speaker's points. There are exceptions—a major policy speech will be covered in detail—but the usual, everyday talk can be covered in a few hundred words.

Sometimes, something that **happened** provides the main element for the story. During a political campaign in Wisconsin, the Republican candidate for senator was reciting the failings of his opponent and closed with, "I challenge him to deny these charges."

Suddenly, from the back, his opponent rose and shouted, "I deny every one of those charges," and he made his way to the stage. The **happening** obviously became the lead, and the confrontation between the two made up most of the story.

Speeches and speakers come in as many varieties as the offerings of a boardwalk ice cream parlor. There is the Kiwanis Club luncheon talk given by a member of the local chapter of the Audubon Society who discusses the need to save saltwater marshlands, and the recollections of a dentist before the county dental society about the early days of dentistry when Painless Parker cruised city streets in a horse-drawn wagon and extracted molars for 50 cents each.

Whatever the topic, whoever the speaker, the story must include certain essentials.

Gates urges homeowners association to support death penalty, '8,500 plan'

By Nicole Szulc
Herald Examiner staff writer

Los Angeles Police Chief Daryl Gates told some 300 Los Feliz residents last night they could contribute to stemming crime by supporting the death penalty.

At a monthly meeting of the Loz Feliz Improvement Association, which claims to be the largest and oldest home improvement association in Los Angeles County, Gates reminded the audience that two seats on the California Supreme Court recently had been vacated by two justices who favored capital punishment.

"You can help put a stop to crime by letting Governor Brown know how you want those Supreme Court vacancies filled," Gates said.

The police chief had been invited to speak to residents concerned about skyrocketing crime in their neighborhoods who are anxious to organize neighborhood watches or private security patrols. He outlined for them a three-fold plan to put a stop to violence.

Gates said the first point was to change the criminal sentencing structure, so "we can return to a system where if you commit a crime, you get punished."

Secondly, Gates pointed to the so-called "8,500 tax plan," which would provide funds to increase the city's police force to that number.

Next, Gates said, citizens have to learn to "become their brother's keepers," so neighbors know each other and can be "each other's eyes and ears" in trying to cut down neighborhood crime.

Neighborhood watches and security patrols are positive steps in the direction of crime prevention, Gates said, and he pledged the full support of the LAPD in bringing such organizations about.

Finally, Gates told the audience they must look into themselves in order to be able to defend themselves.

"If we hadn't won World War II, we probably wouldn't be here tonight discussing this," he said. "But now the greatest danger we face is from within."

In this speech story by Nicole Szulc of the *Los Angeles Herald Examiner,* Szulc selected the death penalty as the major point of the speech and placed it in the lead. The second paragraph gives the name of the organization sponsoring the meeting. The third paragraph has a direct quote that amplifies the speaker's point, and the fourth paragraph contains background. Notice that the other points made by the police chief are placed near the end of the story.

Speech Essentials

- Name, identification of speaker
- Major point of speech
- Quotes to support main point
- Purpose, time and place of speech
- Nature of audience; prominent people in audience
- Audience reaction
- Background of major point
- Speaker's dress, mannerisms, if important
- Speaker's comments before and after speech, if any
- Additional points made in speech
- Material from question-and-answer period, if any

Writing the Lead

As we've said, the lead of the speech story generally answers the question: Who said what? It does so in S-V-O fashion, the speaker's name or identifying label first and what he or she said next.

Some editors prefer the lead reversed: What was said by whom.

> Rural Americans are not going to let high-voltage lines crisscross their homes, farms and ranches, two Carleton College faculty members said today.

The theory behind this structure is that often what was said is more important than who said it. For broadcast news writing, and increasingly for newspaper usage, the S-V-O structure is preferred.

The identification of the speaker is essential. This gives him or her the credentials to merit our attention. The identifying label usually establishes the speaker's credentials at once in the lead. We use a label when the name of the speaker will mean little to readers or listeners. With widely known people, the name alone usually establishes the person's authority to speak:

Identifying label

The owner of a chain of fast-food restaurants in the Midwest told a convention of food handlers here today that in 10 years a home-cooked meal will be unusual.

Identifying label

A University of Wisconsin historian said today that mass culture is a means through which men and women are manipulated.

Widely known name

Gov. William Blair said today his administration plans to increase aid to the state's colleges and universities that have suffered from federal cutbacks.

In addition to identifying the speaker and stressing the speaker's major point, two other essentials may be placed in the lead:

- Where the talk is given—location
- To whom the speech is given—audience

It is not always possible to jam location and audience into the lead and still make it crisp:

```
    The head of a local architectural firm told members
of the Engineers and Architects Club at their monthly
meeting in the Miller Hotel last night that the
proposed city hall may prove too costly to build.
```

To shorten such leads, drop the location and audience to the second or third paragraph:

```
    The head of a local architectural firm said last
night that the proposed city hall may prove too
costly to build.
    Preston Wilcox told the Engineers and Architects
Club that the cost is estimated at $22 million. He
spoke at the Miller Hotel.
```

The Audience

In our list of essentials, the word *audience* refers to those directly addressed. In Wilcox's talk, the audience is a local club. Audience can also mean the people the speaker hopes to reach through the press. Many speakers have the general public in mind when they speak. Wilcox obviously was intent on warning the public about the costs of constructing a new city hall.

The writer handled this aspect of Wilcox's talk by including background:

```
    Wilcox's talk comes in the midst of a controversy
over whether to go ahead with construction. The
increased cost of labor and supplies has sent costs
soaring.
    Taxpayer organizations oppose the construction
that was authorized by the city council in 1987. But
local unions and the administration of Mayor Fred
Partell favor going ahead.
```

During George Bush's presidential campaign, reporters pointed out that Bush's handlers made sure he spoke before friendly audiences who would be unlikely to heckle or respond negatively to his speeches.

Sometimes, as we have seen, the audience may provide the lead element. An unusually small audience for a presidential candidate's major speech can merit the lead, unless the candidate says something extraordinary. An unexpectedly large audience can be the basis of the lead as well, as can the use of a small hall to make the audience seem to be a crowd.

Heckling or boredom at political speeches may be lead material. Significant questions from members of the audience may reveal more newsworthy information than the speech itself.

Constructing the Story

As in all the types of stories in this chapter, the speech story is built on direct quotes, the words of the speaker. Careful: The sign of the beginner is using a direct quote in the lead. A great orator is able to reach out and grab the audience and shake it with ringing sentences worthy of a lead. Such a speaker comes along once in a decade. Name one.

Most of the time, the writer begins with a paraphrase of the speaker's major point. This is followed closely by a direct quote that best makes the point.

The speech story is a blend of direct and indirect quotes, of the speaker's exact language and the writer's paraphrasings.

Caution Sometimes a writer is tempted to take a clever or flashy quote and put it high in the story to attract the readers' interest. This can create problems. Often, the quote is only the speaker's way of getting attention and may not relate to the news point. Placed high in the story, the quote may mislead the reader. The same caution should be taken with the anecdotes speakers sometimes use to spice their talks. Unless they lead directly to the news point, they should not be used high in the story.

Finding the proper material for the lead can be difficult. Some speakers dart from one subject to another, like a trout moving upstream, now here, now there.

A tipoff to the theme can be the title of the talk, if there is one. Watching the speaker's demeanor can indicate the emphasis of the speech. When the words come slowly and deliberately, the speaker is trying to stress his or her point. When the arms wave or a finger points, listen closely or follow the prepared text, pencil ready to underline.

When in doubt about the speaker's theme, ask the speaker. Post-speech interviews can sometimes turn up better leads than the speech itself.

Occasionally, the writer will find the lead in a point the speaker did *not* emphasize. The manager of a local television station may be speaking to a women's club about the merits of programming for the mass audience. In passing, he may say that his station is cutting back on public affairs programming because "nobody watches those shows anyway."

The writer knows that the change in local programming is of greater interest than a generalized defense of situation comedies and quiz shows. To gather more details, the reporter may stop the speaker on his way out or call him at the station.

When a speaker does not explain a point adequately or the reporter needs additional information, the speaker should be interviewed or telephoned after the presentation. The story should state how the information was obtained. If the follow-up does not work out, the story should state that the point was not clarified. The writer should not hesitate to do this. Otherwise, the reader will presume the writer neglected to explain something important.

An AP reporter covering a speech at an Asian population conference quoted a member of the Islamic Consultative Assembly as saying that the regime in Iran had eliminated 114,000 prostitutes "who were the products of the disgraceful, satanic domination of America and lived at the highest level of wretchedness." To this, the AP reporter added his own comment, "She did not say how this was done."

The texts of important speeches are often distributed to the press ahead of their delivery. Examination of the prepared text gives reporters time to study the material and to write without pressure. It also allows newspapers and broadcast stations to use the material before the talk is given—unless it is embargoed (restricted for use) until after delivery.

When prepared texts are used before delivery, the writer places in the lead or high in the story the phrase "In a speech prepared for delivery. . . ."

Reporters always cover important speeches with eyes on the text and ears on the speaker. News can be made by last-minute insertions to or deletions from the prepared speech.

Fallaci, Oriana. *Interview with History*. New York: Liveright, 1976.

———. *The Egotists*. Chicago: Henry Regnery Co., 1968.

Garrett, Annette. *Interviewing: Its Principles and Methods*. New York: Family Association of America, 1982.

Mitford, Jessica. *Poison Penmanship*. New York: Vintage Books, 1980.

Terkel, Studs. *Working: People Talk About What They Do All Day and What They Think While They Do It*. New York: Pantheon, 1972.

10

From the Office and On the Beat

Beat reporters move quickly to cover breaking news such as accidents and fires, and they develop feature stories from their beats when they have time.

Looking Ahead

The essential elements of many types of stories are described in this chapter.

Accident stories focus on the names of the dead and injured.

Fire stories center on two themes: human casualties and physical damage.

Crime stories usually are written from police reports. Additional reporting gives these stories human interest. Coverage of the **courthouse** beat emphasizes large damage suits and trials for major crimes.

Obituaries give the name, age, address, major accomplishments and survivors of the deceased.

Sports stories are most effective when the writer knows the sport and the players and coaches and when the writer makes the action, rather than supercharged language, propel the story. Game stories require the names of the teams, score, decisive play(s), strategy of players and coaches and the effect on standings.

Briefs or **shorts** include **precedes,** or **advances, personals** and other short items that run no more than five or six sentences. **Folos** are stories that follow up on a theme taken from another story. **Sidebars** emphasize an aspect of the main story printed nearby. **Roundups** combine two or more stories into one by finding a theme common to the stories and using that theme in the lead.

Weather forecasts and stories about unusual or extreme weather include data from official sources and are enhanced by human interest.

Many editors assign their new reporters to the police beat as a way of introducing them to the community. Although at first glance this seems to be the way to see the city from the underside, the beat does give the reporter a quick overview of the city since accidents, fire and crime strike widely and at all levels of society.

Let's look at the traffic accident story first. The accident story is a staple of journalism. More than a million people are killed or injured every year in traffic accidents, and all but the largest newspapers carry stories of these accidents. Only the most minor—the so-called fender benders—are ignored or written in summary form in a column of briefs.

In all accident stories, the names of the dead and injured must be reported. The victims are identified by age, address and occupation. The extent of the injuries and the condition of the injured are also given.

Accidents

Accident Essentials

- Names and identification of dead and injured
- Time and location of accident
- Types of vehicles involved
- Cause (Quote official sources.)
- Source of information
- Names and identification of drivers and of others in vehicles if relevant
- Where dead and injured were taken
- Extent of injuries
- Condition of injured
- Funeral arrangements, if available
- Arrests or citations by officers

If the accident merits a longer story because of its severity, add the following:

- Damage to vehicles
- Speed, origin and destination of vehicles
- Unusual weather or highway conditions
- Accounts of eyewitnesses and investigating officers

Caution Do not try to fix blame, to give the cause of an accident, or to give information about excessive speed or drinking by a driver unless the information comes from an official source.

For minor accidents, only the first six essentials are included, as in this story about a car striking a pedestrian:

James Oates, 46, of 447 Dartmouth Ave. suffered two broken legs Thursday evening when struck by a car while crossing Bailey Avenue near LaSalle Avenue, police said.

He is reported in serious condition in the Erie County Medical Center.

Police reported that John Rinzel, 24, of 211 Doat St., driver, said the man stepped into the path of his vehicle from a parked car. He was not charged.

—*Buffalo Evening News*

For fatal accidents, background about the victim is given, as is information about survivors and funeral arrangements:

A 34-year-old Bullitt County man, Jackie L. Boone, was killed Monday in a car-motorcycle accident near Lebanon Junction.

According to state police at the Elizabethtown post, Boone, of Route 1A, Lebanon Junction, was killed when the motorcycle he was riding was struck from the rear by an auto about three miles north of Lebanon Junction on KY 61.

Deputy Coroner J. B. Close said Boone died at the scene of a broken neck.

The driver of the auto, Marla Seay of New Albany, was not injured. No charges were filed.

Boone, formerly of Louisville, was a maintenance machinist for Naval Ordnance Station and a Navy veteran.

Survivors include his wife, the former Janice Goeing; a son, Jackie L. Boone; his parents, Mr. and Mrs. Witt Boone; four sisters, Miss Juanita Boone, Mrs. Norbert Carey, Mrs. Colleen Gipson and Mrs. Beth Lehner; and a brother, Robert Boone.

The funeral will be at 10 a.m. Friday at O.D. White & Sons Funeral Home, 2727 S. Third St., with burial in Resthaven Memorial Park.

Visitation will be at the funeral home after noon tomorrow.

—*Louisville Times*

Despite the frequency of vehicular accidents, the news writer can often find an interesting fact to begin the story with instead of leading with the name and identification of the dead and injured and the location. Look at how a *Miami Herald* writer started a fatal accident story:

James D. Robinson of Opa-locka was driving in the proper lane when he died.

The car that killed him and seriously injured his wife and two small children was not.

In the next few paragraphs the writer gave full identification of those involved in the fatal collision, the location, where the injured were taken, and the extent of their injuries. The story ended with this paragraph:

> Charges are pending, Broward Sheriff's Deputy Hal Samuels said. Altieri's blood was tested to determine if he had been drinking while driving, Samuels said.

Death or serious injury are not always necessary for an accident story to make the news. Massive traffic tie-ups, with the usual dented fenders and broken brake lights, also interest readers. So do the accident stories that have a humorous twist, as this AP story does:

> MUSKOGEE, Okla. (AP)—A woman who stopped on a slick bridge here to scrape off her windshield drove off without a scratch, leaving 36 dented cars behind her.

Fires

Stories about fires usually are given good play. Fire stories interest readers, possibly because of our fear of fires. Whatever the reason, the beginner will likely find himself or herself handling a fire story within days, whether it is a farmhouse fire that causes $20,000 in damage or an apartment house fire that kills eight people:

> HARRISBURG—A farmhouse six miles northeast of Harrisburg was badly damaged Sunday evening by a fire that began when the occupants of the dwelling were away.
>
> Harrisburg Fire Chief Sonny Hanf said the two-story frame house, at 24661 Rowland Rd., sustained a loss of about $20,000. The building is owned by George Turney of Dallas and rented by Jim and Patsy Rosenberg, Hanf said.
>
> According to Hanf, Jim Rosenberg returned to the house about 7 p.m. Sunday and found a bedroom in flames. Firefighters from Harrisburg and Halsey responded to the alarm.
>
> Hanf said fire damage was confined to the bedroom area, although the rest of the house sustained smoke and water damage.
>
> —*Eugene* (Ore.) *Register-Guard*

PATERSON, N.J. (AP)— Eight people died in a predawn tenement fire and 11 were missing yesterday after a man who had been spurned by a female resident allegedly set the building ablaze with a can of gasoline, authorities said.

Two dozen others were injured, "many of them jumping from windows," said police Sgt. Edward Hanna.

"The firemen were inside the building, crawling around on their hands and knees, feeling for people," he said. "Twenty minutes after I got there, they carried out three kids while the fire was really going. I never saw anything like it in my life."

Paterson Fire Chief Harold J. Kane said the bodies were found after firefighters gained control of the blaze that left more than 100 people homeless.

"We just hope it ends here. But we're waiting on a crane to help us go through what's left of the building,". . . .

Burned Out. When someone is injured or killed, or the damages are large in a fire, this information goes into the lead. Home fire stories include the consequences to the residents— homeless, clothing gone, perhaps a valuable stamp collection or library gone up in smoke. When the consequence has a strong human-interest aspect, that element should be considered for the lead in place of the routine death, injury, damage aspect.
Susan Plageman, The Berkshire Eagle.

Fire Essentials

- Deaths, injuries
- Full identification of victims
- Location
- Type of structure
- Official cause
- Investigation of cause
- Source of information
- How victims were injured or killed
- When and where fire started, and how and when it was brought under control
- Rescue attempts
- Where injured, dead taken
- Extent of injuries
- Damage to structure, cost, insurance coverage
- Number of units and firefighters; amount of water used
- Name(s) of fire company(ies) responding
- Quotes of witnesses, firefighters, residents
- Human interest details
- Time of first alarm; who called fire department

Go back to the fire story datelined HARRISBURG that began this section. One of the essentials is missing—the cause of the fire. If the cause of the fire was unknown at the time the story was written, say so.

Fires are frequent in large cities, especially in winter, but they are not covered unless there is considerable damage, loss of life, traffic congestion, or a large amount of equipment is called out. In small and medium-sized cities, fires are usually covered even when there is no loss of life and damage is minor.

In rural communities, fire is a great enemy, and coverage is thorough. The fire companies that answer the call are identified and the chief's quotes usually are used. A farm fire that destroyed a feed barn, a tractor, a hay baler and 3,000 bales of hay received front page play in the *Georgetown News,* a weekly newspaper in Kentucky. The fire was caused by lightning. Ed Moore, chief of the Scott County Fire Department, was quoted in the story as saying:

"We just call this kind of thing an act of God. I've seen farms with lightning rods go up in smoke. Once the lightning flash causes a dust explosion in the hay, there's just nothing you can do to save the barn."

Quotations add human interest to the stories. In the following story, a quote is used in the second paragraph and the names of the cities from which firefighters were dispatched is also included.

Brush fire threatens home

WAVES—A brush fire driven by northeast winds scorched 12 acres near this Hatteras Island village Wednesday night, threatening several homes, before it was brought under control.

"Everyone on the island was involved," said Bert Austin, Dare County's chief deputy sheriff.

Firemen from Waves, Rodanthe, Salvo, Avon, and Buxton answered the alarm about 7 p.m. National Park Service, Coast Guard, and N.C. Division of Forest Resources personnel assisted.

Austin said the flames reached within 50 feet of one home before the dry swamp grass was doused by firemen.

The fire started when an electric wire fell in the grass. The wire apparently had been damaged by the accumulation of salt, a common problem for utility companies in Dare County.

—*The Virginian-Pilot*
(Norfolk, Va.)

The Lead

When there are several deaths or many injuries the lead usually will focus on this essential. When property is the only loss that usually is the basis of the lead. Fires sometimes threaten homes in areas plagued by forest fires and brushfires, and this often provides the lead material, as in the story from Waves.

If possible, try to work into the lead human interest material—a narrow escape, heroism, pathos, coincidence. Let's see how a reporter does this.

Death of a Smoker

Dennis Love of *The Anniston* (Ala.) *Star* describes how he heard about an unusual fire in a rural area and tells how he gathered the information for his story.

"While on weekend duty one Saturday night, I got a tip while calling funeral homes throughout our seven-county circulation area. An employee said he was handling funeral arrangements for a 76-year-old man who died in a school bus fire the night before.

"An accidental death alone merits a brief story, but this man's age and obvious questions about why he was in the bus required further checking. I called the coroner, the sheriff's department and the fire department—all of which were represented on the scene—and pieced together the basic information.

"The old man, who lived with his brother in a rural part of the county, often slept in an old school bus he had converted into a camping vehicle. On this night he had apparently fallen asleep while smoking and was unable to escape the flames that rapidly engulfed the old vehicle. The coroner said there was no evidence of foul play."

Then Love began to try to reach relatives of the dead man to piece together the details. The coroner supplied the name of one relative who gave Love the telephone number of the family home, which he had not been able to find in the directory. He reached the victim's brother. This was a vital call.

"He gave me a first-hand account of what had happened, and he testified to his brother's love of cigarettes, which they were convinced caused the fire. He also said his brother recently had moved in with him from a nursing home and was not in the best of health and often needed assistance in moving around. I wrote down his comments and was ready to write the story."

Here is Love's story, and alongside it his comments about how he wrote it:

I had some colorful quotes from the brother about his brother's smoking habits, and since that had emerged as the consensus as to the cause of death, I decided to emphasize that angle in my lead paragraph. His age was also significant, as was the school bus setting, so I incorporated all of it in what I consider a somewhat clumsy lead. But it seemed to work.

Next, the sequence of events was in order so I used the clearest and most official source I had—that of the coroner. I let him give the basic facts in the next three paragraphs, throwing in an aside about the victim's health in the third graf.

Then I came back to the smoking angle, using my best quote from the victim's brother. I let him describe the chainsmoking habits, tell about the camper and the events leading up to his discovering the fire in progress.

FRUITHURST—Seventy-six-year-old Tom Jenkins' penchant for chainsmoking has been blamed for the fire which engulfed the old school bus in which he slept early Saturday and in which he died.

Cleburne County Coroner Hollis Estes said he and the Heflin Fire Department were summoned to the Coldwater community near Fruithurst shortly after 4 a.m. Saturday to find the old bus—converted into a camping vehicle—ravaged by flames.

The bus was parked in the front yard of the home of the victim's brother, Hubert Jenkins. Tom Jenkins was living with his brother while he recovered from a stroke he suffered earlier this year, according to family members.

Estes said the bedding in the rear of the bus apparently caught fire from a burning cigarette and spread rapidly throughout the vehicle. The coroner said there was no evidence of foul play and no autopsy would be performed.

"Lord, he (the victim) was always careless with his cigarettes," said Hubert Jenkins Saturday night. "He would just smoke one right after the other. Only thing we can figure is he got out there in the camper and fell asleep or something with one lit."

Jenkins said his brother, who left Golden Springs Nursing Home in April, spent a great deal of time sitting in the bus, which was equipped with a stove, refrigerator and other appliances.

"Friday afternoon, he said he was going out for some fresh air, and I watched him make a beeline for the bus," Jenkins said. "I checked on him later on and he was just sitting on the side of the bunk bed, said he wanted to stay out there a while longer."

Jenkins said his brother later told his daughter "he wanted to spend the night out there."

Around 4 a.m., Jenkins said he awoke to the sound of "something popping. It sounded like his old walking cane he used—I thought he was tapping on the side of the bus to get my attention. Before I could get to the door I could see the trailer" on fire. Jenkins said he believes the popping sound that woke him was .22-caliber cartridges exploding in the bus.

Jenkins said his brother needed some help in "getting around" after the stroke, but was at a loss to explain why the victim was unable to escape the flames.

He said the bus had a front and rear entrance, but the back door was blocked by the bed on which Jenkins slept. Estes said, however, that the body was found on the floor of the bus.

I closed the story with his brother's explanation.

"It just looks like when he woke up he tried to get out, but just didn't make it," said Hubert Jenkins.

Love said his story lets "the people who were involved answer the obvious questions: How and why did Jenkins die where he did, and why couldn't he avoid his death? My last phone call to the family of the deceased brought all that together, and helped to take the story a bit beyond the level of a routine police item."

Here is a story that includes the death of a teen-ager. The cause of death is in the lead. Let's see how the story is developed:

STARKVILLE—A 14-year-old Starkville girl died Monday when a fire ignited by a woodburning heater destroyed her family's home.

The lead identifies the victim as a 14-year-old girl. The next paragraph must give her name:

> Sgt. Mike Collins, of the Stark-ville Police Department, said Denise Lee, the daughter of Martha Lee, was found dead in the rear bedroom of the residence on Hwy. 12 near the Stark Road intersection.

The next logical step is to give the cause of death:

> Lee apparently died from smoke inhalation while trapped in the fire, said Randy McCool, Oktibbaha County deputy medical examiner.

Then some details:

> Two other occupants—including Lee's mother—were able to escape through a door window in the wood frame structure, Collins said. Lee was apparently unable to escape, he added.
>
> —*The Commercial Dispatch,*
> (Columbus, Miss.)

Crime Stories

The main job of the police reporter is to handle reports of violent and property crimes, investigations and detection, and arrests. The police reporter may also cover the police and municipal or criminal courts to follow up the arrests he or she reports.

Almost everyone knows someone who has been a victim of a crime, or has himself or herself been a victim. A third of all households in the United States have been affected by burglary or a violent crime in the 1980s. In towns where people never locked their doors, there is now a thriving business in burglar alarm systems. Automobile owners search for the switch, wiring or siren that will keep a thief from taking off with their Toyotas and Fords. In some cities, women are advised not to wear necklaces or earrings on the streets. Around college and university campuses, the number of rapes has doubled and tripled in recent years.

Note: Criminal and civil law varies from state to state. The descriptions in this section may differ somewhat from those in your state.

During the 1970s, the number of crimes reported to law enforcement officials increased by 50 percent. In the 1980s, the number of crimes plateaued. Yet, a property crime is committed every three seconds and a violent crime every 24 seconds. A rape occurs every six minutes and a murder every 23 minutes.

Almost every community in the country has contributed to these figures. This means that police reporters have had to be more discriminating in their reporting. If they were not, they would not have enough time to report the most newsworthy crimes in their cities and towns.

To help clear the way through this flood of police information, the police reporter usually concentrates on violent crimes and spends less time on property crimes.

Violent Crime refers to events that may result in injury to a person. **Property Crimes** are unlawful acts with the intent of gaining property that do not involve force or threat of force.

Violent Crimes	**Property Crimes**
Murder	Burglary
Rape	Larceny
Robbery	Motor vehicle theft
Aggravated assault	

Crime Reports

Few police reporters have ever seen a crime committed. Yet they write about crimes every day, often with the intensity and drama of an eyewitness. Most of their information comes from crime reports. These are the forms filled out by officers who have investigated the crime. The reporter supplements these reports with interviews with the officers or their superiors and with those who witnessed the crime or were its victims.

Crime Essentials

- Victim(s), full identification
- Nature of crime
- Date, time, location of crime
- Violent crime: official cause of death or injury; weapon used; motivation; background of victim, if relevant
- Property crime: value of loss; method of theft or entry
- Suspects (no names unless charges filed), clues
- Unusual circumstances
- Quotes of witnesses, victim(s), police
- Source of information

The following story about a violent crime begins with the nature of the crime and the victims. In the second paragraph, the victims are identified and their injuries described. The third paragraph describes the possible weapon and the questioning of two suspects.

A man and woman were shot about 10:40 p.m. Monday when gunfire erupted during what police called a "neighborhood-type" argument in a field at 34th and Forest.

The victims were identified as Tony Simmons, 20, of 5117 Woodland, who was listed in critical condition with a gunshot wound to the forehead, and Ms. Debra Williams, 21, of 3327 Tracy, in fair condition with a gunshot wound to the left hand. Both were admitted to the Truman Medical Center.

Police, who said they heard different accounts of the shooting at the scene, said they were questioning two persons in connection with the incident. A pump shotgun believed to have been used in the shooting was recovered on the porch of a home at 3329 Tracy, police said.

—*Kansas City Times*

Robbery

Beginning reporters sometimes confuse robbery, a violent crime, and burglary, a property crime. The difference is this: Robbery is a crime against a person. Burglary is a crime against property.

Robbery involves taking or attempting to take something of value from a person by force or threat of force or violence. The writer approaches robbery stories from two avenues—the value of goods stolen and the prominence of the person involved. Usually, the value of goods taken is the element chosen for the lead, but when a widely known person is robbed, that is the lead, regardless of the amount taken from the person.

Here is a typical robbery story:

A lone gunman held up the Thrifty Liquor Store at 42 First St. this morning and got away with $1,780 in cash, police said.

The owner, Martin Nolan, said that he was closing the store when a man in his thirties bought a bottle of wine. As Nolan opened the register, the man took a revolver from his jacket pocket and told Nolan to hand over the day's receipts.

On leaving, he warned Nolan against following him. But Nolan told police he managed to see the tall, thin man drive off in a 1979 blue compact car with Arkansas plates.

Burglary

Burglary is the unlawful entry of a structure to commit a felony or a theft. (A felony is a crime that is punishable by a year or more in a state or federal penitentiary.) In the case of burglaries, state law usually defines the dollar amount of stolen goods at which the theft passes from a misdemeanor to a felony. In some states, it is $250, in others $500, and so on. (A misdemeanor is a crime punishable by a fine or a term of less than one year in a city or county jail or prison.)

When the loss in a burglary is considerable, the lead focuses on the value of the stolen goods:

Jewelry and personal items worth $50,000 were reported missing from the home of Victor Sewell, 560 Eastern Lake Ave., last night.

Police said Sewell told them he and Mrs. Sewell returned from a visit to friends about 11 p.m. and discovered the window to a bedroom at the rear of the house had been forced open.

Sewell, an attorney, told police he had purchased a matching diamond bracelet and necklace last week in London where he attended a law seminar. He said he had told no one of the purchase.

Police said the bedroom was the only room in the house that had been entered.

Detection

Police are understandably close-mouthed during the investigation of a serious crime, which makes it hard for the reporter to obtain material for a story during the detection-investigation stage.

Sometimes, the police will seek help from the press in locating a suspect and will provide information. Now and then a reporter will learn something the police want to keep confidential. Most police reporters will keep the material under wraps. They risk antagonizing their sources if they use it. In the larger cities, the unwritten code is that a reporter may use anything he or she can learn. If the department cannot keep its people quiet, so be it.

Early information about suspects may compromise not only the investigation but the court case. A reporter must weigh all this before running any but officially sanctioned material.

Detection Essentials

- Progress of investigation
- Suspects
- Additional clues
- Personnel assigned to case
- Summary of crime

Caution Only the most serious crimes are investigated by most big-city police departments. Generally, the greater the public interest, the more likely the police are to push an inquiry. The murder of a prominent person or a police officer will be investigated. But in large cities, the murder of a drug dealer or a drifter may be closed quickly. Burglaries and car thefts have, for all practical purposes, been decriminalized in large cities, unless the criminal is caught in the act. There is almost no follow-up investigation of these crimes.

Some of the best crime stories are of arrests. Again, the information usually comes from a report, in this case an arrest report, which the reporter examines on his or her rounds of the police department. For arrests in serious crimes, the police or district attorney may call a news conference to make the announcement for all the media.

Arrests

Usually, charges are filed on arrest, but sometimes a suspect is held for investigation. A suspect may be detained for a limited period until formal charges are filed. In the arrest story, the writer must be certain that the charges mentioned have actually been filed.

The reporter does not wait until charges are filed to write an arrest story, but the arrest story avoids mention of charges. Notice the key phrases in this lead:

> Ralph Hunter, 24, of 167 Broad St., was arrested last night *in connection with* (or: *in the investigation of*) the armed robbery of a service station last week that netted the robber $18,000.

But once the prosecutor files the charges, don't hesitate to say so in the lead:

> Ralph Hunter, 24, of 167 Broad St., was charged last night with the armed robbery of a service station. . . .

Only a third to a half of those arrested are formally charged with a crime. For most arrests, the prosecutor decides not to draw up a charge because the evidence is inadequate, witnesses will not testify, or additional information makes prosecution inadvisable. This has led some newspapers, such as the *St. Louis Post-Dispatch,* to withhold the names of most of those arrested until a charge is drawn.

Another bit of advice: Double check names and addresses, especially if the person arrested gives the name of a person well known in the community. Verify by calling the suspect at home or at work, or questioning police closely. Some suspects give false names and addresses.

Never write this kind of lead for an arrest story:

> Ralph Hunter, 24, of 167 Broad St., was arrested for the armed robbery. . . .

This lead makes Hunter guilty of the crime.

Arrest. A crime suspect is flushed out of a field by police officers and is handcuffed. Arrests are handled carefully: Names and addresses are double-checked, and the reporter makes it clear that the person has been arrested in connection with some crime. The reporter avoids any implication that the arrested person is guilty. *Joseph Noble, The Stuart* (Fla.) *News.*

Arrest Essentials

- Name, identification of person arrested
- Crime person is charged with
- Details of crime, including name and identification of victim
- Circumstances of arrest
- Officers involved in arrest
- Source of information

For serious crimes, add these:

- Investigation
- Background of suspect
- Motive
- Circumstances of arrest announcement
- Booking, arraignment, any other procedures

The Arrest Lead Generally, the lead to the arrest story is based on the name and identification of the person arrested and the crime that the person is accused of committing.

If the arrest is the result of extraordinary police detection or unusual circumstances, a delayed lead may be put on the story, with the arrest coming as a climax.

Here are some leads that emphasize different essentials:

Name, identification of person arrested

Two teen-agers are in the Dade County jail, charged with first degree murder in the robbery and execution of a meat truck driver whose truck they are accused of hijacking. Robert Borton, 18, of 1981 NW 37th Ct., and his longtime friend, Carlton Derly, 19, of 2149 NW 24th Ct., were arrested Wednesday night.

Circumstances of arrest

A one-armed busboy captured a fleeing gunman, tripping him twice and holding him in a headlock for police, after the gunman held up a restaurant and shot a cook, authorities said today.

Detail of crime

A suspect has been arrested in the weekend slaying of a department store manager who was found shot to death with his 3-year-old son standing over him, police said.

Investigation

Eleven South Americans were in custody today after a four-month investigation by the Sheriff's Department, Narcotics Bureau and U.S. Customs resulted in the seizure of $750,000 worth of cocaine, $139,500 in cash, a rifle, three handguns and a sizeable amount of gold jewelry, Undersheriff Sherman Block said yesterday.

What's Newsworthy? The size of the community and the amount of its crime determine what kinds of arrests become news. In Miami, Detroit, Chicago, Los Angeles and cities of similar size, the arrest of a murder suspect may merit a few lines, if that, unless the victim is prominent or the crime had been given attention.

But in smaller cities and towns even the theft of some jeans and the arrest of a suspect is worth a story:

A Dress Barn employee was arrested Wednesday on a warrant charging him with stealing 49 pairs of blue jeans.

Joseph Scapella, 40, of 95 Trudy Lane was charged with second degree larceny in connection with the theft of the jeans valued at $1,302 and taken from a Dress Barn warehouse March 26, police said.

This story appeared in *The Advocate* in Stamford, Conn. The story is as long as a piece about an arrest for attempted murder in Chicago, which was carried by the newspaper only because of the grisly nature of the crime:

A resident of a West Side halfway house was charged Monday with shoving his roommate out of a third-floor window, then rushing downstairs and stabbing him 11 times as he lay in the alley where he landed.

The police charged Allen Taber with attempted murder. The victim, Fred Krumpe, was in critical condition with multiple fractures.

Analyzing the Arrest Story Here is an arrest story with the list of arrest essentials alongside it:

Circumstances of arrest, nature of crime

A special burglary detail yesterday chased and caught a suspect the officers believe responsible for a rash of house burglaries in the Tacoma Avenue area.

Charges, name and identification of person arrested

Karl Vogt, 31, of 967 Eastern St., was charged with burglary and possession of burglary tools.

Circumstances of arrest elaborated

Police said that Vogt was spotted by a detective in the special unit going from house to house along Tacoma Avenue. When he saw the man enter 98 Tacoma Ave. he radioed for the rest of the detail. Vogt awoke a tenant, John Strong, and then tried to flee but was arrested a block from the building.

The detail was set up for round-the-clock surveillance of the neighborhood after several house burglaries were reported.

Officers making arrest

Detectives who made the arrest included Ray Miller, John Hazar and Bill Smith.

Law-Enforcement Agencies

Crime is handled by a variety of law-enforcement agencies. Local crime is under the jurisdiction of the municipal police force. More than 90 percent of all cities with a population of 2,500 or more have their own police forces. At the county level, sheriff's departments handle duties similar to local police for unincorporated areas and in municipalities with no local police force. The sheriff often operates the county jail. State police and highway patrols handle traffic on state highways and provide assistance to local police and sheriff's departments.

After an arrest, the suspect is **booked** at the police station:

A 23-year-old prison parolee, the object of a statewide manhunt, surrendered in San Luis Obispo County and was booked Tuesday in the murder of a teen-age Hollywood girl, Los Angeles police said.

Mauricio Rodriguez Silva was being held without bail in the Hollywood Division jail. He is expected to be arraigned on a murder charge Thursday, authorities said. . . .

—*Los Angeles Times*

The police reporter usually will cover the booking at the police station. The court reporter will take over for the arraignment, which is the beginning of the court process.

State Judicial System

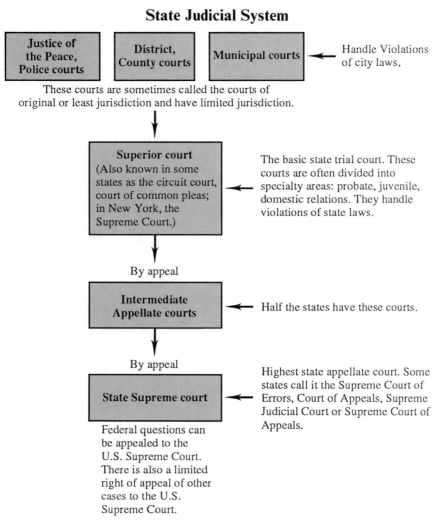

Justice of the Peace, Police courts

District, County courts

Municipal courts ← Handle Violations of city laws.

These courts are sometimes called the courts of original or least jurisdiction and have limited jurisdiction.

Superior court
(Also known in some states as the circuit court, court of common pleas; in New York, the Supreme Court.)
← The basic state trial court. These courts are often divided into specialty areas: probate, juvenile, domestic relations. They handle violations of state laws.

By appeal

Intermediate Appellate courts ← Half the states have these courts.

By appeal

State Supreme court ← Highest state appellate court. Some states call it the Supreme Court of Errors, Court of Appeals, Supreme Judicial Court or Supreme Court of Appeals.

Federal questions can be appealed to the U.S. Supreme Court. There is also a limited right of appeal of other cases to the U.S. Supreme Court.

U.S. Department of Justice, Bureau of Justice Statistics, Report to the Nation on Crime and Justice.

Court Coverage

Criminal law procedure can be roughly divided into two areas for coverage—pretrial and trial. Both areas are given considerable coverage in the case of a major crime.

Pretrial

Arraignment The suspect is arraigned in a local court soon after arrest. The procedure consists of the court's advising the suspect of the charge and in hearing the suspect's plea. Bail is sometimes set at the arraignment.

> A 19-year-old West Roxbury man yesterday pleaded innocent to a second-degree murder and assault and battery charges in connection with the death last winter of a Boston College student.

> The case of Scott O'Leary was continued one month for a pretrial conference following his arraignment before Suffolk Superior Court Judge James P. Donohue. . . .
>
> —*The Boston Globe*

The federal courts have held that the time between arrest and arraignment can be no longer than 24 hours. Many states have laws stipulating that an arraignment and bail hearing must be held without unnecessary delay.

Preliminary Hearing This hearing is sometimes called a probable cause hearing. The judge reviews the facts and may hear testimony. The judge then decides whether there is reasonable and probable cause to bind the suspect over for grand jury action and whether to hold the suspect in jail or to set him or her free on bail. A person without a lawyer may have one assigned.

Arraignments and preliminary hearings are held in what are known as courts of original or least jurisdiction. These are municipal, police, city and criminal courts. These courts can try misdemeanors and sentence those who plead or are found guilty. A higher, state court must try felonies.

Grand Jury A jury, usually of 23 persons, hears the evidence presented by a prosecutor and decides whether to issue an indictment (true bill) or to dismiss the charge (no bill):

> A Cobb County grand jury returned murder indictments Thursday against two men and a woman accused of causing the death of a Marietta woman who took an overdose of cocaine in February. . . .
>
> —*The Atlanta Constitution*

In some states, an **information,** which is a formal written accusation, is submitted to the court by the prosecutor instead of an indictment being returned by a grand jury.

From Crime to Prison

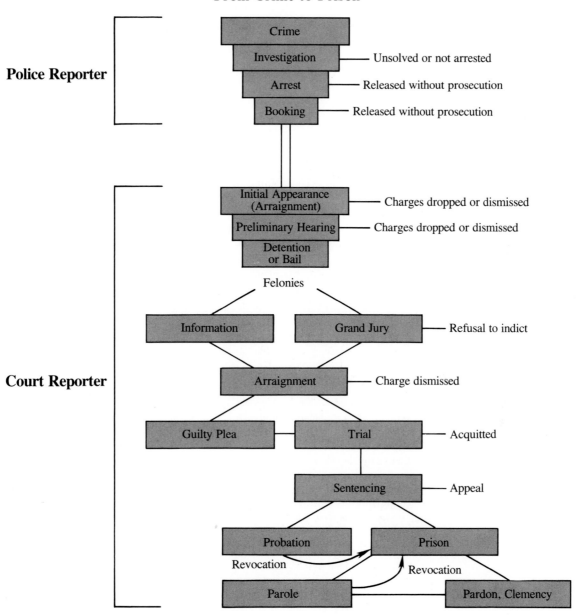

Police Reporter

Crime

Investigation — Unsolved or not arrested

Arrest — Released without prosecution

Booking — Released without prosecution

Court Reporter

Initial Appearance (Arraignment) — Charges dropped or dismissed

Preliminary Hearing — Charges dropped or dismissed

Detention or Bail

Felonies

Information

Grand Jury — Refusal to indict

Arraignment — Charge dismissed

Guilty Plea

Trial — Acquitted

Sentencing — Appeal

Probation

Prison

Revocation

Parole

Revocation

Pardon, Clemency

Re-arraignment The defendant is informed of the charge in the indictment or information, is advised of his or her rights and is asked to plead to the charge. If the plea is guilty and the judge has jurisdiction, the defendant may be sentenced. If the plea is not guilty, the case is set for trial.

Pretrial Hearings A number of different hearings may be held before the case goes to trial. Some are:

Suppression—Consideration of the admissibility of evidence or a confession.

Sanity—Determination of the fitness of the defendant to stand trial.

Jurisdictional—Determination of whether the court has jurisdiction over the case.

Plea Bargaining

During any of these steps in the pretrial procedure the defendant may plead guilty. Often, the defendant is allowed to plead to a lesser charge than the one on which he or she has been indicted. This negotiation of a plea is called **plea bargaining** and is used in most courts to help to clear the calendar of the enormous number of cases before them. A study of 13 cities showed that plea bargaining occurred in from 81 percent of the cases in Louisville to 97 percent in New York City. Here is a story based on a bargain struck by the prosecutor and the defense lawyer:

> A 26-year-old man described by authorities as a Marine deserter has been sentenced to life in Walpole state prison after pleading guilty to second-degree murder in the Oct. 12 death of concert pianist Mary Louise Sellon, 30, of Medford.
>
> The guilty plea last Tuesday of Steven Ballway came less than a week before he was scheduled for trial in Suffolk Superior Court on first-degree murder and rape charges.
>
> *—The Boston Globe*

Sometimes, a deal will be worked out with a defendant in return for his or her cooperation with authorities:

> PHOENIX—A Boulder man charged with seven others in a 56-count indictment has been placed on four years' probation for possessing cocaine and selling marijuana.
>
> Dennis J. Cimmino, 31, was sentenced by Judge Cheryl Hendrix of Maricopa County Superior Court after pleading guilty to the two drug charges and agreeing to help prosecutors. . . .

Should no plea bargain be offered—which often happens when the defendant is a frequent offender—the case moves to trial. In many cities, district attorneys concentrate their sparse resources in prosecuting what is known as the career criminal, the defendant with a long record of felony arrests and convictions.

Jury Selection A jury is chosen from a **wheel** or jury box that contains the names of all registered voters in the jurisdiction. A defendant may waive the right to trial by jury and ask the judge to hear the evidence.

Trial The trial begins with opening statements by the prosecutor and the defense attorney. The reporter usually learns the outline of the case from these statements. They are followed by the prosecutor's presentation of the state's witnesses. (In criminal trials, the state, not an individual, brings the charges.)

The defense then may cross-examine the prosecutor's witnesses, after which the prosecutor may question the witnesses in redirect examination.

The defense then presents its case by calling its witnesses:

The Trial

Out of 100 felony arrests by police, the U.S. Bureau of Justice found the following results:
- 51 were rejected before charging or dismissed in court.
- 49 cases were carried forward. Of these, 45 plea bargained, and there were four trials.
- Of the four tried, three were convicted.
- Of the 45 who pleaded guilty and the three who were found guilty at trial, 24 were put on probation, 13 were sentenced to a year or less, and 11 were sentenced to more than a year in prison.

CLAXTON, Ga.— Annette Moore sat in Evans County Superior Court and read from a pocket-size Bible while her son testified for more than an hour as the sole witness in his own defense.

Before 18-year-old Michael Moore was arrested Feb. 1 and charged with murder in the bludgeoning and stabbing death of his girlfriend's mother, Rebecca Futch, he was his own mother's hope for the future.

Now, in the third and last day of testimony before Judge John R. Harvey, he was staring a possible death sentence in the face and blaming his girlfriend for the crime.

Moore's girlfriend, Sherri Futch, is white. Her mother did not like her seeing Moore, Miss Futch said, because he is black. Moore testified that on the evening of Feb. 1 he and Miss Futch, 17, planned to tell her mother that she was pregnant. . . .

The prosecutor may cross-examine defense witnesses, and the defense is allowed then to make redirect examination of its witnesses.

Both sides are allowed to present rebuttals to testimony. The last step in the trial procedure is the final argument by both sides.

Southern Style Justice

The South accounts for about a third of the crime in the United States but for well over half the felony convictions, the U.S. Justice Department reports. Generally, says the department, the less populated the area, the greater the conviction rate.

	Crime	**Felony Arrests**	**Felony Convictions**
South	34	38	57
West	26	24	15
Midwest	18	18	15
Northeast	22	20	13

(Percent of total number of crimes, arrests and felony convictions, 1986.)

The Jury

Charge to Jury The judge charges or instructs the jury about the law involved in the case.

Jury Deliberations and Verdict The jury retires to a jury room to decide the facts of the case. The jurors must reach a unanimous verdict in all states but Louisiana, Montana, Oklahoma, Oregon and Texas. The jury may ask the judge for further instructions about the law, and it may request that testimony be read to it from the transcript. Since jury deliberations are secret, these occasional requests may tip the reporter to what the jury is considering.

> RIVERSIDE—Douglas Neslund, the 40-year-old founder and director of the Los Angeles-based California Boys Choir, was convicted by a Riverside Superior Court jury of molesting several of his choirboys.
>
> The jury deliberated almost three full days before finding Neslund guilty on four felony counts and one misdemeanor count of child molestation. . . .
>
> —*Los Angeles Times*

Verdict stories include the period the jury deliberated and comments of those involved. When possible, jurors are interviewed. Also included are the accusation, identification of the accused and the background of the crime. Notice in the beginning of this story by Beverly Medlyn of *The Mesa Tribune* that she has stressed the viciousness of the crime and the relief of the child's parents:

> PHOENIX—Frank Jarvis Atwood, an ex-con and a drifter, was convicted Thursday of first-degree murder and kidnapping for snatching an 8-year-old girl off her bicycle in broad daylight and then killing her in the desert northwest of Tucson.
>
> The verdict was the emotional climax of a 2½-year wait by Vicki Lynne Hoskinson's family, which held a press conference after court adjourned to describe the long torment that had finally come to an end.
>
> "I'm on top of the world. Today, justice was served for Vicki Lynne," proclaimed Debbie Carlson, the victim's mother. Carlson, her husband, George, and her daughter, Stephanie Hoskinson, alternately beamed and wept for joy as they faced a battery of cameras and microphones.
>
> Carlson said she was "relieved that Frank Jarvis Atwood will never walk the streets again. He will never be able to victimize another child."

Sentence If the jury returns a verdict of guilty, the judge may sentence the defendant at once or may await a probation report or schedule a presentence hearing at which evidence of aggravating or mitigating circumstances may be considered. In some states, the jury decides the sentence for capital offenses such as murder.

> Eddie L. Green was sentenced Wednesday to a five-to-15-year prison term in the bludgeoning death three years ago of a Buffalo man who, Green claims, had made advances to his girlfriend.
>
> —*The Buffalo News*

Judges sometimes make newsworthy statements. Perhaps the most famous sentencing comment of all was that of a Colorado judge after the trial of Alfred G. Packer, a survivor of the ill-fated group of emigrants in the Donner party who were trapped by snow in 1846 in the Sierra Nevada. Packer was convicted of cannibalism, the only man ever convicted on that charge in U.S. history. The judge sent him to prison with this comment: "Packer, there was only five Democrats in this county, and you et 'em all."

Contemporary historical note: Students at the University of Colorado at Boulder named their dining hall in honor of Packer.

Stories can be written at any stage of the process. If the crime is notorious or involves a prominent person, a reporter may be assigned to stay with the event from arraignment through sentencing.

Criminal Trial Essentials

- Identification of defendant
- Original charge
- New charge if plea bargain
- Nature of crime, details
- Status of proceeding:
    What happened today
    Review of trial
    Next steps
- Name of judge, title of court
- Courtroom scene

Trials are often dramatic, and the reporter should seek to reflect the drama. They are also complex, frequently complicated by legal jargon and technical procedures. The reporter must look beyond the technical points to the human interest, the tale that is unfolding.

Civil Law

Damage Suit Filed

Alvin Kellogg of St. James, Minn., checked into a Rochester motel room on Sept. 13, 1985, planning to have his annual checkup the next day at the Mayo clinic.

That night he suffered a stroke in his room. He claims in a suit filed in Olstead County Court that he was not found until three days later. He is suing the Chambers Corp., which owns the motel, for $500,000.

Kellogg, 67, alleges that the company was negligent because its employees at the Phillips Downtown Motel failed to discover him for three days. Medical reports filed with the suit state that Kellogg was severely dehydrated when he was found. . . .

We have been discussing criminal law procedures. In this area of law, the government is the accuser. In the other major area of law, civil law, the action is usually brought by an individual or a group. Civil law is not seen by the press as having the drama of criminal law, and consequently coverage of the civil courts is spotty, usually confined to the suits brought in what is called **actions at law.** These suits seek the recovery of property and damages for personal injury and breach of contract.

The county courthouse reporter has the responsibility for checking the court clerk's records daily to ferret out the most interesting and significant suits filed. A guide to making judgments is the sum sought by the person filing the suit. But be careful: Lawyers sometimes seek huge sums for the damage allegedly done their client, then agree to a much-reduced figure in pretrial bargaining. In fact, most suits never reach the trial stage.

When a settlement is reached, the story must contain the amount awarded by the jury, the name of the person bringing the suit and the damage inflicted, the defendant, the title of the court in which the suit was heard, the incident leading to the suit:

A 20-year-old Wyckoff woman who was injured in an automobile accident yesterday won a $405,000 jury award in Superior Court in Hackensack from the friend who was driving the car in which she was a passenger.

Megan McMurtrie of 402 Meer Ave. was semiconscious for eight days of a month-long hospitalization after Kathryn Gallant lost control of the Mercedes Benz in which Ms. McMurtrie was riding, causing the car to strike a tree in Franklin Lakes. . . .

The Record

Equity Proceedings

The other area of civil law is called **equity proceedings.** Here, an individual or a group seeks to have the court compel an individual, the government, or an organization to do something or to refrain from an action.

Here is the beginning of a story about the court's issuance of a temporary restraining order:

Dr. John H. Lambette's attorney obtained a court order Friday barring state health officials from suspending the heart specialist's medical license.

State Superior Court Judge Karl Krane granted the order and scheduled a hearing next Tuesday to determine whether the temporary restraining order should be made permanent. . . .

Injunctions are usually issued pending a hearing to determine whether they should be made permanent.

There are two judicial systems: federal and state. Most coverage is of the state system. In cities where federal courts are located, the newspaper usually assigns a full-time staff member to cover the federal court.

Federal Courts

Federal courts hear a wide variety of cases that involve the violation of federal laws—immigration cases, constitutional issues, interstate car theft, drug shipments from outside the country into the country, tax cases, civil rights.

NEW YORK (UPI)—The largest tax fraud case in U.S. history has ended with the conviction of four Wall Street executives and a hung jury in the case of a fifth defendant.

The nine-man, three-woman jury considering the complex trail of $130 million worth of phony tax shelters reached a partial verdict. . . .

DETROIT—One white man was found guilty and another was acquitted in federal court yesterday in a civil-rights trial stemming from the 1982 killing of Vincent Chin, a 27-year-old Chinese-American.

A jury of 11 whites and one black found Ronald Ebbens, 45,

guilty on one count of violating Chin's civil rights. Chin had been bludgeoned to death with a baseball bat after a barroom brawl in what U.S. Department of Justice prosecutors said was a racially motivated slaying.

—*Los Angeles Times*

The federal court system has three tiers: the district courts, where most trials are held; the courts of appeal in 12 circuits to which cases may be taken by appeal, and the final court of appeal, the United States Supreme Court, to which cases are taken by writ of certiorari.

Obituaries

The Washington-based political reporter had finished his talk to the journalism class and asked for questions. He had just completed a five-state tour of the Midwest to sound out political feelings about the president.

"What was the strongest impression you got from your trip?" a student asked.

The reporter paused a moment before answering. "This isn't really a political matter," he said. "But when I was interviewing a woman in her kitchen in Iowa, I glanced over to the wall where she had some things clipped to a wallboard. At the top was a newspaper clipping behind a piece of clear plastic.

"It was the story of President Kennedy's funeral. The paper was yellow and frayed. It told me something about the woman's politics. But it also told me something about journalism. Here was the most basic journalistic story of all, an obituary, and it had been saved for all these years."

Obituaries are among the most frequently read items in newspapers. A third to a half of the readers regularly read them.

The Kentucky Post in Covington for years carried an obituary for everyone who died within the newspaper's circulation area. The *Post* would take special pains to obtain material. Every morning, reporters would call hospitals in the area for death reports, and funeral directors were expected to call the newspaper with material.

After a while, the obituaries began to take too much space. The newspaper decided to reduce the type size of its obituaries from eight points to seven.

"We got all kinds of complaints," says David Brown, the managing editor. "Since then, we haven't fooled with them much."

For the *Post,* obituaries must include all the basic information and be tightly written.

Unlike the *Post,* the *Knoxville News-Sentinel* runs obituaries only of people prominent in the community or of those whose achievements merit attention. "To get a good death story, we stress trying to make the person live. We want it to be a personality piece of sorts a person who had a family and friends and achievements," says Wade Saye, assistant managing editor of the *News-Sentinel.*

"Our goal is to really catch the personality of the person in the story."

For *The Cincinnati Post,* a person need not be prominent to be a good subject for an obituary. "We did an obit once on a bus driver whose name meant nothing to most people," says Leon Hirtl, managing editor of the *Post.* "But we discovered that many people knew him as the bus driver who sang."

The newspapers that run most or all deaths in their obituary columns write them tightly:

> BATCH, FRED J., 83, of 5623 80th St. N, died Thursday (June 21, 1987). Born in Boston, he came here in 1969 from Framingham, Mass. and was a retired musician. He was a member of Boston Musicians Protective Association. Survivors include his wife Nell; two sisters, Beatrice Carlson, Randolph, Mass., and Mildred Villa, Manchester, Mass., and several nieces and nephews. National Cremation Society.

Unless a suicide is committed in a spectacular fashion, the story of the death should be treated no differently from other obituaries. Newspapers and stations usually play down the means of death. But how the person died should be mentioned somewhere in the story.

Some newspapers provide this service with the paid death notice and will run staff-written obituaries only for the people the newspaper considers newsworthy.

But newsworthiness is sometimes an elusive guideline for an obituary. If the president of a local highway equipment firm is worth seven or eight paragraphs, why not the bookkeeper in his firm who emigrated from Hungary as a youth 50 years ago? What made him leave home and family, and how did he fare on arrival? What were his struggles to educate himself? Did he struggle alone, or did he have help? Friends and relatives would know.

"There are a lot of missed opportunities for good stories with obituaries," says Jim Adams, city editor of *The Cincinnati Post*. "It's my philosophy that you treat the obituary the same as any other news story—get quotes and talk to people and try to give a face to the person you're writing about."

Obituary Essentials

- Name, age, address and occupation of the deceased
- Time and place of death
- Cause of death
- Date and place of birth
- Survivors
- Funeral and burial arrangements

These are the bare essentials. For the longer obituary, add:

- Accomplishments and achievements
- Membership in organizations
- Armed forces service
- Anecdotes of friends and relatives

Usually, the basic material is made available by the mortuary handling the death. Material may be available from the advertising department, which may receive a paid death notice from the funeral home. Occasionally, an obituary is called in by a person identifying himself or herself as a friend or relative. Be careful. Unless you know the person well, always verify the information by telephoning a relative or a mortuary. Some people call in phony death reports for the kick they get in seeing an obituary of someone who is very much alive.

Personal Details

Readers are interested in stories about the deaths of local people. Here, in capsule form, is the biography of someone we know or have heard about. We can read that the local Chevrolet dealer grew orchids as a hobby and had won prizes at local shows, or that the retired music teacher had set a national collegiate record for the 100-yard dash 50 years ago.

Obituaries balance these personal details with the obvious necessities—name, age, address, occupation, survivors, funeral arrangements.

The following obituary from the *Lexington* (Ky.) *Herald-Leader* includes the kind of detail that reveals, in just a few paragraphs, the story not only of a local businessman but of a class of people who pulled themselves up from humble beginnings:

Store Founder 'Al' Wenneker Dies at Age 76

Alex "Al" Wenneker, a prominent Lexington businessman, died here yesterday. He was 76.

With a rented storefront on Main Street measuring only 12 feet by 30 feet, eight kitchen chairs, empty boxes used as shelves and a relatively small stock of shoes, Wenneker and his wife Mary opened for business back in 1935. The business, located at 155 East Main Street until 1979, was called Wenneker's Sample Shoe Store.

Although no longer at the Main Street location, Wenneker's Shoe Stores have become a very successful business chain here with locations at three of Lexington's shopping malls.

Wenneker was a member of Temple Adath Israel.

A native of St. Louis, Mo., he was the son of William Wenneker, a Russian immigrant, and Libby McDowell Wenneker.

Besides his wife, survivors include two sons, James E. Wenneker and William R. Wenneker, both of Lexington; four sisters; and three grandchildren.

The funeral will be at 3 p.m. Tuesday at W. R. Milward Mortuary—Broadway. Burial will be in Lexington Cemetery. Visitation is from 3 to 5 and 7 to 9 p.m. today.

Cause of Death

Reporters often discover that finding out the cause of a person's death is the most difficult part of reporting for the obituary. The family sometimes feels ashamed, embarrassed or fearful that the way a person died will reflect poorly on that person's life, or on the family. The family of a teen-age girl who committed suicide asks that the obituary say simply that she died "suddenly." The widow of a man who died of cancer insists that the obituary say death came "after a long illness," a euphemism that has become less frequent as the number of cancer deaths has increased and the word "cancer" no longer is whispered. Most newspapers or stations have policies on how to handle these situations.

Deaths from diseases that may indicate a lifestyle many people consider unsavory are often troublesome for the reporter. Deaths caused by cirrhosis of the liver or AIDS, for example, present problems. Cirrhosis is associated with alcoholism, and AIDS victims are for the most part homosexuals or intravenous drug users.

Perhaps because AIDS is such a recent disease, or because of the stigma attached to it, acquired immune deficiency syndrome is not mentioned as a cause of death in many obituaries, except when the person who died was prominent. Instead, the obituary may list the cause of death as pneumonia, Kaposi's sarcoma, or another of the so-called opportunistic infections that the AIDS virus allows to invade the body. Many larger stations and newspapers are realizing that a death from AIDS is no different than a death from cancer, or from a heart attack or car accident, and encourage funeral homes and families to list AIDS as the cause of death.

When Thomas Schippers, a well-known orchestra conductor, died of cancer, *The New York Times* received several letters asking whether Schippers had been a smoker. The information should have been included in the obituary, the *Times* admitted. The newspaper had included this information in the obituaries of heavy smokers who died of lung cancer, an editor stated.

Light Touch

The obituary does not have to be written in somber tones of black. If the deceased was known to be genial and easygoing, why not write an obituary to match his or her life? Here is the beginning of such an obituary from *The Milwaukee Journal:*

Services for Paul W. LaPointe, widely known Milwaukee restaurateur who was better known as "Frenchy," will be at 11 a.m. Tuesday at the Wittkopp Funeral Home in Plymouth. Burial will follow in St. John's Cemetery in Elkhart Lake.

LaPointe, 72, died Saturday, apparently of a heart attack, at his summer home on Elkhart Lake. He lived in Milwaukee at 2629 N. Summit Ave.

A self-described workaholic, LaPointe owned and operated Frenchy's Restaurant at 1827 E. North Ave. from 1945 until he retired in 1975. In February 1979 he decided retirement was not for him and opened Paul's Small Cafe at 1854 E. Kenilworth Place, just around the corner from his old restaurant.

In an interview in 1980, LaPointe spoke of his futile attempt at retirement.

"Just wait until you get to be 65 or 70 and you're just looking at four walls," he told a reporter. . . .

The Obituary Lead

Generally, a person's occupation, accomplishments or distinctive contribution to the community is placed in the lead to identify him or her:

Occupation

Raymond T. Baron, former president of Paxton and Baron Co., book publishers, died yesterday in his home at 75 Arden Lane. He was 78 years old.

Accomplishment

Mortimer Heineman, an advertising executive who helped create the slogan "Promise her anything, but give her Arpège," died yesterday following a heart attack. He was 74 years old.

Contribution

Florence Gable Cerrin, long active in the local chapter of the American Red Cross, died yesterday at her home at 65 Eastern Parkway at the age of 94.

Funeral and **burial arrangements** can also be the basis of the lead. Some newspapers will try to vary their leads so that instead of every lead beginning with the report of someone's death, an occasional obituary will begin with the date, time and place of the funeral and burial.

Services for Albert D. Scott, 79, of 156 W. Central Ave., will be held tomorrow at 11 a.m. in the Boulder Funeral Home.

Burial for the retired pharmacist will follow in the Piedmont Cemetery in Oberlin.

Scott died yesterday at his home after suffering a heart attack. . . .

When the death has occurred a few days before, the lead usually will be based on the funeral and burial arrangements.

Delayed leads are rarely used for obituaries. If the delayed lead is in good taste, it is acceptable:

Margaret Wilson did get her last wish.

When she was told she had terminal cancer, the 73-year-old former high school teacher asked

that she be buried in her ancestral family plot in Ireland.

Next Tuesday, her ashes will be. . . .

Sudden Death When death strikes a young or middle-aged person suddenly, the story can be as much news story as obituary, as we saw with fatal accident stories. With sudden death stories, the cause of death is essential and must go into the lead. Here is how Rick Hampson of the AP began his story about the shooting of John Lennon:

```
     NEW YORK--(AP)--John Lennon, the singer-
song writer who helped make the Beatles musical
superstars and pop-culture legends in the
1960s, was killed in a late-night spray of
gunfire outside his luxury apartment building.
     He was the co-author with Paul McCartney of
such famous songs as ``I Want To Hold Your
Hand,'' ``Yesterday'' and ``Let It Be.''
     Minutes after the shots rang out, police
took a suspect into custody. Early today, they
charged Mark David Chapman, 25, of Hawaii, with
murder. No motive was known immediately.
```

Written under pressure shortly after Lennon was shot, the reporter had to balance the facts about the slaying and Lennon's background, which was obtained from the AP library.

Here is the beginning of the story about the death of Elvis Presley written by Les Seago of AP soon after the death was reported:

```
    MEMPHIS, TENN.--(AP)--Elvis Presley, the
Mississippi boy whose rock 'n' roll guitar and
gyrating hips changed American music styles,
died Tuesday afternoon of heart failure. He was
42.
    Dr. Jerry Francisco, Medical Examiner for
Shelby County, said the cause of death was
''Cardiac Arrythmia,'' an irregular heartbeat.
He said ''That's just another name for a form
of heart attack.''
    Francisco said the three-hour autopsy
uncovered no sign of any other diseases, and
there was no sign of any drug abuse.
    Presley was declared dead at 3:30 P.M. EDT
at Baptist Hospital, where he had been taken by
a fire department ambulance after being found
unconscious at his Graceland mansion.
```

Presley's fame endures.
Graceland, the home the singer built in Memphis, Tenn., attracts thousands of visitors a year. It is also the destination of 75 letters mailed to Presley each day. One said, "I love you very much, and I hope you are well and kind to yourself." Some describe Presley's followers as a mortuary cult. The bottom-line observers marvel at the Presley industry: Visitors pay $11.95 for a package tour and can select from an assortment of trinkets that include Graceland ashtrays and bedroom slippers with Elvis heads on their toes. The Presley estate licenses more than 200 products.

Localizing the Obituary

When a widely known person dies, a local follow-up is sometimes possible. The person may have been born or gone to school in town. Here is how a Springfield paper handled the death in another state of a former resident:

> Robert Cowan, who served as governor from 1956–60, died today in a retirement home in St. Augustine, Fla. Cowan was born in Springfield and attended school here before moving to Gulfport in 1915. . . .

Sometimes, the local connection is less specific, as when the nation mourned the death of President John F. Kennedy. Then, local observances were the subject of many stories.

Covering Sports

No one can predict the kinds of stories he or she will be covering. Even those who have no interest in reporting sports events may find themselves in the press box at a football game or at courtside for a college basketball tournament.

"If you're not a sports writer when you begin working as an AP newsman or newswoman, you become one—quickly," the AP tells news staffers.

A sportswriter once asked Carl Furillo, the great outfielder for the Brooklyn Dodgers, how he learned to play the tough right-field wall in Ebbetts Field. "I worked, that's how," Furillo replied.

And that, says the writer, Roger Kahn, is how a reporter learns to write sports stories. The first efforts may be as fumbling as the lead that a high school correspondent called in to a newspaper after his high school team had won a no-hit game:

> In the best-pitched game these
> old eyes have ever seen. . . .

Or the sport being covered may be as confusing as it was to Becky Teagarden, a sportswriter for the *Columbus* (Ohio) *Citizen-Journal* when she covered her first basketball game.

"I didn't know what was going on," she recalls. But she had the good sense to corner the coach after the game. She asked him, "Tell me, what happened out there?"

The high school reporter learned, too. His first task was to learn to keep himself out of the story. The reader is interested in the athletes and the game, not in the writer.

For most beginning sportswriters, the important lesson is that good sports writing is good writing. This means getting to the point quickly, stressing human interest, avoiding sports jargon and clichés, and giving the reader some insight into the game or the personality being described.

In other words, sports writers follow the principles of good writing that have been described in previous chapters.

School Sports

Sports writers who aspire to cover the Cleveland Indians, Dallas Cowboys or Golden State Warriors break in on school or non-professional sports. Although many people follow professional sports, many more are fans of local high school or college teams. These fans expect the same quality of reporting and writing the fans of professional teams are given.

Many newspapers hire part-timers, most of them students, to cover school games. Don Watz, a junior at Florida State University, was assigned to cover a high school baseball game in the afternoon and a college baseball game that evening. He describes how he went about it:

> My day started with traveling from Tallahassee to Live Oak (80 miles) for the 2 p.m. high school game. That game lasted about two-and-one-half hours. At about 5:15 I finished with my interviews and hit the highway.
> I then had 80 miles to travel to Jacksonville. The FSU-Jacksonville game started at 7 p.m.

By the time I traveled crosstown through rush-hour traffic and reached the University field, the game was just completing the first inning. I had to finish my high school game story (I started it during the high school game).

While the FSU game went on I finished up my high school story. By the sixth inning I sent it to the office in Tallahassee.

Then, I had the FSU game to worry about. The game took 12 innings and had 17 runs scored. It finished at 11:30 and I had a midnight deadline.

I made it.

How did he do? Judge for yourself. Here is the beginning of his high school game story:

LIVE OAK—It was a mismatch on paper, and by the end of the game, the scoreboard reflected that. Second-ranked Leon won the District 2-AAA baseball title Friday afternoon, thumping Suwannee 13–1.

The underdog Bulldogs were no match for Leon, which has won three straight district titles and six of the last eight. The game lasted just five innings due to the 10-run mercy rule. The Bulldogs could manage just one hit off Leon starter Brad Culpepper. The single by Jason McCarl came with one out in the fourth and brought home the only Bulldog run.

"I tried to keep them off-balance," said Culpepper. "They are a good ballclub and a good hitting club; after a while they would get used to a fastball pitcher."

Culpepper struck out eight in the five innings but at times Suwannee did manage some hard shots—all of which were scooped up by the solid Lion defense.

"We played two games back-to-back and haven't made an error. We had outstanding defense," said Leon coach Ronnie Youngblood. . . .

Who's Looking at Sports on TV

	Number (millions)	Percent of Adults
Professional football	63.2	37
Baseball	62.7	37
College football	48.9	29
Boxing	37.2	22
College basketball	36.2	21
Professional basketball	34.7	20
Professional wrestling	28.8	17

Loser. For every winner, there is a loser, and a story in the loss—despair, frustration, overconfidence, bad luck, illness. A loss in sports is not a tragedy, but players and fans do take it seriously and so the reporter must be careful neither to overdramatize nor understate the loss.
Robert Burke, Sunday Courier & Press, Evansville, Ind.

Notice that Watz did not write a simple lead with only the score. He had an idea of a mismatch when he went to cover the game, and that's what he saw unfold. That became his lead. Despite his hurry, he did manage some postgame interviews.

Now, over to Jacksonville for the college game. Again, Watz wrote a lead that is imaginative. Here are the first few paragraphs:

JACKSONVILLE—When Florida State began its current three-game road swing, Chris Pollack was told he probably would be needed in a relief role. He liked the idea.

Not only did he like it, he's good at it. The senior lefthander pitched 7⅔ innings and earned the win, beating Jacksonville 9–8 in a Friday night game that took 12 innings.

"When they told me I might be coming in relief I was excited," Pollack said. "Coming in with two on and two out and the score tied is exciting. After starting all of last season and most of this one, I looked forward to it."

The leads that Watz put on his stories are informative and entertaining. Look at the game story essentials below and see how many Watz handled in his first few paragraphs.

Game Story Essentials

- The score
- Names of teams, type of sport
- When and where the game took place
- Key incident or play
- Outstanding player(s)
- League
- Scoring
- Effect of game on league standings
- Strategy
- Crowd size; behavior, if a factor
- Statistics
- Injuries
- Winning or losing streaks
- Duration of game
- Record(s) set
- Postgame quotes

The quality of the written story depends on the quality of the reporting. The reporter who knows the players well, who keeps up on the strategy coaches use for different opponents, and who knows the sport he or she is covering, is able to write an interesting story.

Some Statistics

The odds against a high school athlete becoming a professional ball player are 12,000 to 1.

Thirty percent of college basketball and football players are functionally illiterate.

Seventy percent of all basketball and football players in big-time college sports never graduate.

Teams that go to the Rose Bowl get $5 million–$6 million each for the bowl game.

The Sports Lead

Any of the essentials can be the major element that is placed in the lead of the story. Let's look at a Monday newspaper that carried the results of Sunday's games.

None of the stories began with the score alone. All used a record, an incident, a play, an outstanding player, or an injury along with the score:

Outstanding Player

HOUSTON—The running back Allen Pinkett, starting for the injured Mike Rozier, scored his third touchdown of the game on a 6-yard run with 31 seconds to play today as the Houston Oilers rallied to defeat the Los Angeles Raiders, 38–35.

—AP

Key Play

EAST RUTHERFORD, N.J.— With less than a minute and a half left in their game against San Francisco this afternoon, it seemed as if the Giants might escape with a victory, despite a flawed performance.

The Giants' victory seemed almost certain when San Francisco wasted two plays on its final possession: Jerry Rice dropped a 10-yard pass and Joe Montana was stuffed for no gain on the next play.

But Montana threw a 78-yard scoring pass to Rice with 42 seconds to play as the 49ers won, 20–17, before 75,943 fans at Giants Stadium.

—UPI

Duration of Game

NEW YORK—The game had stretched into the sixth hour when with one swing of the bat Claudell Washington smashed a two-run home run to give the New York Yankees a 5–4 comeback victory over the Detroit Tigers in the 18th inning.

It was the longest game in the season so far at 6 hours 1 minute.

—UPI

When writing for a weekly newspaper or when the game is a few days old before it reaches the newspaper's columns, the lead will emphasize a personality or perhaps the consequences of the home team's victory or loss—injuries for the next game, change in standings, changes in starting players.

Behind the Score. Scores are remembered for a few hours, says a sports writer. But the emotions endure. By capturing the human element in the game, the writer may tell a story that moves beyond the athletic field. This picture by Morris Berman of the *Pittsburgh Post-Gazette* captured the moment that a battered Y. A. Tittle of the New York Giants sensed his career as a quarterback was at an end. Many games have good follow-up story possibilities, as this game between the Giants and the Pittsburgh Steelers did. Some originate in locker-room interviews following the game, and others require additional reporting.

Be Imaginative

Imagination is vital to the sports story. There are so many sports, such a multitude of games that after a while the sports pages seem to swim in team names and numbers. Sports is the story of men and women straining mind and body to reach beyond their limits, of unusual people and strange events. The stories should reflect this.

When Nolan Ryan pitched his record fifth no-hit baseball game, the story was as much his nonchalance as the accomplishment. When the Montreal Expos cannot win a game against the Los Angeles Dodgers in their home park, the story of still another loss is the story of jinxes and superstitions.

"People forget about game scores in one hour," says T.J. Simers of *The Commercial Appeal* in Memphis. "But a story about emotion may stick with them for two hours." Simers is being sarcastic about the durability of a news story, but he does have a point.

The writer who captures the human dimension of the event creates a story the reader will remember, and this is what we all strive for in journalism—the story that makes the reader sit up and take notice.

Leads can focus on the small details unseen by fans in the stadium or watching on television:

> Paul Williams leaned a foot too
> far to his right last night, and that
> was the ball game.

This was the beginning of a story about a baseball team trailing 1–0 in the bottom of the ninth with two out. Williams had walked, the next batter had two balls and no strikes. And suddenly the game was over because Williams was picked off first base by the pitcher.

Don't Be A Rooter

Favoritism, rooting or any sign of partiality are out. Athletes and their activities are given the same treatment as anyone subject to news coverage.

When the student newspaper at the University of Arkansas at Little Rock revealed that several student athletes had been caught cheating on a biology test, a sports columnist for the *Arkansas Democrat* attacked the newspaper for its story. The column earned the writer a Dart from the *Columbia Journalism Review,* which described the piece as "offensive" for criticizing the newspaper and for arguing "passionately" in defense of the athletes.

Favoritism has compromised reporters so that they ignored drug and payoff scandals among college and professional teams. A longtime college basketball coach said that many sports writers had winked at payoffs and academically ineligible players. (Scandals have rocked many major colleges: SMU, Tulane, Clemson, the University of Maryland, the University of Minnesota, TCU, and Memphis State in recent years. The exposures, many by non-partisan reporters, led *The New York Times* to suggest: "Pay athletes outright and let them stop masquerading as students and amateurs.")

When possible, the sportswriter tries to match the drama of the game with his or her account of it. The difference between the fans' observations and the sports story is the knowledge that the sportswriter takes to the game. This insight must be shown in the story. For this reason, sportswriters often like to begin their stories with the little things that are the turning points of the game, such as the base runner's too-long lead that abruptly ended a possible ninth-inning rally.

Increasingly, delayed leads are put on sports stories. The first paragraph or two may contain an incident, anecdote, a key play or a strategic move. Then, in the second or third paragraph, the writer gives the score. Next, a few paragraphs are devoted to the important points of the game—the scoring, significant substitutions, injuries or changes in the standings.

If most fans already know the result of a game, it is a good idea to focus on a key play or turning point in the game:

Some clutch free-throw shooting by Paul Threet and a lucky bounce helped Park School clinch the co-championship of the Independent Athletic Conference basketball league.

Threet made both attempts in a one-and-one situation Thursday with seven seconds left in overtime as Park defeated visiting St. Mary's for the Deaf 62–61 in a game here. . . .

—*Buffalo Evening News*

Sportswriters are enthusiasts. Sometimes they write as though they are covering the end of the world, not a game. This kind of enthusiasm leads to excesses:

Shrillness This is a common ailment, especially of some television announcers. In football, every other play is accompanied by a rise in the voice. A writer can be shrill, too. A story written with high-pitch intensity from lead to end irritates the reader. Every game has pauses, lulls, even dull periods. The story should not be dull, but it should not scream at the reader.

Overstatement Games sometimes are made into battles of titans, and the language of the story is exaggerated and pumped up. Writing of this sort often flows shamelessly in stories about the games of traditional rivals—Green Bay Packers–Chicago Bears; Stanford–University of California at Berkeley; Red Sox–Yankees; New York Knicks–Boston Celtics; Kansas–Missouri; Rangers–Flyers; Iowa State–University of Iowa.

Mindless Emotionalism Fans do become excited by games. They have even been known to hurl beer cans at players and officials. Some fans become so involved with the action that it becomes a life-and-death conflict for them. Sportswriters should reflect the intensity and the seriousness of sports, but they must also keep their distance. These are, after all, only games.

Extra Dimension

Most of those who turn to their newspapers to read of yesterday's games already know the results. They might have seen one game on television and heard the scores of others on television or radio. The reporter's task is to add an extra ingredient.

Emery Filmer, a sports reporter for *The Advocate* in Stamford, Conn., was covering a local team in the state baseball playoffs. On Tuesday, the team, the Stamford Catholic High School Crusaders, had upset the defending state champions, 2–1. Then, on Wednesday, Stamford lost 7–2 in the semifinal. Filmer was writing for the Thursday newspaper. *The Advocate* is an afternoon newspaper, which meant that most fans following the local team already knew it had lost.

How would you handle this situation? A story that begins this way would be barely adequate:

> Andrew Warde High School defeated the Stamford
> Catholic High School Crusaders yesterday in the
> semifinal state baseball playoffs by a score of 7-2.

There is nothing wrong with this lead, except that it repeats what many readers already know. How about this one:

> The Crusaders from Stamford Catholic High School
> hung up their gloves yesterday and will have to wait
> another year before trying for the state high school
> baseball championship. The Crusaders lost to Andrew
> Warde 7-2 in a semifinal playoff game yesterday.

Although this lead is also adequate, it says little more than the previous lead. All it does is add a picturesque but trite phrase, "hung up their gloves."

Filmer was able to write an effective lead because he understood the key to the Crusaders' loss, the absence of their leading pitcher. He added a dimension to his story because of his knowledge of the team and the game. Here is how Filmer's story begins:

Warde eliminates Catholic, 7–2

By Emery Filmer
The Advocate

Here are the two sides of the Stamford Catholic High School Crusaders:

On Tuesday night, they played a near-perfect game in upsetting the defending state Champion Westhill Vikings, 2–1, in an FCIAC first-round playoff game. But on Wednesday, they fell behind 5–0 in the first inning and ended up on the short end of a 7–2 score against Andrew Warde, a club they had beaten 8–3 last month.

So, what's the difference?

Roger Haggerty perhaps. After all, he wasn't pitching Wednesday.

"Knowing that we did not have to face Haggerty tonight was a definite factor in our favor," admitted Warde coach Ed Bengermino after his team had qualified for its first appearance in the FCIAC championship game.

Haggerty pitched a brilliant two-hitter against the heavy-hitting Vikings on Tuesday to vault the Crusaders into Wednesday's semifinal against the Eastern Division champions, Warde. It was Haggerty's sixth victory of the year and lowered his ERA to 1.82.

But, unfortunately, he can not pitch every day. And therein lies the difference in the Stamford Catholic Crusaders.

Wednesday, Catholic manager Mickey Lione tabbed lanky right-hander Matt Reed to start against Warde. Now Reed has had a better-than-average season (3.95 ERA), but his three wins were the second most on the team.

The difference was apparent immediately. The first five Crimson Eagle batters to face Reed all reached base, and all scored.

"Reed just didn't throw strikes," said Lione. "He was constantly falling behind 2 and 0 and 3 and 0 on everybody. So he had to come in with a lot of fat pitches."

Although he only walked one batter, Reed was never ahead of a hitter through the first five batters.

John Martin led off with a double and Mark Carlson followed with run-scoring single. So after two batters, Reed had allowed one run and two hits, which were the seven-inning totals for Haggerty a night earlier.

After a walk and a Greg Cantwell single, Joe Braun singled in the second run. After Reed retired the next man on a ground out which made it 3–0, Dan Schetino closed out the first-inning onslaught with a two-run single.

Before half of the crowd had arrived, Warde led, 5–0.

"We got beat by Haggerty last year and this year and both times he just blew us away," Bengermino admitted.

Tips on Covering Games

Here is some advice from the AP on covering a few sports:

Baseball lives on numbers and that is where you'll generally find your lead: a low number (e.g., a one-hitter for a pitcher) or a high number (e.g., four home runs for a batter). Account for all scoring and remember to mention outstanding defensive plays and unusual incidents such as fights or injuries.

Basketball is a sport where points come too rapidly to mention all the scoring, so focus on the players with the biggest or most important numbers and key stretches where the game is won or lost.

Bowling is an easy sport to describe because it basically involves two plays, a strike and a spare. Total pins and decisive plays, such as missing a key spare or covering a difficult split, are essential to any bowling story.

Football stories should begin with a summary, a graf or two that disposes of the most important things that happened in the game. For football (and basketball as well) every lead must have a hero in it. Include anything unusual.

Track and field: Lead with a record-breaker, a multiple individual winner or a team's domination of a meet. Most track events are short and merely listing the performance is enough. But be sure to mention the color, too, such as a shot putter winning with a mammoth heave on his final attempt or a miler coming from back in the pack on the final lap to win by inches.

In the Newsroom

When the reporter arrived at his desk early one morning he could tell he would not be out on his beat for at least two hours. On his desk sat a batch of announcements and press releases, a couple of notes from the city editor and a telephone message. Without taking time for his usual chat with the reporter at the next desk, he set to work.

First, he looked through the releases. One was about a regional history conference that would be held on the campus of the local college. Another concerned a skating party to be held Sunday for a charity. The third was about a speech to be given by the governor next week. He put these in one pile, took a slip of paper and wrote *advances* on it and clipped the material together.

Another sheet contained a release from an army base about the promotion of a local soldier. He scribbled the word *personal* across the top of the press release. He knew that he could handle these releases quickly. The others would take a little more time. One was an obituary, another required some calls to localize a wire story, and the third required a call to the weather bureau for a story the city editor wanted for the newspaper's early edition.

Better get the easy ones out of the way first, he decided. He turned to the advances and the personal item. These would require short pieces. In fact, these tightly written pieces are called **briefs** or **shorts.**

Briefs

The trick to writing briefs, he had been told his first day on the job, is to give the reader the basics. "No frills, no ornamentation. The Five W's and an H and get out of there fast," an experienced reporter had told him. No more than two or three paragraphs, unless the advance is about a big meeting of the city council that is coming up, or the personal is about the appointment of a new minister to the largest church in town, or the marriage in town next month of the 72-year-old senior U.S. senator.

Precedes

The reporter then looked over the seven-paragraph press release from the local college about the history conference. He wrote a precede:

> The eighth annual Midwestern Conference of History Teachers will be held on the Hampden College campus next Thursday and Friday.
>
> Registration will take place in McGuire Auditorium Wednesday afternoon and Thursday. The fee is $5. Sessions will be held in the Liberal Arts building.
>
> The main speaker will be Professor Felix S. Woodward of Oxford University. He will speak Thursday evening on "Breaking the Plains."

The smaller the newspaper, the longer the precede. Here is how the skating benefit story was written:

> A fund-raising skating party to assist the Norwalk Community Hospital will be held Sunday at the Wheels Roller Skating Center at 61 Converse St.
>
> There will be two sessions, from 7 to 9 p.m. and from 9:30 to 11:30 p.m. Music will be provided by "Soul Sounds." Admission is $3.
>
> The income will be used to furnish a children's playroom in the hospital.

Here is an advance from *The Berkshire Eagle,* a daily newspaper with a circulation of 31,000 that stresses local news. The *Eagle* has room for stories like this:

A talk on bobcats in Massachusetts, part of the Berkshire Sanctuaries predator series, will be given tonight at 7:30 in the members room at Pleasant Valley Wildlife Sanctuary in Lenox.

Chet McCord, who is in charge of research for the state Division of Fisheries and Wildlife, will be the speaker.

While a graduate student at the University of Massachusetts, McCord studied bobcats on the Prescott Peninsula near Quabbin Reservoir in central Massachusetts. Using collars with radio transmitters, he studied the bobcats' movements and habitat preferences.

Fee for the talk is $1 for Massachusetts Audubon Society members and $2 for non-members.

The precede, or advance, tells people about events they may want to attend or at least want to know about. Knowing that the local school board will be considering a change in the busing policy, parents may call or write board members to express their opinions if they cannot attend the meeting. A family may not want to go roller skating but might send a donation to the community hospital after reading the short item about the benefit.

Precede Essentials

- Event or activity planned
- Date, time, place of activity
- Purpose
- Sponsor
- Fee, admission charge, if any
- Background, if a significant event

Personals

Names make news. In big cities, the names that make news are those of public figures—television personalities, the wealthy, politicians, athletes, the social set. In smaller towns, the names are those of neighbors, and their comings and goings are recorded in detail. These news items are called **personals.**

Here is the beginning of a personal item in *The New York Times,* daily circulation 950,000:

There were people who looked like George Burns, Goldie Hawn, Woody Allen and Katharine Hepburn. And there were quite a few who looked like Prince Charles and Lady Diana Spencer.

The party Tuesday night at Ted Hook's Backstage restaurant. . . .

Here are two personal items from the Hinsdale correspondent on the weekly *Dalton News-Record* in Massachusetts:

Airman First Class Edward G. Barrett and Mrs. Barrett have returned to their home in Hampton, Va., after spending a week with their grandparents, Mr. and Mrs. Richard Boker.

The Ladies Aid Society will have a food sale during the annual town meeting this Saturday. Ethel Perth and Julia Anderson are in charge of the event. Nancy Jenkins is in charge of the snack bar where homemade doughnuts and coffee will be available. Hours are 1 p.m. to 5 p.m.

Births, engagements and weddings, awards, retirements, promotions, confirmations, bar and bat mitzvahs, appointments—all are duly recognized.

"Small is beautiful," says Avice Meehan, managing editor of *The News-Record*. "Mainly we concentrate on the little things—items about the Boy Scouts, the high school junior that the Lions Club has selected to represent the club in the All-State Band at the district convention, the names of officers of the local Historical Commission."

The personal cements communities. It tells people about the successes, and sometimes the tribulations, of the family down the street.

Some newspapers use personals imaginatively. When Waconah Regional High School held its graduation, *The News-Record* ran a paragraph about the plans of each of the graduates for colleges and careers.

Frank Availe, son of Frank and Karen Availe, County Road, Becket. Undecided.

Debra Wuinee, daughter of Mr. and Mrs. Robert Wuinee of 32 East Deming St., Dalton. BCC to study accounting.

Personal Essentials

- Name, identification
- Newsworthy activity
- Connection of individual(s) to activity
- Special or unusual activities in connection with the event

Personals are usually handled in a straightforward manner. If there is a special or unusual activity connected to the event, that can become the lead— the wedding held on the lawn of a summer home, the birthday party celebrated atop a mountain.

For weddings, the names of the bride and groom and the location of the wedding are carried in the lead. Also essential to the story are the background of the couple and the names of the parents:

Ann Margarita Poray and Marvin Abercrombie were married yesterday in St. John's Church.

The bride is a teacher in the Fairfield Junior High School. She was graduated from Weston College. Abercrombie is a loan officer at First National Bank in Fairfield. He is a graduate of Brown University.

The bride is the daughter of Mr. and Mrs. Phillip Poray of 62 Antonio St. The bridegroom is the son of Dr. and Mrs. Albert Abercrombie of Boston.

For engagements, the parents of the bride-to-be usually make the announcement and this is placed in the lead:

Mr. and Mrs. Burton V. Carroway announced the engagement of their daughter, Faye Elizabeth, to Robert Becker, son of Mr. and Mrs. Stanley Becker.

The wedding is planned for Sept. 21.

Ms. Carroway, 435 Eastern St., is a librarian with the state legislative service. Becker is a salesman for Reed Chevrolet and lives at 67 Marion Ave.

Small-town newspapers carry stories about the celebration of wedding anniversaries (usually 25th, 35th, 40th and 50th).

Mr. and Mrs. W. J. Stagg were honored by their children in celebration of their golden wedding anniversary Saturday in the Reorganized Church of Jesus Christ of the Latter-Day Saints. At the celebration, they renewed their wedding vows.

Mildred Forrest and William J. Stagg were married July 25, 1937, in Lawrence, Kan. They have three married children and five grandchildren.

Most briefs can be handled quickly because few require additional information. The material that has been included in the announcement or press release usually is sufficient. Two points to remember:

1. If there is any indication of an unusual situation or circumstance in the material, check it out. There might be a good story hidden there.

2. Avoid running the press releases in the form given to you. They should be rewritten after the facts are checked.

There are other stories that can be written from the office but require reporting and checking. Let's begin with a story that needs to be **localized.**

The logic of localizing news stories is simple. Readers prefer to read about people and events close to them. Proximity, we learned, is a basic news determinant.

A reporter is handed a wire service story that lists the names of 11 people who were killed in Ohio when the bus they were riding in collided with a truck. Two of those who died were local residents.

The reporter calls the AP to ask if anyone from the local area was injured. He also makes a few calls to gather background information on the two people who were killed and the funeral arrangements.

An essential task is to make sure that the names are spelled correctly. They are often garbled in wire stories in such situations. Another is to verify that the people involved are actually from the home community. Mistakes do happen.

Here is the wire story:

```
     YOUNGSTOWN, OHIO--Eleven people were
killed when the chartered bus in which they
were riding collided with a truck on U.S. 80
last night.
     The driver of the truck and 15 passengers
were injured. The bus had been rented by a
church group, the Presbyterian Fellowship
League, that was holding a conference in Akron.
     Witnesses told investigating officers the
truck seemed to veer into the bus as the bus
tried to pass it.
     Names of the dead are:
     Alvin Bailey, 59. . . .
```

The localized version began this way:

Two local residents were killed last night when the bus in which they were passengers collided with a truck on U.S. 80 near Youngstown, Ohio.

The dead are: Alvin Bailey, 59, of 12 Belford Place and Charlene Dearborn, 21, of 68 Topper St.

The Associated Press reports they were attending. . . .

News writers can localize major national and international events, as Ingrid Peritz did for *The Gazette* in Montreal. The Islamic revolution in Iran caused a rift among Iranian students studying abroad. Some became followers of the fundamentalist Ayatollah Khomeini, the aged absolute ruler of the country, and some opposed his rule, which they described as tyrannical. The students at the university Peritz was attending often had heated debates, and this gave her an idea for a story for an anniversary of the revolution in Iran.

Here is how her story began:

The famous scowl and penetrating eyes of Iran's leader dominate Mohammed Abbaszadeh's sparsely furnished living room in his Montreal West apartment.

It is as though Ayatollah Ruhollah Khomeini, the 81-year-old patriarch of Iran's Islamic revolution who seized power three years ago yesterday, watches over Iranians in Montreal as carefully as he does his countrymen at home.

"I support Khomeini with all of my power," says Abbaszadeh, 27, a devout Moslem who has lived in Montreal for three years. "His is the only way."

Yet that "way" stabs through the very heart of Montreal's 2,000-member Iranian community, dividing the Iranians into two camps: Abbaszadeh's Khomeini followers pitted against an anti-Khomeini majority.

A bitter student rivalry between the two Khomeini factions in the city has been fuelled by anti-Khomeini charges that the Iranian government is tampering with student allowances, and claims the Iranian embassy is cancelling student passports in acts of political persecution. For their part, the Khomeini followers in Montreal brand the anti-Khomeini students as terrorists and agents of the U.S. Central Intelligence Agency.

After this general overview, Peritz tells individual stories, beginning with Reza:

Reza, 25, shuffles nervously in his plaid shirt and rumpled jeans, clutching his chemistry books under one arm. His jet black hair is dishevelled, his large eyes weary and bloodshot, as though the pressures of exams have worn him out.

But it is not exam time at Concordia—Reza is beset by worries that most students never dream of.

"They (Iranian authorities) know who we are," he says in a whisper, his eyes darting back and forth. "They know everybody against the regime . . . they take our passports and force us back to Iran. But if we return, they will execute us at the airport."

Under no circumstances will Reza reveal his last name—his family will be persecuted in Iran, he warns, if his words reach the authorities back home.

Reza says his fears are matched by dozens of Iranian students. Like him, many were drawn to Montreal by its promise of a coveted university degree. Some followed cousins and brothers; others were lured by our universities' one-time relaxed admission policies. . . .

Localizing Essentials

- Name of local person or situation that justifies localizing
- General situation or background
- Source of information—name of wire service or organization

A **folo** is a story that follows up on a theme in another story. If a national educational organization reports that a growing percentage of high school graduates is putting off college, the enterprising reporter who sees the wire story hits the telephone to call area high schools, junior colleges and four-year schools. Folos usually run the day after the original story appears.

When President Reagan sent Congress a budget that would have cut back on services to the needy, reporters sought to determine the local consequences. Here is how one newswriter began her follow-up story:

Needy local residents would be severely hurt by Reagan administration proposals in Congress that would cut and restrict many federal programs.

This was the opinion of officials of several public and private organizations concerned with social, economic and health services for the poor here. Margaret Murtagh, executive secretary of the Family and Children's Services agency, a private organization, said:

"Half of the proposed reductions affect the poor. The budget seems to single these people out."

Another local agency, the Hospital and Home. . . .

Some people sit at home and paste stamps into albums, while others fly model airplanes. Most hobbies are perfectly safe. But some people climb mountains. Why?

This question occurred to several editors after an icefall entombed 11 mountain climbers under 70 feet of ice on Mount Rainier one Sunday in June, and just a few hours later five others died after a climbing party plummeted 2,000 feet down Mount Hood.

Reporters were told to find some local mountain climbers. Their answers made an interesting folo to the wire stories of the tragedies. Here is one local folo:

Contrary to the view of one well-known mountain climber, climbers do not attempt to scale mountains just because they are there.

"First, you have the beauty," said John Simac, 78 Harper Ave., who has climbed Mount Rainier in the state of Washington a dozen times, as well as other mountains.

"Then you have the challenge. Sometimes, it is almost too great," Simac said.

Then the challenge defeats the climber with frostbite and frustration. But sometimes the loss is greater. Last Sunday, 11 men climbing Mount Rainier were entombed when. . . .

Notice the insertion in the fourth paragraph of the **news peg,** the reason for the folo.

Folo Essentials

- Reaction, response, local aspect of an event
- Event or situation that gives the folo its news peg

These are the minimum essentials of the folo. The rest of the story should include the elaboration and buttressing of these essential elements.

The *Boston Herald American* jumped on a story involving the city administration after it issued a dress code that city hall employees were supposed to adhere to. The dress code contained the following provision for female city employees:

> Wearing apparel must be clean, neat and of a "business look" nature. Pants suits, dungarees, slacks or shorts will not be permitted at any time.

As soon as the code was issued, the *Herald American* assigned reporters to do a story on the new code. The newspaper also assigned a reporter to ask fashion designers for their reactions.

If the reaction story had appeared the next day, it would have been a folo. But since the reporter was able to report and write the story so quickly, the reaction appeared alongside the story about the code. The accompanying story became a **sidebar.**

Sidebar

A sidebar is a story that emphasizes an aspect of another story that is printed nearby. When Bonnie Britt did a series of articles for the *Houston Chronicle* on the dangers of insulation used in the construction of mobile homes, she wanted to get the reaction of the mobile home industry, which was being sued by a number of Texas mobile home owners.

Britt sought out the attorney for the industry. Although he was unwilling to comment, Britt dug into his background for the following sidebar that appeared alongside one of her articles in the series:

> One of the ironies in the formaldehyde story is the involvement of former Atty. Gen. John Hill, who while in office obtained 440 injunctions and $5 million in civil penalties against polluters.
>
> Hill is the lead attorney hired to defend the Texas mobile home industry in the 70 or so lawsuits filed by mobile home buyers irritated by indoor pollutants.
>
> The second irony underlying Hill's defense of the industry is that formaldehyde irritation struck close to home. In this case, his grandchildren's home. Hill's grandchildren (ages 1 and 4) became sick after exposure to urea formaldehyde foam insulation in their parents' brick home, according to plaintiff attorneys Robert Bennett and Andy Vickery.
>
> When asked why he would take so prominent a role in the cases if this were true, Hill would only say "No comment." . . .

The essentials for the sidebar are the same as those for the folo. The news peg of the original story and the reaction or response are placed high up and close together.

The **roundup** is frequently used to combine several stories into one. The roundup is based on finding an element common to two or more events and then writing a lead that reflects the common element.

When a heavy fog covered the East Coast there were ship collisions in New York harbor and off Virginia. The AP put the two stories together. The common element in the lead was the fog:

The Staten Island ferry collided with a freighter in New York harbor and two freighters collided off Virginia Wednesday morning, as dense fog cloaked the East Coast. More than 80 persons were injured in the accidents, none seriously, and all four ships were damaged.

In New York, the ferryboat American Legion, carrying 2,500 rush-hour commuters, was near the Statue of Liberty when it collided with the freighter Heogh Orchid at about 7:20 a.m. injuring 83 persons, officials said.

"It looked like a large gray shadow coming out of the fog," said ferry passenger Matthew Bendix, 17.

Four of the 83 injured were hospitalized in satisfactory condition, and the others were treated and released, hospital officials said.

A Greek cargo vessel, the Hellenic Carrier, was taking on water and leaving a trail of diesel fuel as it limped toward Norfolk, Va., after it collided with another ship at about 7:20 a.m., said spokesmen for the 5th Coast Guard District headquarters at Portsmouth, Va.

The Greek ship's crewmen huddled in lifeboats for more than two hours before being rescued, Coast Guard officials said. Two were slightly injured, one suffering a sprained ankle and another treated aboard a Navy destroyer with a tetanus shot for cuts.

Mahfooz Hussain, who was at the wheel of the Hellenic Carrier when the two ships crashed, said there was a heavy blanket of fog over the area.

Notice that the lead includes both incidents. The body of the story amplifies each accident separately, one after the other.

Roundups are frequently used for traffic accident stories. You can spot them after a weekend or a holiday, or when bad weather has caused a number of accidents:

Crews in North Dakota found the bodies of two people yesterday who died in a blizzard that dumped up to 25 inches of snow. The same blizzard paralyzed northeastern Wyoming, where it claimed three lives. Further east, thunderstorms raged over Tennessee, leaving one man dead and another critically injured after they were struck by lightning.

—Associated Press

Weather Stories

The spectators in the large auditorium were filing out after having watched the second round of competition for Miss Iowa. The lines moved slowly, and people were chatting. But they weren't talking about Miss Muscatine's chances of making it to the finals, or the fact that Miss Dubuque seemed embarrassed about parading in front of a few thousand people in a skimpy bathing suit.

They were looking out the windows of the auditorium watching a hailstorm gather force, and the talk was about the weather.

"It'll tear up the beans pretty bad," one man said. "Wind like that is worse than hail when you come down to it."

The mobility of the population has made people interested in weather outside their immediate vicinity. The traveler going to California wonders what the weather is like in San Francisco, and the Florida-bound family checks to see whether their Christmas holiday will be spent under blue skies in 80-degree weather.

Most of us have friends or relatives in other cities and states. When a windstorm hits Washington, a flood strikes the midwestern states or a drought wilts crops and people in the Southwest, we sympathize and might even write or call our relatives or friends.

In short, weather affects us all, and newspapers and stations have responded to this. Newspapers publish half-page weather maps in color, and radio and television stations flood us with weather reports. There are even all-weather stations.

Locally, people want to know how the weather affects them—what the forecast is and the full story when there is anything out of the usual. If it is turning warmer, people will put on lightweight clothing. If rain is forecast, umbrellas and overshoes come out of the closet. If the weekend looks grim, the sports fans stock up on beer and snacks for a weekend of television sports.

Weather stories are often routinely written, but they need not be. When a heavy snowfall hit New York City, Meyer Berger, a gifted writer who covered local news for *The New York Times*, wrote that the storm "left tremendous drifts in the countryside, and in main urban avenues it veiled skylines, tufting skyscrapers and steeples with enormous white caps."

The daily weather forecast was taken out of the routine by H. Allen Smith of the *New York World-Telegram,* who wrote what may be the best one-liner in all of journalism:

> Snow, followed by small boys on sleds.

As you can see, there are two types of weather stories, the daily forecast and the longer piece for unusual or extreme weather. Here are the essentials for both types:

Weather Essentials

- Forecast for next 24 hours
- Long-range forecast
- Most recent temperatures, humidity and precipitation
- Record highs and lows, if any

When weather is severe, the writer must consider the consequences. The effects are included along with the basics:

- Deaths, injuries, property damage
- Amount of precipitation (or drought)
- Strength of wind, depth of snowfall and height of drifts
- Any record(s) set
- Predicted duration of severe weather
- Consequences:
  - Traffic—roads, bridges blocked, accidents
  - Travel—air, bus, rail, local travel curtailed or stopped
  - Mail—any delivery or collection changes
  - Public services—power, water and telephone outages
  - Business—crops, tourism affected; business shut down
  - Schools—closings or changed hours
  - Aid—declaration of disaster area or aid from government

Writers try to show the consequences of unusual weather by introducing human interest, the effect of the weather on people. When unusually warm weather settled over western Massachusetts, *The Berkshire Eagle* reporter wrote that "large numbers of baby carriages blossomed forth on North Street and mopeds were seen put-putting about."

When the temperature reached 99 degrees in Baltimore one June day, a reporter for *The Baltimore Sun* had a novel idea for his story. He talked to youngsters at the zoo, and these interviews became his lead.

The Many Faces of Weather:

City Pleasures. When the temperature in Baltimore flirted with 100 degrees, youngsters took to the fire hydrants. In large cities, obliging fire departments will turn on the hydrants, realizing that there are few swimming pools available. *Richard Childress, The Baltimore Sun.*

Stranded. Midwestern weather can turn nasty in the winter. Heavy snowstorms block highways and leave motorists and their vehicles stranded. Unusual weather makes for good stories. Also, travelers rely on news accounts in making their plans. *Photo by Jay Koelzer of the Rocky Mountain News. Used with permission.*

Hot, Cold, and Wet

Collapse. Heavy, prolonged rains frequently cause floods whose damage can be awesome, in property and in lives. When this bridge went down on a busy New York highway, traffic was interrupted for months. Officials alerted the photographer. *Photo by Sid Brown of the Schenectady Gazette. Used with permission.*

Storm. Nature is fickle, bestowing bumper crops one year, and undoing a man's labors in minutes the following year. This Kansas farmer's sunflower crop was destroyed by a hailstorm, which bombarded his and neighbors' crops. *Photo by Charlie Riedel of The Hays Daily News. Used with permission.*

Summary

Different as they may seem at first glance, these dozen-plus types of stories have much in common. All are written in anticipation of the reader's or viewer's questions. This means: All persons in the story are fully identified, the events reported are backgrounded, and the possible consequences of the event or situation are presented.

The best sources are used, and they are quoted when possible. Drama and human interest are essential.

Underlying all news writing is the understanding that you can write good stories only if you *know* what you are writing about and if you have control of the writing techniques that make up the craft of journalism.

Suggested Reading

Anderson, David, ed. *The Red Smith Reader*. New York: Random House, 1983.

Kahn, Roger. *The Boys of Summer*. New York: New American Library, 1973.

Oran, Daniel. *Law Dictionary for Non-Lawyers*. St. Paul, Minn.: West Publishing Co., 1975.

Whitman, Alden. *Come to Judgment*. New York: Viking Press, 1980.

Part Four
Specialties

11
Broadcast Writing

Broadcast journalists offer their viewers and listeners up-to-the-minute news from neighborhoods, city hall, the state capital, the White House and battlefronts across the world.

Looking Ahead

Stories written for radio and television are written in conversational style, clearly and simply so that the listener or viewer can easily understand the story.

Complicated news stories are simplified by emphasizing only one or two themes. Leads are short and the present tense is used whenever possible. Attribution usually is placed first in the sentence so that the listener or viewer knows at once the source of the information.

News Check. Monica Kaufman and assignment editor Morris Pyle of WSB-TV in Atlanta go over the wire news before preparing the 6 p.m. news program.
Karen Clark.

Monica Kaufman anchors the 6 p.m. and 11 p.m. newscasts on WSB-TV in Atlanta. Her news day begins at 2:30 p.m. and ends at 11:45 that night. But that's deceptive. She is always working.

"My day starts with reading the morning paper," she says, "and listening to the all-news radio station. If I have time, I tune in the cable news on television."

By the time she shows up at the station early in the afternoon, Kaufman has a good idea of the day's news.

"My first stop at the station at 2:30 is the assignment desk to see what stories we're covering." These stories will be used on the 6 o'clock newscast.

"My second stop is the producer's desk to see what copy I have to write to fit between stories that reporters have turned in."

Her third stop is the wire machines where the news services spew reams of copy. She tears off the stories that she wants to use.

"Then it's writing time." Kaufman may rewrite the lead-ins that local reporters have written. These are the brief introductions to the reporters' stories. She will change them to conform to her speaking style.

If she is working on a special story of her own, she leaves the station to conduct interviews and to do her research.

"About 5 p.m., we begin to firm up the show. I write a 30-second promo, which is a tease to interest people in the 6 p.m. newscast. I do the promo live at 5:28:11.

"When I come back up to the studio, it's time to look at the scripts that the reporters have written. They have been torn apart. White copy goes to the telesynch operator. Blue to the show director. Green to the anchor who reads the piece. Goldenrod goes to the anchor who is listening. Pink to the show producer. Yellow to the editor."

Kaufman is on the set at 5:50 when she does a final read-through of the script.

After the show, she has little time to relax before preparing for the 11 p.m. news program. Usually, she goes out on a story for the late evening show.

"I try to make the 11 o'clock program different with new material. We update the 6 o'clock news whenever we can."

At 11:30 p.m., she takes a breather, and by midnight she is on her way home.

"At home, I try to read some magazines to keep up with what is going on in the world."

Life for Kaufman is not always rush and more rush. Now and then, she slows down to take on a major project that requires in-depth reporting and thoughtful writing. Often, these stories turn out to be series, one segment being presented each day.

Clarity Is the Goal

Much of what we have been discussing in this textbook applies to writing for the eye. Although we are discussing writing for the ear and the eye in this chapter, the principles of broadcast writing are no different from those of print journalism—clarity, accuracy, honesty of expression. There are, however, some differences in the application of these principles.

The first rule of broadcast news is that the story must be clear at once. Unlike the reader, the listener has no second chance to go over the material. Radio and television news is written on the wind—here for the instant, then gone.

There are several ways the broadcast news writer makes his or her copy clear.

Language   Broadcast news writers **use everyday words,** the language of conversation. Colloquialisms and contractions are acceptable. The style is informal. Look at some brief news items broadcast on the CBS television news program "Newsbreak":

Mail carriers are still making their rounds, while postal unions and management are still going round and round. There was tentative agreement on a new contract early today, but later the deal fell through. Now negotiations have resumed, and the unions say they have no plans for a strike.

Nato foreign ministers, meeting in Rome, today said nyet to Moscow—rejecting the Soviet demand for a moratorium on deployment of nuclear arms in Europe.

A Singapore Airlines jumbo jet left Southeast Asia today with a new way to help passengers pass the time. The plane, bound for San Francisco, is fitted out with six slot machines—for high fliers.

Ideas   Broadcast news writers **simplify the complex.** The story written to be read plunges right into the heart of the event. The broadcast story often has a brief capsule before the theme is stated.

When the mayor and the city council disagreed over a proposal to increase the city sales tax from 3 to 4 percent—a week after another disagreement over taxes—the radio copy of a local station began this way:

The mayor and the city council are feuding again. This time, the issue is the city's sales tax.

After this brief introduction to the heart of the story, the writer went into the details:

The city council last night turned down a proposal to increase the city sales tax from 3 to 4 percent. Mayor George Grogan said the city faces trouble unless it takes in more revenue.

And the only way the mayor can see to add to revenue is to raise the sales tax.

But the council voted six to one against the increase.

"Good writing," says former NBC correspondent Linda Ellerbee, "is the basis of what television is about. Good writing is not insulting your audience; good writing is not talking down to your audience; good writing is not being arrogant. It is the most important thing there is because it will give you a seamless newscast."

Count the number of sentences in the story. Then count the number of words in each sentence. There are six sentences, and they contain the following number of words: 9, 9, 20, 14, 18, 10. Clearly, most of the sentences are short, much shorter than the sentences would be in the same story written for a newspaper. The average number of words per sentence in this radio news copy is 13 to 14.

This leads us to the next point.

Brevity **Sentences are short** for broadcast stories. Long sentences cannot be read easily by the announcer, and the listener has a hard time following them. Here, side-by-side, are the UPI news wire and broadcast accounts of a major story from Atlanta:

News Wire

ATLANTA (UPI)--Wayne B. Williams, flanked by his defense team and surrounded by sheriff's deputies in a packed courtroom, pleaded innocent today to charges that he murdered two of 28 young blacks whose slayings kept Atlanta on edge for almost two years.

Williams, wearing a dark suit and a shirt open at the collar, appeared before Fulton County Superior Court Judge Clarence Cooper under extremely tight security.

Movements into and out of the courtroom were tightly controlled, with deputies using electronic metal detectors to search each of the about 300 reporters and spectators who jammed the small room.

During the 10-minute session, the charges were read to Williams. . . .

Broadcast Account

The man charged in two of the Atlanta slayings has pleaded innocent. Wayne Williams appeared in a packed courtroom today to answer to the charges that he killed two of 28 young blacks. The courtroom was under extremely tight security that included a search of everyone who entered. The judge tentatively scheduled the trial to begin October 5th. The 23-year-old Williams remains the only person charged in any of the 28 slayings that terrorized Atlanta for almost two years.

The news wire story continues for 20 more paragraphs. The first four sentences of the broadcast account contain 106 words. The average sentence length is around 26 words. The five sentences of the broadcast story total 81 words. That averages to a bit more than 16 words per sentence.

We know the way to write short sentences. Follow the S-V-O style. Look at the broadcast version. Every sentence begins with a subject, and the verb usually follows the subject immediately.

Broadcast news has been described as a headline service. It is intended to give the listener or viewer only an outline of the event. A half-hour newscast may have as many as 20 news items crammed into the 22 to 23 minutes allotted to news. The CBS "Newsbreak" program runs four to six items in 68 seconds. One day there were seven. That's a bit less than 10 seconds for each story, one or two sentences a story. Altogether, the news script for a Newsbreak program contains about 170 words, which is the equivalent of a three-to-four-inch story in a newspaper.

In other words, there are more words in a routine traffic accident story in a newspaper than there are in the entire Newsbreak program, and on the longer television news programs most stories have fewer words than a newspaper story about a non-controversial appointment by the governor.

All the news on a half-hour newscast would not fill the front page of a newspaper.

Brevity—tight writing—is a result of clear thinking. In order to write broadcast copy, the writer must be able to reduce news stories to their essence. The broadcast writer always asks himself or herself: **What happened here? Who said or did this?**

The answer, in simple S-V-O form, is the basis of the story.

The thinking process is the same, whether the news is gathered by a local reporter or is rewritten from the press association wires.

When stories are rewritten from the AP and UPI wires for television newscasts, these stories are described as **tell** stories or **readers.** That is, the anchor tells the listener about them, instead of showing tape. **Tell** stories do not excite viewers, broadcast people believe. So the tell story must be as brief as possible. Few tell stories run more than 20 or 30 seconds, which limits them to 50 to 75 words, the equivalent of one or two newspaper paragraphs.

In the "CBS Evening News" program we read about in Chapter 1, there were eight tell stories. Not one ran more than 30 seconds. Even the stories with videotape were short. The lead story—the signing of a tax bill—ran two-and-a-half minutes, 365 words. The same story in *The New York Times* had 1,000 words. *The Washington Post* story of the event contained 1,200 words.

Handling Attribution

Here's how the AP tells its broadcast writers to handle attribution:

Attribution on broadcast circuits must be every bit as clear as on newspaper wires. But the use of titles is less formal and the attribution should be expressed in a conversational manner—usually at the start of a sentence, rather than hanging at the end, as in newspaper copy.

Thus, "The National Aeronautics and Space Administration" becomes "NASA" or "the space agency" on first reference, and it's worked into the story where it falls naturally.

Consider this example:

Newspaper Style:

Seven people died and 35 were injured in a bus crash on a slippery highway outside New York City today, the Metropolitan Transportation Authority said.

Broadcast Style:

TRANSIT OFFICIALS SAY SEVEN PEOPLE DIED AND 35 WERE HURT IN A BUS CRASH ON A SLIPPERY HIGHWAY OUTSIDE NEW YORK CITY TODAY.

Tense Use the **present tense** whenever appropriate. Broadcast writers frequently use the present tense in their leads. Newspaper stories almost always contain the past tense throughout. The broadcast version of the Atlanta murders story used the verb *has pleaded,* which is the present perfect tense. The news wire story said that Williams *pleaded* innocent, which is the past tense.

The reason for using the present tense is simple. Broadcast news is supposed to give the listener or viewer the sense of immediacy, of events being covered as they happen. Sometimes, the present tense would sound silly, so the writer has to use the past tense. Evening news programs use the past tense in looking back on events that occurred during the day.

If the mayor announced at a noon news conference that he will not seek re-election, the radio news account would begin this way:

Mayor George Grogan **says** he will not seek re-election. The mayor **made** his intention clear at noon today in a news conference. He **said** he wants to go back to running the family business.

Notice the present tense in the first sentence. The tense then switches to the past in the next two sentences when it describes the actual news conference statement. The logic behind using the present tense in the lead sentence is that his statement still holds true at the time of broadcast. The present tense does not violate the truth.

In its seventh "World in Brief" of the day, the UPI's broadcast news staff wrote these leads on some of the news items:

Present tense
> Portuguese air traffic controllers **are** engaged in a two-day boycott of U.S. flights in sympathy with the walkout by American controllers.

Present tense
> A survey done by the University of Michigan **says** American consumers feel much better about the economy than they did a year ago.

Present tense
> Country music star Willie Nelson reportedly **is** ill.

Present perfect tense
> Elvis Presley's manager, Colonel Tom Parker, **has** vehemently **denied** allegations he defrauded Presley.

Several items did begin with the past tense. The writer thought there was no alternative for these leads, called yesterday leads:

> Five hundred people **attended** a memorial service honoring Elvis Presley at Memphis State University yesterday.

> A youth evangelist and one hundred members of the First Assembly of God Church in Guthrie, Oklahoma, **made** a bonfire of rock music albums yesterday.

Incidentally, notice how short these leads are. They contain 22, 23, 8, 13, 15 and 25 words. Most newspaper leads run 30 to 35 words.

Although radio and television stations have staff members who report, write and broadcast news, much broadcast news originates from outside the station. Except for the networks, which have correspondents scattered over the world and in major U.S. cities, most stations rely on the AP and UPI for their national and foreign news and for much state and regional news.

This news is rewritten by broadcast news writers and put into broadcast form. Smaller stations usually subscribe to a broadcast wire and use the material just as it comes in. Large stations usually subscribe to both the AP and UPI news wires, and the writers rewrite wire copy for broadcast.

One reason bigger stations rewrite the news wires is that news directors prefer that their writers see the original story, before it has been filtered by a broadcast rewrite person at the wire service. The wire service rewrite may neglect an aspect of special interest to local listeners.

Yesterday first sentences: "People tune in expecting to hear the latest news, the later the better," says Mervin Block in his book, *Writing Broadcast News: Shorter, Sharper, Stronger.* "If you have to lead with a story that broke yesterday, try to update it so you can use a 'today.' Or use the present perfect tense. It expresses an action carried out before the present and completed at the present or an action begun in the past and continuing into the present. . . . A script musn't deceive listeners by substituting 'today' for 'yesterday,' and you musn't try to pass off yesterday's news as today's. Exercise ingenuity in figuring out how to write a first sentence without harking all the way back to yesterday."

Rewriting the Wires

Shortly after 9 o'clock one morning in August, the press association news wires began to move a story they marked "urgent." Two Navy jets had shot down two Libyan jet planes in a dogfight over the Mediterranean Sea. The U.S. Defense Department stated that the Soviet-made Libyan planes had attacked the F-14 fighter planes, which had fired back.

In the CBS newsroom in New York, Mervin Block was preparing the "Newsbreak" television newscast, which goes on at 11:57 a.m. As he watched the wires move the story, he knew that it could not be told in the 10 or 15 seconds each item on Newsbreak is usually allotted. By 10 a.m., the AP had moved three leads on the story, and by 10:30, the UPI was transmitting its fourth lead.

This was a big story. Did it mean Libya was planning to attack a neighboring country and wanted no U.S. surveillance? Was Libya's president eager to demonstrate his nation's defiance of the United States, which he had described as the most dangerous country on earth?

Block had to monitor the wires for developments. Because the story was going to take more than a couple of sentences to tell, he could not wait long before sitting down with the thousands of words of AP and UPI copy to draft his broadcast story.

The people involved with the program—producer, editor, anchor and writer—agreed that the story would be given 40 or 45 seconds, which is long for a **tell** story. This meant Block had to boil down the wire stories to about 135 words.

After taking one last look at the wire and ripping off the latest leads, he went to the typewriter and began to write. He had half an hour, but he had been thinking about the story since he saw the first "urgent." He knew that he had to tell CBS television viewers the essential facts—that U.S. planes had downed two Libyan jets.

"There are some things I would change now," Block says. "Maybe I would use plane instead of craft on the first page of copy.

"But in broadcasting there are no second chances. I was reading a book the other day with the title *Done in a Day,* about newspapers. It describes the work that has to be done, all in a day, to produce a newspaper. But in broadcasting, it's done in minutes, sometimes seconds."

Block says that he always looks for the short word and that he tries to write short sentences that conform to the S-V-O sentence structure. For example, at one point in the script he used *taking part* instead of *participating.*

His script is shown in figure 11.1.

The broadcast news writer has to keep in mind that the story is to be read aloud by someone. This means that the copy should be prepared in a certain way. Stations differ in their rules for copy preparation but here are some suggestions.

BLOCK'S COMMENTS	SCRIPT

BLOCK'S COMMENTS

This headline--admittedly a fragmentary sentence--gives the viewer a quick preview. The wire services said "off the coast of North Africa," but I jettisoned "the coast of" as needless. Near the top, I cite the source of the story. In broadcasting, attribution precedes assertion. Again, I took pains to name the source for the second assertion. My producer, however, might have thought the second sourcing was redundant, and he deleted it. Or he thought I was running long. Apparently, no reporter saw the dogfight, so we must make clear who told us. The wires quoted the Department of Defense, but I condensed it to "Pentagon," which has more punch. The wires also quoted the State Department; I reduced that to "Washington." We're constantly struggling for tighter scripts, even on two-hour newscasts. Although a viewer can't see quotation marks, I use them so the anchor can change his delivery. I use direct quotations seldom, and I say "quote" or "unquote" rarely.

After I gave the gist of the accusation, I reported the other side's response. And I tacked on a bit of background about the territorial claim. I couldn't take time to elaborate on the claim or to report on U.S.-Libyan relations. Nor did I waste time with name-dropping or name-calling. Until now, I hadn't identified the type of U-S jet. At 11:57 a.m., most of our viewers are probably housewives, and, chances are, few, if any, know an F-14 from an F-4 or even a 4-F. The wires said the Nimitz is nuclear-powered, but I saw no need to waste words about its propulsion. The AP said the encounter was "60 nautical miles" off Libya. I know that a nautical mile is about a mile and a seventh, which would make it nearly 70 miles. I wrote "almost"; years ago, my editor on the CBS Evening News told me an anchor can get a better grasp

SCRIPT

A jet battle off North Africa: The Pentagon says two Libyan jets fighters attacked two U-S Navy F-14 jets over the Mediterranean today. and the ~~Pentagon says the~~ Navy jets shot down both Libyan craft. Washington says the attack against the U-S jets was ''unprovoked'' and that it took place in ''international air space over international waters.'' Libya says the U-S jets violated air space over its waters, but Washington does not recognize Libya's territorial claim. The U-S jets, Ef-fourteen Tomcats from the carrier Nimitz, were taking part in Sixth fleet exercises. The Navy says its jets were almost seventy miles off Libya when the Soviet-made Libyan jets fired at them.

(MORE)

Figure 11.1 Mervin Block explains how he chose the few words allowed him to convey the pertinent facts of the news story within the 45-second time limit.

Figure 11.1 *Continued*

on "almost." That editor also told me, repeatedly, that viewers are only half-listening. So I strive for simplicity. My maxim: Make it minimal. That's one reason that in the first sentence I didn't mention "F-14." But the director dug up a photo of an F-14, so he prevailed upon the producer to insert "F-14" high up. He obliged, and I was shot down.

The Navy says neither of its planes was hit. The State Department has protested, and it warned Libya against any new attack.

Copy Preparation

Name or initials of writer in lower right-hand corner.
Slug of story in upper left-hand corner.
Time the story takes to run is placed above slug.
Date in lower left-hand corner.

Use wide margins in preparing radio copy. The margins are normally set for 45 to 50 units and the length of lines is kept as uniform as possible. Depending on the speed of the anchor, each line will take about three seconds to read. Knowing this, the anchor can estimate how long it will take to read the story.

Television copy is prepared on two-thirds or half of the right-hand side of the page. The left-hand side is used for instructions, such as the name of the anchor or correspondent and whether the copy will be read over a video-tape (*VO* for voice over).

Each page is numbered and slugged at the top. The word *more* is written and circled at the bottom of pages of stories that are continued.

Each page should end with a complete sentence. If the page ends in the middle of a sentence, the anchor will be forced to pause as he or she reaches for the next sheet of copy.

So much for the basics of preparing copy. Next, some rules about writing style.

Style Rules

These rules have been used by broadcast news writers for many years to avoid confusion for the announcer reading the copy and to help the listener quickly grasp what he or she hears:

Numbers are spelled out.
Abbreviations are not used.
Titles are placed before names.
Initials of agencies and organizations are not used unless they are widely known.
Quotes must be clearly introduced as direct quotes. "As the senator put it," "In the words of the president," "To quote the prime minister. . . ."

News Up-to-the Minute

News Center. Fast-breaking news from around the world funnels into the newsroom just before the "World News Tonight" with Peter Jennings is to go on the air. Some of the news is from the ABC television news staff, and other material is from the wire services that the network subscribes to. Editors cull the vast flow for the few items that will be used. *Capital Cities/ABC, Inc.*

On Location. Anchorman Dan Rather reads the latest returns during the presidential primary. For big stories like this, networks will sometimes locate their key people on the scene. Major news events—disasters, airline crashes, and the like— are often given blanket coverage by television. Even local stations are now able to give on-the-scene reports because of the new satellite technology. *CBS News.*

Writing Guidelines

We have already seen that broadcast news is written in simple, conversational language. The sentences are short, and they are usually in the S-V-O form.

Every word has a purpose. Broadcast news is timed to the word. Avoid using lengthy phrases and clauses to begin sentences. Get right to the point. When a source is being used, put it at the beginning of the sentence. Use action verbs. Stay away from adjectives and adverbs unless they are essential.

The HELP WANTED NEWS section of *Broadcasting* magazine lists the qualifications of people the stations seek. Here are some phrases from these advertisements: top-notch writer; best writing and production skills; a reporter who can do journalism; crisp, clear writing; journalist first, and on-air talent second; strong writing abilities.

Introductory phrase

Avoid: Stressing the increased number of cars on campus, the Student Council has asked for more parking spaces near dormitories.

Improved: The Student Council wants more parking spaces near student dormitories.

Attribution

Avoid: There are two cars for every parking space, says Student Council President Tom Jarrett.

Improved: Student Council President Tom Jarrett says there are two cars for every parking space.

Action verb

Avoid: The Council was unanimous in its vote for the proposal.

Improved: The Council voted unanimously for the proposal.

Adjective

Avoid: Dean Albert Levine reacted with strong criticism of the vote.

Improved: Dean Albert Levine criticized the vote. (Or: Dean Albert Levine condemned the vote.)

Leads A listener should not be overwhelmed with a long lead to a story. Complex stories can be introduced with a general statement, such as:

> The parking-space issue has heated up. Dean Albert Levine said this afternoon. . . .

> The Russians want no part in the U.S. plan for feeding the hungry of the world. Soviet leaders said. . . .

Do not begin a story with the name of an unknown person. If you must, precede the name with the person's title or some identifying label. You can begin with a name if the person has what Block calls "star quality." That means the president, the pope, the governor of your state, a senator or congressman, your mayor.

For a story about the death of Robert Moses, who built many of the major highways in and out of New York City and a number of its major buildings, Block realized only New Yorkers would be familiar with the name, and then not all of them, as Moses had been out of public life for many years. He was writing for a network news program. Here is how he began the obituary:

> The man credited with building even more than the Pharaohs of Egypt—Robert Moses—died in a New York City suburb today at the age of 92.

Here the identifying label is an arresting description. People will listen.

Do not start a story with a quotation. The listener cannot see or hear quotation marks and may think the words are those of the broadcaster. Some writers start with a quote and their next sentence is "Those were the words of. . . ." or "This advice, warning, challenge came from. . . ." Block says the technique does not work because it confuses listeners.

Short Leads Keep Listeners Tuned In

Here is some advice the AP passes on to its broadcast writers about writing leads:

The shorter the better. The function of the broadcast lead is to capture the listener's interest by providing the essence of the story's status at that hour.

Don't summarize the day's major development in a long, complex sentence. Instead, provide a short and compelling reason for the listener to keep listening.

For example, when a long-delayed space shuttle mission was ended earlier, the story could have been written this way:

```
     Space agency officials have ordered a
Thursday landing for the space shuttle
``Columbia,'' cutting the mission by one
day in order to shorten the preparation
time for the next launch of the trouble-
plagued spaceship.
```

But consider how much more effective the story is written like this:

```
     They were late to work, and now
they're leaving early. The crew of
``Columbia,'' which finally got off the
launch pad 25 days late last weekend, is
now preparing to come home a day ahead of
schedule. Space agency officials say
moving the landing to Thursday morning
will give engineers an extra day to get
the shuttle ready for its next launch.
```

Note the use of the present tense and familiar terminology.

Storytelling Names make news in newspaper stories, but the fewer names in a broadcast story the better. Listeners are confused by lists of names and by a cast of characters in a story. The fewer people in a story, the clearer the story.

If Roger Grimstead, a spokesman for the governor, says something, simply write: The governor's office says. . . .

If the secretary of defense, Allen Weinstein, issues a comment in a story about the president's defense bill and there are already too many names, just write: The Pentagon commented that. . . .

Also, the fewer facts, the better. A newspaper story may have a major theme and two, three, even four secondary themes. The broadcast story should have a major theme and perhaps one other theme.

What It Takes

For those considering a career in broadcast journalism, the ability to write well under pressure is essential. A study by Professor Stephen Lamoreux of Colorado State University found that broadcast editors want writers who can write simple sentences in a conversational style, men and women who can write lively, colorful copy and who have imagination.

Mastery of the writing craft is not enough, says Block. "The writer has to have a wide knowledge. He or she should know what is going on in the world. Also, the writer should understand how things work—government, the criminal justice process, zoning boards, state government.

"The data bank in the writer's mind has to have a jillion bits of information because the writer must be able to retrieve a lot of data, and do it almost subconsciously."

For television reporters who do on-camera reports, the ability to organize a story mentally—that is, without a typewriter—is essential. Often, TV reporters covering breaking stories have to go on the air live.

The best way to do this, says John Chancellor, a veteran NBC-TV journalist, is to make a brief outline of what is to be said. "The whole story needn't be outlined," he says, "but the lead and the closing line should be settled." He says that a few minutes on an outline will pay off with "a very well organized piece of work."

The Key Is Reporting

At this time, it is worth remembering that writing is based on reporting. Good reporting makes for good writing. Good writing cannot make up for weak or lazy reporting.

When WCPO-TV in Cincinnati learned that a hospital orderly who was accused of killing one man was also involved in 20 other deaths at the hospital, it turned reporters loose on the story. "We worked very hard. We worked very carefully," said Terry Connelly, the general manager. "We spent many months on it."

The result was a half-hour newscast based on the station's three-month investigation. The reporters linked the orderly to a score of deaths. "No one else had done the legwork so we were three months ahead of everybody," said Jack Cahalan, the news director.

A grand jury investigation followed the newscast, and soon thereafter the orderly pleaded guilty to 24 murders and was connected to as many as 70 other deaths.

The Angel of Death, as he was described, was sentenced to three consecutive life sentences.

Summary

Broadcast writers try to follow these guidelines:
- **Use everyday language.** Instead of *impact on*, the writer uses *affect*. Instead of *interface*, the writer uses *match*.

- **Simplify complex stories.** One way to do this is to begin a story with some background material: "Last month, the city council decided to revise the city's zoning regulations. Last night, it adopted a new master plan that will affect all new commercial and residential development in the city." Another technique is the headline to introduce a story: "Schools are open again." This could begin a story about the settlement of a long teachers' strike.

- **Use short sentences.** The listener cannot follow a long sentence. Any sentence over 25 words should be broken into two sentences. One way to cut down on the number of words in a sentence is to eliminate unnecessary words: *At this point in time* becomes *now, revenue enhancement* is changed to *taxes,* and such redundancies as *totally destroyed, cold, hard facts* and *first annual* are corrected. Introductory phrases and clauses are dropped. Stick to the S-V-O sentence construction.

- **Favor the present tense.** Give the reader the sense of immediacy by using the present tense for leads when possible.

- **Keep items brief.** Find the major theme of the event and concentrate on it.

Suggested Reading

Barnouw, Erik. *Tube of Plenty: The Evolution of American Television.* New York: Oxford University Press, 1975.

Block, Mervin. *Writing Broadcast News: Shorter, Sharper, Stronger.* Chicago: Bonus Books, 1987.

Donaldson, Sam. *Hold On, Mr. President.* New York: Random House, Inc., 1987.

Persico, Joseph E. *Edward E. Murrow: An American Original.* New York: McGraw-Hill, 1988.

Savitch, Jessica. *Anchorwoman.* New York: G.P. Putnam's Sons, 1982.

Sperber, Ann M. *Murrow: His Life and Times.* New York: Freundlich Books, 1986.

12

Visual Reporting

Photojournalists show the human condition— people at play, men at war; our joys, our sorrows. In this famous photograph, Dorothea Lange showed more than the migrant peapicker mother of seven, destitute in California, aged at 32. This is the despair of the Great Depression of the Thirties. This is the face of hopelessness.
The Library of Congress.

Looking Ahead

The photojournalist uses the camera to give us pictures that provide information and insights about people, events and ideas. The photojournalist sees and portrays the world in visual terms.

Good news and feature photos are truthful, informative, interesting and have significance or impact. They may be educational or entertaining. They are technically sound.

Photojournalists know people, how they live, work and play. Their photographs reflect this sensitivity and understanding. The picture-storyteller also is a master of his or her equipment, knowing just which lens, shutter speed and aperture are appropriate for each shot.

From earliest times, people have used pictures to record their thoughts and experiences—the hunt etched on the walls of caves, mourning women scratched on pottery, ceremonies painted on wood and canvas. Modern men and women make pictures, too, millions of them. We also place them on our walls. And we send them off to speak to distant friends and relatives. Pictures tell our stories. They are a universal language.

The Picture Is Universal

Pictures extend our reach. They allow us to see events that have passed into history, to travel to places we will never visit, to experience the emotions of others. They communicate feelings, set moods. Dorothea Lange's photo of the mother and children of a migrant labor family that opens this chapter takes us back half a century to the Depression to show us the haunting face of a young mother, aged by adversity, looking into a future that seems without hope.

Today's picture-storytellers work for newspapers, magazines and television stations. Called photojournalists, they combine the skills of journalist and photographer. The news writer seeks to capture the essence of the event in words; the photojournalist uses the camera to capture the essence of the event in visual terms. On small dailies and weekly newspapers, reporters are expected to take photographs to illustrate their stories.

Photographs reveal as well as inform. They let us live with people different from ourselves, experience events half a world away and those too small and too fast for the eye and brain to capture in their natural state. They hold for us the leap of the ballet dancer, the fetus in the mother's womb, the finish of a close race.

The photojournalist's picture enables us to understand and emotionally identify with the event. By using scene or setting and the expression, gesture and body language of those in the picture, the photojournalist communicates with us at a personal level. Sometimes, a news photograph comes to symbolize the issues and the problems of a period in history.

The photographs in the textbook tell us something about what makes a good picture, and they reveal something about what it takes to be a good photojournalist.

A good picture is first a truthful portrayal of an event. It is a pictorial record of the event the photojournalist is reporting. Beyond this, the good photograph can be described as interesting, informative, educational. It may be entertaining.

The good photograph has impact; it has a message. It is technically sound and aesthetically right. The good picture makes proper use of light and dark, the horizon, curves and diagonals. There are logic and rhythm in the picture. It has a point of interest.

U.S. Navy Photograph

Arthur Rothstein, The Library
of Congress

Morris Berman, Pittsburgh
Post-Gazette

Pictures played a major role in the birth and growth of the *Daily News,* once the top circulation daily newspaper in the country. The founder of the *News,* Joseph Medill Patterson, publisher of the *Chicago Tribune,* was an avid moviegoer. He was so impressed with the impact of the motion picture that he established the *News,* in 1919, as a "picture newspaper."

Some photographs reach us in the same way that a song or symphony, a novel or short story touch us. The news photo of the death throes of the battleship *Arizona* at Pearl Harbor portrays a humbled United States and the beginning of a struggle for survival with a powerful adversary.

Arthur Rothstein's picture of a farmer and his sons making their way through swirling sands became a symbol of the struggle of the country's farmers when the blowing soil made the Southwest into a dust bowl. The barefoot boys, the younger one shielding his eyes against the stinging sands, the father's shapeless clothing and the hopelessness of his slouch tell the story. Photographs like this one made the public aware of the need for rehabilitation of rural areas and led Congress to adopt new farm legislation.

Morris Berman's photo of the sacked quarterback transcends the game and the season. The sagging body and the agonized face tell us the athlete knows his speed and agility are gone, that the body will no longer respond.

Reporting Visually

Clearly, the photojournalist has to be able to recognize the news and to freeze in visual form the news point.

In addition, the student thinking of a career in photojournalism should have a creative streak, Rothstein said, and a practical bent as well. The photojournalist has to know something about photographic equipment to be able to make minor repairs. A knowledge of light, optics and the chemistry of photography are indispensable.

Rothstein said the photojournalist must have the talent and ability to portray events and ideas in "unusual visual terms." "Most important," he said, "is the knowledge of human beings and how they live, work and play."

That knowledge must be built on sensitivity, the capacity to identify with what is being photographed. "Every photographer in each situation becomes a vicarious participant in the event," says Michael Geissinger of the photography faculty at the Rochester Institute of Technology. The news photo of the woman awaiting word about the men trapped in a Centralia, Ill., mine shaft is "an example of the emotion a photographer must experience in order to produce a profound picture," Geissinger says.

Anguish. Sometimes, the reaction of those on the scene tells us as much, or more, about the event than a photo of the event itself. Gary Hart's wife looks on as he announces his withdrawal from the presidential primaries following revelations about his escapades with a young model. Ken Papaleo of the *Rocky Mountain News* stationed himself where he, alone among the photographers, could shoot this scene. In the other photograph, Sam Caldwell of the *St. Louis Post-Dispatch* found a face on the crowd of friends and relatives who waited at a mine entrance after an explosion trapped miners. The toll was 111 dead.
Photo by Ken Papaleo of the Rocky Mountain News. Used with permission.

The photograph portrays the grief and tension of one woman. But it represents all those who look fearfully into the unknown. The harsh and cutting light, the "pitiful hands that don't seem to know what to do with each other," as Claude Cookman says, the eyes focused on some awful scene as much in her mind as in front of her—all these prepare us for the awful news of death underground. The explosion took the lives of 111 miners.

Breaking News

When Ken Papaleo was assigned to cover a news conference at which Gary Hart announced his withdrawal as a Democratic presidential candidate, Papaleo was able to capture the anguish on the face of Mrs. Hart for *Rocky Mountain News* readers. The picture was all the more powerful because Hart withdrew as the result of revelations about his relations with a young woman.

Lucky shot? Hardly. Other photographers stationed themselves in front of the lectern from which Hart spoke. Papaleo picked a spot off the side, where there were no other photographers, so that he could capture Hart and his wife. His picture of Mrs. Hart was an exclusive. Incidentally, when Hart later re-entered the race, many photographers turned their cameras on Mrs. Hart.

Sam Caldwell of the *St. Louis Post-Dispatch* used the same idea—the reaction shot—when he was assigned to cover a major mine disaster in Centralia, Ill. His picture of a woman looking intently and fearfully at the mine site has become a photographic classic.

Helping the Reader

Cookman, a picture and graphics editor with AP Wirephoto and *The Louisville Times* and *The Miami Herald,* says, "Every photo incorporates at least two aspects: content and pictorial treatment." For newspapers, the content must be significant.

Pictorial treatment involves "training the eye and mastering the technical side of the medium in order to organize reality into a visually interesting photograph," Cookman says. This process involves the photojournalist in selection—choosing what is significant, paring away the extraneous. Using light, composition, camera angle and space, the photojournalist is able to help the reader to recognize the significant.

The starting point for the photojournalist is the same as it is for the news writer: Know what you want to say and use the techniques and craft to say it. That is, the photojournalist must be clear about the point he or she is trying to make in the photograph and must have command of the technical aspects of photography.

Just as the news writer has the help of modern technology to speed his or her thoughts from fingertips to printed form, the photojournalist has versatile cameras, lenses of amazing diversity, an array of film and a modern laboratory to help tell the story in picture form.

"But these techniques are used only to obtain more freedom, to make the mechanics of taking a picture so simple that they (photojournalists) can concentrate on the subject, the idea and the event," says Rothstein.

Techniques and technology are not ends in themselves. Fritz Lang, the movie director, declared as a moral of technique, "Every camera movement must have a motivation, a reason."

Concentrate on Subject

Prep and Shoot. The photojournalist is able to hit it off with people quickly, to gain their trust so they are willing to be photographed. Photojournalists say they combine the talents of the psychologist and the sociologist. Here, Karen Leff, a young freelance photographer, chats with a merchant, gains her confidence, then shoots her picture. Leff graduated from Boston University School of Public Communication in photojournalism and works as a freelancer. "Since freelance photography is not consistent enough to pay the rent, it means working in a job, usually not related to photography, part-time," Leff says. "One of the reasons I stick with freelance photography is that each assignment means a new adventure and a new set of personalities, locations and events."

Advice for the Beginner

For the beginner, the task of learning begins not with shooting yards of film and spending hours in the darkroom. The starting point is internal—thinking, feeling and looking before the shutter is snapped. Know what it is you want to show, the experts say, and then examine what you have done with that in mind. Ask yourself, what do I want the print to say?

"Simplicity is a virtue in any type of communication," Cookman says. "It's also a good place to start in photography. Begin by recording what you see that interests you, and most often that will be people." He suggests practicing on one person, then trying to capture the interaction of two people.

"After you've learned to get them to relax and to stop worrying that your camera will make them look ugly or ridiculous, then concentrate on telling as much about them as you can through expression, body language, setting, clothing and other props." Try to record a range of emotions and experiences.

"To tell a complete story, make sure there is action in all your pictures. For every subject let there be a visual verb," Cookman recommends.

The Photo Editor

Photographers are assigned by the picture editor, who tries to select the photographer who will do the best job on the particular assignment. Some photographers specialize in sports; others do their best work on feature assignments. The photographer may accompany the reporter. If they have time, the two will discuss picture possibilities before leaving the office. On the scene, they may also exchange picture ideas, though the reporter often is too busy reporting and the photographer too involved in shooting.

Back in the office, the photo editor looks over the negatives or prints. The final decision as to which shots are used, how they are cropped and printed is the editor's.

Not only must the photo editor have an eye for the photograph that best symbolizes the event, but the editor must also be able to resist the dramatic picture that distorts the event.

If it is true that journalism is history in a hurry, then it follows that sometimes the historical or universal is overlooked in the rush to deadline. This is the backdrop to an interesting story about Berman's photograph of Y.A. Tittle, the New York Giants quarterback.

Berman was standing near the Giants' 35-yard line when Tittle dropped back to pass. "It had been a dull contest," Berman recalls. "But since Tittle had a reputation as a great passer, I trained my lens on him." As Tittle let the ball go, a 270-pound defensive end slammed into him. Tittle crumpled to the ground, unable to see his pass snared by a Steeler defender, who ran into the end zone.

"I just kept shooting Tittle," Berman says. "He was bleeding, and his helmet had been torn off. He was unable to stand. Then he just bowed his head as if something very serious had happened."

The photo, made with a 200mm lens at f8 at 1/1000, was passed over by Berman's photo editor. "I couldn't believe it," Berman recalls thinking.

"For some reason he preferred the shots of Tittle surrounded by his teammates and being carried off the field." The photograph of Tittle on his knees was picked up by other publications and won many awards and hangs in the Football Hall of Fame.

As does the news writer, the photojournalist moves through four steps in handling a story: **The Process**

- Idea generation
- Planning, preparing
- Observation
- Writing

The photographer develops an idea or concept; decides on the appropriate lenses, speed and aperture and selects locations from which to shoot; decides when to shoot, and then does the darkroom work that will enhance the story's point.

For a feature, the photojournalist moves carefully and deliberately through these stages. On a breaking news event, the thinking and the decisions come quickly, seemingly instinctively.

Considerable planning went into a series of photographs by Robert E. Kollar, chief photographer of the Tennessee Valley Authority. For a study—the idea—about the economics of Appalachia for *Forum,* a TVA publication, Kollar planned to show a proud people caught in poverty. He wanted to animate the article, he said, to "bring it to life" in a sensitive, non-sensational photo essay. **Poverty in Appalachia**

The community of Roses Creek, Tenn., was selected as representative. Kollar realized he would need the confidence of the people so that he could photograph them. A TVA employee who had worked in the area accompanied Kollar and helped him to gain the trust of Roses Creek residents.

"Roses Creek is one of many communities that grew up around the Clear Fork River on the Tennessee-Kentucky border when mining was in its heyday," Kollar wrote in an article accompanying his photographs.

"Now most of the mines are gone—and the good jobs with them. Their passing has left scars on the people and the land. The carved-up earth of unclaimed strip mines stares out from the sides of mountains like open wounds. Few people have jobs, and many go hungry. They wear secondhand clothes and drive worn-out cars. Many homes don't have electricity, running water, or indoor plumbing. . . ."

Small home gardens are important to the people of Roses Creek. "If we hadn't had our garden, we really would have gone hungry," Letta Casey told Kollar, who took several photos of women in their gardens.

Appalachia Mountain Family

Letta Casey was one of the people photographer Robert E. Kollar selected as representative of the people in the Appalachia mountain communities. After he gained their trust, Kollar said, they felt comfortable with his cameras and equipment. "They were even eager to tell their story and to work with me," he said. For a photo of Casey and her two children, Kollar asked them to stand together on their porch. "I was trying to illustrate some of the family's surroundings. I wanted the setting to be as natural as possible. The whole idea of the series of photos was to document the conditions the people live in without being degrading to those people." In the family photo, Kollar used a 35mm lens with 1/125 shutter speed and an opening of f11. Tri-X film was rated at 400. *Photos by Robert E. Kollar, Tennessee Valley Authority. Used with permission.*

Kollar said he found Casey "a strong-willed person, full of determination, despite her limited financial means. She may be poor in terms of money, but not in spirit. I wanted to show this.

"We were standing in front of her house talking about her hopes and plans for her two sons when her face took on a determined expression. I knew if I worked fast I had my photograph.

"In anticipation of this very thing, I had put my 180mm, f2.8 lens on one of my three cameras, a Nikon FE2."

Kollar shot half a dozen frames, checking the exposure between shots.

"This all happened in a matter of probably five seconds or less. Then, the expression was gone, and I never saw it again."

Kollar used a motor drive, and he opened the lens a little wider than the meter indicated because the light was coming from the side and back, just where he wanted it.

"I had to burn the hair and the headband slightly, but the photo turned out exactly as I had envisioned it. The highlight on her hair added drama, and there was still plenty of light on her face. The headband added interest to this photo because it seemed so out of place in this setting."

Daisy Pierce and Her Okra

Roses Creek people do not have enough income to feed their family nutritious food, and their home gardens are vital in meeting their food needs. TVA helped the people start their gardens and taught them how to maintain plots. Daisy Pierce grows okra and other crops. "Why, I share with them, you know," she says. "And then if they have something I am out of, well, then they share it with me."

The photograph was tricky, Kollar says. Pierce's face was in shadow and the background was bright, a three-stop difference in the brightness levels. "To overcome this condition without destroying the mood and feeling of the photo, I used just a little fill light bounced from a flash card bent backward atop my strobe. The primary exposure was basically for the sunlight, although I backed off slightly—opened up some." The exposure was 1/250 at f11 with Tri-X.

Photo by Robert E. Kollar, Tennessee Valley Authority. Used with permission.

The Camera

Most photojournalists use the 35mm camera, a single-lens reflex (SLR) with a fast lens. The same lens is used for viewing the scene and exposing the film; what you see in the viewfinder is what you will see in the print. The camera usually has a built-in exposure meter that measures the light on the scene and allows the photographer to determine how to expose the film. Some cameras are automated so that the proper amount of light is automatically let in.

Aperture

The lens opening or aperture affects the amount of light reaching the film. The lens opening is measured in numbers preceded by the letter "f," called f-stops. The smaller numbers have the wider apertures, letting in more light than the larger numbers: f1.4 lets in twice as much light as f2. Each lens setting on the camera indicates half the light of the preceding setting: f1.4, 2, 2.8, 4, 5.6, 8, 11, 16, 22, 32, 45.

The other element that controls the amount of light that strikes the film is the shutter speed.

Shutter Speed

The shutter speed affects the length of the exposure, the amount of time the shutter is open. The shutter openings are measured in fractions of a second. The markings of 15, 30, 60, 125, 250, 500, 1000 refer to 1/15, 1/30, etc. of a second. The B marking allows the photographer to keep the shutter open as long as the shutter release is pressed down.

The correct exposure is a combination of lens opening and shutter speed. Since much of the photographer's work involves action in poorly lit areas, the shutter speed usually is 125 and the lens opening is wide, f2.8 or f4. The shutter speed of 125 or 250 may not stop the action and it may have to be 500 or 1000. To obtain sufficient light, the lens opening has to be made wider—f1.4 or thereabouts. But the wide lens opening cuts down on the depth of field, the area of sharpness. Compromises and adjustments are always being made.

Freezing Action. After two days of steady rain, Sid Brown, a photographer for the *Schenectady* (N.Y.) *Gazette* decided to check for flooding along a creek that flows through two counties served by his newspaper. Officials were worried about damage to bridges. He found nothing to shoot in one area and decided to move upstream. "Without any warning, we heard a loud, resounding bang and the creaking groan of steel beams crashing and bending," Brown recalled. Part of a bridge had given way. Brown knew the rest of the span would crumble and stationed himself nearby. "After about 15 minutes, the vigil paid off, when the last section let go with a roar I hope never to hear again." He caught the crumbling bridge in a series of shots with a Nikon F3, his 35-105 zoom lens set at 105mm. He shot at 1/1000, f5.6 on Tri-X.

Depth of field refers to the area between the nearest and the farthest points in the picture that are in sharp focus. Depth of field is affected by three factors that the photographer can control:

Depth of Field

> Lens opening: Smaller the f-stop number, shorter the depth of field.
> Focal length: Shorter the focal length, deeper the depth of field.
> Lens-to-subject distance: Farther away, deeper the depth of field.

In Berman's photo of the football player, the viewer's eye is directed to the player because the background is purposely out of focus. At the same time, the background is clear enough to tell us we are at a game.

Most cameras have a depth of field scale on the lens that tells the photographer the extent of the area of sharpness at each f-stop. By using this scale, the photographer can deliberately put areas out of focus, such as a distracting background, or make sure some parts of the scenes are sharp.

Don Ultang, a Pulitzer Prize-winning photojournalist and a photography instructor at Drake University, suggests using the "one-third rule" to make a quick determination for the point of focus so that the various elements in a picture are sharp.

1. Estimate the distance between the nearest and farthest subjects.
2. Take one-third the difference between the two figures.
3. Add the one-third figure to the nearest distance and set this figure on the distance scale.

For example: To take a picture where the nearest subject is five feet away and the farthest 20 feet, the difference is 15 feet. One third of 15 is five. Add the difference (five) to the distance to nearest subject (five) and set the camera at 10 feet.

For grab shots in quick-shooting situations, Ultang often will preset his distance scale at 12 or 13 feet. (The one-third rule does not work in low-light situations with wide-open apertures.)

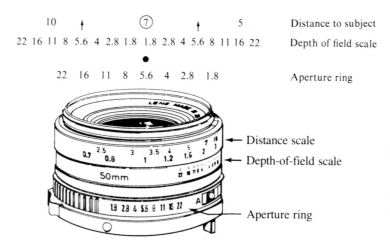

Distance to subject

Depth of field scale

Aperture ring

Distance scale

Depth-of-field scale

Aperture ring

Figure 12.1 Depth of Field. The area of sharpness, the depth of field, can be determined for different apertures by reading the depth of field scale on the lens barrel. When the lens opening or aperture is set at f5.6, for example, and the distance is set at 7 feet, the area of sharpness on the scale is from about 6 to 9 feet, as indicated here.

Pinpoint Sharp. Mike McClure was able to close his lens to f16 because of the bright sun shining the day he set out to shoot fresh snow in the Tetons. The f16 lens opening meant he was able to keep in sharp focus the brush in the foreground, the moose in the middle area, and the snow-covered mountains in the background, giving the photo a three-dimensional feel. McClure used a film with a speed of ASA 125 to produce a negative free of graininess, which made for a clearer enlargement.

One of the adjustments photojournalists are always making uses the concept of reciprocity. Since the apertures (f-stops) double or halve the amount of light reaching the film and the shutter speeds do the same thing, they can be adjusted together to accomplish the purpose the photographer has in mind. If the reading is f4 at 125th of a second and the photographer must stop high-speed action, the shutter speed will be set at 250, which lets in half the amount of light at 125. To compensate for this, the lens is opened one stop to f2.8, which lets in twice as much light as f4.

But f2.8 has a narrower depth of field than f4, and if depth of field is essential for the photo, the f-stop will have to be left at f4 and the shutter speed at 125, which may result in a blurred image of the action. The photographer must decide what he or she wants the picture to show.

Reciprocity

Lenses are usually described in terms of focal length—normal, long and short. The 50mm lens is considered the normal lens because it most nearly duplicates human vision. The long lens, 100mm and up, is known as the telephoto lens. This lens brings distant objects close and compresses the scene. The longer the lens, the greater the magnification and the narrower the angle of coverage. The short lens is known as the wide-angle lens. It takes in more of the scene than the other lenses.

The shorter the focal length, the greater the area that can be photographed and the smaller the objects will appear. The photographer can move the camera toward or away from the scene, or he or she can change lenses to bring about the effect desired. Sometimes, the simplest step is to change the lens. But each lens has limitations as well as advantages.

Lenses

Focal Length

Normal The normal lens is usually designed with large maximum lens openings, which permit photos in low-level light situations. Distant objects are small; objects outside the area directly ahead, 47 degrees in the angle of view, are not registered on the film.

Limitations

Long Distant objects are increased in size, but the area photographed is smaller the longer the lens that is used: 85mm, 29 degrees; 200mm, 12 degrees; 1000mm, 2.5 degrees. Also, the longer the focal length the shallower the depth of field. Since the larger image magnifies slight hand movements, a fast shutter speed is necessary when the camera is hand held. (A practical guide: Use a shutter speed at least as fast as the reciprocal of the focal length—with a 200mm lens, shoot at 1/250 or faster.)

What Lenses Put on Film

Magnification. The size of the object on the film depends on the focal length of the lens. As the focal length increases, the size of the object on the film increases. A 135mm lens—a telephoto lens—will produce an image almost three times the size of the image produced by a 50mm lens, which is called the normal lens. A 300mm telephoto lens will produce an image six times that produced on the film by the normal (50mm) lens. Also, as the focal length increases the angle of view narrows and a smaller area is encompassed in the photograph. To photograph a wide area, a wide angle lens is used. While giving a larger area in the photograph, the wide angle lens also makes the size of the object smaller. These photographs were taken from the same spot using four different lenses.

28 mm—wide angle

50 mm—normal

135 mm—telephoto

300 mm—telephoto

Lenses. The fisherman on the left was photographed with a 135mm lens, the one on the right with a 28mm lens. The 135mm telephoto shot tells us about the uninviting weather that brings out only the most intrepid surf fisherman. The shot on the right with the wide-angle lens tells another story, that of the loneliness of the winter fisherman.

Short This lens is useful in crowded areas where the photographer is close to the scene. The shorter the focal length the greater the depth of field. The photographer can preset the wide-angle lens and be sure distant and close subjects will be in focus. However, wide-angle lenses when used close to the subject will make the subject disproportionately larger than objects of the same size in the background.

Photographers use a variety of other lenses:

Zoom: Combines a range of focal lengths in one lens. Zoom lenses have the advantage of eliminating the need to change lenses. They are not practical in extremely low light conditions.

Macro: Is used for close-ups. This lens is corrected to eliminate the distortion of subjects close to the lens.

Fisheye: Has an extended wide angle of view; some of them extend to 180 degrees. Objects close to the lens and those far away are distorted. The image appears as a circle instead of the usual rectangle.

Different situations call for different lenses. Since the long lens compresses space, a telephoto lens is often used to convey a sense of cramped space. To photograph a person's face, the normal lens on a camera close to the subject would make the person's features nearest the camera (nose and forehead) disproportionately large. A medium-long lens (85–135mm) would give better results. Also, the longer lens would allow the photographer to be farther away from the subject, which would lessen the person's discomfort.

Without . . . with. Filters are used to enhance effects the photographer wants to achieve. A yellow, orange or red filter will bring up clouds and darken the sky. Filters are used to correct picture contrast. A yellow-green filter is used for outdoor portraits. Photographers shooting news pictures do not bother with filters since most of these shots are taken on the run with flash. But for picture essays and with feature stories filters can be used. These photographs were taken on the French River in Ontario, Canada, for a feature story the author was preparing.

Black and white film does not respond to the colors around us the same way that the human eye does. If you have ever taken a black and white photograph of a beautiful blue sky with powder-blue clouds you know how true that is. The sky looks a uniform and washed-out white. A filter would have solved the problem.

Filters

Filters for black and white film correct picture contrast. The proper filter would have brought up the clouds—a yellow, orange or red. A yellow-green filter is useful for portraits outdoors as it will correct skin tones and bring out facial expressions. For indoor portraits under lights, a green filter does the same work.

The ultraviolet filter is used for pictures of the seaside. It absorbs ultraviolet rays and makes landscapes sharp and clear. It also eliminates fogginess.

For dramatic effect, a red filter makes white even whiter on a dark background.

On spot news assignments indoors, no filters are necessary. But on feature assignments when there is plenty of time, filters pay off with dramatic shots.

Film is described by its speed—its sensitivity to light. Fast films have speeds of ASA 400 and up. The faster the film, the less exposure or light needed to produce an image. A medium-speed film would be ASA 125; slow film, ASA 32. Fast films allow the photographer to take pictures in dimly lit areas, but there is an increase in graininess and a decline in the contrast and in the sharpness of the image in the print. Fast film makes large prints grainy, even mottled. The slow or medium-fast film shows more detail.

Film

In some situations, even ASA 400 is not fast enough. Photographers can "push" a film to as much as ASA 1600 by using a high-energy developer for their film. When Karen Leff was photographing boxers at a gymnasium where the lighting was dim, she pushed her film to 1600 so that she could use a fast shutter speed and the hands of the boxers would not be blurred. She shot the picture of the boxer taping his hands at 1/125th of a second at f2.8. Had she used the film at its normal speed, 400, she would have had to use a shutter speed of 1/30th, too slow to stop the motion. If she wanted to retain the shutter speed of 1/125th, she could have opened the lens to let in more light. But that would have meant an aperture of f1.4, which was not available on the 100mm telephoto lens she was using.

Increasingly, photographers are shooting color film as newspapers print more and more color photos to attract readers. "How can you tell he's bleeding if it's in black and white?" a photographer asks.

There is another reason photographers are using color film. It is more economical to send out one photographer with color film than two, one with black and white and the other with color. Since it is easy to make black and white prints from color negative film, nothing is lost and a great deal is gained when the camera is loaded with color film.

Pushed. For this picture of a boxer in a dimly lit gymnasium, Karen Leff needed a fast shutter speed and a lens opening wider than her 400 film permitted. She was able to take the picture by pushing her film to a speed of 1600.

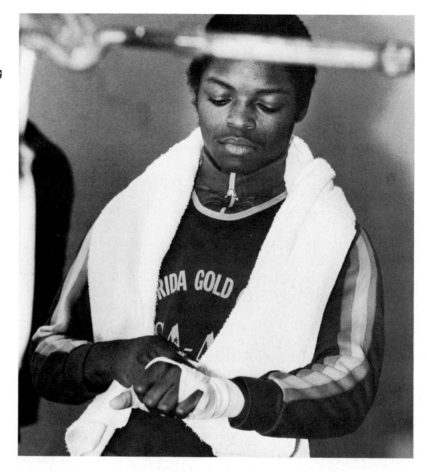

At the Associated Press, black and white film is a thing of the past. Hal Buell, assistant managing editor for news photos, says that in most instances the prints made from color negative film are even better than those enlarged from black and white negatives.

Technology Rampant

Faster and faster film. Point and shoot cameras. New cameras, new lenses every month. There seems no end to the advances in photography. And yet . . .

Some of the most memorable pictures were taken with the simplest equipment, even with a shoebox with a pinhole. Some early equipment was so bulky and heavy it had to be carried by pack animals when early photographers went into the countryside to photograph.

The key element is obvious, the photographer. No mechanism has yet replaced the man or woman who is able to see clearly the faces and events of the times and who can transfer these insights to film. The photographer records the happenings of the day—accidents, fires, wars, birth and death. The

Social Document. Some pictures do more than supplement the news story. They provide new insights, new ways of looking at the world. The photograph can capture a face or a scene with arresting impact. Lewis Hine's photograph of a child at work in a southern cotton mill is simple, yet devastating. At first, says Cookman, there is nothing so terrible about the scene depicted. ''The factory does not seem particularly dangerous, and we cannot see the girl's face closely enough to tell whether she is fatigued, malnourished or otherwise ravaged by her experience,'' he says. But what is not shown is important: ''Our associations of what a good childhood should be like—education and play and freedom from drudgery.'' The picture was taken in 1908, when children labored in mines and factories. This knowledge combines with our emotional reaction to the picture to make it a powerful statement.

The photo is pictorially simple. The long loom directs the eye to the picture's focal point, the girl. The strong light from the window not only sets up an interesting pattern but reminds us of the world outside, where children play. The narrow corridor seems to imprison the child.

Hine, a documentary photographer who took pictures of immigrants at Ellis Island and children and adults laboring in American industry, is considered by some to be the country's greatest photographer. His social commentaries on film of children in factories helped lead to changes in child labor laws. Hine took 15,000 pictures from 1900 to 1940. Recognition came too late. He died a pauper in 1940.
Lewis Hine, International Museum of Photography at George Eastman House.

photographer also has recorded our problems. "The camera has a devastating effectiveness in portraying evils," said Frank Luther Mott, a noted historian of journalism. "It is the best crusader of our times. Think of any abuse—social, economic, political—and sound and honest pictures which will bring the evils to our eyes suggest themselves immediately."

Lewis Hine's photograph of a child working in a cotton mill still speaks to us today, though it was taken more than 80 years ago. And despite the limits of the photographic technology then the picture is technically excellent.

Photographers continue to show us the problems society grapples with. Some of Jeff McAdory's photographs that accompanied the stories of poverty in Tunica, Miss., describe the timeless as well as the timely, as in his photograph of a child and her doll.

Photo Essay

The photo essay or picture story is a series of pictures with a common theme that documents an event or tells a story about a person or a place. While single photos are effective, the series can reveal subtleties and make distinctions that one photograph cannot.

Usually, the picture story is built around the strongest single photo, the picture that describes or defines the theme. The photographer keeps this in mind while shooting, as well as the necessity to take pictures that will make the display interesting and exciting. A wide-angle lens may be used for one shot, a telephoto for another. Pictures are taken from a variety of positions. Close-ups that focus on a single aspect of the subject vary the perspective. Called detailing, these close-in shots give the viewer an intimate relationship with the subject, and in some cases provide a view that would be difficult if not impossible otherwise.

The essay may use various lighting techniques—the light from windows, room light, silhouette.

The film is printed and the pictures cropped according to a layout that emphasizes the theme and presents the photos in varying sizes and shapes. The theme photo is placed in a dominant area and is surrounded by supporting photographs.

Hope Resides In The Young

A reporter-photographer team found poverty and ill health during their stay in Tunica, Miss., one of the poorest areas in the nation. The infant mortality rate was three times that of the middle-class white areas nearby, and 45 of 100 families lived in poverty. Despite the overwhelming problems, the journalists found hope among the people. This photograph by Jeff McAdory symbolized the hopes of many in the community—its children. The determination and strength in this child also was symbolic of the community.

Photo by Jeff McAdory, The Commercial Appeal, Memphis, Tenn. Used with permission.

From Vietnam to Kansas Prison

Joel Sartore of *The Wichita Eagle-Beacon* used most of the techniques in the photojournalist's camera bag for his photographs of a Vietnamese woman convicted of hiring a man to burn a restaurant. The man hired two young Vietnamese to assist him, and when the gasoline and diesel fuel ignited the two were trapped inside the building and died.

The trial attracted attention because the woman was a member of a Vietnamese family that had fled that war-torn country and was welcomed to Kansas by a Salina church.

Sartore was able to obtain permission from the presiding judge to photograph inside the courthouse. He also was granted permission to photograph in correctional institutions in which the woman was placed.

Sartore shot several rolls of film, used several different lenses, and pushed the Tri-X film to 800 and 1600 because of lighting conditions. In the proof sheet reproduced here of scenes at the trial of Huong Thuy Pham the lens was a 35mm, f2 on a Nikon F3 camera body. The film was pushed to 800, and the shutter speed was 125. Frame 8a–9 was selected to show the "curiosity and confusion Huong experienced," Sartore says.

One of many proof sheets that Joel Sartore made for the photo editor to illustrate the story. The photo of the woman peering into the courtroom was used on the first page of the three-page article. Note how many shots were unused. The economy of 35mm photography is such that newspapers are willing to allow photographers to shoot rapidly and frequently. Photo editors know that the good photographer will bring back the insightful shots that give the reader a glimpse of the event and the people involved—even under the most trying circumstances.
Photos by Joel Sartore of The Wichita Eagle-Beacon. Pages from the newspaper. Used with permission.

Good art is big art. This is one of the principles that photo editors use in marrying photographs to text. The top photo works because of the small figure against the featureless background, which symbolizes the emptiness of prison life. The photographs below reveal portions of her trial and an aspect of her home life.

Huong Thuy Pham, imprisoned for arson, says, "To be in jail in America is better than to be free in Vietnam." But she longs for home.

District Judge Paul Clark presided over the many hearings. Pham was given a 5- to 20-year sentence for her role in an arson that killed two.

Pham peeks back in after her attorney sent her out of the courtroom during a hearing. The native of Vietnam is confused by the lengthy legal process.

HUONG

Freedom lost: from war to America to prison

TOPEKA — Huong Thuy Pham glided, smiling, into the visitor's room, her pair of silver bracelets jangling. When she blinked, her eyes became two half-moons of mauve.

Once again, she'd dressed herself in black, head to toe. Not the black suit, patterned hose and spike heels she'd worn at her arson trial, but black jeans and a jacket with satin lapels and padded shoulders.

At the Kansas Correctional Vocational Training Center, inmates don't wear uniforms. The prison jumpsuits are always too big, anyway, for this 4-foot-11-inch Vietnamese refugee who once sold rice at a street market in Saigon.

Andy and Mindy, her children, have been told she's going to school in Topeka. When they visit her every other weekend in the dormitory-style complex, they wonder why she can't come home with them and study in Wichita. They live with their father, Pham's childhood sweetheart and ex-husband.

Pham's parents are ashamed that their oldest daughter has broken the law and gotten herself into

● FREEDOM, 6E, Col. 1

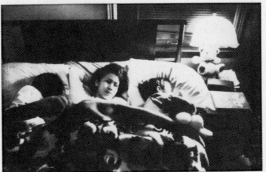

Three days before a court appearance, Pham waits for sleep between her children in the family bed. They moved in with her sister's family after the bank foreclosed on Pham's home.

Story by Sharon Hamric   Photography by Joel Sartore

Visual Reporting   361

From Proof Sheet . . .

Campaigning. To spend a day with Mike Hayden, Charlie Riedel and the reporter had to negotiate with the candidate's press secretary for several weeks. Given permission, Riedel had to travel with little equipment since there was no room for excess baggage in the candidate's plane and car, which Riedel and the reporter rode in. Because Riedel could not carry lighting equipment, most of the shots were taken with available light. The stops were brief and quick-moving, Riedel says, and the result was that he had little time to think of composition but had to shoot on the run. He used Ilford HP-5 film an ASA 400 and 1600. He shot with a Nikon F3 and used 18mm, 105 and 180mm lenses.

Photos by Charlie Riedel of the Hays Daily News. Used with permission. Front page from the Hays Daily News used with permission.

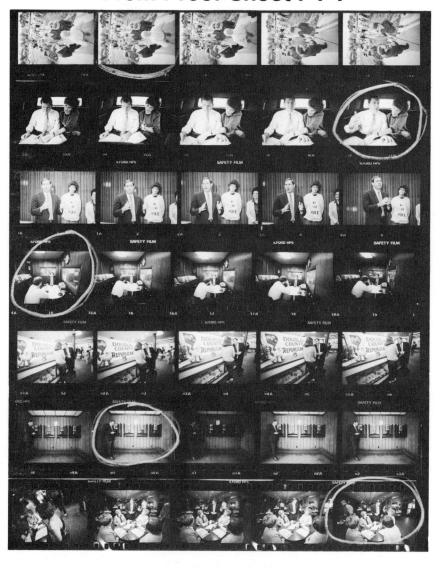

. . . to Printed Page

A western Kansan campaigns for governor during a typical

Day on the Trail

During the ride from Lincoln to Salina, Hayden talks about the campaign with his driver while his wife, Patti, checks their schedule for the rest of the day.

ABOVE: Lincoln High School students line up to meet Republican gubernatorial candidate Mike Hayden during a visit to Lincoln Wednesday morning. **RIGHT:** Campaigning during his lunch hour, Hayden shares a laugh with patrons of a Salina restaurant.

by SEAN REILLY

photos by CHARLIE RIEDEL

Before lunch, Hayden checks with his office from a restaurant entrance.

Whether campaigning from the steps of a limestone courthouse or within the confines of plush university auditorium, gubernatorial candidate Mike Hayden maintains a high level of energy.

On Wednesday, Hayden, 42, an Atwood native and the Republican nominee for governor, traveled to eastern Kansas to drum up support for his campaign against Democrat Tom Docking, 32, Wichita.

With only days left before Tuesday's general election, experts say the race is too close to call.

Five days before the election, just a day after the last debate between the two candidates in Salina, Hayden hit the trail to visit the final county in the state, Lincoln.

The morning began uneventfully with people gathering in the parking lot of a private club in Salina. They were part of an entourage of Republican supporters and state representatives waiting to greet him.

Dressed in a conservative two-piece, pin stripe suit and a red tie, Hayden went quickly from one supporter to another, smiling and striking up small talk with some.

Just as quickly as he darted out of the Cadillac of Saline County Republican Chairman Nancy Macy, Hayden was telling everyone it was time to depart.

Macy was chauffeuring Hayden and his wife, Patti, 38, to Lincoln and back in her climate-controlled vehicle.

"We feel just tremendous," Hayden said of the campaign. Whenever he spoke of the efforts to get him elected, Hayden used "we," referring to himself and his campaign workers.

Hayden obviously was happy about Tuesday's debate with Docking. When he discussed the event, there was a hint of confidence, but Hayden did not proclaim himself, nor Docking, as the winner.

"We got our point out to the voters. We felt our opponent exposed the lack of experience he has," Hayden said. "It was one of the better debates."

The Grand Old Party candidate said there were 12 debates conducted during the campaign, six of which were conducted formally.

Riding through countryside nearly identical to his hometown in northwest Kansas, Hayden talked of the things his campaign had forced him to miss.

Without hesitation, Hayden said the biggest sacrifice he had made since announcing his candidacy a year ago was being separated from his two daughters, Chelsi, 11, and Anne, 5. The girls are in Atwood, being taken care by members of Hayden's family.

"The biggest sacrifice is being separated from our children. We've been separated for six months. They came down to Topeka for the weekend, Saturday afternoon to Sunday morning.

"It's been so hard the last few months. We've only see them one or two days each month in the last few months," Hayden said.

"I knew the price would be very high. The challenge is very, very great. I knew it wasn't going to come easy," he said.

Besides missing the children, Hayden talked about how he missed fishing and hunting near his hometown and his 3-year-old hunting dog, Ivy.

As planned, Hayden and his entourage arrived in Lincoln, the county seat of Lincoln County, on time.

Parked in front of a picturesque courthouse, Hayden immediately got out of the car and began greeting well wishers. The crowd, which was at first

about 20 people, swelled to more than 50, especially with the arrival of a Lincoln High School government class.

Grabbing a microphone as a worker adjusted two nearby speakers to reduce the feedback, Hayden began to talk about the plight of farmers and small towns.

County workers peered out the windows of the nearly century-old limestone courthouse.

"We've been on the campaign trail for about a year. This has been a family effort. With this trip, Patti and I, or at least one of us, have been to every single county in Kansas," Hayden said.

"We are going to do everything we can to be the third individual from western Kansas to be elected governor," he said.

CAMPAIGN DAY
Continued on page 11

At 5 p.m. Hayden gives his third broadcast interview of the day at a Lawrence radio station.

Wearing a gift from a supporter, Patti Hayden watches while her husband speaks to several hundred people at a Republican gathering in Lawrence.

Hayden talks to a group of campaign workers at the Douglas County Republican Headquarters.

Quick Thinking

Stabbing. After a man stabbed a woman and fled, investigators showed the suspect's picture to people in the area where the man's car was located. Keith Warren was shooting the scene with a wide angle lens when he noticed an officer was carrying the photograph in a visible position.

Warren quickly switched to his 300mm lens and focused on the photograph. In the darkroom, he blew up the negative for that day's newspaper. *Photos by Keith Warren, The Commercial Dispatch, Columbus, Miss. Used with permission.*

A Photo Biography

Detailing. After gaining the confidence of an elderly homeless man, David Blumenkrantz was able to take photos of him without his objection. Blumenkrantz wanted to show the wear and tear of the man's lifestyle and focused on his face and

hands. He used his 105mm lens. The telephoto lens brought the subject closer. It also avoided making the nose and forehead disproportionately large, which a normal lens would. The pictures were taken at f5.6 at 1/250.

What's Wrong with These Photos?

Cabin. For a photo essay on life in the back country, the photographer took this interior shot. The kerosene lamp indicates the lack of electricity and the woodstove the source of heat. A saw and an ax add to the feeling of the occupant's lifestyle. But one ingredient is missing. What is it?

Classics. These memorable photographs of historic events could be made even better, says Claude Cookman, a photo and graphics editor. He says there is no question that the pictures are moving still lifes of part of the past taken under enormous pressure and that probably there was little time for the darkroom to work on them. Given time, what would you do? *Left, Wilmer Counts, The Arkansas Democrat, right, Sam Caldwell, St. Louis Post Dispatch.*

Interview. On a spot news assignment, the photographer took this picture of a spokesman at a rally protesting a campus racial incident during which protestors padlocked a classroom building.

Surprise. While shooting for a piece about local softball games, Joel Sartore saw a young woman sprint out toward one of the players, a local dentist. This was the dentist's birthday, and his friends had sent him this "Strip-O-Gram" as a gift.
Photo by Joel Sartore of The Wichita Eagle-Beacon. Used with permission.

Soldiers. Jole Kilthau took this photograph for a class at the Rochester Institute of Technology to illustrate several basic mistakes beginners in photography make.

Whoa

Before going on to the next page, jot down your suggestions for changes you would make to improve these photographs. Use common sense along with the technical knowledge you have picked up from this chapter and from lectures and other reading.

Here are a few problems that photographers pointed to in the pictures on the preceding pages:

Cabin: The empty chair cries out for someone to sit in it, the person whose lifestyle is being pictured. The dog adds some life to the shot, but it calls out for human interest. Look at the two photographs at the bottom of the page; it is obvious how the person adds life to the shot.

Soldiers: Michael Geissinger of the Rochester Institute of Technology says that all the elements necessary for a successful photograph are present but they are assembled awkwardly. In the background, the automobile next to the boy's head is distracting. Failure to notice the background is a common beginner's mistake. Also, the bright street distracts.

The gap between the subjects is too great. The viewer is attracted by the youngster's upward glance but has to work too hard to find the adult, Geissinger says. Once the adult is located, his head is too near the top of the photo and the viewer's eye moves off the page. Also, the adult's hat is cut off.

Interview: The focus of the photograph is lost in background and foreground images. The student in the background is much too sharp, and the blurred heads in the foreground get in the way. The photographer used a 135mm lens to move close in. A longer telephoto lens would have helped in a number of ways. It would have eliminated the heads in the foreground because they would be out of the frame, and the shorter depth of field would have blurred the student's head in the background. Another way to rid the photo of the student would have been to increase the shutter speed and open the lens wider since the wider the lens opening, the shorter the depth of field.

Empty and Cold

Person Adds Warmth

Surprise: When Sartore submitted this photo to his editors at *The Wichita Eagle-Beacon* it was part of a picture story on softball in Wichita. "I had brought it back thinking it might have a chance of getting into the paper. (This was during my internship, and I was still pretty green about such matters.) The picture got to the assistant managing editor level and went no further. It was too risqué to be used, I was told. In general, we don't run pictures with any nudity."

Classics: These pictures should have been improved with cropping, says Cookman. The photo of the woman at the mineshaft was run in 1947, but today it would probably have been cropped before use, he says. Many of the faces to the left of the principal subject would have been cropped or burnt down in the printing process to make them less noticeable.

A similar step would have been taken to the left of the downed man in the Little Rock photograph. The photo would have been cropped inside the left edge of the utility pole, and this would strengthen the picture by "not allowing our eye to escape from the central message to the area to the left." The pole would become a solid border on the left side of the picture.

Cropped for Greater Impact

13

Advertising

I grew up believing I was going to be somebody. But it seemed like no one would give me a chance. Until finally I found Someone to turn to.

SUPPORT
The National Urban League

WE CAN MAKE A WORLD OF DIFFERENCE.
Help us help them. ⊜ National Urban League, 500 E. 62nd St.,
New York, N.Y. 10021

Advertising is used to create goodwill for a company or organization as well as to sell goods and services. When such advertising is designed for public service organizations, advertising agencies donate the work of their employees and the media donate time and space for the advertisements.
Used with permission of the National Urban League and Young & Rubicam.

Looking Ahead

Advertising brings sellers and buyers together. It helps sellers to compete for a share of the market by encouraging people to try new products, to maintain product loyalty or to switch brands. Most advertisements are the product of a process involving:

• **Research**—observations, interviews, focus groups to help the advertiser understand consumer behavior.

• **Positioning**—selection of an audience and a theme or concept to make the product or service appear favorably among comparable products and services.

- **Media selection**—from among the television and radio programs, newspapers and magazines that the target audience watches, listens to and reads.
- **Composition of the advertisement**—the teamwork of creative directors, copywriters, photographers, artists.

We have been reading about men and women whose job it is to inform. In this and the following chapter we will examine the work of the practitioners of another art, the art of persuasion.

Those who are in advertising and public relations ask us to do something: Buy this brand of jeans, ask for that tube of toothpaste, think kindly of this candidate, appreciate the work of that organization.

Though superficially alike, advertising and public relations differ significantly. The advertiser buys time and space to reach the public. Public relations operates more quietly, behind the scene. "The advertising man must know how many people he can reach *with* the media, the public relations man must know how many people he can reach *within* the media," says the author Martin Mayer.

The advertiser reaches the public through the media, and the media depend on advertising for survival. Newspapers receive about three-fourths of their income from advertising, a fourth from circulation. Commercial broadcast stations receive all their revenue from advertising.

"**Advertising,** like other good things, may be practiced wrongfully, harmfully; but the fact remains that in its proper use the highest order of journalistic public service is performed. In advertising, truth should abide and be controlling, temptation should be resisted and virtue extolled to the nth degree. In advertising, the science and art of journalism may be more readily prostituted, for it is here the devil of journalism plays his most alluring tunes to catch the credulous and the unwary."—Adolph S. Ochs January 13, 1925

How Advertising Works

The purpose of advertising, and the goal of the advertising employee, is to put seller and buyer together. James Webb Young, whose ideas are still used by advertising people, said advertising works in five ways to do this:

1. By making the product or service familiar to the people.
2. By reminding people about the product or service.
3. By spreading news about the product or service to the people.
4. By overcoming inertia in potential customers.
5. By adding value to a product that is not in the product. (A sleek sports car is not sexy in and of itself. But if a person feels sexy driving such a car because of advertising, then advertising had added a value to the product that didn't exist.)

B. O. = P. U. = $

The TV commercial shows a sweaty man walking up to his daughter after jogging. The child pulls back and blurts out, "P. U. Your shirt smells icky." The shirt then undergoes a transformation. It is washed in Surf. Daughter and father embrace.

By positioning itself in an area none of the other detergents wanted to enter—body odor—Surf shot to No. 2 in the $3.3 billion detergent market. Most detergent advertisements claim to make clothes fresh and fragrant. Procter & Gamble, makers of Tide, No. 1 in the field, monopolized the clean, white bright claims, said an advertising man. But Lever Brothers found for Surf a niche in smell and spent more than $100 million on promotion and advertising. "Body odor isn't pleasant and detergent companies didn't really want to talk about it in the past," said the agency executive.

Positioning

"We've reached the point where no one, including the manufacturers, thinks there is a bit of difference between advertised products. And so no one says anything because no one can think of a claim that anyone will believe."— Dave Vadehra, president Video Storyboard Tests, which measures the effectiveness of TV ads, commenting on the disappearance of product claims in television advertising.

Advertising is used by sellers to influence buyers to select their products or services. The choice usually is made from among several similar goods and services, which means that the advertiser must position his product so that the buyer decides to choose the seller's particular product or service.

To position the product successfully, to reach the buyer successfully, the advertiser tries to understand consumer behavior. Buyer characteristics that advertisers study include sex, age, education, where potential buyers live, the kinds of homes they occupy, their family makeup, their attitudes toward the seller's product. On the basis of market research an advertising program is drawn up.

When the Borden food company decided to go heavily into the snack food market with Spirals, it quickly found that teen-agers are the biggest consumers of salted snacks. The company's advertising agency set up a focus group of teen-agers to find out about their snacking habits. (A focus group consists of a representative sample of the kinds of people the service or product is aimed at.) The agency learned that youngsters like the nacho flavor of Spirals. They compared the flavor favorably with that of Doritos and Tostitos, made by Pepsico's Frito-Lay, the leader in the snack field.

The agency's job was to direct the market to the new product. The copywriter came up with the line, "Spirals are going to turn your taste around." This was followed by, "Move over flat nacho chips. New Spirals are here." In the background, teen-agers whirl around to a hard beat.

Prune sales had been declining for three decades, despite advertising campaigns and television commercials. The California Prune Board was disturbed, and it hired Hal Riney & Partners, an advertising agency in San Francisco, to turn things around.

"People thought prunes just weren't worth buying," says Kirk Citron, senior writer with the agency. "Obviously we needed to tell people something to change their minds.

"So the first thing we did was go talk to people. Hundreds of people. And we found that one thing could make a difference: a thoughtful, reasoned discussion of the benefits of prunes."

Prunes have plenty of fiber, he found. Fiber is on the minds of people these days because medical authorities say that the typical fast-food diet (usually low in fiber) is a lousy diet, and a leading cause of cancer is an unbalanced diet.

"When we told people prunes have more fiber than almost any other food, it turned all the negatives about prunes into positives," Citron says. "Prunes had something people wanted; fiber. So it was easy to find what the advertising should say."

Citron had defined the objective—to increase sales of prunes—and he had found a theme for his advertising campaign—the high fiber content of prunes. Every advertisement has a specific objective whose purpose is to move the reader or viewer of the advertisement to approval or to action. Every advertisement is built on a specific idea or theme.

The theme that is selected implies that if the consumer acts on the advertising he or she will be pleased. The theme may be the low price of beef at the local market—which promises the satisfaction of saving money. Or the theme could be the sweet smell of a wash—which promises to demonstrate a women's love of her family.

Some advertising people say they sell an emotion, not a product.

"We don't buy the product. We buy the satisfaction the product will bring us. And that's what the commercial should display," said Ted Bates, head of the agency that bears his name.

"We're using a whole battery of psychological techniques—some new and some new—to understand the emotional bond between consumers and brands," says Paul Drilling, director of strategic planning for McCann-Erickson. "You have to sell on emotion more than ever because it's a world of parity products out there. The days of having a competitive edge and a special product benefit are long gone."

Rosalinde Rago, director of advertising research at the Ogilvy and Mather advertising agency, says, "Brands are not just commercial products we buy and use, they are our companions in life as well."

Putting Prunes on the Table

Here's a list of the foods that are a better source of fiber than prunes:

Prunes have more fiber per serving than almost any food you can name. And prunes have four of the five types of fiber your body uses. Plus potassium and vitamin A. Not to mention the fact that they're about the best-tasting source of fiber under the sun. Which explains why our list is so short.

Prunes. The high fiber fruit.

Selling prunes became easier once the concept of fiber was introduced. Fiber became the theme of the advertising of California prune growers. *Used with permission of Hal Riney & Partners.*

Promising Pleasure

Minneapolis-St. Paul is the most popular test market for food and drug products. Over a 27-month period, 92 products were tested in these Minnesota twin cities. Other cities frequently used: Portland, Ore., 91; Columbus, Ohio, 69; Syracuse, N.Y., 62; Kansas City, Mo., 60. Cities are selected for testing on the basis of the similarity of their residents to the overall population in age, education and income.

Automobile advertisements promise neighbor-envy. Perfume and cologne advertisements promise the attraction of the opposite sex. Insurance advertisements promise a feeling of security.

Noxema shaving cream promises men a great deal. One advertisement promised too much. The commercial showed a man emerging from the woods and eyeing Farrah Fawcett. "I haven't seen a woman in nine years," he says. She returns his hungry look. Suddenly a can of shaving cream bursts through the earth's crust, surging from the forest.

No go, said the network's censors.

Image Making

Advertisements combine information and image making. When Campbell Soup Co. entered the frozen food market—a $2 billion a year business—it faced stiff competition. Campbell chose to package gourmet foods, a market that has grown enormously as consumers become more conscious of their diets.

Campbell informed buyers of the nutritional value and the quality of its product. And it sought to build an image of the product to appeal to intelligent, cultured consumers.

One commercial had a string quartet in the background. Another was filmed aboard a yacht. These images differ considerably from those of the 1950s when Swanson developed the TV dinner. Then, commercials for frozen food stressed quantity. Commercials showed families sitting in front of the television sets helping themselves to large portions of spaghetti and fried chicken.

Once the objective and the theme are set, the advertisement is composed. Illustrations are selected, copy written, the commercial recorded and shot. The advertisement is then placed.

Media Selection

If the product is frequently used—painkillers, soap, toothpaste—the media buyer will use network television to try to reach many of the country's 72 million households. If the product is world cruises, which only those with large disposable incomes can afford, then the advertiser might select the *National Geographic,* whose readers' income is $300 billion a year, the magazine says.

Manufacturers of expensive, fashionable women's clothing seek out *Vogue.* Indeed, so many place their ads in the magazine that a fall fashion issue will contain well over 800 pages. J. C. Penney, on the other hand, will advertise its inexpensive daily wear in local newspapers, and Sears will use direct mail.

Ricochet, an international arts magazine that sells for $5 a copy, attracted advertisements from Leica—one of the most costly cameras on the market—and from the makers of high-priced cars and vodka.

Shades of Opinion

"Advertising is a meter of social and cultural change . . . though advertising is rarely controversial. Only when a new idea no longer is threatening do marketers exploit it through advertising. They oversimplify and stylize the idea in order to sell products and make profits."—*The Wall Street Journal.*

"In the factory we make cosmetics; in the store, we sell hope."—Charles Revson, founder of Revlon.

"Again and again advertising has been an agency for inducing Americans to try anything and everything—from the continent itself to a new brand of soap. As one of the more literate and poetic of the advertising copywriters, James Kenneth Frazier, a Cornell graduate, wrote in 1900 in 'The Doctor's Lament':

This lean M.D. is Dr. Brown
Who fares but ill in Spotless Town.
The town is so confounded clean,
It is no wonder he is lean,
He's lost all patients now, you know,
Because they use *Sapolio*."
—Daniel J. Boorstin, historian.

"Advertising can either increase or decrease the degree of sanity with which people respond to words. Thus, if advertising is informative, witty, educational and imaginative, it can perform its necessary commercial function and contribute to our pleasure in life without making us slaves to the tyranny of affective words. If, however, products are sold largely by manipulating affective connotations . . . the influence of advertising is to deepen the already grave intensional orientation widely prevalent in the public. The schizophrenic is one who attributes a greater reality to words, fantasies, daydreams and 'private worlds' than to the actualities around him."—S. I. Hayakawa, semanticist.

"Advertising . . . projects an image of what life *could* be and associates this image with its product."—Peter B. Hammond, anthropoligist.

"The advertisements are by far the best part of any magazine or newspaper. Advertisements are news. What is wrong with them is that they are always good news."—Marshall McLuhan.

Agencies place advertisements for maximum effectiveness. Used car advertisements often are placed in the sports sections of newspapers, laundry detergent on television during the daytime soap operas. When Young & Rubicam initiated its "Lovin' from the Oven" campaign for Pillsbury it put the commercials for microwave oven products—cakes, popcorn, brownies and pizzas—on the Miss America Pageant.

Teamwork

The advertisement is the result of teamwork. In fact, teamwork is involved from the very time the client selects an agency. At that time, the client meets with the people who will be handling his or her account, media planners and the creative team. When the program is worked out, the media or medium selected, the creative team takes over.

The team plots the strategy:

Who is the audience? For prunes, it was adults conscious of their diets. For jeans, it's young men and women. For Mercedes automobiles, the audience is high-income earners.

What's the theme? For prunes, it was they are good for you. For jeans, Sportswear Ltd. created a television character named Sergio Valente to project the message of sexual attraction. For Mercedes, the idea is high efficiency and status.

What's the message? "It was easy to decide what the advertising should say," says Citron about the idea for selling prunes to people. "Then came the hard part: deciding how to say it."

Saying It: The Content

What should the copy say? What kind of pictures should illustrate the message? What should Sergio Valente say? Or should he simply walk around in his jeans against a rock beat background?

The creative team has the job of bringing the advertising to life.

"The copywriter and the art director will assimilate and generate ideas," says Nelda King, associate creative director at Young & Rubicam, one of the largest advertising agencies in the United States.

Over at Hal Riney & Partners, Citron pondered how to say it. "How many ways are there to say, 'Prunes are high in fiber'?"

"Would you believe 300? That's how many headlines we wrote. And we came up with a dozen visual ideas. We had to do more than just give people information. We had to grab their attention and capture their imagination."

Citron decided that the copy would be longer than usual. He had to give buyers a lot of information, and the kind of people he was seeking to reach would not be frightened off by a lot of text—if it was interesting.

Sergio, on the other hand, had only to saunter down the street with a blonde on each arm sighing his name. Sergio is seen from the rear with the name of the jeans on his back pocket.

"Sex sells. Everyone knows that," said the manufacturer.

"I make Sasson jeans, I make Calvin Klein jeans, and I make Jordache jeans, and they're all the same." —an apparel manufacturer quoted in *Hype,* a book by Steven M.L. Aronson.

THE BEST DRESSED MAN IN TOWN!

—WEARS A SUIT OF—

Clothes Cut and Made

— BY —

SAM'L BLACK,

THE TAILOR,

206 FOURTH STREET,

NEAR BROWN'S HOTEL,

Tombstone, A. T

WHERE YOU WILL FIND THE BEST SELCETED STOCK OF IMPORTED WOOLEN Cassimeres, Diagonals, Broadcloths, Scotch and English Cheviots, Fancy Suitings and Trousering, and the Latest Fashions at Bed Rock Prices. A perfect fit and first class workmanship guaranteed. Scouring and Steaming by the latest process, and Binding and Repairing at Reduced Rates. Call and examine the Goods and Prices before going elsewhere.

206 Fourth Street, near Brown's Hotel.

Arizona Mail and Stage Line.

J. D. KINNEAR & CO., Proprietors.

Lowest Stage Rates.

TOMBSTONE TO BENSON DAILY!
TOMBSTONE TO CHARLESTON DAILY!
TOMBSTONE TO HUACHUCA TRI-WEEKLY!
TOMBSTONE TO HARSHAW TRI-WEELLY!
TOMBSTONE TO CONTENTION CITY DAILY!
TOMBSTONE TO BISBEE TRI-WEEKLY.

Coaches can be Chartered from Benson to Tombstone and Return by Giving Two Days Notice.

Fastest Time and Best Stock.

OFFICE WITH WELLS, FARGO & CO., TOMBSTONE.

MARSHALL WILLIAMS, AGENT.

The content of newspaper advertisements has changed little over the years. More than a century ago, these advertisements appeared in *The Tombstone Epitaph,* then in the Arizona Territory. The pictures (woodcuts) illustrated the goods and services offered for sale. The message was simple and direct, presented in a headline that caught the eye.
The Tombstone Epitaph. Used with permission.

A Vocabulary for Copywriters

The psychology department at Yale University identified 10 words as the most personal and persuasive. They are:

New. Human beings continuously crave novelty.

Save. Everybody wants to save something, whether it be time, energy or money.

Safety. This word indicates long-lasting product quality . . . and personal well-being.

Proven. Documentation works.

Love. Everybody wants the inner satisfaction this word connotes.

Discover. Stimulates feelings of adventure and excitement.

Guarantee. Today's consumers often demand a guarantee of some kind.

Results. Ultimate results are every consumer's desire.

You. This is possibly the most persuasive word of all in ad copy.

Health. The health consciousness of the '80s can be applied to a wide variety of products.

The Results

Money alone does not buy success in the market, said Philip Dougherty, who wrote the advertising column in *The New York Times*. If that were so, he said, Procter & Gamble, which spends more money than any other advertiser, would never market a dud. Despite spending large sums on Pringles, a potato chip, the snack never took off. Nor did Body Flowers, a deodorant-cologne that the Gillette Company launched in 1983 with an $11 million budget. Aimed at the 12–34 women's market, staggered along until the company stopped advertising.

Did the advertising work? For Citron, "The results were astonishing. Every month since the advertising started, prune sales went up, 10, 12, 17 percent.

"*Advertising Age* named prunes as one of the 10 hottest products in supermarkets for the year," he said. Also, the advertisements won a number of awards.

Sportswear Ltd. thought it would sell $2.5 million worth of its Sergio Valente jeans a month. But after the commercials appeared, orders piled up at the rate of $2.5 million a week. Sportswear's success led to a flood of television commercials for signature jeans. Companies were spending as much as 15 percent of their sales on advertising. (Levi Strauss & Co., the largest U.S. maker of jeans, budgets about 2 percent of sales on advertising.)

"The prize goes to the biggest spender," said an investment broker whose firm handles major industries. The managing director of Sportswear, Martin Heinfling, who created the jeans and suggested the character of Sergio, takes this a step further.

"People don't care about quality," he told *The Wall Street Journal*. "All they wanted was this television hype."

Maybe. There is actually no solid evidence that advertising alone can sell goods. Consumers, studies show, care about quality and cost, and unless they are given both they turn their attention elsewhere sooner or later.

Product advertising and institutional advertising make up the two broad classes of advertising. The purpose of product advertising is to sell goods or to make the buyer favorably disposed toward the product. The purpose of institutional advertising is to make friends for the company or organization, to create good-will.

Product advertising can introduce a new product, maintain market position or improve it. Right Guard earned more than half a billion dollars for The Gillette Co. after its introduction in 1960, and then it ran into competition. Its market share declined and Gillette poured $30 million into advertising in one six-month period. Sales improved somewhat.

But when Gillette sank $11 million into a campaign to sell a combination deodorant-cologne for women, the response was lukewarm.

Some products once in favor seek to make comebacks, and the vehicle of their attempted return is specialized advertising.

A decade ago, Schlitz and Pabst Blue Ribbon sold a lot of beer, around 17 million barrels a year each.

They did well through the 1970s, but their image is one of another and older generation, and half of all the beer drinkers in the United States are 18 to 34 years old. Pabst's sales sunk to 4 million barrels and Schlitz almost disappeared, down to a million barrels a year.

Image and Reality

"It's the real thing. Coke is." Commenting on the Coca-Cola commercial, Ann Nietzke wrote in the *Saturday Review:* "In the back of our minds we are all looking for the real thing—genuine affection—and would be ready and willing to buy any products that might help us find it."

An article in *The Wall Street Journal* about the producer of television commercials for politicians said his commercials have "striking photography with almost no message about issues or ideology." In reply, the producer, Bob Goodman, said: "This tube is a very emotional thing. We measure passion, not facts. What I am trying to do is show this man the best way I can, to capture his essence. Feelings win elections. What I strive for is an emotion, not a position."

"It pays to give your brand a *first-class ticket* through life. People don't like to be seen consuming products which their friends regard as third-class."—David Ogilvy of Ogilvy, Benson & Mather, advertising agency.

"If you actually ate the 'TV diet'—with the amounts of each food you eat proportionate to the advertising dollars spent on each food—you would be dead long before your time."—Beverly Moore, a lawyer-nutritionist.

Advertisers are checked and regulated by a variety of groups and agencies. The Food and Drug Administration looks into any questionable claims for products in its jurisdiction. The Federal Trade Commission devotes about half its funds to halting deceptive practices in advertising. Local Better Business Bureaus check complaints about advertising, as do many consumer organizations. Newspapers, magazines and broadcast stations and networks examine advertisements for acceptability and usually reject advertising that they find in questionable taste or that make outlandish claims. Finally, advertising personnel subscribe to a code of ethics.

"The backbone of Pabst's sales has been men in their 40s, 50s, and 60s, but they're literally dying off," said Hal Asher, the head of Asher/Gould Advertising, Pabst's agency. "What we have to do is make young people feel it's acceptable to drink their father's brand." His agency prepared advertisements depicting racing roller skaters who pass a large bottle of Pabst as they skate. Another TV commercial has two brewery workers dancing. The woman strips off a white smock to reveal a leotard. She rips the shirt off a co-worker.

Skaters and dancers pulse to the slogan: "What'll you have? Pabst Blue Ribbon."

Schlitz stresses nostalgia: A young man polishes his 1956 Chevy, people watch Willie Mays playing baseball. The idea was to remind people of what is thought to have been a better and less troublesome period, the 1950s. "We have a dual audience for these ads," says the director of creative services at Stroh Brewery Co., which makes Schlitz, "older drinkers who were part of that era and young people who are enamored of the '50s."

Selling Compassion

Next, an example of public service advertising. Nelda King, whose job is to develop ideas to sell products, is also involved in the agency's work for the National Urban League, an organization devoted to promoting equal opportunity for blacks through employment training, counseling of the aged and handicapped and through a variety of other activities. Young & Rubicam donated King's time and that of the others who work with her to prepare television and print advertisements for the League. The space and time for the advertisements were donated by the media.

King's first task was to find a theme for the League's institutional advertising, which was directed at gaining support for its activities and programs. Research in 1980 about general attitudes toward minorities had shown a negative reaction to the theme of affirmative action, she said. "To many people this meant 'special treatment' for minorities," she said. (The resentment was considered still valid at the time the advertisements were planned.) But people do have a sense of fair play, she said, and from this a theme emerged: Be Fair.

Despite advertising and publicity for the Urban League in the past, few people had any idea of the League's activities. So the new advertisements needed to be informative as well as persuasive.

"One way to do this would be to use statistics," King said. For example, the League counsels 50,000 teen-agers. "But figures are not too motivating," she said. After discussions with League officials and her creative team, it was agreed that the idea of helping people who had nowhere to turn would be stressed. Three areas were chosen: pregnant teen-agers, the aged and unemployed young adults.

Against a backdrop of the song "Who Can I Turn to When Nobody Needs Me?", 15- and 30-second videotapes and print advertisements were planned. The Urban League, said the voiceover and the print advertisements, is "someone to turn to."

From Storyboards to Stills to Television

After the creative team at Young & Rubicam advertising agency decided on a theme for public service advertisements for the National Urban League, the artist made sketches or roughs of the major ideas. These sketches, called storyboards, combined visual effects, music and words. The sketches became the basis for still photographs that illustrated the key ideas. For print advertisements, the photographs and their captions were sent to newspapers and magazines. They were also used to advise television stations of available 15- and 30-second videotapes. The agency made advertisements for three major areas of concern to the League—unemployed young adults, the aged and pregnant teen-agers. *Used with permission of the National Urban League and Young Rubicam.*

Y&R

CL/PROD URBAN LEAGUE   ART Brumfield
TITLE "Who/Teen Girl"   COPY Rothstein
LENGTH :15   TYP

JOB NO
DATE
PAGE 1 OF 1

(MUSIC UNDER)

SONG:

WHO CAN I TURN TO...

ANNCR: VO: The National Urban

League. We can make a world of

difference. Please support us.

(MUSIC UP)

SONG:

BUT WHO CAN I TURN TO...

IF YOU TURN AWAY?

"PREGNANT GIRL"   Available in :30 & :15 seconds versions.   CNUL-6330/6315   (note: only the :30 is closedcaptioned)   30 Seconds

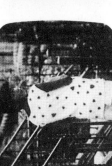

MUSIC: WHO CAN I TURN TO, WHEN NOBODY NEEDS ME...

ANNCR. (VO): The Urban League gives pregnant teens and their babies hope for a better future.

Please support us. We can make a world of difference.

MUSIC: BUT WHO CAN I TURN TO, IF YOU TURN AWAY?

Print advertisements for the Urban League are examined by Nelda King, *bottom left,* of Young & Rubicam and John Jacob, *bottom right,* president of the National Urban League. Others in the photograph are from various groups involved in the project. *Camera 1. Used with permission of Young & Rubicam.*

The creative team thought up the theme, "We can make a world of difference." The copy writer tried to convey a poetic feeling through the language in the advertisements and in the way the lines broke on the print advertisements.

Jobs and Salaries

Opportunities in advertising are good, salaries adequate to excellent. In a recent Sunday issue of *The New York Times,* the help wanted section contained eight columns of advertising jobs, with salaries ranging from $18,000 to $200,000. The average starting salary in the field, a study has shown, is $14,700.

The work is not for everyone, those in the field say. Advertising copywriters must be able to work quickly, and work long hours.

"You have to write ad after ad and meet deadlines that force you to be fast," says Tom McElligott of Fallon McElligott in Minneapolis. "And every ad is based on the basis of sales—period."

On his first job as a junior copywriter for a Minneapolis department store, McElligott said he learned the basics, among them that "superlatives were a sin. You can't claim one thing is 'best' today and something else 'best' tomorrow."

It was on this job, he said, that he learned the "philosophy that customers should be treated with honesty and respect."

Arlen, Michael, *Thirty Seconds*. New York: Farrar, Straus & Giroux, 1980.

Mayer, Milton. *Madison Avenue U.S.A.* New York: Harper & Brothers, 1958.

Ogilvy, David. *Confessions of an Advertising Man.* New York: Atheneum, 1963.

Suggested Reading

14

Public Relations

Planning a program is one of the four activities in the public relations process. The program is based on research to find out what the public thinks of the organization or individual for whom the program is planned. Here, Mary Huchette of Burson-Marsteller outlines the audiences at which she is aiming her public relations program.
Photo of Burson-Marsteller employees. Used with permission.

Looking Ahead

Public relations seeks to establish goodwill for the client by creating and molding attitudes. The public relations practitioner examines the interests, concerns and attitudes of the various publics that the organization serves and then recommends a program to reach these groups. The practitioner carries out the program in a variety of ways—through press releases, news background sessions, brochures, employee publications, speeches and videotapes.

"We are advocates," says Harold Burson, head of Burson-Marsteller, the largest public relations firm in the world with 2,000 employees in 21 countries. "We are being paid to tell our client's side of the story. We are in the business of changing and molding attitudes, and we aren't successful unless we move the needle, get people to do something.

"But we are also a client's conscience, and we have to do what is in the public interest. I define public relations as an effort to influence opinion—to influence the attitudes of people. That's all it is.

"We can do three things to public opinion.

"We can try to change it, if it suits our purposes to do so.

"We can try to create new opinion, where none exists.

"Or we can reinforce existing opinion." Burson said.

Joseph P. McLaughlin, president of a public relations agency, defined his work this way:

"We may speak of the PR man's role as an interpreter to his client or clients of society and events; an evaluator of the meaning and consequences of social and economic change; a prognosticator of future troubles; a prudent and imaginative preparer of programs designed to deal with problems before they descend in full force upon his employer; a transmission belt to carry the client's messages to various publics and to convey back to the client the re-actions of those publics to his programs and activities. He undoubtedly, at various times, depending upon the scope of his responsibilities, is all of these. But primarily he is an advocate."

The Beginnings

The purpose of public relations has not changed since Ivy Lee and George F. Parker opened their doors in 1904 and since John W. Hill, founder of Hill and Knowlton Inc., advised his first clients more than 60 years ago that his job was to help influence the public to think well of them. *Public Relations News* puts it this way:

> Public Relations is the management function that evaluates public attitudes, identifies the policies and procedures of an individual or an organization with the public interest and executes a program of action to earn public understanding and acceptance.

"The good reporter tells you. The publicity man sells you."—Donald H. Higgins, *Finance Magazine*.

Hill had a formula for what he called "lasting and substantial success" for his clients:

1. Integrity and truth. "Public opinion is entitled to the facts in matters of public concern," he said.

2. Soundness of policies, decisions and acts viewed in the light of the public interest.

3. Use of facts that are understandable, believable and presented with imagination.

The Scope of Public Relations

The Public Relations Society of America lists the major job classifications of the public relations specialist as writing, editing, placement of material, promotion of events, speaking, production (photography, layout for print, production for broadcast and motion pictures), program development and institutional advertising.

Public relations covers a variety of activities that include: public information, public affairs, investor relations, corporate communications, employee relations or communications, marketing or product publicity and consumer service or customer relations.

Whatever the term, the basic activity consists of communicating information about an organization or an individual in the best light.

Schools, churches, hospitals, college athletic departments, labor unions, hunting and fishing resorts, television networks, rock bands, the armed forces, the Red Cross and the bottlers of soft drinks use public relations practitioners.

The many and varied tasks of the public relations specialist include: producing an in-house newspaper or magazine for employees; dealing with community relations; designing, writing, producing company reports; lobbying; staging events for the media; supervising junkets for the press.

Some specialize in planting items with gossip columnists. Others are at the call of the sports writers who cover the local college teams. These sports information directors have statistics at their fingertips and can summon an athlete for an interview in 20 minutes. Some are geniuses at staging events that seem—and sometimes are—newsworthy: a corporation's donation of funds for minority scholarships; a beer company's annual contest for the largest fish caught during the summer; a television star's visit to the geriatric or pediatric ward of the local hospital; a transcontinental walk for nuclear disarmament. All of this is accompanied by press releases, photo opportunities, background kits, videotapes.

The task is to manage relations with the public so that the reputation of the client is enhanced, the image is positive. To bring this about, public relations counselors analyze trends, preferences, feelings, attitudes through research; indicate the consequences of these findings to the client and devise a program that will promote the client's interests.

Robber Barons

Public relations traces its origin to the period of public cynicism and anger about big business practices. By the early 20th century, the United States had grown into an industrial giant. But it was growth with pain.

Low wages; trusts and monopolies; child labor in mines, fields and factories; the 12-hour workday; resistance to collective bargaining and workers' strikes by owners who had the help of the state militia, federal troops and their own armed detective agencies. Signs were posted on factory doors saying, "If you can't come in Sunday, don't come in Monday."

All this and more had stigmatized business.

John Spargo's book, *Bitter Cry of the Children,* described what he saw at Pennsylvania and West Virginia coal mines at the turn of the century:

Published monthly for active and retired employees of Reader's Digest

PEGASUS

July 1987

Summertime – and the listening's easy

The New York City Opera National Company's sweet voices filled our Pleasantville grounds July 10 for our second Concert in the Park.

Seven cast members and a full orchestra serenaded more than 2,500 active and retired Digesters, their families and special guests with two hours of selections from world famous operas and Broadway shows.

(continued on back cover)

The New York City Opera National Company (top) serenaded Digesters and special guests, who picnicked on our Pleasantville grounds while enjoying beautiful music. Dorothy and Neil Hennessy (above), corporate communications, prepare an elegant picnic dinner, while young Douglas Gollogly (left), son of Nan and Neil Gollogly, on-site electrician, nibble on some finger-lickin' chicken.

Employee communications include the production of newsletters, newspapers and magazines for the employees of the firm or organization. *The Reader's Digest* magazine *Pegasus* has a small full-time staff and many correspondents in the Digest's departments and divisions. Bookkeepers, messengers and secretaries rub shoulders in *Pegasus* columns with editors, sales managers and advertising representatives. *Used with permission of Reader's Digest.*

PEOPLE

Research is an essential early step in drafting a public relations program. Large agencies maintain a reference library like this one used by Stacy Sperling and Kyle Kunz of Burson-Marsteller. Sperling is working on the General Electric lighting account and Kunz is doing some research for the American Telephone & Telegraph account. *Photo of Burson-Marsteller employees. Used with permission.*

In their book, *PR: How the Public Relations Industry Writes the News,* Jeff and Marie Blyskal quote the Coleco public relations executive who was behind the Cabbage Patch doll selling job: "When Bryant Gumbel or Jane Pauley . . . says, 'Here's the season's hottest item,' it means more to consumers than if Coleco says the same thing. The credibility that achieves far outweighs an advertisement." (New York: William Morrow and Company, 1985.)

Crouched over the chutes, the boys sit hour after hour, picking out the pieces of slate and other refuse from the coal as it rushes past the washers. From the cramped position they have to assume most of them become more or less deformed and bent-backed like old men. . . . The coal is hard and accidents to the hands, such as cut, broken, or crushed fingers, are common among the boys. Sometimes there is a worse accident; a terrified shriek is heard, and a boy is mangled and torn in the machinery or disappears in the chute to be picked out later, smothered and dead.

The boys were 10 and 12 years old and were working for 50 and 60 cents a day.

The biggest of the big businessmen were described as "robber barons," a mark of the aristocracy of wealth that had developed and a description of the means by which their wealth had been accumulated.

Jay Gould, the railroad tycoon, announced: "Labor is a commodity that will in the long run be governed absolutely by the law of supply and demand."

John D. Rockefeller had destroyed competition in the oil business and had constructed a monopoly, the Standard Oil Company, that controlled refineries, pipelines and the transportation of oil. The Ohio Supreme Court dissolved his monopoly in 1899, but he quickly formed a holding trust. Workers were exploited. Many lived in company towns where they paid high rents and exorbitant prices for food. They could not live or shop elsewhere. The Rockefeller fortune was enormous; the Rockefeller name was reviled.

By 1911, his billions secure, Rockefeller—the richest man in the word—left the business to his son, John Jr., and managers. He sought to cleanse his name. He turned to Ivy Lee, who, in that year, had formed his own public relations firm. Lee went to work for Rockefeller.

Lee, a former New York newspaperman, had a formidable task, not the least of which was overcoming the charge of journalists that he had compromised his integrity. Reporters felt Lee had sold out.

"They saw this new occupation called public relations as a form of black magic," said Burson. Public relations, reporters decided, was "an attempt to make things seem what they weren't—to make people who behaved badly look good," said Burson, who himself left the newsroom of the *Memphis Commercial Appeal* and subsequently formed his own public relations firm.

"PR" became a pejorative term. Its practitioners were known as flacks. Some of the early practitioners resorted to their imaginations more often than to facts in their attempts to market their clients. Not all the criticism was undeserved, says Burson. Public relations has been engaged, he says, in "a quest for legitimacy."

The press was usually happy to use the odd feature stories that some creative public relations practitioners (often called publicity men or press agents) dreamed up. A baby elephant might be hired to attract reporters to the opening of a new business, or the manufacturer of cold cuts would announce the selection of a salami queen, who was available for cheesecake photos—pictures that showed ample female epidermis.

In the 1920s, a press agent dreamed up what he thought was a great news story to publicize a Warner Brothers movie, "Down to the Sea in Ships." He planted a fake whale atop Pikes Peak and told newspapers that a whale had been sighted on the mountain. The press agent hired a youngster to sit on the whale's back and spurt seltzer into the air.

As the media matured, so did public relations. The relationship between the media and public relations remains close. The press depends on public relations people for tips and information.

When AT&T was split up by court order, some of the so-called Baby Bell companies invaded the turf of others. Southwestern Bell tried to market its Yellow Pages in New York. Tom Barritt of Burson-Marsteller sent a "pitch letter" to a reporter at *The Wall Street Journal* suggesting this might make a good business story and offering to set up interviews with company officials. The battle of the yellow books emerged as one of the more amusing stories about the consequences of the breakup.

Kyle Kunz, another Burson-Marsteller employee, distributes video news releases of the Army Reserve to television stations. One video showed Reserve troops in Ecuador helping out after a flood. His job is to make the videotapes have legitimate news value.

As more people in public relations have journalism degrees, says Mary Huchette, one of Kunz's fellow workers, the suspicion lessens. "Since we know news values, we can talk one-to-one with journalists," she says.

The public relations worker and the journalist are interdependent. As much as a third to a half of all the material used by newspapers and broadcast stations originates with a public relations or public information specialist. The journalist must rely on the accuracy and truth of the information supplied by the public relations specialist, especially since much of what is contained in press releases is accepted at face value.

True, journalists often rewrite the press releases they receive. But they are usually too busy to verify all material in a release. Studies indicate that fewer than half of the press releases reporters receive are subjected to additional reporting by the journalist. In short, journalists rely on the public relations specialists to do their jobs honestly and fairly. This reliance is sometimes considerable because the public relations worker has access to sources that the reporter may not, and often the public relations person is a specialist in a field with which the reporter is only superficially acquainted.

A general assignment reporter may be assigned to report a development in the nuclear industry, a new organism created through genetic engineering, a complicated local tax plan. In many cases, the reporter will turn to a public information specialist employed by the company, the university or the city for background and direction.

PR Makes News–or Something

The constant need of the wire services for news works to the advantage of public relations firms. Here is a story the AP ran that is based on a PR practitioner's brainstorm. Decide for yourself whether it is news:

NEW YORK (AP)—Give Americans an extra hour and what do they want to do? Not much, it turns out.

In a recent nationwide telephone survey, 1,283 people were asked what they wanted to do with the extra hour they'll get Sunday when daylight-saving time ends. A majority—51 percent—said they just want to be alone—or asleep.

Others were looking foward to such exciting pursuits as "appreciating simple things" (9 percent), "doing fun things . . . goofing off" (6 percent) and "watching television" (2 percent).

Eleven percent said they want to spend the time with a sexual partner or "someone special," but they weren't asked what they wanted to do with that person.

Seven percent want to spend the time with friends; 4 percent with family.

Two percent want to play sports and 2 percent want to do nothing.

Two percent wouldn't say what their plans were, but considering the other responses, nobody is likely to care.

The survey was conducted for Tissot, a Swiss watch company, by Edwards Associates of San Diego.

Public relations cannot control the uses to which its material is put by the press. When NBC called a press conference to promote its series "Little House on the Prairie," it made the star, Michael Landon, available to reporters. Instead of asking about the program, reporters wanted to know why Landon had appeared in commercials promoting Ronald Reagan. Furious, Landon stormed out of the conference.

Most beginning public relations practitioners engage in a wide range of activities, from seeing that the coffee is warm at a news conference to writing a speech for a client.

The new employee will handle calls from news organizations and the public; write and deliver releases to newsrooms; write brochures, assist on research projects; read newspapers and report on developments of interest to the firm or the organization. And more.

The beginner will be asked to help write reports and letters; draft presentations; produce displays and audiovisual material of many types; arrange for meetings; conduct surveys, and go over questionnaire results.

All of this is done under deadline pressure. "Under such high pressure conditions," says the Public Relations Society of America, "nine-to-five schedules go out the window. . . . Meetings, community functions, business lunches, travel assignments, special speaking and writing commitments and unscheduled work on 'crisis' situations often mean long hours."

Chuck Cordt handled sports information for Washburn University of Topeka. His job summary hints at his many tasks:

Sports Information Director

Under the direction of the director of athletics, the sports information director shall coordinate all public relations, publicity, news releases and related activities for the varsity athletic program players and games.

The director's job is to keep the media informed of Washburn's athletic activities, and to do that he produces media guides, writes press releases and makes a lot of phone calls. He also has to coordinate interviews with coaches and players. He is on the sidelines and in the press box during all football and basketball games where his major task is to compile statistics.

Before games he supplies reporters with pre-game information and makes sure that radio and television personnel have the proper hookups for their broadcasts.

Sports publicist Chuck Cordt goes over statistics from last night's basketball game before working on a sports release that will be distributed to reporters covering the team's next game. Before the season, Cordt compiles data from the preceding season with other material for a guide that is sent to all newspapers and broadcast stations in the area.
Photo by Mike Robinson and sports material used with permission.

Sports fans are statistics buffs, and the sports' information offices distribute reams of them. The 1987–88 basketball team compiled a 27–4 record. Fans wanted to mull over the team's accomplishments, and the office supplied them.

When Washburn's basketball team managed to lure a top high school prospect, the office was ready with a detailed press release.

How It's Done

Stripped to its essentials, the public relations process has four tiers:

Research—Determination of what the public thinks of the seller, the individual, the organization.

Program—A public relations program or policy is adopted.

Communication—Positive information consistent with the program is distributed through appropriate channels.

Response—Reactions to the communicated material are evaluated.

Earth Technology

When the Earth Technology Corporation wanted to develop a hazardous waste disposal market, its chief marketing officer devised a plan that she described as "sophisticated, a soft-sell approach."

"An image and communications assessment was conducted among our clients," says Diane C. Creel, head of marketing. "It was found we were still perceived as a smaller, somewhat less sophisticated, less established company than our competitors."

The firm also learned it had little name recognition in the hazardous waste market. Creel said the research found that 80 percent of its business was from "repeat client work," and that a significant amount of business was from fewer than 500 clients.

Direct mail was used by Earth Technology Corporation to reach its target audience with a series of four photographs. Each photo was accompanied by a brief written commentary. One began: "In some ways our step has been too heavy on this, the third planet from the sun. We have created challenges in the geotechnical and earth sciences that were unimaginable a short time ago."
Photo by Jeff Corwin used with permission of the Earth Technology Corporation.

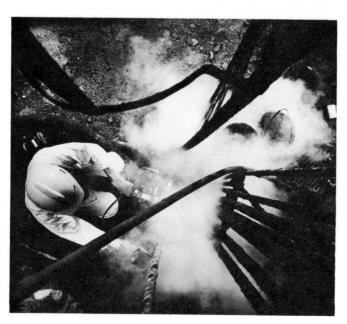

The company decided to reach out to its key clients to produce an image that Earth Technology is "a cut above" its competitors. The study showed that 64 percent of the firm's clients "were influenced by direct mail above any other form of promotional communications."

Since the engineering industry is "rather staid," Creel said, "we did not want to be flashy. It was important that the copy deliver a soft-sell message."

The Communication

Given all this information from their research, Creel and her colleagues decided to send a limited edition photo essay by mail to their clients.

"We wanted our clients to have something they could keep that was special to them," Creel said. It would also be a tangible reminder of Earth Technology.

Response

A photographer and a copywriter were hired. The firm sent out four photos in four separate mailings. The response was gratifying to the company. "Many of the photo essay recipients sent letters of appreciation for the series and praised Earth Technology for being dedicated to professionalism," Creel said. The photo essay also won a number of awards.

Most important, the company's business improved. Its hazardous waste revenues increased during the year from $900,000 to $14.8 million.

The NFL and Drugs

The National Football Players Association, AFL-CIO, which represents 1,600 football players, is often embroiled in disputes with the team owners and the league commissioner. The task of the public relations staff of the association is to keep the players, their agents and retired players informed of matters affecting them, particularly when there are labor disputes. The staff distributes press releases to respond to an issue or to reach the players in the off season when they are scattered around the country. The staff also seeks positive publicity for players by publicizing their awards and activities, such as their participation in charities.

The staff had to jump into action one recent summer when Commissioner Pete Rozelle announced that he was ordering random drug testing. Rozelle was reacting to the news stories about the drug-related deaths of a gifted college basketball player and a professional football player. The players union had not been notified of the testing, and when it heard about the commissioner's action, the union decided the testing violated the collective bargaining agreement between the NFL and the association.

"It was crucial that we respond immediately," said Beverley Pitts, a member of the Ball State University journalism faculty who works in the association's public relations office during the summer months. "The players were going into training camp where the tests would be given in a few days."

The union filed suit to halt the testing. Just before the case was to be heard, an agreement was reached. The union's public relations office was on the courthouse steps with a release giving the players' position and the details of the agreement.

"The public relations director, who wrote the release, was trying to accomplish several things," Pitts said. "First, he wanted the 2,000 players in the NFL to know immediately that they did not have to submit to random testing. The best way to reach the players is through the national media."

Also, the union wanted its version of the conflict to reach the public first. The release quoted the union spokesman, Gene Upshaw, a former player, so the statement would have credibility.

The information the union wanted to pass on was put in quotations from Upshaw "so there would likely be little rewrite" that might have altered the union's points, Pitts said.

News Releases

Just about everyone in public relations writes news or press releases, and for some it is a major part of the their daily work.

Since many news releases cross the desks of editors at newspapers, magazines and broadcast stations, the release had better say something important, interesting or unusual and say it well enough to catch an editor's attention.

The graduating class of 1987 at Columbia College included 325 women, the first women to graduate from the college in its 233-year history. Moreover, many of the prize winners for academic excellence were women, and women played a major role in leading volunteer organizations. It was clear to Fred Knubel, director of public information at Columbia University, that the women's performance could be a major news item. His office sent out a release that began this way:

They came to Columbia College four years ago: more than 300 women pathbreakers in the first year of coeducation at the centuries-old school. Now, as they prepare to graduate tomorrow (Wednesday), they're at the head of the class.

The top two students in the first fully coeducational class to graduate from Columbia College are women. They're also math and science whizzes, and the daughters of professors in the school. The senior class president is a woman, as is the president of the United Minorities Board, the head of the Community Volunteer Service Center and the leaders of many other campus organizations and activities.

In all, some 325 College women expect to earn bachelor's degrees from Columbia this week, about 42 percent of the 765 graduates. In interviews recently with some of these pioneers, they recalled their first days on campus and experience as part of the historic Class of 1987.

"Being 'the first' was certainly part of the attraction of coming to Columbia," said Ritu Birla, whose family lives. . . .

The reporter handling the graduation for *The New York Times* liked the female success angle and used it as the basis of his story. He interviewed several of the women whose names were mentioned in the release. Here is how the *Times* account begins:

At Columbia College, the last Ivy League school to become co-educational, the impact of the first group of women to graduate yesterday was keenly felt.

The graduating class's top academic positions, valedictorian and salutatorian, were held by women, and according to Roger Lehecka, dean of students, most of the seniors who received awards this year are women.

The fact that the reporter's version differed from his did not bother Knubel. His job—creating a positive image for the university—was done.

Journalism training comes in handy for those writing press releases.

"We always use news style, tight leads, concise paragraphs," says Pitts. Information for the release is gathered in the same way as reporters gather material for their stories.

"Background data is researched, quotes and additional information are gathered through interviews, and a draft is written that is reviewed by the director of public relations and other staff members," she said.

The public relations practitioner must have several skills in addition to writing competence, especially in smaller organizations. If the job calls for editing on the employee magazine, the public relations practitioner may shoot the photos, write the story and design the layout.

Some of the critics of public relations contend that the whitewashing by the public relations expert covers truths that often are better opened to the public.

Past and Present

Ivy Lee generated vast publicity for John D. Rockefeller with a gimmick. Lee had Rockefeller hand out dimes to everyone he met. The newspapers loved to run photos of Rockefeller bending down to pat some tow-headed youngster while handing him a dime.

The work of the public relations practitioners was awesome in the case of Rockefeller and the Rockefeller interests. It is easier to find references to Rockefeller's dimes than a description of the Ludlow Massacre in histories, for example.

In Ludlow, Colo., a band of strikers, their wives and children were attacked by state troops in their tent camp outside Rockefeller's Colorado Fuel and Iron Company mine.

Dissatisfaction with the public relations information supplied by the women's fashion industry led to the creation of *The Clothes Report* and similar newsletters, magazines and special supplements. Called advertorials or info-mercials, the material is sponsored by a single corporation. *The Clothes Report* and its kin differ from the traditional publicity kit in that the kits tend to focus on the product whereas material in the info-mercial covers general trends and uses the sponsor's products as illustrations. The newsletter format gives an aura of legitimacy to the editorial content. As a result, local newspapers can—and do—reprint the material, including the name of the sponsor and its products. (The use of the material unedited raises serious ethical questions for the publications that print the material.)
PRADS Inc., The Clothes Report. Used with permission.

the clothes report

prepared by the Editors of RetailWeek/Clothes

DENIM '88: THE MANY FACES OF SPRING/SUMMER

By GRACE KOLBE
the clothes report

CONE MILLS PHOTOS

CONTRASTS IN COLOR DIRECTION AND BODY-CONSCIOUS STYLING are the dominant fashion trends in denim for Spring/Summer '88, according to Noel Rosenbower, Cone Mill's director of communications. Using the heavyweight 14-ounce weave, manufacturers are focusing on the opposite ends of the light-dark spectrum. Regardless of color, jean cuts tend to be close-fitting; jackets are shorter and tighter; tops are cropped.

The ensemble at left, from Candies®, features the new capri-length pants that fit like a second skin, coordinated with an abbreviated western jacket. Both are in indigo-dyed denim that has been "dynamite" washed to a very pale, variegated blue. The choice of a technicolor-striped camp shirt adds the dash of bold contrast that is de rigueur this season.

The shrink-to-fit® construction of Levi's® original 501®, at right, ensures a close-to-the-curve look. In this outfit, the dark hue of the black denim stone-washed jean is juxtaposed against the crisp white of the cropped top. The floral suspenders add that important note of bright color.

The overall effect of both approaches is clean and streamlined, whether a woman buys pieces pre-coordinated by the manufacturer or puts together her own separates. Individuality is more subtle, less strident, and is best attained through careful selection of tops and accessories.

the clothes report is published by PRADS Inc., former publisher of RetailWeek and Clothes. REPRINTING of text and photographs is PERMITTED. Please send tear sheets to 21 Charles Street, Westport, CT 06880 · (203) 264-0377. Publisher: Lewis E. Kaplan. Editor: Carolyn Carpentieri Potter. Vol. 1, No. 4. HALFTONES AT 150 LINE. FOUR-COLOR SLIDES AVAILABLE.

The story begins when the company and other mine operators refused to recognize the worker's union, which wanted an eight-hour workday, the abolition of the criminal guard system, strict enforcement of state mining laws (which were being ignored by a state government sympathetic to the operators), a weighman of the miners' selection, and the right to live where they wished and to buy goods where they pleased.

The owners refused to meet the miners' request, and in September 1913 8,000–10,000 miners and their families trooped out of the southern Colorado canyons and set up tent camps. They knew what they could expect: The miners dug trenches around the camps and holes inside the tents for women and children in case of an attack by the state militia, which the governor was certain to call out.

John D. Rockefeller Jr. was adamant and the strike continued. Foreign miners were hired, and the operators employed special guards to patrol their properties. Tension grew, and the strike dragged into the following year. On April 20, a shot was fired at the Ludlow tent camp, and the Massacre began. The 200 militiamen were outnumbered by the strikers, but the militia was armed with machine guns, and as the guns swept the camp a fire broke out, trapping the women and children in their tents.

Just how many died is uncertain. *The New York Times* of April 22, 1914, reported 45 dead, "more than two-thirds of them women and children, a score missing and more than a score wounded" in the 14-hour battle.

The strike failed. Rockefeller did not recognize the union. The battle at Ludlow became known as the Ludlow Massacre.

This is history, and times have changed. Big business is said to be enlightened, and some of the enlightening has originated with the advice of public relations practitioners that the firms act in the public interest. A study by Michael Ryan of the University of Houston found most public relations practitioners state that "developing programs that are good for society is good business; that a corporation that is socially responsible is more credible."

Some agencies advise their employees to understand the consequences of dealing at a distance with people. Person-to-person communication makes people less prone to exaggeration, to truth-stretching. But when the copywriter sits down to write about a product, he or she is isolated from the buyer or user and the temptation is to enter a world of words. There, the copywriter manipulates language, free of the possible stares of disbelief and incredulity of an audience.

The writer can be a master sytlist, can be a fountain of information on subjects large and minute. But unless he or she has an awareness of and a respect for the people at whom the work is directed, the best-crafted news release, the most persuasive advertisement is stripped of value.

What Employers Look For

Most advertising and public relations agencies test job applicants. The interviewer looks over the applicant's college record, work experience and references. A journalism major is helpful. For the large agencies, experience may be necessary, but this is not always required. However, for the applicant without previous work in the field, some sign of commitment to advertising, journalism or public relations is usually essential.

Mary Huchette went to Burson-Marsteller directly after graduation from Ohio University. Though she lacked professional experience, she was able to demonstrate her commitment: In high school, she did public relations work for the school district and was the school correspondent for her local newspaper.

Commitment to the job is essential, says Terrie M. Williams. But the long hours and tiring work are balanced by challenging assignments and unlimited opportunity, she says. She realized her ambition to have her own agency. It handles entertainment and sports figures and corporate accounts. Among her first clients were Eddie Murphy, the actor-comedian; Miles Davis, a legendary jazz master, and Essence, publisher of a national black women's lifestyle magazine.
Photo of Terrie Williams by Bruce Williams. Used with permission.

The agency also looks for imagination, an ability to get along with people, creativity and an appetite for work.

Terrie M. Williams, who at 32 was the youngest vice president in the history of Essence Communications, works long hours. She arrives at her office at 9:30 in the morning and often works until 10 or 11 at night. She worries about "burnout, running yourself ragged. The job can totally consume you."

"You have to have endurance," says Connie Byerlee of Burson-Marsteller. You also have to be able to do journalistic tasks.

In talking about the problems that beginners have, John Atropoeus, editorial director for Burson-Marsteller, says, "Some don't seem to have the energy to check so-called facts."

Arthur V. Ciervo, director of public information and relations for The Pennsylvania State University, suggested several precautions in hiring news bureau writers:

"Always give a writing test. Because writing is a large part of any staff member's work in a news bureau, he or she must be a good writer. . . . Some directors ask the applicant to read a certain speech and write a news story based on it. Others have the applicant write a feature article, based on interview notes or other sources of information. . . . Look for writing style, speed and accuracy."

Atropoeus judges the written tests taken by applicants for jobs at his agency. The test consists of several parts:

Editing a paragraph to correct misspellings and misplaced pronouns; eliminate unnecessary words; improve and correct word usage.

Writing a picture caption from a set of facts.

Writing a 250-word press release on a new product.

Correcting redundancies.

Writing a news release on a speech.

"The most common mistake I see on the speech story is the lead that begins, 'So-and-so spoke last night on the subject of such-and-such.' " Artopoeus said. "Too many don't know what news is and what a lead is."

"Most of today's senior public relations practitioners started in journalism," says the Public Relations Society of America. "The experience gained in writing, personal contact, and other aspects of work for metropolitan or smaller newspapers, general or trade magazines, and broadcasting media is still deemed important by a majority of public relations employers."

Agencies do hire public relations majors, of course. The demand has been steadily growing. There are an estimated 150,000 practitioners in public relations, although so many people are associated with the field that some estimate the actual number at closer to half a million.

Salaries begin at around $15,000, and for those who become the directors of small or medium-sized companies the salary is about $40,000. The practitioner with a large firm can earn $150,000 a year and up.

Up the Career Ladder

Here is the pay scale for a large agency and the period an employee usually is on the job before being considered for promotion:

Account representative—$18–20,000; six months to one year.

Assistant account executive—mid $20s; one year.

Account executive—high $20s to mid-$30s; one to two years.

Senior account executive—high $30s; unlimited.

Account supervisor—unlimited.

A year or so of experience in journalism usually leads to employment as an assistant account executive.

NEW YORK UNIVERSITY

GRADUATE SCHOOL OF BUSINESS ADMINISTRATION
Student Handbook

Published by the Office of Student Affairs
Graduate School of Business Administration
New York University
100 Trinity Place
New York, N.Y. 10006
(212) 285-8823

From Backgrounders to Brochures

The range of activities by the public relations specialist is considerable, says Richard Kwartler, director of public affairs for the School of Business at New York University. "The days are long gone when all that a public relations office had to worry about was putting out a few news releases a month," he says. Kwartler, an experienced newsman who worked for the *Plain Dealer* in Cleveland and *Newsday* in New York, supervises activities that include reporting, writing, editing and publishing. *NYU Business* is mailed to 50,000 alumni twice a year. His office designs brochures, posters and reports as well.

The office also handles calls from reporters for background information from faculty members. "Why all this activity?" Kwartler answers his question: "The battle of the business schools is intense. Big name schools compete for good students and top-flight faculty members. A study shows that in picking a business school students rely heavily on stories they read about the curriculum, faculty and alumni in newspapers, magazines and school publications."
Material from the Office of Public Affairs, Leonard N. Stern School of Business, New York University. Used with permission.

Aronson, Steven M. I. *Hype.* New York, Wm. Morrow & Co. Inc., 1983.

Packard, Vance. *The Hidden Persuaders.* New York: Pocket Books, 1957.

Suggested Reading

Part Five
Laws and Codes

"Then I got that awful phone call."

"SHE'D NEVER CALLED ME BEFORE. We'd just been together a couple of times.

So she tells me she's pregnant.

I mean. I didn't know what to say. There's just this silence on the phone until she asks if I died.

She sounds like she's burnt out on crying and you don't know what to do. It's like you're a blank.

The worst part is I wake up in the morning and it just rushes at me. Quit school. Get married. Run away from it. I don't know.

I didn't know then and I don't know now.

All I know is all the ways it shouldn't have happened. All those easy ways. But it's a little too late for that, I guess.

Too late this lifetime, for me."

Nobody has all the answers about sex. But keep in mind that a million teen girls get pregnant every year. Which means a million guys don't hear the end of it. Here's your choice. You can take responsibility when it's easy or you can wait until it's impossible. Don't make a big mistake. Buy a condom. You can get them at any drugstore or from your local Planned Parenthood. If you need help or information, call us. That's what we're here for.

 Planned Parenthood®
Federation of America

810 Seventh Avenue,
New York, NY 10019

15

Libel, Ethics and Taste

Decisions of reporters and their editors can lead to offended readers and listeners and libel suits unless they are made with some idea of the community's sense of propriety and a knowledge of libel law. A grasp of the morality of journalism helps guide reporters also. *Editor & Publisher.*

Looking Ahead

The laws of libel and privacy, codes of ethics and guidelines on matters of taste place limits on the journalist.

Libel is the publication of false and malicious material that damages a person's reputation. A person who can prove he or she has been injured by a story or photograph can collect damages in a libel suit. Stories that are based on facts and are thorough, fair and impartial are free of libel.

Privacy is the right of the individual to be left alone. A reporter cannot invade a person's home or use listening or recording devices to intrude on a person's privacy.

Ethics are not enforced by laws. They are understandings among journalists as to what is proper journalistic behavior. Some of these agreements are formulated in codes. The personal beliefs and traditions of journalists also constitute ethical commitments.

Taste—what society considers proper in the use of language and subject matter—changes with time and depends on the nature of the audience and who is involved in the event. Generally, material that is considered vulgar, obscene, profane, or offensive is permissible only if it is absolutely essential to the news story.

• The news story was like a dozen others that the newspaper had printed—a local resident had been arrested for drunk driving. But this one led to a libel suit.

• For several months, the reporter was underground. He had used a false identity to work his way into membership of the Ku Klux Klan for a series of articles on the organization that preaches hatred of blacks, Jews and Catholics. Some journalists questioned the methods he used to gather information for his articles.

• On their 6 p.m. news broadcasts, two Cleveland television stations reported that a coroner's examination of a 69-year-old woman murdered in a parking lot determined that the body was actually that of a man. The victim was Stella Walsh, a former women's Olympic track champion and a well-known member of Cleveland's Polish-American community, which assailed the news reports of the two stations.

• Reporters for *The Miami Herald* staked out the area around the Washington, D.C., home of Gary Hart, the leading candidate for the Democratic presidential nomination. They saw a young woman enter in the evening. The reporters did not see her leave. They printed what they had observed.

What was wrong, if anything, with these news stories? In this chapter, we will be looking at (1) libel laws, (2) journalistic ethics and (3) guidelines for matters of taste to find the answers. First, to libel.

Libel

The news story reported that L.D. Sylvester of 536 Western Ave. had been arrested for drunk driving the night before and had posted bond. Several weeks later, Sylvester's lawyer sued the newspaper for libel. Sylvester said he had never been arrested. In fact, he had been out of town the evening that the newspaper had him careening down the center of town.

An error had been made, the editor learned on a quick check. There was nothing to do but settle out of court for several thousand dollars. The newspaper had no defense.

What had happened was simple, but devastating. In his haste at the police station, the police reporter had scribbled the man's name and address on his note pad. Drunk driving stories are not major events, and the reporter had been hurrying to get on to more important arrests.

Back in the office, the reporter could not read the scribbled address and looked in the telephone book for the address of L.D. Sylvester. He found the address as 536 Western Ave., which went into the story.

Actually, the arrested person was T.D. Sylvester of 561 Eastern Ave.

The incident reveals the cause of most libel suits: sloppy reporting and careless writing, the failure to check or verify potentially dangerous material.

Definition of Libel

Libel is the publication of material that injures a person by causing:

1. Financial loss.
2. Damage to reputation.
3. Humiliation, mental anguish or suffering.

Newspapers do publish stories that cause people to lose their jobs and that damage their reputations and humiliate them. The Ohio congressman who put his mistress on his Washington payroll in a do-nothing job was exposed by reporters and defeated for re-election. No job and a tarnished reputation. Even so, the congressman did not sue for libel because the story was true. He knew a suit would be hopeless. The reporters had the sworn statement of the woman and proof from the payroll records.

A true story can be printed or broadcast without fear. When the story is untrue, however, there is trouble. In the Sylvester incident, the story of his arrest was the only erroneous one of a dozen arrest stories that weekend. The other people undoubtedly were humiliated by the news of their arrests. Unlike Sylvester, they had no grounds for a libel suit. The printed reports were accurate.

The *Enquirer* and Carol Burnett

Inaccuracy can be costly. The *National Enquirer* carried this item in one of its columns:

At a Washington restaurant, a boisterous Carol Burnett had a loud argument with another diner, Henry Kissinger. She traipsed around the place offering everyone a bite of her dessert. But Carol really raised eyebrows when she accidentally knocked a glass of wine over one diner—and started giggling instead of apologizing. The guy wasn't amused and "accidentally" spilled a glass of water over Carol's dress.

A month later, the newspaper published a retraction admitting its report was wrong. But Burnett sued for libel. The television star testified that despite the retraction, the item had caused her anguish and diminished reputation.

The jury hearing the Burnett case felt that she had been so seriously defamed and had suffered such humiliation that it awarded her $300,000 in compensatory damages (for injuries actually suffered) and $1.3 million in punitive damages (to punish the *Enquirer*). The award was later lowered to $200,000 by a California appeals court.

Key Supreme Court Rulings on Libel

New York Times Co. v. Sullivan, 376 U.S. 254 (1964)—Requires public officials to show that the publication printed a defamatory statement knowing that it was false or with reckless disregard for the truth.

Curtis Publishing Co. v. Butts and *AP v. Walker,* 388 U.S. 130 (1967)—In deciding these two cases together, the Court established its meaning of "reckless disregard of truth." Justice John Harlan applied three criteria to the problem: Was publication of a story urgent—a rush news item—or was there time for a reporter to check his facts? (The Butts case involved a magazine; the AP case involved a fast-breaking news story.) Was the source of a story reliable or suspect? Was a story probable on its face or improbable enough to warrant further investigation? Butts won his case; Walker lost his.

Gertz v. Welch, 418 U.S. 323 (1974)—The Court held that a **private person** could win a libel suit without showing actual malice. The court returned to an emphasis on the status of a libel plaintiff rather than the subject matter involved. It required **public figures** as well as **public officials** to meet the actual malice liability standard. Public figures, the Court said, are of two types: public figures for all purposes, those who "occupy positions of persuasive power and influence"; and **limited public figures,** those who voluntarily step into the public spotlight in order to influence the resolution of a public issue.

There are three basic defenses against libel suits:

Libel Defenses

1. **Truth** If the reporter can show that the defamatory material is true, the offended person may sue but usually cannot win. It is not enough for the reporter to say he or she thought the material was truthful or that someone said it was true. There must be proof of its truth. Truth is almost always an absolute defense in a libel suit.

2. **Privilege** Anything said in a **public and official** legislative or judicial situation—whether it is true or false—can be reported. Legislative bodies include the city council, county commissions, state legislature and congress. In the courts, statements by attorneys, the judge and witnesses and any documents filed with the court are privileged.

3. **Fair Comment and Criticism** Critics who assess the work of artists, authors, performers, sports figures and others who offer their services to the public may comment on the work or performance. The criticism must be based on facts and must not attack the personal life of the individual whose work is being assessed. The comment must not be malicious.

In all of these defenses, the reporter is on safe ground if the report is a full, fair, impartial and accurate account of the event. If the story is so one-sided that it could be proved that the reporter intentionally singled out the critical or defamatory material, the reporter could be in trouble if sued.

The Sullivan Ruling

In 1964, the U.S. Supreme Court granted reporters some leeway for their mistakes. In a famous case, *The New York Times* v. *Sullivan,* the Court ruled that if a **public official** is the victim of a libelous story, the official must prove that the account was published with "actual malice." To prove actual malice, the official must prove in court that the material was published with:

1. The knowledge that it was false, or
2. The reckless disregard of whether the material was true.

The Sullivan decision took away from the individual state courts their control over libel actions. In its ruling, the Court said that a constitutional issue was involved—freedom of the press. This is why so many libel decisions are appealed to federal courts.

For a while, the Court's ruling about "actual malice" was extended to public figures and to private individuals involved in public or official matters.

However, recent court decisions have restricted the definition of a public figure, so that now some public figures and most private individuals need only prove that the defamatory material was published or broadcast because of carelessness or negligence.

Public Officials

Elected officials—mayor, governor, members of congress, legislators, city council members, etc.

High-level appointed officials—supervisors, inspectors, medical examiners, cabinet members, etc.

Police officers

Judges

Careful: Not all public employees are public officials.

Public Figures

People with power and influence—newspaper columnists, authors, radio and television personalities, popular performers, union officials

People involved in important public controversies who seek to influence the outcome—a person who vigorously and publicly opposes or supports a referendum, bond issue, candidacy

---

Public figures can be libeled unless the reporter is careful. The figure must be involved in some public issue. Defamatory material about the person's private life would not be protected unless the personal actions had some bearing on matters of public concern.

Any story that contains material that might injure someone's reputation should be treated carefully. Hasty, careless reporting and writing are dangerous. Some suggestions:

Avoiding Libel

Confirm and verify all possibly defamatory material. A reporter should double-check anything that:

1. Questions a person's fitness to handle his or her job.

2. Alleges a person has committed a crime or has performed some act that constitutes a crime.

3. Implies or directly states that a person has a mental illness or a loathsome disease.

Make sure that questionable material can be proved true.

Be especially careful of arrest reports, damage suits and criminal court hearings. These stories cause more libel suits than all others, and almost all are the result of careless reporting or writing. Check names, addresses; make sure the defendant and plaintiff are properly identified.

Watch out for charges, assertions, claims. Just because someone says something and you quote the person accurately does not mean you have avoided libel. If a district attorney tells you he is investigating a business that has a long string of lawsuits and you quote the official, you may lose a libel suit if the owner proves he has never been sued. If the district attorney makes the same statement in a court proceeding, or if he files charges and makes any allegations in them, the material may be used because it is protected by the defense of privilege.

Don't try to sneak in defamatory material by suggestion with such words as *allegedly,* **or** *reported.* These are not protections against libel.

When charges and accusations are made in a privileged situation, it is a good idea to check with the person being defamed. This demonstrates your fairness.

Watch out for words that a court may hold to be libelous. Some of these words and their context:

Subject	Dangerous Words
Commission of a crime	Swindler, thief, loan shark, shoplifter, bigamist, gangster, ex-convict
Performance in job or profession	Incompetent, failure, quack, shyster, hack, bribery, slick operator
Diseases that could cause a person to be ostracized	Wino, leper, sickie, AIDS victim, addict
Damage to a person's credit	Unreliable, bankrupt, gambler, cheat, failure
Lack of chastity	Loose, B-girl, hooker, seducer, immoral, streetwalker, adultery, prostitute, gigolo, pimp
Lack of mental capacity	Screwy, nutty, strange, incompetent, out-of-it
Incite ridicule or contempt	Phony, coward, hypocrite, communist, fascist

Don't color the article with opinions. Watch out for personal enthusiasms that cause you to lose control of the writing.

Be careful of statements by police or court officials outside court.

Truth is a defense, but good intentions are not. You may not have meant to defame someone, but when your well-intended writing proves to be untrue, your intention is no defense.

A retraction of an error is not a defense. It may lessen damages and could eliminate punitive damages.

Another danger area for reporters is the private lives of individuals. Reporters cannot indiscriminately pry, peek and probe into the personal affairs of anyone they choose to single out.

Privacy

In their search for news, reporters gather material about the personal lives of people that can be embarrassing or unpleasant to those involved. Newspapers routinely carry hospital admissions, divorce actions, arrests and traffic violations. Reporters search out and interview the parents of children killed in automobile accidents and fires. Sunday supplements and magazines detail the sex lives of the stars and the drug habits and alcoholism of athletes. Television carries the shame and the grief of those involved in tragedy and crime into millions of living rooms.

These stories can be published and broadcast because the people are involved in legitimate news events. The drunk driver has no claim to privacy when he or she is arrested. The details of a divorce case may be published. The horrors of a nursing home fire and the sorrow of relatives may be shown on television.

A Florida newspaper published the picture of a scantily clad woman being led by police from an apartment house where she had been held captive. The woman sued, claiming the picture had embarrassed and humiliated her. Her lawyer told a jury that there was no argument about the truth of the incident but that the picture had invaded her privacy. The jury agreed and awarded the woman $10,000 in damages.

The verdict was appealed and the appeals court reversed the decision. It found that the photograph was part of a legitimate news story and that its publication was not so outrageous as to show intentional "infliction of emotional distress."

However, when the press digs into private acts that are of no public interest or that are of no legitimate concern to the public, there can be trouble, even when the account is accurate. The law of libel protects a person's reputation and character. The right of privacy gives the person the right to be left alone, unless the person is involved in a legitimate news event.

The right to privacy protects people from several kinds of activities that journalists engage in:

Publicizing private matters   Public disclosure of private facts and acts of an individual that are considered offensive can lead to legal trouble. Sensational material about a person's love life, health, business affairs or social activities can constitute invasion of privacy. If the acts are private and of no legitimate concern to the public, the material is dangerous.

If a rock star talks about his drug habit, or an athlete discloses he is struggling with alcoholism, the information can be used. The courts have ruled that personal material can be used if it concerns a **newsworthy person,** is of **public concern** and **is not "highly offensive to a reasonable person, one of ordinary sensibilities."**

If the activity takes place in public or the information is in a public document—no matter how sensational or offensive—it can be used.

Intrusion   If the reporter forces himself or herself into a private area to gather news, this is intrusion. The intrusion need not be physical. The use of tape recorders, hidden microphones, cameras and any other kind of electronic equipment without the person's permission is intrusion, even if the material is not used.

When a reporter misrepresents his or her identity to gain entrance, eavesdrops on personal affairs or trespasses, this is intrusion.

Publicizing false material   When a reporter tries to dramatize an event by inventing material, or when a television station produces a docudrama—a fictionalized account of an actual person or event—and defamatory material is used, the person may be placed before the public in what the law calls a "false light." A person may also be placed in a false light when he or she is linked to a defamatory situation. For example: A documentary on drug dealers operating on a city street may inadvertently show an innocent pedestrian walking down the street.

Appropriation   Use of someone's name or picture for advertising or for commercial purposes or for one's own use constitutes appropriation, unless consent is given. Legitimate news events can be covered, and no permission is needed. However, a feature story that uses the name and activities of a well-known person can be the cause of problems if the purpose of the story is to promote the newspaper's sales. In this situation, a court may rule that the story was designed to exploit the commercial value of the person.

An excellent guide to the laws of libel and privacy is *Synopsis of the Law of Libel and the Right of Privacy* by Bruce W. Sanford, published by Scripps-Howard Newspapers. The paperback edition is distributed by World Almanac Publications, 200 Park Ave., New York, N.Y. 10166. Sanford is with the law firm that represents Scripps-Howard and has lectured and written extensively on libel and privacy.

Reporters increasingly are looking into the private lives of public figures and while much of what they publish and broadcast is free of legal problems, these reports pose ethical problems. Deciding what is right and wrong is one of the most difficult tasks a reporter faces.

When reporters described what apparently was the extramarital affair of Gary Hart, there was no legal problem involved. Although Hart's activities with the woman involved his private life, as a public figure, Hart's acts were legitimately of concern to the public.

Journalistic Ethics

• A reporter for the Oceanside, Calif., *Blade-Tribune* wrote a column for the newspaper that was almost a word-for-word copy of a column by Art Buchwald. He was asked to resign.

• A columnist for the *Daily News* in New York invented characters and quotes in a story about a street clash between British soldiers and a gang of youths in Belfast, Northern Ireland. He was forced to resign.

• A sports writer for *The Evening Tribune* in San Diego wrote a piece that contained material that had been published in *Inside Sports*. For using "certain phraseologies" from the magazine, he was suspended from his job.

• A *Washington Post* reporter who won a Pulitzer Prize in 1981 for her moving story about an 8-year-old heroin addict was fired when it was discovered that her story was fiction. The *Post* returned the prize.

• Walter Cronkite accepted an appointment to the board of directors of Pan American World Airways after he stepped down from his long tenure as the anchor of the "CBS Evening News." Cronkite became a special correspondent for the network, and some of his work was to involve coverage of space programs with which Pan American had contracts. Cronkite was criticized for accepting the post on the ground it was a potential conflict of interests for him to accept money from an enterprise he would be covering. Six months after joining the Pan American board, Cronkite resigned from it.

These situations involve matters of journalistic ethics. Each is an example of a violation of one of the underlying rules of conduct for the journalist.

The journalist is expected to be truthful, to do his or her own work, to avoid pursuing any activity that would raise questions about his or her integrity. These and other ethical principles are outlined in various codes that newspapers, broadcast stations and national journalism organizations have adopted.

The basketball player was a drug addict, Kevin Simpson heard. But Simpson, who covered professional basketball for the *Rocky Mountain News,* sat on the story. When he confirmed the story with the player's manager, Simpson was asked to hold off until the star athlete could enter a clinic. Simpson complied, in return for the manager's promise of an exclusive story. "The story was not more important than the player's getting help," Simpson said.

The codes prescribe responsibility to the reader or listener, accuracy, fairness and compassion.

In its code, the American Society of Newspaper Editors lists six areas of ethical behavior:

Responsibility   The task of the journalist is to serve the general welfare by informing people so they can make judgments about the issues confronting them. Journalists should not abuse their power for selfish motives or unworthy purposes.

Freedom of the press   Freedom belongs to the people, and journalists must make sure public business is conducted in public. They must be vigilant against those who exploit the press for their purposes.

Independence   Journalists must avoid conflicts of interest. They should accept nothing from sources nor engage in any activity that compromises or might seem to compromise their integrity.

Truth and accuracy   The journalist must seek to keep the good faith of readers by assuring them that the news is accurate, free from bias, and that all sides are presented fairly.

Impartiality   News reports and opinion should be clearly distinct. Opinion articles should be clearly identified as such.

Fair play   Journalists should respect the rights of people in the news and be accountable to the public for the fairness and accuracy of their reports. Persons accused in the news should be allowed to respond.

(The Code of Ethics of the Society of Professional Journalists is included in Appendix D.)

But codes are not complete guides to ethical behavior. No code, for example, can say whether *The Miami Herald* behaved ethically when it spied on Hart. The newspaper's reporters hid in bushes and cars to watch Hart.

In the ensuing furor, Hart dropped out of the race. His advisers told him that questions had been raised about his judgment and his personal life that he could never satisfactorily answer.

The reaction of journalists was less decisive. A reporter for *The Cincinnati Post* said: "Hart's bedmates are nobody's business—unless he gets AIDS." The editor of the *Albuquerque Tribune* said: "Sure, the *Herald's* methods were unorthodox. But they were necessary." Nicholas Von Hoffman, a syndicated columnist, described the reporters as "gonad-seeking practitioners of sex-snoop journalism."

Several prominent journalists refused to condemn the original story, but they said they would not accept an assignment to spy on an individual's personal activities. This brings us to one of the bedrocks of ethical behavior, a personal code.

A Newspaper's Code of Ethics

The following guidelines are excerpted from the code of ethics of *The Des Moines Register:*

An individual's own good judgment and integrity are the keystones of this code because it would be impossible to spell out every single question that might arise. . . .

Our management and employees must remain free of obligation to any special interest . . . avoiding all possible conflicts of interest or even the appearance thereof. . . .

MEALS—This code will continue the present company policy of having staff members pay for their own meals. . . . When it [is] impossible to pay for a meal beforehand or at the time . . . appropriate payment [shall be] sent later.

TRAVEL— . . . There are times when staffers ride with sports teams on chartered aircraft or with public officials on military aircraft or in chartered private aircraft with a political figure. On such occasions, the company will send a check covering our staffer's share of the transportation.

TICKETS—It shall be our policy that no staffer accept any free ticket to any event.

OUTSIDE EMPLOYMENT AND ACTIVITIES— . . . No employee will hold membership on boards of directors of corporations, or assume leadership or activist roles on boards or organizations about which this employee might be called upon to write stories, take pictures, edit copy or make editorial judgments.

. . . Working for a political candidate or party would be a clear conflict of interests for almost any staff member. . . . There is a flat rule against any employee producing publicity material for any public official, politician, government agency or sports team. . . . [No staff member shall] make public statements of opinion that will compromise that staff member's credibility on the job.

Personal Code

Most of us know right from wrong. Our moral sense might have been influenced by our parents, schools or religious training. Some of our guidelines come from reading. For some young men and women, friends exert a powerful influence in establishing what is right and wrong.

For two days, a 16-year-old student at Milpitas High School in California bragged to his classmates he had raped and strangled his 14-year-old girlfriend. He then led several friends to a remote spot in the foothills near San Jose and showed them her body.

Eight youngsters saw the body of the girl. Some covered it with leaves to hide it. One dropped a rock on her head to make sure the corpse was really that of a human.

Not one of the youngsters informed the police.

An assembly-line worker was shown the body by a student who had been taken to the scene by the 16-year-old. The worker called the police.

When word got out that the body had been recovered, some of the high school students criticized the worker for notifying the police. One described him as a "snitch . . . a fucking narc." The worker said that he had been hassled for his action. "I don't know if I'd do it again," he said.

Sheriff's Sgt. Gary Meeker wondered, "What the hell has happened to these kids?"

Sgt. Ron Icely of the Milpitas Police Department thinks he knows. "Usually when people are witnesses to a homicide, they come forward right away," he said. "But you have this code of honor (that says) forget about the girl on the side of the ravine and let's protect our buddy."

Although loyalty to friends is an honorable quality, we must respond to a greater demand on our loyalty, and this is our responsibility to society. Journalists can use their social responsibility as a basis for establishing a personal code of behavior.

Responsibility and Independence

Journalism is a public service. Its practitioners are independent of commitments or obligations to any special group. The journalist places responsibility to the public above and beyond loyalty to an employer, a political party or friends.

Passing on information is the journalist's duty. Thus, if a source or a friend asks that something be withheld from print or broadcast, the journalist must weigh the request against his or her commitment to inform the public.

If an editor, publisher or news director kills a story or removes information from a story on the ground that it will hurt business, advertising or friends of the newspaper or station, the journalist must confront the situation from the same moral perspective—the obligation to report truths.

In both cases, the action the journalist must take is clear: See that the information reaches readers and listeners. As a result, some journalists have lost sources and some have quit their jobs rather than be a party to a cover-up.

Sometimes, this independence can be strained to the breaking point, as it is when reporters learn about something that the government wants kept secret because of "national security." In such cases, the reporter is confronted by a dilemma. In a democracy, the public is entitled to know what its government is doing. At the same time, revealing this information endangers security, according to the government.

This brings us to a second basic point in the formulation of a personal code. The point is that journalists serve their readers and listeners by checking on power. They maintain an adversary relationship to power. The power may be held by a dean, a corporation president, the mayor or the president.

Watching Power

The founders of this country made sure that journalists would be free of government interference or supervision so that the press could be a check on power.

If we go back to the first part of this chapter where we discussed libel, you can see the willingness of the federal courts to grant journalists wide freedom, even the freedom to make mistakes that libel officials. In the Sullivan ruling, the Supreme Court said that the press needs to be free of restrictions so that it can provide "the opportunity for free political discussion to the end that government may be responsive to the will of the people. . . ."

Reporters and their newspapers have confronted power at the highest levels, even at the risk of compromising what officials have said is "national security."

Given such power, the press can be an unchecked power itself. If government has no control over the press, what then is to protect the public from a free-wheeling, irresponsible press? Very little. And this is precisely why codes and guidelines—whether they are written and handed to reporters along with a stylebook, or are the reporter's personal beliefs—are so important.

We have discussed two essentials for a personal code of ethics—responsibility to the public and independence from power. A third is the mission to seek truth.

Search for Truth

Most reporters understand that they should be truthful. But what is truth? At one level, it is the accurate reporting of what a source says in an interview. But the truth-seeker must do more. On important stories, the reporter is obligated to dig into causes, to peel away the layers of the event that conceal the truth.

A tenement burns down. One person is killed. The reporter quotes the investigators about the cause—faulty wiring. Other buildings in the neighborhood have been damaged by fire. The reporter senses a pattern and checks records, looks at property transfers, examines insurance claims. She finds that most of the fires are listed as being of suspicious origin, that the buildings have been heavily insured, and that they are owned by local police officers.

Newspapers lack "sustained outrage over basic injustices and fundamental idiocies," said W.E. Chilton III, publisher of *The Charleston* (W.Va.) *Gazette*. "We hit an issue and then pass on to something else. We show the attention span of a postal clerk. . . . We're sitting on our mountains of money and our tremendous power, and we might just as well be silent for all the impact we're having on our society."

Her stories exposed the sordid affair. Some of the officers sued for libel, but a New Jersey court tossed out the suit after finding the stories were accurate.

Reporters have little tolerance for any person or any action that hurts people. This is the fourth point in our personal code. Journalists are concerned with the victims of unfair, illegal, discriminatory actions. They consider such actions pollutants in the community.

Poses and Disguises

At the beginning of this chapter, mention was made of the reporter who adopted a false identity to expose the Ku Klux Klan in his state. The use of poses and disguises is an old device frequently used by investigative reporters. A *Wall Street Journal* reporter obtained a job in a factory in Texas and then revealed the company's harsh personnel practices and anti-union bias. A reporter for *The Washington Post* feigned mental illness and was admitted to a large mental hospital. She described the inadequate care given patients.

Lately, newspapers are questioning the use of this technique. They do not feel free to criticize others for illegal and underhanded actions in business and public life if they are themselves using questionable tactics to gather news.

Spies, snoops and informers are not respected in our society. Yet the newspaper whose reporters use poses and disguises do spy and snoop and then tell the story. It seems unethical, and it is. But it can be justified, under certain circumstances.

The reporter who is trying to formulate a personal ethical code might want to consider this point: When a critical condition exists in which lives are endangered by a person or an organization, the journalist may use a tactic or a technique that otherwise would be considered unethical.

If the tactic will remove or publicize the danger, then the reporter may find justification for purposely misleading people from whom he or she intends to elicit information.

The journalist has a responsibility to the general society to serve as its watchdog, and sometimes this requires the warning bark of a brief story. At other times, it may be necessary to bite deeply into the situation. We punish the dog that bites unnecessarily, but we reward the watchdog that grabs the gunman by the arm, or threatens the thief's throat.

In the case of the Klan, its members have advocated violence against minority groups, and some Klansmen have been sentenced to prison for murder. The reporter who joined the Klan by using a pose may be thought of as providing a public service.

When such techniques are used, they should be described to the reader or listener. A tactic or technique used by a reporter that he or she is ashamed to admit in print or on the air should not be used in reporting.

Guidelines for a Personal Code of Ethics

Here are some additional points for the beginning journalist to consider for a personal code of ethics:

The willingness to admit errors.

The determination to follow the facts, even if they lead in a direction you personally dislike or disagree with.

A commitment to make yourself improve as a journalist so that you can better serve those who rely on you as their eyes and ears.

Resistance to praise, the attractions of money, popularity and power— if any of these should stand in the way of writing the truth.

An identification with those who suffer.

The desire to make your community a better place for all its people— youngsters in school, the sick, the poor without jobs, the elderly without hope, the victims of discrimination.

One last word on developing a personal code. Each of us knows when he or she is giving the best possible effort. Sometimes we cannot do our best because we have not pushed ourselves.

Only the journalist knows when he or she is not doing his or her best. To accept anything of ourselves but the best we are capable of achieving is unethical because the journalist's duty is to keep readers, listeners and viewers informed and only untiring effort informs fully.

The student and the professional journalist must always be checking themselves: Is this story telling people all they need to know about the event? Should I make one more telephone call, check another document? Is this the precise word, or should I try harder to find a word that describes the situation more accurately? Am I being honest with the reader in the way I've structured this story, or have I emphasized a secondary element because it is more dramatic? Am I silent with all the others when conscience and duty demand that I speak?

Self-examination

"In Germany they came first for the Communists, and I didn't speak up because I wasn't a Communist. Then they came for the Jews, and I didn't speak up because I wasn't a Jew. Then they came for the trade unionists, and I didn't speak up because I wasn't a trade unionist. Then they came for the Catholics, and I didn't speak up because I was a Protestant. Then they came for me, and by that time, nobody was left to speak up."—Martin Niemoeller, German Protestant clergyman imprisoned by Hitler 1938–45.

The Obscene, the Indecent and the Profane

Go back a few pages to the section on journalistic ethics. Reread the part that is titled "Personal Code." Was there something in this material that offended you, some word that bothered you?

Flip the pages back still further. Look at the photographs in Chapter 2 about the executions in Liberia. Were you uncomfortable when you looked at any of them?

In both places there is material that some people may consider offensive, a word and some photographs that are in questionable taste. The word is used in a quotation from a youth who condemned the worker who called the police to report a body in the foothills. He describes the worker as a "snitch . . . a fucking narc." The photographs are the grim, if not horrifying, pictures of the execution of members of Liberia's old guard.

Most people are bothered by obscene language and by explicit representations of death. Why, then, was the material used? Why did some newspapers that ran the story of the youngsters in Milpitas make the quote read: "f------ narc," whereas others used the actual language of the youth? And why did the Pulitzer Prize jurors think so much of the execution pictures they awarded the photographer a prize, while others turned away from the photographs in horror and condemned their use as another example of journalistic bad taste and sensationalism?

Because such questions are easier to raise than they are to answer, many people, and even some editors, have declared: Nothing obscene, profane or indecent should be published or broadcast.

When newspapers received an advertisement for a James Bond movie some advertising departments were worried that the picture on the display advertisement might anger readers. It showed scanty tights across the rear of a rifle-toting female. (See the picture that opens this chapter.) Some newspapers put their artists to work. Some painted trunks, some short pants on the woman. And a few simply covered her butt with copy.

If the news is supposed to give the public a picture of reality, then a head-in-the-sand attitude deprives the public of essential information. Not only that, it is hypocritical. At the same time that some readers and listeners (and some editors as well) condemn the gossip columnist and are appalled by the picture of the dead child lying in the street, they applaud the movies and soap operas that routinely parade incest, adultery, murder and nudity.

They did it 20,000 times on television last year.

How come nobody got pregnant?

Teenage pregnancy in the U.S. has reached epidemic proportions, shattering hundreds of thousands of lives and costing taxpayers $16 billion per year. Instead of helping to solve this problem, the TV networks have virtually banned any mention of birth control in programs and advertising. We need to turn this policy around. You can help.

I. On television, sex is good, contraception is taboo.

There's a lot of sex on television. We all know that. What most people don't realize is that while the networks have been hyping sex, they've banned all mention of birth control in advertising, and censor information about it in programming. (It is permitted in the news.) Millions of dollars in sexually alluring ads are okay. Ads for vaginal sprays and hemorrhoidal products are okay. So are the ads which use nudity here and there to sell products. And characters like J.R. Ewing have been seducing women a few times an hour for eight years.

In 1978, researchers counted 20,000 sexual scenes on prime-time network television (which does not even include soap operas), with nary a mention of consequences or protection. It's even higher today. The only sexual mystery left seems to be how all these people keep doing it without contraception while nobody gets pregnant.

With all that worry-free hot action on television, it's no wonder American youngsters are having sex earlier and more often. *And* getting pregnant. Kids watch an average of four hours every day. That's more time than they spend in school or doing anything else in life, except sleeping. That's four hours per day inside a world where no one ever says "no," where sex is loose and often violent, and where sexual responsibility is as out-of-date as hula-hoops. Today's TV message is this: "GO FOR IT *NOW.* GO FOR IT AGAIN. AND DON'T WORRY ABOUT ANYTHING."

Guess Which of These Are in "Good Taste"
(According to the Networks)

PREP-Z | VAGINAL SPRAY
TAMPONS | CONDOMS

The tv network execs have decided that all advertisements for contraceptive products are in "bad taste" and they have banned them. Vaginal sprays, hemorrhoidal products, tampons are all in "good taste," according to them. So are toilet paper ads, underwear ads and nudity in everything from soap and cosmetic ads to beer ads. As for network drama and comedy programs which emphasize sexual doings? "Good taste." But mentioning "contraception" or "birth control" within programming (except news) is censored. ▶ The networks have not yet got the message. Our country is suffering a major problem of teen pregnancy, and television network policy is making it worse. Hyping sexuality while censoring information about responsibility is giving a terrible double message. ▶ The networks need to hear from you. Now. Please use the coupons above, write letters, phone. Your response can turn things around.

But there is plenty to worry about. The teen pregnancy rate in this country is now the highest of any country in the industrialized world. In the U.S. more than a million teens get pregnant every year. The consequences are tragic: high rates of school drop-outs, broken families, welfare and abortion. Who pays the tab? You do. About $16 billion yearly.

Of course television is not the only cause. When it comes to sex, there's a terrible breakdown of communications between parents and kids. There's also an appalling lack of timely, comprehensive sex education in schools. So kids are learning about sex the hard way—by experience. But television is making matters worse. Both because of what's on TV, and because of what is not.

II. Censorship by the Networks

The television industry is very sensitive about people telling them what they cannot broadcast. But the TV industry itself feels free to censor content.

Last year, the American College of Obstetricians and Gynecologists (ACOG)—a most prestigious physicians organization—prepared an ad campaign to educate kids about how to prevent pregnancy. They wanted to use print media, radio, and television. The brochure for the campaign said this: (1) Kids *can* resist peer pressure. They can take the option of postponing sex until they're ready. (2) The pill *is* a safe contraceptive for young women. And (3) sexually active young *men* should also be responsible—use condoms. These were useful statements.

The TV commercials ACOG prepared were even milder. All they suggested was that *unintended pregnancy* can interfere with career goals for women, and they offered to send the brochure. But, amazingly, the network execs said the ads were too "controversial," because they made mention of the word "contraceptives." These are the same networks which routinely show thousands of murders, rapes and acts of kinky sex. And 94% of the sexual encounters in soap operas are among people not married to each other. Are *those* presentations non-controversial? Do *those* represent some kind of higher moral value?

Finally, after long negotiations, the three networks agreed to let the spots run. But only after the dreaded "C-word"—"contraception"—was censored. Instead, the networks substituted this dynamic phrase: "There are many ways to prevent unintended pregnancy."

As for network policies censoring "birth control" within programs? No change. As for the rejection of commercials for contraceptive products like condoms, foams, the pill? No change. As for the reduction of irresponsible sexual imagery? No change. As for a sense of balance between sexual hype and realistic useful information? No change.

III. Blaming the public tastes

Network executives argue that they've a responsibility to uphold high standards of public taste. The mention of birth control (except in the news) would somehow violate that. Is that true? Does the public really want uneducated pregnant teenagers? And a tax bill for $16 billion?

A recent Louis Harris Poll showed exactly what the public wants. Most Americans believe that television portrays an unrealistic and irresponsible view of sex. And 78% would like to see messages about contraception on TV. A similar percentage wants more sex education in schools. So it's not the public which resists more responsible sexual imagery. It's the television executives who resist it. Why? Maybe it's just a creative problem for them. We think they can solve it. Right now they don't even mention birth control when it's exactly appropriate. Why can't J.R. ask his latest conquest if she is prepared? Why can't she ask him? The screenwriters can work it out.

The television industry once said the public couldn't handle images of people wearing seatbelts, and they figured that one out. The case of birth control should be simpler than seatbelts, since 90% of adults already accept its use. It's mainly teenagers who don't.

IV. What you can do

Television executives keep trying to avoid their own responsibility, telling us that TV imagery has nothing to do with shaping teens' attitudes, that television doesn't influence them. But this is ridiculous. Television is the most powerful medium ever invented to influence mass behavior. It's on that basis that the networks sell their advertising.

Television influences all of us every day. And it is a major influence on teenagers about sexuality and responsibility. It may now be a more important influence than school, parents, or even peers. The problem is that television is putting out an unbalanced view which is causing *more* problems for teenagers and society. The situation has got to change.

It's time we turn to the small number of men who control this medium and tell them they have a responsibility to the public beyond entertainment, titillation, pushing products and making money.

They need to know you are out there, and that you are concerned. It will make a tremendous difference. Use the coupons. Write letters and make phone calls. And join Planned Parenthood's efforts in your area.

Thank you.

Planned Parenthood®
Federation of America, Inc.

This ad paid for by private contributions. ©Copyright 1986 Planned Parenthood Federation of America, Inc.

Contraceptive advertising is favored by a majority of Americans. A Louis Harris poll found that people would rather see contraceptives advertised on television than beer, wine or feminine hygiene products. Yet when family-planning agencies tried to place 30-second advertisements on contraception, many stations turned them down. Newspapers and magazines have handled such advertising gingerly. This advertisement was rejected by most newspapers and magazines. *Newsweek* refused to allow one advertiser to put the word *sex* in a headline. *Time* and many other publications accept condom advertising only if the text refers to disease protection but not to contraception.

Used with permission of Planned Parenthood Foundation of America, Inc.

Death and Its Aftermath.
The Dover, N.H., newspaper, *Foster's Daily Democrat*, ran this picture of a University of New Hampshire student being pulled from the water after the university rowing shell was swamped by a gale. Readers objected to the picture, saying it was in poor taste. Managing Editor Rod Doherty replied: "We used the photo because it was explicit in its depiction of the event. It showed the conclusion of a tragedy that need not have occurred. Our obligation is to collect and print the news."
Tim Lorette, Foster's Daily Democrat.

Here is a summary of a week's activities on a few of the TV soaps:

AS THE WORLD TURNS: When Iva tells him that she saw Frannie swimming, Seth pays a visit. Clad only in a towel, Sabrina really turns him on. Before she can identify herself, the sex-starved farmer draws her into a passionate clinch. Then they assume a supine position and embark on a love-making frenzy.

DAYS OF OUR LIVES: Jo cooks dinner for Neil and brings it to the hospital for him. But Grace steals Curtis away before Jo arrives and takes him home for a romantic evening. The two end up in Neil's bedroom and start to make love. Curtis confesses he still has feelings for his ex-wife, Liz. . . . But Neil overcomes his anxieties and the two end up making love, both happy with their new relationship.

GENERAL HOSPITAL: Rosa muses over her choices while studying for her first English test. With Corey's help, she hopes to ace it. Melissa spots the two together and is hurt. Zack, the class druggie, watches Melissa run out, and follows. He has just the thing to cheer her up, Zack promises, handing Melissa a joint. They light up.

THE YOUNG AND THE RESTLESS: Worried that Nina might spill the beans to Cricket about their one-night stand, Phillip tells Cricket that the night of their fight he got drunk. He passed out and spent the night at Cricket's apartment with Nina, Phillip admits, but insinuates that nothing happened.

Many viewers do their housework—and homework—with one eye on these daily dramas. College students schedule their classes around their favorite soaps. And vacationers insist that their cottages come equipped with color TV sets so they can follow "Days of Our Lives" and "One Life to Live."

Clearly, there are words, subject matter and pictures that should be off-limits. But how do we determine what they are? Do we refrain from using any material that would offend someone? Benjamin Franklin had no use for the meat-cleaver approach. "If all printers were determined not to print anything until they were sure it would offend nobody, there would be very little printed," he said.

These days much of what is newsworthy does involve unsavory matters. Crime is a major problem in our society, and many of the crimes are unspeakably violent and vicious. Do we refrain from running the brutal rape, the beheading of a 5-year-old, the robbery gang that drove ballpoint pens through the ears of helpless patrons of a supermarket?

We do, however, need guidelines for the use of frank language, subject matter that is offensive and pictures that are gruesome.

Vulgar Language

Most people find obscenities, profanities and language that refers to the sex act or to bodily functions to be unsavory.

Much of the hostility to such language stems from the desire to keep this kind of language from becoming acceptable speech. Taste is the sum of many value judgments about what is acceptable language or behavior. If such language is seen and heard frequently by young people, it becomes a part of their vocabulary and, possibly, will influence their behavior. Thus, adults—who are responsible for establishing values for their children—are anxious to hold the line against obscenity and profanity.

On the other hand, such language is part of everyday life. How do newspapers, radio and television stations tread the thin line between the extremes without falling on either side—offending well-intentioned people or cutting readers and listeners off from reality?

Let's start with the quote from the youngster angry at the man he described as a "snitch." *The Miami Herald,* which carried the quote as "f----- narc," tried to walk the line. It did not run the obscenity, but by using the first letter and the exact number of dashes it was obvious to nearly all readers what the youngster actually said. I used the word *fucking* in this section. Why? Primarily to convey the intensity of the youth's feeling, but also because of the audience, the readers of this book. The *Herald's* readers range from grade school students to senior citizens. Some of the adults have strong feelings about obscenities. The newspaper prefers not to risk offending them.

The readers of this book obviously are acquainted with such language. To have used dashes instead of the actual word would have been, it seemed to me, insulting, condescending. In addition, students are entitled to know the precise details of subjects they are studying. To sum it up, the word was used

The New York Times permits the use of obscenity or vulgarity "only when the printing of the objectionable word or words will give the reader an obviously essential insight into matters of great moment—an insight that cannot be otherwise conveyed."

AIDS has had considerable impact on decisions about what is fit for readers and viewers. The word *condom* had been taboo until health authorities talked of their use as a method of safe sex. In discussions of the transmission of the disease, homosexual practices were described and although the press was slow to discuss such subjects as oral, anal and vaginal intercourse, gradually many newspapers and stations became more forthright.

In a long piece, the staid *New York Times* interviewed women on their use of condoms. "I keep them with me," the newspaper quoted a fashion designer as saying. "I have them in my house. I won't have sex without them." The designer, and other women, were identified by name, obviously with their approval—perhaps a final comment on the development of notions of the acceptable in our time.

because it was **essential to the situation** and because the **nature of the audience** was such that the word would not be considered offensive. These concepts are put in boldface because they are important guides in deciding whether to use certain kinds of language in newspapers.

When Mark Patinkin and Christopher Scanlan of the *Journal-Bulletin* in Providence, R.I., interviewed the director of a job-training agency about unemployment among blacks, the official was frank, firm and forceful. This was reflected in his language. They quoted him as saying:

"It's a deep, deep problem," he said. "People don't realize it's an American problem. They say it's a black problem. It's a goddamn American problem and it requires the best energies of everybody to jump in and try and resolve it."

The profanity undoubtedly offended some readers of the newspaper. However, the writers chose to use it because of the intensity of feeling it revealed. The word was essential to the interview, they felt.

Some words are offensive in certain contexts, not in others. What do you think of this headline and lead from the *St. Petersburg Times?*:

Marie Osmond Says She Is a Virgin

Saying, "I have just as many passions as any other woman," Marie Osmond declares she is a virgin and a "square lady" in February's issue of *Ladies Home Journal*.

Celebrities raise the shades on their personal lives to allow journalists and the public to peek in. But that does not mean that every scene in every room need be described. Osmond has no objection to talking about her virginity, but what purpose does it serve in a newspaper? It adds nothing we need to know about the world.

So, what's the point? Marie Osmond's virginity is used to titillate readers. In this sense, such newspaper stories do meet the competition—magazines, soap operas, movies.

If the publisher desires to set a news policy in this direction, then editors and news writers must follow the policy. We now have a third guideline for determining what should be used—**the policy of the publication or station.**

Up to this point, we have been assuming that everyone agrees on what is offensive. The material we have used is clearly offensive to most people. But what is in poor taste to one person may be acceptable to another. The 16-year-old gang member and the Episcopal minister probably do not share the same definition of what is profane and what is obscene.

The truth is that there is no agreement on taste. There never will be. Just as some like licorice and others find it abominable, and just as some people will stand in the rain all night to buy tickets for a football game or a Madonna concert while others consider this a form of madness, so there is no consensus on matters of journalistic taste.

However, we can say that opinions are changing, that overall there is a greater tolerance for what had been considered tasteless and offensive.

In 1905, the Brooklyn Public Library decided to ban from the children's room *The Adventures of Huckleberry Finn* and *Tom Sawyer* by Mark Twain. The librarians decided that the books were "bad examples" for children. (The guardians of public morality often contend that their actions are intended to protect the young from contamination.)

When Twain heard about the action of the librarians, he was contrite, and he made a public statement of his contrition.

"I wrote *Tom Sawyer* and *Huck Finn* for adults exclusively, and it always distresses me when I find that boys and girls have been allowed access to them," he wrote. "The mind that becomes soiled in youth can never again be washed clean. I know this by my own experience, and to this day I cherish an unappeasable bitterness against the unfaithful guardians of my young life, who not only permitted but compelled me to read an unexpurgated Bible through before I was 15 years old.

"None can do that and ever draw a sweet breath again. . . ."

Twain was poking fun at the zealous guardians of public morality. *Huckleberry Finn* and books by J. D. Salinger, Kurt Vonnegut and others are constantly under attack by zealots. Those who seek to ban books have been taken to the courts, which have held that book-banning is unconstitutional.

Subject Matter

Subject matter that was once deemed unfit for readers' consumption is now their daily fare. Even the most conservative newspapers carry the unsavory details of trials and the sordid aspects of crime. *The New York Times,* which promised at its founding that it would not "soil the breakfast table," has carried stories about teen-age prostitution (male as well as female) and some of the bizarre antics of celebrities.

The details of the rape of a 7-year-old child by two 6-year-olds and an 8-year-old were carried by the AP and were printed by many newspapers. Here is the beginning of this sordid story:

SYRACUSE, N.Y. (AP)—Two 6-year-old boys and an 8-year-old boy are accused of raping a 7-year-old girl in the back of a school bus and again in an apartment building, police say.

"If they're not the youngest, then they are certainly among the youngest" rape suspects in the state,

Syracuse police investigator Rod Carr said.

The incident allegedly occurred Monday afternoon when the four children were riding home from school.

After allegedly raping the girl on the back floor of a moving city school bus, the three boys forced her into an apartment building where they attacked her a second time, according to a report issued by Carr.

Police were vague on the details of the alleged rape, and some medical experts said Wednesday a rape by boys so young would be physically "unusual." Dr. Gerald Nathanson, a pediatrician at Montefiore Hospital in New York City, said rape involving boys aged 6 to 8 would be "highly improbable."

But Carr said doctors at Crouse-Irving Memorial Hospital here confirmed the girl had been raped. The girl was taken to the hospital after her mother discovered her crying in bed, he said.

"We just received the medical reports, and, as unlikely as it may seem, it indicates that a rape took place."

The mother of the girl, whose name was withheld, said her daughter used to play alongside the three boys. . . .

This is a horrible story, clearly offensive to almost anyone. Why run it? Most of the newspapers that used it were not trying to peddle papers. They were, rather, trying to call attention to something terrible about the society we live in, to cry out that something must be very wrong if children can behave this way.

This leads to another guideline for our consideration: **Material that warns us or serves as a deterrent** may be used despite its tastelessness. Indeed, it is the shock value of the offensive material that drives home the point.

The Sex Industry

When Charles Bernsen of *The Commercial Appeal* was assigned to do a series of articles on the commercial sex industry in Memphis he had to see just what was being sold.

He says he went out to see his first peep show:

I remember coming out of the place, pausing to blink away the bright sunlight, and thinking: "How in the hell am I going to put what I just saw in the newspaper?"

The dilemma only got worse. I visited 12 more peep shows during the next eight weeks, including two that had "live show" booths in which patrons were urged to masturbate while they watched a naked woman writhe in feigned sexual ecstasy on the other side of a glass partition.

I went to 17 nightclubs that featured topless and/or bottomless dancers. In addition to watching the stage show, a patron could pay $5 for a four-minute "table dance" during which he often did more than just simulate the sex act with the

naked waitress dancing between his outstretched legs.

I subscribed to a Memphis firm's obscene phone call service. (Pay them $20 and they send you a telephone number. Call the number and a woman will tell you what she'd like to do to you if only you were there with her.)

I subscribed to the same company's referral service for "swingers." (Pay them $20 and they send you the names and telephone numbers of folks in your area who are interested in getting together for a little mate swapping or group sex.)

I went to a public swingers club that said it offered "twosomes, threesomes, foursomes and moresomes" and did.

Bernsen and the newspaper were trapped in a dilemma. The commodity being peddled was bound to repel many readers, but the story had to be told because of the consequences of commercial sex. Much of it, Bernsen found, was controlled by organized crime, and its activities included "murders, beatings and attempted bombings." Also, it was big business in Memphis, grossing about $10 million a year.

"A business that big needs to be covered," Bernsen said. "That doesn't mean propriety should be tossed out the window.

"It doesn't do any good to write a story if your readers are going to gag on their orange juice and refuse to read it. But the business of selling sexual titillation can be reported fully and accurately without being titillating."

The policy that was adopted for the series was this: "If it was important to understanding how a part of the sex industry operated, we described or explained it in as much detail as possible. If it was superfluous, we avoided explicit detail that might be offensive."

This brings us to another guideline: **Explicit details of tasteless matters are avoided unless absolutely relevant to the story.**

Man or Woman?

Just what is relevant? This question came up with the story that we mentioned at the beginning of this chapter: the murder of Stella Walsh, the Olympic track champion and a prominent member of Cleveland's Polish-American community.

After the two television stations reported the coroner's finding that the examination revealed the body of 69-year-old Walsh was that of a man and not a woman, the community became angry and hostile. People called and wrote to protest against the station's revelation.

The only local television station that did not mention the result of the autopsy was WJKW-TV, whose news director said that although the station knew of the sex angle it did not use it because: "We didn't think it was germane to the story. It was essentially a story of crime and violence."

Cleveland's two daily newspapers agreed with the news director's sentiments. An editor of the *Plain Dealer* said that the paper "felt there should be dignity in death."

To these objections, the assistant news director of WEWS-TV said that the coroner's findings were the story.

The full story was run by *The Philadelphia Inquirer, The Boston Globe* and *The New York Times*. Only then did the Cleveland papers use the details.

Unquestionably, the coroner's findings were relevant. On the other hand, the local newspapers and WJKW were undoubtedly sensitive to their audience, the Polish-American community. In the balancing of these legitimate claims, the journalist usually decides to use the material, for, after all, the journalist's job is to tell truths, no matter how unpleasant.

Legitimate or Irresponsible? When the *Columbus Citizen-Journal* ran this picture of the body of a 9-year-old girl who had been struck by a car, readers wrote and called to protest. They described it as tasteless and irresponsible journalism. Many readers said that such realism is unnecessary. The newspaper replied that the photo was a stark reminder to parents and to children of the dangers of city streets. *Photo by Hank Reichard of Scripps Howard Newspapers.*

Photographs

The picture was stark and tragic: A child's body, half covered by a blanket, lay in the street where she had been struck and killed by a car.

As soon as the newspaper arrived in the homes of readers, the complaints began. Callers, then letter writers, complained that using the picture was irresponsible, that it was sensational journalism. Richard R. Campbell, editor of the *Columbus Citizen-Journal,* said "the most common accusation was that the picture was tasteless.

"One reader called us coldhearted and tasteless and urged us not to forget discretion and compassion." Another reader said, "You have won first prize in the journalistic bad taste contest. Your prize for achieving this distinction is an all-expense paid trip to 'Sensational City' for the photographer and the editor who saw fit to print the picture."

Campbell said that the decision to run the photograph was his. His reasons, he said, were these:

There could be no more dramatic way to point out to mothers and fathers and children, to drivers and pedestrians, the danger of carelessly stepping into the street. The proverb says one picture is worth more than 1,000 words. Here was such a picture.

Secondly, it was part of our role of writing history.

One father who appreciated our reason for using the photo said he showed it to his small sons, separately, and took the time to explain to each what happened to the little girl and why. That is what we expected the reaction to be.

If we look back at the guidelines for using material that may be in questionable taste, we can see that one of the reasons editors used the picture was that they hoped it would serve as a warning, a deterrent. The horror of the picture might register, as no written warnings can, the dangers to youngsters of playing in the street or darting out into the street.

Campbell also mentions the fact that this was part of local history. Of course, not every incident and accident is recorded by newspapers or television. The newspaper or broadcast station, like the historian, is selective. The editor chose to run this picture because it was a graphic demonstration of a part of every community's history—the appalling toll of traffic deaths.

"We gave our readers a slice of Tuesday's life in Columbus that they did not want to see," a reporter said about the protests. "Hank Reichard took the image of that broken little girl and hurled it in our faces so that we would have to look at her, too.

"Hank made us care that a little girl had died when she should not have died, in a place that was terribly wrong for a child's death. He made us suffer."

Some of the same reasons can be given for the other photographs in this book that might have offended readers—the pictures by Larry C. Price of the execution on the beach in Liberia. These pictures did indeed show us history in the making, and they showed us man's dark and lethal side.

Sports pictures do not usually provide problems of taste. But Harry Baumert's photograph of an angry basketball coach caused problems for editors at *The Des Moines Register*. The photograph was of Iowa State University coach Johnny Orr gesticulating toward a referee—the "finger photo," as it was dubbed.

Although the editor of the newspaper approved the picture for publication, the sports editor killed it. "While it was a dramatic photo, it was clearly obscene. I didn't feel there was sufficient news value to risk alienating the bulk of our readers," the sports editor concluded.

An associate editor of the *Register* decided to ask editors over the country whether they would have used the picture. The result: 129 said no; 31 said yes, and 61 said perhaps.

Of those who would have turned it down, 32 said they had used the photograph of Nelson Rockefeller, then vice president, making the same gesture to heckling students. AP Newsphotos ran the Rockefeller picture, but not the Iowa State shot. Why?

No-no. Or maybe. In Des Moines, the *Register* sports editor turned thumbs down on the coach's gesture. The AP found in a survey of editors' reactions to use of the picture: 129, no; 31, yes; 61, maybe.
Harry Baumert, The Des Moines Register.

Rockefeller was widely known, his actions covered by the press. The coach, says Hal Buell, AP assistant general manager for Newsphotos, is hardly in that class. Buell says, ". . . a picture of nobody giving nobody the finger is still a picture of nothing. So we wouldn't carry it, basically because it lacks news value."

Summary

Here are some guidelines for questionable language, subject matter and photographs:

The material must be essential to the story being told. Without the material, the point would not be made or would be diluted.

The audience must be taken into consideration. If the great majority of readers or listeners would be offended, the material should not be used.

If the material serves as a warning, then it may be used despite its offensive nature.

Details of crimes, sex acts and other shocking actions should not be used unless absolutely relevant.

If the event has historical significance, it should be used.

Suggested Reading

Davis, Elmer. *But We Were Born Free.* New York: The Bobbs-Merrill Co., 1954.

Denniston, Lyle. *The Reporter and the Law.* New York: Hastings House, 1980.

Hulteng, John. *Playing It Straight.* Chester, Conn.: The Globe Pequot Press, 1981.

Sanford, Bruce. *Synopsis of the Law of Libel and the Right of Privacy.* New York: Pharos Books, 1984.

Stylebook

addresses Abbreviate *Avenue, Boulevard, Street* with specific address: *1314 Kentucky St.* Spell out without specific address: *construction on Fifth Avenue.*

Use figures for the address number: *3 Third Ave.; 45 Main St.* Spell out numbers under 10 as street names: *21 Fourth Ave.; 450 11th St.*

age Use figures. To express age as an adjective, use hyphens; a *3-year-old girl.* Unless otherwise stated, the figure is presumed to indicate years: *a boy, 4, and his sister, 6 months.*

Further guidelines: *infant:* under one year of age; *child:* ages 1 to 13; *girl, boy:* under 18; *youth:* 13–18; *man, woman:* over 18; *adult:* over 18, unless used in specific legal context for crimes such as drinking; *middle-aged:* 35–55; *elderly:* over 65; avoid when describing individuals.

a.m., p.m. Lowercase with periods.

amendment: Capitalize when referring to specific amendments to the U.S. Constitution. Spell out for the first through ninth; use figures for 10th and above: *First Amendment, 10th Amendment.*

brand name A non-legal term for a trademark. Do not use them as generic terms or as verbs: *soft drink* instead of *Coke* or *coke; photocopy* instead of *Xerox.*

capitalization Generally, follow a down style.

Proper nouns: Use capitals for names of persons, places, trademarks; titles when used with names; nicknames of people, states, teams, titles of books, plays, movies.

century Lowercase, spelling out numbers less than 10, except when used in proper nouns: *the fifth century, 18th century,* but *20th Century-Fox* and *Nineteenth Century Society,* following the organization's practice.

The **purpose** of the stylebook is to provide uniform presentation of the printed word. It sets standards for the use of abbreviations, capital letters, titles, punctuation and dates.

The stylebook eliminates arbitrary decisions. It is the guide that newspapers and the wire services use routinely to settle questions of usage.

chairman, chairwoman Use *chairman* or *chairwoman* instead of *chair* or *chairperson; spokesman* or *spokeswoman* instead of *spokesperson,* and similar constructions unless the *-person* construction is a formal title.

Use *chairman* or *spokesman* when referring to the office in general. To avoid sexism, a neutral word such as *representative* is often the best choice.

co- Use a hyphen when forming nouns, adjectives and verbs that indicate occupation or status: *co-star, co-written.* No hyphen for other constructions: *coeducation, coexist.*

congress Capitalize when referring to the U.S. Senate and House of Representatives. The term is correctly used only in reference to the two legislative branches together.

Capitalize also when referring to foreign governments that use the term or its equivalent.

Constitution, constitutional Capitalize when referring to the U.S. Constitution, with or without the *U.S.* modifier. When referring to other constitutions, capitalize only when preceded by the name of a nation or state. Lowercase *constitutional.*

court names Capitalize the full proper names of courts at all levels. Retain capitalization if *U.S.* or a state name is dropped.

dates *July 6, 1957,* was her birth date. (Use commas.) *She was born in July 1957.* (No comma between month and year.)

Abbreviate month with specific date: *Feb. 19.* Spell out all months when standing alone. With dates, use abbreviations: *Jan., Feb., Aug., Sept., Oct., Nov., Dec.* Spell out *March, April, May, June, July.*

directions and regions Lowercase *north, south, northeast,* etc. when they indicate compass direction: *Police followed the car south on Route 22.*

Capitalize when they refer to regions: *Southern accent; Northeastern industry.*

With names of nations, lowercase except when they are part of a proper name or are used to designate a politically divided nation: *tourism in southern France,* but *South Korea* and *Northern Ireland.*

fireman Use *firefighter* since some women hold these jobs.

fractions Spell out amounts less than 1, using hyphens, *one-half, two-thirds.* Use figures for amounts larger than 1, converting to decimals whenever possible: *3.5* instead of *three and one-half* or *3½.*

Figures are preferred in tabular material and in stories about stocks.

holidays and holy days Capitalize them. In federal law, the legal holidays are New Year's, Martin Luther King's Birthday, Washington's Birthday (President's Day), Memorial Day, Independence Day, Labor Day, Columbus Day, Veteran's Day, Thanksgiving and Christmas.

States are not required to follow the federal lead in designating holidays, except that federal employees must receive the day off or must be paid overtime if they work.

Jewish holy days: Hanukkah, Passover, Purim, Rosh Hashana, Shavuot, Sukkot and Yom Kippur.

initials Use periods and no space: *H.L. Mencken; C.S. Lewis.* This practice has been adopted to ensure that intitials will be set on the same line.

nationalities and races Capitalize the proper names of nationalities, peoples, races, tribes, etc. Lowercase *black, white, red,* etc. Lowercase derogatory terms such as *honky* and *nigger.* Use them only in direct quotations.

See *race* for guidelines on when racial identification is pertinent in a story.

non- Hyphenate all except the following words, which have meanings of their own: *nonchalance, nonchalant, nondescript, nonentity, nonsense, nonsensical.*

numerals Spell out *one* through *nine* except when used to indicate age or with dates. Use figures for *10* and above.

Spell out a number when it begins a sentence: *Fifteen members voted against the bill.* Use figures when a year begins a sentence. *1980 began auspiciously.*

Use figures for percentages and percents.

For amounts of $1 million and more, use the *$* sign and figures up to two decimal places with the *million, billion, trillion* spelled out: *$1.65 million.* Exact amounts are given in figures: *$1,650,398.*

When spelling out large numbers, separate numbers ending in *y* from next number with a hyphen: *seventy-nine; one hundred seventy-nine.*

percentages Use figures—decimals, not fractions—and the word *percent,* not the symbol; *2.5 percent; 10 percent.* For amounts less than 1 percent, place a zero before the decimal: *0.6 percent.*

When presenting a range, repeat *percent* after each figure: *2 percent to 5 percent.*

policeman Use *police officer* instead.

political parties and philosophies Capitalize the name of the party and the word *party* when it is used as part of the organization's proper name: *the Democratic Party.*

Capitalize *Communist, Conservative, Democrat, Liberal* etc. when they refer to the activities of a specific party or to individuals who are members of it.

Lowercase the name of a philosophy in noun and adjective forms unless it is derived from a proper name: *communism; fascist.* But: *Marxism; Nazi.*

prefixes Generally do not hyphenate when using a prefix with a word starting with a consonant.

Except for *cooperate* and *coordinate,* use a hyphen if the prefix ends in the same vowel that begins the following word: *re-elect,* not *reelect.*

Use a hyphen if the word that follows is capitalized: *pan-American; anti-Catholic.*

Use a hyphen to join doubled prefixes: *sub-subclause.*

president Capitalize only as a title before an individual's name: *President Ronald Reagan,* but *The president said he would spend New Year's at his California ranch.*

race Race, religion and national origin are sometimes essential to a story but too often are injected when they are not pertinent. When in doubt about relevance, substitute descriptions such as *white, Baptist, French.* If one of these descriptions would be pertinent, use the original term.

religious references DEITIES: Capitalize the proper names of monotheistic deities, pagan and mythological gods and goddesses: *Allah, the Father, Zeus.* Lowercase pronouns that refer to the deity: *he, him, thee, who,* etc.

Lowercase *gods* when referring to the deities of polytheistic religions. Lowercase such words as *god-awful, godlike, godsend.*

RITES: Capitalize proper names for rites that commemorate the Last Supper or signifiy a belief in Christ's presence: *the Lord's Supper; Holy Eucharist.* Lowercase the names of other sacraments.

HOLY DAYS: Capitalize the names of holy days: *Hanukkah.*

OTHER WORDS: Lowercase *heaven, hell, devel, angel, cherub, an apostle, a priest,* etc.

seasons Lowercase *spring, summer, fall, winter* and their derivatives. Capitalize when part of a formal name: *St. Paul Winter Carnival; Summer Olympics.*

senate, senatorial Capitalize all references to specific legislative bodies, regardless of whether the name of the nation or state is used: *U.S. Senate; the state Senate.*

Lowercase plural uses: *the Iowa and Kansas state senates.* Lowercase references to non-governmental bodies: *the student-faculty senate.*

Senatorial is always lowercase.

sexism Avoid stereotyping women or men. Be conscious of equality in treatment of both sexes.

When writing of careers and families, avoid presuming that the wage-earner is a man and that the woman is a homemaker; *the average family of five* instead of *the average worker with a wife and three children.*

Avoid physical descriptions of women or men when not absolutely relevant to the story.

Use parallel references to both sexes: *the men and the women,* not *the men and the ladies; husband and wife* not *man and wife.*

Do not use nouns and pronouns to indicate sex unless the sex difference is basic to understanding or there is no suitable substitute. One way to avoid such subtle sexism is to change the noun to the plural, eliminating the masculine pronoun: *Drivers should carry their licenses,* instead of *Every driver should carry his license.*

Personal appearance and marital and family relationships should be used only when relevant to the story.

state names Spell out names of the 50 U.S. states when they stand alone in textual matter.

The names of eight states are never abbreviated: *Alaska, Hawaii, Idaho, Iowa, Maine, Ohio, Texas, Utah.*

Abbreviate other state names when used with a city, in a dateline or with party affiliation. Do not use Postal Service abbreviations.

Ala.	*Kan.*	*Nev.*	*S.C.*
Ariz.	*Ky.*	*N.H.*	*S.D.*
Ark.	*La.*	*N.J.*	*Tenn.*
Calif.	*Md.*	*N.M.*	*Vt.*
Colo.	*Mass.*	*N.Y.*	*Va.*
Conn.	*Mich.*	*N.C.*	*Wash.*
Del.	*Minn.*	*N.D.*	*W.Va.*
Fla.	*Miss.*	*Okla.*	*Wis.*
Ga.	*Mo.*	*Ore.*	*Wyo.*
Ill.	*Mont.*	*Pa.*	
Ind.	*Neb.*	*R.I.*	

statehouse Capitalize all references to a specific statehouse, with or without the state name. But lowercase in all plural uses: *the New Mexico Statehouse; the Arizona and New Mexico statehouses.*

suspensive hyphenation The form: *The 19- and 20-year-olds were not served alcoholic beverages.* Use in all similar cases.

Although the form looks somewhat awkward, it guides readers, who may otherwise expect a noun to follow the first figure.

teen, teen-ager (noun), **teen-age** (adjective) Do not use *teen-aged.*

temperatures Use figures for all except *zero.* Use the word *minus,* not a minus sign, to indicate temperatures below zero. *The day's high was 9; the day's low was minus 9.*

time Exact times often are unnecessary. *Last night* and *this morning* are acceptable substitutes for *yesterday* and *today.* Use exact time when pertinent, but avoid redundancies: *8 a.m. this morning* should be *8 a.m. today* or *8 o'clock this morning.*

Use figures except for *noon* and *midnight. 12 noon* is redundant.

Separate hours from minutes with a colon: *3:15 p.m.*

titles

ACADEMIC TITLES: Capitalize and spell out formal titles such as *professor, dean, president, chancellor, chairman,* etc., when they precede a name. Lowercase elsewhere. Do not abbreviate *Professor* as *Prof.*

Lowercase modifiers such as *journalism* in *journalism Professor John Rist* or *department* in *department chairwoman Kim Power,* unless the modifier is a proper name: *French Professor Ann Marie Jones.*

COURTESY TITLES: do not use the courtesy titles *Miss, Mr., Mrs.* or *Ms.* on first reference. Instead, use the person's first and last name. Do not use *Mr.* unless it is combined with *Mrs.: Kyle Scott Hotsenpiller; Mr. and Mrs. Kyle Scott Hotsenpiller.*

Courtesy titles are used on second references for women in most newspapers. Use these guidelines:

Married women: On first reference, identify a woman by her own first name and her husband's last name: *Betty Phillips.* Use *Mrs.* on first reference only if a woman requests that her husband's first name be used or her own first name cannot be determined: *Mrs. Steven A. Phillips.*

On second reference, use *Mrs.* unless a woman initially identified by her own first name prefers *Ms.: Rachel Finch; Mrs. Finch* or *Ms. Finch.*

If a married woman is known by her maiden last name, precede it by *Miss* on second reference unless she prefers *Ms.: Sarah Wilson; Miss Wilson* or *Ms. Wilson.*

Unmarried women: Use *Miss* or *Ms.* on second reference, according to the woman's preference.

For divorced and widowed women, the normal practice is to use *Mrs.* on second reference. Use *Miss* if the woman returns to her maiden name. Use *Ms.* if she prefers it.

If a woman prefers *Ms.,* do not include her marital status in a story unless it is pertinent.

Note: A number of newspapers drop *Mrs. Miss* and *Ms.* as well as *Mr.* on second reference. In 1985, the AP stylebook added: If the woman says she does not want a courtesy title, refer to her on second reference by last name only.

GOVERNMENTAL TITLES: Capitalize when used as a formal title in front of a person's name. It is not necessary to use a title on second reference: *Gov. Fred Florence; Florence.* For women who hold official positions, use the courtesy title on second reference, according to the guidelines for courtesy titles: *Gov. Ruth Arnold; Miss Arnold, Mrs. Arnold, Ms. Arnold.* (Some newspapers do not use the courtesy title on second reference.)

Abbreviate *Governor* as *Gov., Lieutenant Governor* as *Lt. Gov.* when used as a formal title before a name.

Congressional titles: Before names, abbreviate *Senator* as *Sen.* and *Representative* as *Rep.* Add *U.S.* or *state* if necessary to avoid confusion.

Short form punctuation for party affiliation: Use abbreviations listed under **state names** and set off from the person's name with commas: *Sen. Nancy Landon Kassebaum, R-Kan., and Rep. Charles Hatcher, D-Ga., attended the ceremony.*

Capitalize and spell out other formal government titles before a person's name. Do not use titles in second references: *Attorney General Jay Craven spoke. Craven said. . .*

Capitalize and spell out formal titles instead of abbreviating before the person's name only in direct quotations. Lowercase in all uses not mentioned above.

OCCUPATIONAL TITLES: They are always lowercase: *senior vice president Nancy Harden.* Avoid false titles: *bridge champion Helen P. George* should be: *Helen P. George, Sioux Falls bridge tourney winner.*

TITLES OF WORKS: For book titles, movie titles, opera titles, play titles, poem titles, song titles, television program titles and the titles of lectures, speeches and works of art, apply the following guidelines:

Capitalize the principal words, including prepositions and conjunctions of four or more letters.

Capitalize an article or word of fewer than four letters if it is the first or last word in a title.

Place quotation marks around the names of all such works except the Bible and books that are primarily catalogs of reference material, including almanacs, directories, dictionaries, encyclopedias, handbooks and similar publications.

Translate a foreign title into English unless a work is known to the American public by its foreign name.

Do not use quotation marks or italics with the names of newspapers and magazines.

TV Acceptable as an adjective but should not be used as a noun.

vice Use two words, no hyphen.

vice president Follow the guidelines for **president.**

well- Hyphenate as part of a compound modifier: *well-dressed; well-read.*

words as words When italics are available, italicize them. Otherwise, place in quotation marks: *Rep. Ellen Jacobson asked journalists to address her as "congresswoman."*

years Use figures. Use an *s* without the apostrophe to indicate spans of centuries: *the 1800s.* Use an apostrophe to indicate omitted numerals and an *s* to indicate decades: the *'80s.*

Years are the only figures that may be placed at the start of a sentence: *1959 was a year of rapid city growth.*

Punctuation

Keep a good grammar book handy. No stylebook can adequately cover the complexities of the 13 punctuation marks: apostrophe, brackets, colon, comma, dash, ellipsis, exclamation point, hyphen, parenthesis, period, question mark, quotation marks, semicolon. The following is a guide to frequent problems and usages:

Apostrophe Use for (1) possessives, (2) to indicate omitted figures or letters and (3) to form some plurals.

1. *Possessives:* Add apostrophe and *s* ('s) to the end of singular and plural nouns or the indefinite pronoun unless it has an *s* or *z* sound.
The woman's coat. The women's coats.
The child's toy. The children's toys.
Someone's pistol. One's hopes.

If the word is plural and ends in an *s* or *z* sound, add apostrophe only:
Boys' books. Joneses' farm.

For singular common nouns ending in *s,* add an apostrophe and *s* ('s) unless the next word begins with s:
The hostess's gown. The hostess' seat.

For singular proper nouns ending in *s,* add only an apostrophe:
Dickens' novels. James' hat.

2. *Omitted figures or letters.* Use in contractions—*Don't, can't.* Put in place of omitted figure—*Class of '88.*

3. *To form some plurals:* When figures, letters, symbols and words are referred to as words, use the apostrophe and *s.*

    a. Figures: *She skated perfect 8's.*
    b. Letters: *He received all A's in his finals.*
    c. Symbols: *Journalists never use &'s to substitute for the ands in their copy.*

Caution: The pronouns *ours, yours, theirs, his, hers, whose* do not take the apostrophe. *Its* is the possessive pronoun. *It's* is the contraction of it is.

Note: Compound words and nouns in joint possession use the possessive in the last word:

- *Everybody else's homes.*
- *His sister-in-law's book.*
- *Mondale and Kennedy's party.*

If there is separate possession, each noun takes the possessive form:
Carter's and Kennedy's opinions differ.

Brackets Check whether the newspaper can set them. Use to enclose a word or words within a quote that the writer inserts: *"Happiness [his note read] is a state of mind."* Use for paragraph(s) within a story that refer to an event separate from the datelined material.

Colon The colon is usually used at the end of a sentence to call attention to what follows. It introduces lists, tabulations, texts and quotations of more than one sentence.

It can also be used to mark a full stop before a dramatic statement: *She had only one goal in life: work.* The colon is used in time of day: *7:45 p.m.;* elapsed time of an event: *4:01.1,* and in dialogue in question and answer, as from a trial.

Should the word immediately following a colon be capitalized? Only if what follows is a complete sentence. For example:

> *No—He found three pens: red, blue and black.*
>
> *Yes—Tourism looks promising next year: Construction of motels/restaurants is booming.*

Comma The best general guide for the use of the comma is the human voice as it pauses, stops and varies in tone. The comma marks the pause, the short stop:

> *1. He looked into the hospital room, but he was unable to find the patient.*
>
> *2. Although he continued his search on the floor for another 20 minutes, he was unable to find anyone to help him.*
>
> *3. He decided that he would go downstairs, ask at the desk and then telephone the police.*
>
> *4. If that also failed, he thought to himself, he would have to give up the search.*

Note that when reading these sentences aloud, the commas are natural resting points for pauses. The four sentences also illustrate the four principles governing the use of commas:

1. The comma is used to separate main clauses when they are joined by a coordinating conjunction. (The coordinating conjunctions are: *for, nor, and, but, or.*) The comma can be eliminated if the main clauses are short: *He looked into the room and he froze.*

2. Use the comma after an introductory element: a clause, long phrase, transitional expression or interjection.

3. Use the comma to separate words, phrases or clauses in a series. Do not use a comma before the coordinating conjunction in a series: The flag is red, white and blue. Also, use it in a series of coordinate adjectives: *He was wearing a long, full cape.*

4. Set off non-essential material in a sentence with comma(s). When the parenthetical or interrupting non-restrictive clauses and phrases are in the middle of a sentence two commas are needed. *The country, he was told, needed his assistance.*

Other uses of the comma:

Use a comma with full sentence quotes, not with partial quotes: *He asked, "Where are you going?" The man replied that he was "blindly groping" his way home.*

To separate city and county, city and state. In place of the word *of* between a name and city: *Jimmy Carter, Plains, Ga.*

To set off a person's age: *Orville Sterb, 19, of Fullerton, Calif.*

In dates: *March 19, 1940, was the date he entered the army.*

In party affiliations: *Bill Bradley, D-N.J., spoke.* To set off a title: *Jane Tyrone, the chairwoman, spoke at the meeting.*

Caution: The comma is frequently misused by placing it between two main clauses instead of using the period, or a coordinating conjunction. This is called comma splice:

> WRONG: *The typewriter was jammed, he could not type his theme.*

> RIGHT: *The typewriter was jammed. He could not type his theme. The typewriter was jammed; he could not type his theme. The typewriter was jammed, so he could not type his theme.*

Dash Use a dash (1) to indicate a sudden or dramatic shift in thought within a sentence, (2) to set off a series of words that contains commas and (3) to introduce sections of a list or a summary.

The dash is a call for a short pause, just as are the comma and the parenthesis. The comma is the most often used and is the least dramatic of the separators. Parentheses set off unimportant elements. The dash tends to emphasize material. It has this quality because it is used sparingly.

1. *He stared at the picture—and he was startled to find himself thinking of her face.*

The man stood up—painfully and awkwardly—and extended his hand in greeting.

2. *There were three people watching them—an elderly woman, a youth with a crutch at his side and a young woman in jeans holding a paperback—and he pulled her aside out of their view.*

3. *He gave her his reasons for being there:*

—He wanted to apologize;

—He needed to give her some material;

—He was leaving on a long trip.

(Note: This third form should be used infrequently, usually when the listing will be followed by an elaboration.)

The dash is also used in datelines.

Ellipsis Use the ellipsis to indicate material omitted from a quoted passage from a text, transcript, play, etc.: *The minutes stated that Breen had asked, "How many gallons of paint . . . were used in the project?"* Put one space before and one space after each of the three periods. If the omission ends with a period, use four periods, one to mark the end of the sentence (without space, as a regular period), three more for the ellipsis.

The ellipsis is also used by some columnists to separate short items in a paragraph.

Do not use to mark pauses or shifts in thought, or for emphasis.

Exclamation point Much overused. There are reporters who have gone through a lifetime of writing and have never used the exclamation point, except when copying material in which it is used. The exclamation point is used to indicate powerful feelings, surprise, wonder. Most good writers prefer to let the material move the reader to provide his or her own exclamation.

When using, do not place a comma or period after the exclamation point. Place inside quotation marks if it is part of the quoted material.

Hyphen The hyphen is used (1) to join words to express a single idea or (2) to avoid confusion or ambiguity.

1. Use the hyphen to join two or more words that serve as a single adjective before a noun: *A well-known movie is on television tonight. He had a know-it-all expression.*

Caution: Do not use the hyphen when the first word of the compound ends in *ly* or when the words follow the noun: *He is an easily recognized person. Her hair was blonde black.*

2. (a) Avoid ambiguity or (b) an awkward joining of letters or syllables by putting a hyphen between prefixes or suffixes and the root word.

a. *He recovered the chair. He re-covered the chair.*
b. *Re-enter, macro-economics, shell-like.*

Parenthesis Generally, avoid. They may be necessary for the insertion of background or to set off supplementary or illustrative material.

Use period inside closing parenthesis if the matter within the parentheses is a complete sentence. Other punctuation goes after the closing parenthesis unless the punctuation refers to the material in the parentheses: *Abbie Hoffman (remember him?) is 50 years old.*

Period Use the period at the end of declarative sentences, indirect questions, most imperative sentences and most abbreviations.

The period is placed inside quotation marks.

Question mark The question mark is used for direct questions, not indirect questions.

> DIRECT: *Where are you going?*
> INDIRECT: *He asked where she was going.*

The question mark goes inside quotation marks if it applies to the quoted material: *He asked, "Have you seen the movie?"* Put it outside if it applies to the entire sentence: *Have you seen "Phantom of the Opera"?*

Quotation marks Quotation marks set off (1) direct quotations, (2) some titles and nicknames and (3) words used in a special way.

1. Set off the exact words of the speaker: *"He walked like a duck," she said. He replied that he walked "more like an alley cat on the prowl."*

2. Use for book and movie titles, titles of short stories, poems, songs, articles from magazines and plays. Some nicknames take quotation marks. Do not use for nicknames of sports figures.

3. For words used in a special sense: *An "Indian giver" is someone who gives something to another and then takes it back.*

Punctuation with quotation marks:

The comma—Use it outside the quotation marks when setting off the speaker at the beginning of a sentence. *He said, "You care too much for money."* Use inside the quotation marks when the speaker ends the sentence: *"I just want to be safe," she replied.*

The colon and semicolon—Always place outside the quotation marks: *He mentioned her "incredible desire for work"; he meant her "insatiable desire for work."*

The dash, question mark and exclamation point—inside when they apply to quoted matter only; outside when they refer to the whole sentence: *She asked, "How do you know so much?" Did she really wonder why he knew "so much"?*

For quotes within quotes, use single quote mark (the apostrophe on a typewriter) for the inner quotation: *"Have you read 'War and Peace'?" he asked.* Note, no comma is used after the question mark.

Semicolon Usually overused by beginning reporters. Unless there is a special reason to use the semicolon, use the period.

Use the semicolon to separate a series of equal elements when the individual segments contain material that is set off by commas. This makes for clarity in the series: *He suggested that she spend her allowance on the new series at the opera, "Operas of the Present"; books of plays by Shaw, Ibsen and Aristophanes; and novels by Tolstoy, Dickens and F. Scott Fitzgerald.*

Speaking Punctuation

Russell Baker, the writer, says that "when speaking aloud, you punctuate constantly—with body language. Your listener hears commas, dashes, question marks, exclamation points, quotation marks as you shout, whisper, pause, wave your arms, roll your eyes, wrinkle your brow." Here are some of Baker's tips for punctuating on paper.

"Generally speaking, use a comma where you'd pause briefly in speech. For a long pause or completion of thought, use a period.

"The semicolon separates two main clauses, but it keeps those two thoughts more tightly linked than a period can.

"The dash SHOUTS! Parentheses whisper. Shout too often, people stop listening; whisper too much, people become suspicious of you.

"A colon is a tip-off to get ready for what's next: a list, a long quotation or an explanation.

"Too many exclamation points make me think the writer is talking about the panic in his own head.

"Don't sound panicky. End with a period. I am serious. A period. Understand?

"Well . . . sometimes a question mark is okay."

Appendix A

Preparing Copy

1. Use copy paper, newsprint or some other non-glossy paper. Triple space. Use large margins left and right.

2. Make a copy of all your work. Keep the copy.

3. In the upper left-hand corner of the first sheet of all assignments, place your name, slug of story, news source and date. Thus:

Chamberlain
PHA-attended
12/21/89

4. On the first page, begin one-third down the page. Write on one side of the paper only.

5. If the story consists of more than one page, write and circle *more* at the bottom of the page that is being continued. On the next page, put your name, slug and "2" at top left of page. Thus: Chamberlain-PHA-2. For the next page, make it 3, and so on.

6. End each page with a complete paragraph, not in the middle of a sentence.

7. Do not correct mistakes by backspacing and typing over. Cross out and retype. Never write over.

8. For simple errors, use copy editing symbols. (See Appendix F) Do not confuse these with proofreading marks. Use pencil to edit your copy.

9. Never divide words at the end of a line. Hit the margin release and continue or cross out and begin word anew on the next line.

10. Keep copy clean. Retype hard-to-read sections and paste over.

11. Do not write more than one story on each sheet of paper.

12. End stories with an end mark: 30, #, or END.

13. Follow the stylebook.

**Preparing Copy
on a Typewriter**

VDT. A reporter for *The Wichita Eagle-Beacon* uses the video display terminal to add information to his computer file. Reporters use the VDT to store material as well as to write their stories.
Photo by Joel Sartore of The Wichita Eagle-Beacon. Used with permission.

Preparing Copy on a Video Display Terminal

Most newspapers have traded in their typewriters for electronic equipment. The video display terminal (VDT) consists of keyboard and screen. The keyboard is used much like a typewriter, although it also has keys with special instructions for setting the type, moving copy around and editing.

The screen displays the copy as it is typed. Depending on the terminal model, 14 to 30 lines of copy can be seen on the screen.

The copy may be stored on a magnetic disk, a magnetic card or in some other storage device. It can then be called up for copy editing, which is also carried out on the screen of the terminal.

The edited version is sent to the phototypesetter, which sets the story according to the instructions of the news writer or editor. The story is produced on photosensitive paper that is placed in a processor.

In the processor, the paper is developed and a positive image or print is produced. The printed material is proofread and then placed on sheets for makeup.

For the news writer, keyboarding a story is faster and easier than using the typewriter. Since most systems have a programmed set of instructions that justifies lines and hyphenates words, the writer does not have to return the carriage but types in an endless line. Corrections and other changes are made with the use of a cursor, a patch of light that can be moved anywhere on the screen.

On newspapers whose terminals connect to a large storage computer, news writers can call up various reference materials, such as the newspaper's clippings on a subject. Reporters also can store their notes or partially completed stories, and with the use of their personal codes can call these up.

When the story is finished, it is read on the screen by a copy editor who also puts into the terminal the instructions about how the copy is to be set. These instructions are called *formats* or *parameters*.

A list of computer terms is included in the glossary.

Appendix B

Moving the Story

After a local story has been written, it is turned in to the city desk. If it has been written on a video display terminal, the city desk calls it up for examination on the screen.

The city editor or assistant city editor reads through the copy to see that it is satisfactory, that the lead contains the main news point and that all questions the reader may have are answered. If the story is inadequate, it is sent back to the news writer for further work. If acceptable, the story moves to the next stage, the news desk, where the type of headline and the story's length are determined. Then the story moves to the copy desk. On smaller newspapers, the city editor decides on the type of headline and the story length.

Linkage. The computer provides the central nerve system for the newspaper newsroom. It links reporters, editors and production of the newspaper. Reporters type their stories, and editors call them up for editing and headline writing.
Photo by Joel Sartore of The Wichita Eagle-Beacon. Used with permission.

Figure B.1 How a Story Moves. The reporter's story goes through several hands before it appears in the newspaper. The city editor or assistant city editor examines it, a news editor reads through it at the news desk and then a copy editor reads it closely and writes a headline for the story.

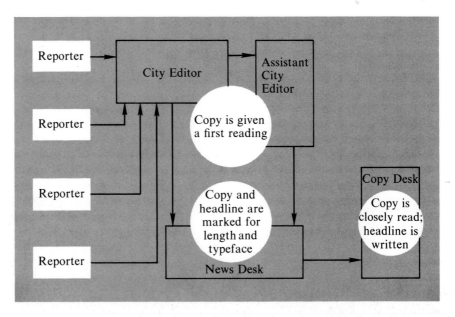

At the copy desk, the story is given a thorough reading. Grammar, punctuation and spelling are checked. The writing is made to conform to the newspaper's style—*Street* may be abbreviated to *St., fourteen* changed to *14*.

If the paper is tight that day, the copy editor trims the story, usually from the bottom. Unnecessary adjectives and adverbs are removed, even when the paper is open—meaning there is plenty of room for news. Redundancies (*true facts, circulated around, 7 a.m. in the morning*) are corrected. Sentences in the passive voice are changed to the active: "The burglar was seen by one of the children" becomes "One of the children saw the burglar."

A copy editor may spot something the city editor missed. If the problem is minor, the copy desk will solve it, but if it is major the story may be sent back to the writer. If the education reporter used too much jargon—the specialized language of educators—the copy editor replaces the technical wording with everyday words and phrases. When the editing is completed, the copy editor writes a headline for the story.

Non-local stories are usually taken from the wire service machines, AP, UPI or others. If the newspaper subscribes to more than one wire service and the news editor wants to combine the dispatches of two or more of them into a single story, the news editor may ask the managing editor to assign the job to a news writer.

On large newspapers, such as the one diagrammed in figure B.1, a regional editor goes over news from correspondents in nearby communities, the business editor handles news from the business staff and from the wires that the news editor or wire editor has turned over to the business desk, and the sports editor handles sports copy.

Each of these specialized departments may have a copy desk of its own. On smaller newspapers, all copy is channeled to a single copy desk.

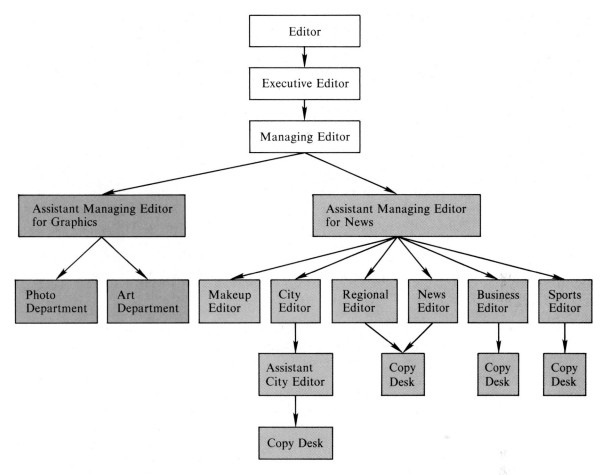

Figure B.2 Newsroom Organization. Newspaper newsrooms are organized along these lines of authority; the editor at the top and various departmental editors and their copy desks under the editor. This diagram shows the organization of a large newspaper. Smaller newspapers may have just one copy desk—called a universal desk—that handles all copy but sports and social news.

As the news day develops, the makeup editor decides how to lay out the newspaper—where to put the stories. Material for the inside pages is laid out first: columns, editorials, comic strips and secondary stories.

On large newspapers, the decision about where to put, or **play,** stories is made at a story conference or news conference. There, the editors of the various sections present the best of their stories to the managing editor. The city editor discusses last night's city council meeting, the national news editor mentions a story from Washington about the federal budget. On some newspapers, a foreign editor is also present.

The managing editor decides what stories will go on page one and which will be given top play. The number one story is usually placed in the upper-right-hand side of the page.

Composition. The final touches are being put on the extra that the *Rocky Mountain News* of Denver published when the space shuttle Challenger exploded.
Photo of the Rocky Mountain News composing room. Used with permission.

On smaller newspapers, the decisions on play are less formal. The managing editor and the city editor chat with each other during the day and then instruct the makeup editor about their decisions.

In both cases, the photo editor, or assistant managing editor for graphics, informs the managing editor or another editor about the local and wire photos or graphics and charts that are available to accompany the major stories.

Once the decisions have been made about play, it is up to the makeup editor to produce a pleasing display of the news for page one and for other section pages—those pages that begin different sections of the newspaper.

Increasingly, newspapers are being edited and made up on video screens. Just as the terminal keyboard has replaced the typewriter, the terminal is replacing the copy editor's pencil and the layout sheets, called **dummies,** of the makeup staff.

When the newsroom work is completed, the laid-out stories are placed on plates, which are usually made up by photocomposition, and then are sent to the pressroom.

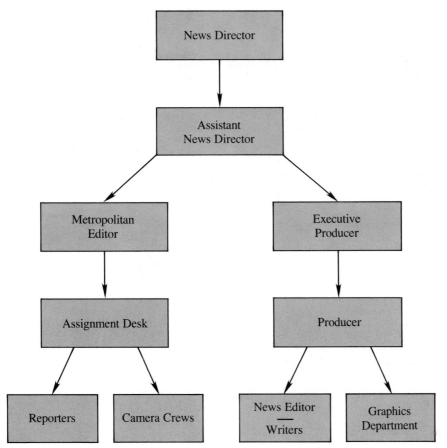

Broadcast Copy

Broadcast news stories move from the writer to the news editor or to the person who will be reading the copy. The copy is edited to see that it can be read aloud without difficulty. Factual errors are corrected, and the copy is checked for broadcast style. Numerals are written out. The number *20* becomes *twenty*; *500,000* becomes *500 thousand*.

Correspondents in the field write their own copy and read it on the air. Sometimes, they "wing it," meaning they speak without written copy.

In smaller stations with no news staff, announcers take wire copy directly from the AP or UPI Teletype machines and read it with little advance checking. This is called "rip and read," and it is the cause of many of the bloopers that are collected on records and sold as entertainment.

Appendix C

How to Use the Freedom of Information Act

The FOIA permits "any person" to request access to agency records. In practice, this includes U.S. citizens, permanent resident aliens and foreign nationals, as well as corporations, unincorporated associations, universities and state and local governments and members of Congress.

Who can Make a Request?

The FOIA requires an agency to respond to an initial request within 10 working days and to an administrative appeal within 20 working days.

How Quickly Will an Agency Respond?

An agency may take an additional 10 days to respond to either the initial request or the administrative appeal in "unusual circumstances" involving the agency's need to obtain records from field facilities, process separate and distinct records, or consult with another agency or two or more of its own components having a substantial interest in the request.

If the agency fails to comply with the applicable time requirements, the requester is deemed to have exhausted his administrative remedies and may seek satisfaction in court. In such a case, however, if the agency can show that "exceptional circumstances" exist and that it is exercising due diligence in responding to the request, the court may retain jurisdiction and allow the agency additional time to complete its review of the records.

Otherwise, upon any determination by an agency to comply with a request, the FOIA requires that the records "shall be made promptly available" to the requester.

The first order of business in making an FOIA request is to determine which agency should receive it.

Where to Write

If you are uncertain about which agency may have the information you seek, go to the library and check records you want, and find out the specific mailing address for its FOIA office.

Describing What You Want

The FOIA simply requires that a request must "reasonably describe" the records being sought. This means that the description must be sufficiently specific so that a government employee who is familiar with an agency's filing system will be able to locate the records within a reasonable amount of time. There is no requirement that you explain why you are seeking the information, but such an explanation might be necessary if you want the agency to waive its fees or comply more fully with your request. The more precise and accurate the request, the more likely you are to get a prompt and complete response, with lower search fees. If you do not give a clear description of the information that is being requested, the agency will contact you for clarification.

Plan Your Request Strategy

• Try to limit your request to what you really want. If you simply ask for "all files relating to" a particular subject (including yourself), you may give the agency an excuse to delay its response and needlessly run up search and copying costs.

• If you know that the request involves a voluminous number of records, try to state both what your request includes and what it does not include.

• Try to be specific about the "search logic" you want the agency to follow. Use *and/or* to describe the different subject matters under request. By using the word *and* between different topics (for example, "mail openings *and* surveillance"), you may receive information that falls into both categories but receive none of the documents which relate *only* to "mail openings" or *only* to "surveillance."

• If you want material released to you in an order of specific priorities, inform the agency of your needs; for example, you might want to have materials reviewed and released to you in chronological or geographical order, or you may simply not want to wait for *all* of the records to be reviewed before any are released.

• Decide whether you want to write a local or regional office of a given agency instead of (or in addition to) the headquarters. Headquarters will ordinarily have policy-making information, plus information of a more general nature than the local officials have chosen to report; the field offices ordinarily have the working files.

Identify What You Want Clearly

• If there are published accounts—newspaper clips, articles, congressional reports, etc.—of the material requested, these should be cited specifically. If they are brief, it may also be helpful to enclose copies of relevant sections.

• If you know that portions of the requested records have already been released, point this out. (It may eliminate or reduce search fees.) Give information, if possible, to identify that release (i.e., date, release number, original requester).

• If you know the title or date of a document, who wrote it, the addressee, or the division or field office of the agency in which it originated, such information should be included.

Sample Request Letter

Tele. No. (business hours)
Return Address
Date

Name of Public Body
Address

To the FOI Officer:

This request is made under the federal Freedom of Information Act, 5 U.S.C. 552.

Please send me copies of *(Here, clearly describe what you want. Include identifying material, such as names, places, and the period of time about which you are inquiring. If you wish, attach news clips, reports, and other documents describing the subject of your research.)*

As you know, the FOI Act provides that if portions of a document are exempt from release, the remainder must be segregated and disclosed. Therefore, I will expect you to send me all non-exempt portions of the records which I have requested, and ask that you justify any deletions by reference to specific exemptions of the FOI Act. I reserve the right to appeal your decision to withhold any materials.

I promise to pay reasonable search and duplication fees in connection with this request. However, if you estimate that the total fees will exceed $_____ , please notify me so that I may authorize expenditure of a greater amount.

(Optional) I am prepared to pay reasonable search and duplication fees in connection with this request. However, the FOI Act provides for waiver or reduction of fees if disclosure could be considered as "primarily benefiting the general public." I am a journalist *(researcher or scholar)* employed by *(name of news organization, book pubishers, etc.),* and intend to use the information I am requesting as the basis for a planned article *(broadcast or book). (Add arguments here in support of fee waiver).* Therefore, I ask that you waive all search and duplication fees. If you deny this request, however, and the fees will exceed $_____ , please notify me of the charges before you fill my request so that I may decide whether to pay the fees or appeal your denial of my request for a waiver.

As I am making this request in the capacity of a journalist *(author or scholar)* and this information is of timely value, I will appreciate your communicating with me by telephone, rather than by mail, if you have any questions regarding this request. Thank you for your assistance, and I will look forward to receiving your reply within 10 business days, as required by law.

Very truly yours,

(Signature)

Appendix D

Code of Ethics

The following is the code of ethics of the Society of Professional Journalists (Sigma Delta Chi, 1987):

The Society of Professional Journalists, Sigma Delta Chi, believes the duty of journalists is to serve the truth.

We believe the agencies of mass communication are carriers of public discussion and information, acting on their Constitutional mandate and freedom to learn and report the facts.

We believe in public enlightenment as the forerunner of justice, and in our Constitutional role to seek the truth as part of the public's right to know the truth.

We believe those responsibilities carry obligations that require journalists to perform with intelligence, objectivity, accuracy, and fairness.

To these ends, we declare acceptance of the standards of practice here set forth:

I. RESPONSIBILITY: The public's right to know of events of public importance and interest is the overriding mission of the mass media. The purpose of distributing news and enlightened opinion is to serve the general welfare. Journalists who use their professional status as representatives of the public for selfish or other unworthy motives violate a high trust.

II. FREEDOM OF THE PRESS: Freedom of the press is to be guarded as an inalienable right of people in a free society. It carries with it the freedom and the responsibility to discuss, question, and challenge actions and utterances of our government and of our public and private institutions. Journalists uphold the right to speak unpopular opinions and the privilege to agree with the majority.

III. ETHICS: Journalists must be free of obligation to any interest other than the public's right to know the truth.

1. Gifts, favors, free travel, special treatment or privileges can compromise the integrity of journalists and their employers. Nothing of value should be accepted.

2. Secondary employment, political involvement, holding public office, and service in community organizations should be avoided if it compromises the integrity of journalists and their employers. Journalists and their employers should conduct their personal lives in a manner which protects them from conflict of interest, real or apparent. Their responsibilities to the public are paramount. That is the nature of their profession.

3. So-called news communications from private sources should not be published or broadcast without substantiation of their claims to news value.

4. Journalists will seek news that serves the public interest, despite the obstacles. They will make constant efforts to assure that the public's business is conducted in public and that public records are open to public inspection.

5. Journalists acknowledge the newsman's ethic of protecting confidential sources of information.

6. Plagiarism is dishonest and unacceptable.

IV. ACCURACY AND OBJECTIVITY: Good faith with the public is the foundation of all worthy journalism.

1. Truth is our ultimate goal.

2. Objectivity in reporting the news is another goal, which serves as the mark of an experienced professional. It is a standard of performance toward which we strive. We honor those who achieve it.

3. There is no excuse for inaccuracies or lack of thoroughness.

4. Newspaper headlines should be fully warranted by the contents of the articles they accompany. Photographs and telecasts should give an accurate picture of an event and not highlight a minor incident out of context.

5. Sound practice makes clear distinction between news reports and expressions of opinion. News reports should be free of opinion or bias and represent all sides of an issue.

6. Partisanship in editorial comment which knowingly departs from the truth violates the spirit of American journalism.

7. Journalists recognize their responsibility for offering informed analysis, comment, and editorial opinion on public events and issues. They accept the obligation to present such material by individuals whose competence, experience, and judgment qualify them for it.

8. Special articles or presentations devoted to advocacy or the writer's own conclusions and interpretations should be labeled as such.

V. FAIR PLAY: Journalists at all times will show respect for the dignity, privacy, rights, and well-being of people encountered in the course of gathering and presenting the news.

    1. The news media should not communicate unofficial charges affecting reputation or moral character without giving the accused a chance to reply.

    2. The news media must guard against invading a person's right to privacy.

    3. The media should not pander to morbid curiosity about details of vice and crime.

    4. It is the duty of news media to make prompt and complete correction of their errors.

    5. Journalists should be accountable to the public for their reports and the public should be encouraged to voice its grievances against the media. Open dialogue with our readers, viewers, and listeners should be fostered.

VI. PLEDGE: Adherence to this code is intended to perserve and strengthen the bond of mutual trust and respect between American journalists and the American people.

The Society shall—by programs of education and other means—encourage individual journalists to adhere to these tenets, and shall encourage journalistic publications and broadcasters to recognize their responsibility to frame codes of ethics in concert with their employees to serve as guidelines in furthering these goals.

Appendix E

Grammar

A verb must agree in number with its subject. Writers get into trouble when they are unsure of the subject or when they cannot decide whether the subject is singular or plural.

Uncertainty often arises when there are words between the subject and the verb:

> WRONG: **John,** as well as several others in the class, **were** unhappy with the instructor.
> RIGHT: **John,** as well as several others in the class, **was** unhappy with the instructor.

The subject is *John,* singular.

> WRONG: **The barrage** of traffic noises, telephone calls and similar interruptions **make** it difficult to study.
> RIGHT: **The barrage** of traffic noises, telephone calls and similar interruptions **makes** it difficult to study.

The subject is *barrage,* singular.

A collective noun takes a singular verb when the group is considered as a unit and a plural verb when the individuals are thought of as separately.:

> RIGHT: **the committee** usually **votes** unanimously.
> RIGHT: **The family lives** around the corner.
> RIGHT: **The family were** gathered around the fire, some reading, some napping.

461

The pronouns *anybody, anyone, each, either, everyone, everybody, neither, no one, nobody, someone* and *somebody* take the singular verb.

A pronoun must agree in number with its antecedent.

WRONG: **The team** has added two players to **their** squad.
RIGHT: **The team** has added two players to **its** squad.
WRONG: **Everyone** does **their** best.
RIGHT: **Everyone** does **his** or **her** best.
WRONG: **Each of the companies** reported **their** profits had declined.
RIGHT: **Each of the companies** reported **its** profits had declined.

Dangling Modifier

Another trouble spot is the dangling modifier—the word, phrase or clause that does not refer logically or clearly to some word in the sentence. We all know what these look like:

Walking through the woods, the trees loomed up.

The phrase in bold face is a dangling participle, the most common of these errors. There are also dangling infinitive phrases:

To learn to shoot well, courses in markmanship were offered.

The way to correct the dangling modifier is to add words that make the meaning clear or to rearrange the words in the sentence to make the modifier refer to the correct word. We can easily fix the two sentences:

Walking through the woods, **the runaway boy** felt the trees loom up at him.
To learn to shoot well, **the police** were offered courses in markmanship.

Misplaced Words

Related parts of the sentence should not be separated. When they are separated, the sentence loses clarity.

Adverbs such as *almost, even, hardly, just, merely, scarcely, ever* and *nearly* should be placed immediately before the words they modify:

VAGUE: He **only** wanted three keys.
CLEAR: He wanted **only** three keys.
VAGUE: She **nearly** ate the whole meal.
CLEAR: She ate **nearly** the whole meal.

Avoid splitting the subject and verb:

AWKWARD: **She,** to make her point, **shouted** at the bartender.
BETTER: To make her point, **she shouted** at the bartender.

Do not separate parts of verb phrases:

AWKWARD: The governor said he **had** last year **seen** the document.

BETTER: the governor said he **had seen** the document last year.

Avoid split infinitives:

AWKWARD: She offered **to** personally **give** him the note.

BETTER: She offered **to give** him the note personally.

Note: Read the sentence aloud if you are unsure about the placement of certain words. Generally, the problem can be solved by placing the subject and verb of the main clause together.

Parallel Construction

The parts of a sentence that express parallel thoughts should be balanced in grammatical form:

UNBALANCED: The people started **to shove** and **crowding** each other.

BALANCED: The people started **to shove** and **crowd** each other.

UNBALANCED: The typewriter can be used **for writing** and **to do** finger exercises.

BALANCED: The typewriter can be used **for writing** and **for doing** finger exercises.

Pronouns

A pronoun should agree with its antecedent in number, person and gender. The most common errors are shifts in number and shifts in person.

WRONG: **The organization** added basketball and hockey to **their** winter program.

RIGHT: **The organization** added basketball and hockey to **its** winter program.

WRONG: When **one** wants to ski, **you** have to buy good equipment.

RIGHT: When **one** wants to ski, **he or she** has to buy good equipment.

A common error is to give teams, groups and organizations the plural pronoun:

WRONG: **The team** played **their** best shortstop.

RIGHT: **The team** played **its** best shortstop.

WRONG: **The Police Department** wants recruits. **They** need 1,500 applicants.

RIGHT: **The Police Department** wants recruits. **It** needs 1,500 applicants.

Sentence Fragments   A phrase or a subordinate clause should not be used as a complete sentence:

> FRAGMENT: The book was long. **And dull.**
> CORRECT: The book was long **and dull.**
> FRAGMENT: The score was tied. **With only a minute left to play.**
> CORRECT: The score was tied **with only a minute left to play.**
> FRAGMENT: He worked all night on the story. **And then collapsed in a heap.**
> CORRECT: He worked all night on the story **and then collapsed in a heap.**

Note: Sometimes writers use a sentence fragment for a specific writing purpose, usually for emphasis: **When in doubt, always use the dictionary. Always.**

Sequence of Tenses   One of the most troublesome grammatical areas for the beginning journalist is the use of tenses. Improper and inconsistent tense changes are frequent. Since the newspaper story is almost always told in the past tense, this is the anchoring tense from which changes are made.

> WRONG: He **looked** into the briefcase and **finds** a small parcel.
> RIGHT: He **looked** into the briefcase and **found** a small parcel.

Not all changes from the past to present are incorrect. The present tense can be used to describe universal truths and situations that are permanently true:

> The Court **said** the Constitution **requires** due process.

When two actions are being described and one was completed before the other occurred, a tense change from the past to the past perfect is best for reader comprehension:

> The patrolman **testified** that he **had placed** his revolver on the table.

Broadcast writers, who tell most of their stories in the present tense, can handle similar situations with a change from the present tense to the present perfect:

> The company **denies** it **has paid** women less than men for comparable work.

In the course of the story, the tense should not make needless shifts from sentence to sentence. The reader is directed by the verb, and if the verb is incorrect, the reader is likely to be confused:

Moore said he **shot** the animal in the back. It **escaped** from the pen in which it was kept.

The reader wonders: Did the animal escape after it was shot, or did it escape and then it was shot? If the former, inserting the word *then* at the start of the second sentence or before the verb would help make it clear. If the animal escaped and then was shot, the second sentence should use the past perfect tense to indicate this:

It **had escaped** from the pen in which it was kept.

Appendix F

Copy Editing

Although most professionals use the word processor and make corrections on a screen, many students prepare copy on a typewriter. Those whose copy spins out of a typewriter should use copy editing marks.

Here are some examples of how copy editing marks are used. Story A is the news writer's original version. The numbers refer to the errors that the reporter caught before handing the story to the copy editor.

Story B is the way the story was edited by the reporter. It contains changes the reporter thought were necessary in the original copy. Story C is the way the story appeared.

Copy Marking

capitalize	U. S. district court judge Frank	District Court Judge
transpose / insert word	J. Broyles will hear (arguments oral) ∧ *Monday*	oral arguments / Monday
delete word and close up	on a suit ~~Monday~~ filed by a woman	suit filed
correction	who wants to build a new Mont_e_ssori	Montessori
new paragraph	School east of Freeport. Jane	
lowercase / separate	Fraker Levine, President of|a	president / of a
insert apostrophe / insert comma	children's group, filed suit last week	children's / group, filed
delete letter and close up	alledging that city officials illegally	alleging
separate / bring together	revoked|a building permit she said s he	revoked a / she
spell out	obtained last July from the (CHA) for	City Housing Authority
abbreviate	the school at 301 Maple (Avenue).	Ave.
abbreviate	In January, the (City Housing Authority)	CHA
use figures	said it had (eleven) objections but	11
retain / addition	decided ~~to~~ issue ∧ anyway. *stet* *the permit*	to / the permit

A

1.
A man who spend through Brockton with his car hood up
2.
was arrested Sunday morning after losing control of his
3.
car and crashing into the front lawn of a North Brockton
4.
home, Brockton police said today.
5.   *6.*
    Arrested was Josehp Small, 45, of Rockville. He was

charged with drunk driving. His car came to rest on the
7.   *8.*
law of the home of Peter Ronney, 16 Eastern Avenue. There

was no damage to the Ronney home, police said.

B

1.
A man who sp**e**~~n~~d through Brockton with his car hood up
2. *he had lost*
was arrested Sunday morning after ~~losing~~ control of his
3. *(landed on)*
car and ~~crashing into~~ the front lawn of a North Brockton
4.
home, ~~Brockton~~ police said today.
5.   *6.*   *(was arrested and)*
~~Arrested was~~ Josehp Small, 45, of Rockville, ~~He was~~

charged with drunk driving. His car came to rest on the
7. *n*   *8.*
law of the home of Peter Ronney, 16 Eastern (Avenue.) There

was no damage to the Ronney home, police said.

C

A man who sped through Brockton with his car hood up was arrested Sunday morning after he lost control of his car and landed on the front lawn of a North Brockton home, police said today.

Joseph Small, 45, of Rockville, was arrested and charged with drunk driving. His car came to rest on the lawn of the home of Peter Ronney, 16 Eastern Ave. There was no damage to the Ronney home, police said.

Explanation of Editing Marks

1. The word is sped. Black out the *n* and close up the word.

2. I would rather have "lost" than "losing." It goes better with the past tense of the main verb of the sentence.

3. How can you crash into a lawn? Makes no sense. "Landed on" may not make strict sense; after all, he wasn't flying a car. But it's graphic.

4. Don't need Brockton. After all, he was driving in Brockton. No other police could make the arrest. Wasted word.

5. "Arrested was. . . ." is what is called *Time*-ese because *Time* magazine reverses subject and verb. Too cute. Stick with S-V-O. I'll start a new paragraph with the man's name and make one sentence out of two here.

6. Transpose the letters in his first name.

7. That's *lawn*. Insert *n*.

8. Make that *Ave*. The stylebook abbreviates avenue and street in addresses.

Stabbing

A

A Brockton man died from stab wounds Monday night after a dispute with his former girlfriend, Barbara Garth, 39, [1] 25 Elm St., had turned violent.

Lee Sam Bensley, 42, died at Bayfront Medical Center Monday evening after the fight, [2] and his former girl- [3] friend was later arrested and booked for investigation into the murder. [4] The incident occurred in Bensley's [5] apartment at 423 W. 120 St.

Police said the two had been seeing each other but split [6] up two months ago when Miss Garth learned he was married.

Explanation of Editing Marks

1. I don't need her name in the lead. No one ever heard of her, and it clutters the lead. I'll save it for the second paragraph.

2. This phrase is a repetition of material in the lead. Tighten up and put a period at the end.

3. This is a run-on sentence. Begin a new sentence here and put in her name.

4. Oops. Murder is the finding of a jury after a trial, or a charge. She's only been booked. Call it a "death" and that is safe.

5. Hard to call what seems to be a killing an "incident." I can't say "death" because I've used that. Major surgery necessary.

6. Do I really need this on what may have been a drunken brawl? Might as well let the desk decide. Our newspaper does not use courtesy titles on second reference. So *Miss* is deleted.

B

A Brockton man died from stab wounds Monday night after a dispute with his former girlfriend, ~~Barbara Garth, 39,~~ [1] ~~25 Elm St.,~~ had turned violent.

Lee Sam Bensley, 42, died at Bayfront Medical Center. ~~Monday evening after the fight, and his former girl-~~ [2] The woman, Barbara Garth, [3] 39, 25 Elm St., was ~~friend was later~~ arrested and booked for investigation into the ~~murder~~ death. [4] Bensley was fatally [5] stabbed in his ~~The incident occurred in Bensley's~~ apartment at 423 W. 120 St.

Police said the two had been seeing each other but split [6] up two months ago when ~~Miss~~ Garth learned he was married.

C

A Brockton man died from stab wounds Monday night after a dispute with his former girlfriend had turned violent.

Lee Sam Bensley, 42, died at Bayfront Medical Center. The woman, Barbara Garth, 39, 25 Elm St., was arrested and booked for investigation into the death. Bensley was fatally stabbed in his apartment at 423 W. 120 St.

Police said the two had been seeing each other but split up two months ago when Garth learned he was married.

A

Boots

1.
For 5 weeks they have been walking, despite the summer

heat, the mosquitoes and their aching, blistered feet.
2.   *3. 4.*
Up over hills. Down sharp rocky hillsides. And along
5.   *6.*
narrow ledges. From 6 a.m. in the morning until 4 or 5 P.M.
7.   *8.*
in the evening they walk. The fifteen soldiers have hiked

15 miles a day, even more. They are on the road to ...
9.
Nowhere!
10. 11.
The soldiers have been walking in circles, since the

middle of July they have been walking over a test course.
12.
They are testing a newlydesigned combat boot. By the time
13.
they have completed their rounds the men will have walked
14. 15.   *16.*
nearly 750 miles. "Its wild, wild", said one of the soliders.

The tests are being conducted on the Aberdeen Proving

Ground in Maryland. The new boot is made of a brown suede.
17.
"No more boot polishing, that's the only thing that makes
18.
this worthwhile," said another.

B

1.
For ⑤ weeks they have been walking, despite the summer

heat, the mosquitoes and their aching, blistered feet.

Explanation of Editing Marks

1. Spell out numbers from one through nine. Stylebook rule.

2. Insert a comma between adjectives.

3. *And* does not work. It spoils the parallel structure and rhythm set by the previous two sentences.

4. Capitalize the letter *a*.

5. Redundancy; a.m. means before noon.

6. Lower case P.M.

7. Redundancy; p.m. means after noon.

8. Use the numeral for numbers 10 and above.

9. Delete the exclamation point. Let the reader supply it, the stylebook says.

10. There are two sentences here. Use a period instead of a comma.

11. Capital letter for beginning of sentence.

12. Separate.

13. I want the reader to pause here. There may or may not be a grammatical reason for this, but commas can be used to stop the reader for an instant.

14. New paragraph. The quotation introduces a new idea.

15. Troublesome word. Here I need the contraction for *it is*. Insert apostrophe.

16. Transpose. When ending quotations, the comma goes inside the quote mark.

17. Delete the comma, put in a period and close up.

18. Another what? The prior reference to a soldier is too far away.

Up over hills. Down sharp, rocky hillsides. And along narrow ledges. From 6 a.m. in the morning until 4 or 5 P.M. in the evening they walk. The (fiftteen) soldiers have hiked 15 miles a day, even more. They are on the road to ...

Nowhere!

The soldiers have been walking in circles since the middle of July they have been walking over a test course. They are testing a newly designed combat boot. By the time they have completed their rounds, the men will have walked nearly 750 miles. "It's wild, wild," said one of the soldiers.

The tests are being conducted on the Aberdeen Proving Ground in Maryland. The new boot is made of brown suede. "No more boot polishing, that's the only thing that makes this worthwhile," said another soldier.

C

For five weeks they have been walking, despite the summer heat, the mosquitoes and their aching, blistered feet.

Up over hills. Down sharp, rocky hillsides. Along narrow ledges. From 6 a.m. until 4 or 5 p.m. they walk. The 15 soldiers have hiked 15 miles a day, even more. They are on the road to . . .

Nowhere.

The soldiers have been walking in circles. Since the middle of July they have been walking over a test course. They are testing a newly designed combat boot. By the time they have completed their rounds, the men will have walked nearly 750 miles.

"It's wild, wild," said one of the soldiers.

The tests are being conducted on the Aberdeen Proving Ground in Maryland. The new boot is made of brown suede. "No more boot polishing. That's the only thing that makes this worthwhile," said another soldier.

Glossary

These definitions were provided by the press associations and working reporters and editors. Most of the brief entries are from the *New England Daily Newspaper Study,* an examination of 105 daily newspapers, edited by Loren Ghiglione (Southbridge, Mass.: Southbridge Evening News Inc., 1973).

Print Terms

add An addition to a story already written or in the process of being written.

A.M. Morning newspaper.

assignment Instruction to a reporter to cover an event. An editor keeps an assignment book that contains notations for reporters such as the following:

> Jacobs—10 a.m.: Health officials tour new sewage treatment plant.
>
> Klaren—11 a.m.: Interview Ben Wastersen, possible Democratic congressional candidate.
>
> Mannen—Noon: Rotary Club luncheon speaker, Horlan, the numerologist. A feature?

attribution Designation of the person being quoted. Also, the source of information in a story. Sometimes, information is given on a not-for-attribution basis.

background Material in a story that gives the circumstances surrounding or preceding the event.

banger An exclamation point. Avoid. Let the reader do the exclaiming.

banner Headline across or near the top of all or most of a newspaper page. Also called a line, ribbon, streamer, screamer.

B copy Bottom section of a story written ahead of an event that will occur too close to deadline for the entire story to be processed. The B copy usually consists of background material.

beat Area assigned to a reporter for regular coverage. For example, police or city hall. Also, an exclusive story.

body type Type in which most of a newspaper is set, usually 8 or 9 point type.

boldface Heavy, black typeface; type that is blacker than the text with which it is used. Abbreviated bf.

break When a news development becomes known and available. Also, the point of interruption in a story continued from one page to another.

bright Short, amusing story.

bulldog Early edition, usually the first of a newspaper.

byline Name of the reporter who wrote the story, placed atop the published article. An old-timer comments on the current use of bylines. "In the old days, a reporter was given a byline if he or she personally covered an important or unusual story, or the story was an exclusive. Sometimes if the writing was superior, a byline was given. Nowadays, everyone gets a byline, even if the story is a rewrite and the reporter never saw the event described in the story."

caps Capital letters; same as uppercase.

caps and lower case Initial capital in a word followed by small letters. See lowercase.

clip News story clipped from a newspaper, usually for future reference.

cold type In composition, type set photographically or by pasting up letters and pictures on acetate or paper.

column The vertical division of the news page. A standard-size newspaper is divided into five to eight columns. Also, a signed article of opinion or strong personal expression, frequently by an authority or expert—a sports column, a medical column, political or social commentary, and the like.

copy Written form in which a news story or other material is prepared.

copy desk The desk used by copy editors to read copy. The slot person is in charge of the desk.

copy flow After a reporter finishes a story, it moves to the city desk where the city editor reads it for major errors or problems. If it does not need further work, the story is moved to the copy desk for final editing and a headline. It then moves to the mechanical department.

correction Errors that reach publication are retracted or corrected if they are serious or someone demands a correction. Libelous matter is always corrected immediately, often in a separate news story rather than in the standard box assigned to corrections.

correspondent Reporter who sends news from outside a newspaper office. On smaller papers often not a regular full-time staff member.

crony journalism Reporting that ignores or treats lightly negative news about friends of a reporter or editor. Beat reporters have a tendency to protect their informants in order to retain them as sources.

crop To cut or mask the unwanted portions, usually of a photograph.

cut Printed picture or illustration. Also, to eliminate material from a story. See trim.

cutline Any descriptive or explanatory material under a picture.

dateline Name of the city or town and sometimes the date at the start of a story that is not of local origin.

deadline Time at which the copy for an edition must be ready.

dirty copy Matter for publication that needs extensive correction.

edition One version of a newspaper. Some papers have one edition a day, some several. Not to be confused with issue, which usually refers to all editions under a single date.

editorial Article of comment or opinion usually on the editorial page.

editorial material All material in the newspaper that is not advertising.

enterprise copy Story, often initiated by a reporter, that digs deeper than the usual news story.

exclusive Story one reporter has obtained to the exclusion of the competition. A beat. Popularly known as a scoop, a term never used in the newsroom.

feature Story emphasizing the human or entertaining aspects of a situation. A news story or other material differentiated from straight news. As a verb, it means to give prominence to a story.

file To send a story to the office, usually by wire or telephone, or to put news service stories on the wire.

filler Material used to fill space. Small items used to fill out columns where needed. Also called column closers and shorts.

flag Printed title of a newspaper on page one. Also known as logotype or nameplate.

free advertising Use of the names of businesses and products not essential to the story. Instead of the brand name, use the broad term camera for Leica or Kodak.

futures calendar Date book in which story ideas, meetings and activities scheduled for a later occurrence are listed. Also known as a futures book or tickler. Kept by city and assignment editors and by careful reporters.

good night Before leaving for the day, beat reporters check in with the desk and are given a good night, which means there is nothing further for the reporter from the desk for the day. On some newspapers, the call is made for the lunch break, too. Desks need to know where their reporters are in case of breaking stories.

graf Abbreviation for paragraph.

Guild Newspaper Guild, an international union to which some reporters and other newspaper workers belong. Newspapers that have contracts with the Guild are said to be "organized."

handout Term for written publicity or special-interest news sent to a newspaper for publication.

hard news Spot news; live and current news in contrast to features.

head or headline The display type over a printed news story.

head shot Picture featuring little more than the head and shoulders of the person shown.

HFR Abbreviation for "hold for release." Material that cannot be used until it is released by the source or at a designated time. Also known as embargoed material.

identification Personal data used to identify a person: name, title (if any), age, address, occupation, education, race, religion, ethnicity. The identifying characteristics used are those relevant to the story. Generally, we use name, age, occupation, address. To lend authority to the observations or statements of sources, we give their background. Use race, religion, national origin only when relevant to the story. In obituaries and crime stories, the readers want as much identification as possible. In general news stories, logic should indicate relevancy: Toledo readers are not interested in the home address of the North Carolina senator who collapses in a hotel and dies. But the newspaper in his home town of Raleigh will insert the address in the press association copy.

insert Material placed between copy in a story. Usually, a paragraph or more to be placed in material already sent to the desk.

investigative reporting Technique used to unearth information sources often want hidden. This type of reporting involves examination of documents and records, the cultivation of informants, painstaking and extended research. Investigative reporting usually seeks to expose wrongdoing and has concentrated on public officials and their activities. In recent years, industry and business have been scrutinized. Some journalists contend that the term is redundant, that all good reporting is investigative, that behind every surface fact is the real story that a resourceful, curious and persistent reporter can dig up.

italics Type in which letters and characters slant to the right.

jump Continuation of a story from one page to another. As a verb, to continue material. Also called runover.

kill To delete a section from copy or to discard the entire story; also, to spike a story.

lead (pronounced leed) First paragraph in news story. A direct or straight news lead summarizes the main facts. A delayed lead, usually used on feature stories, evokes a scene or sets a mood.
Also used to refer to the main idea of a story: An editor will ask a reporter, "What's the lead on the piece?" expecting a quick summary of the main facts. Also: A tip on a story; an idea for a story. A source will tell a reporter, "I have a lead on a story for you." In turn, the reporter will tell the editor, "I have a lead on a story that may develop."

localize Emphasizing the names of persons from the local community who are involved in events outside the city or region: A local couple rescued in a Paris hotel fire; the city police chief who speaks at a national conference.

lowercase Small letters, as contrasted to capitals.

LTK Designation on copy for "lead to come." Usually placed after the slug. Indicates the written material will be given a lead later.

makeup Layout or design. The arrangement of body type, headlines and illustrations into pages.

masthead Formal statement of a newspaper's name, officers, place of publication and other descriptive information, usually on the editorial page. Sometimes confused with flag or nameplate.

morgue Newspaper library.

mug shot See head shot.

new lead See running story.

news hole Space in a newspaper allotted to news, illustrations and other non-advertising material.

obituary Account of a person's death; also called obit.

offset Printing process in which an image is transferred from a printing plate to a rubber roller and then set off on paper.

off the record Material offered the reporter in confidence. If the reporter accepts the material with this understanding, it cannot be used except as general background in a later story. Some reporters never accept off-the-record material. Some reporters will accept the material with the provision that if they can obtain the information elsewhere they will use it. Reporters who learn of off-the-record material from other than the original source can use it.
No public, official meeting can be off the record, and almost all official documents (court records, police information) are public information. Private groups can ask that their meetings be kept off the record, but reporters frequently ignore such requests when the meeting is public or large numbers of people are present.

op-ed page Abbreviation for the page opposite the editorial page. The page is frequently devoted to opinion columns and related illustrations.

overnight Story usually written late at night for the afternoon newspapers of the next day. Most often used by the press services. The overnight, or overnighter, usually has little new information in it but is cleverly written so that the reader thinks the story is new. Also known as second-day stories.

play Emphasis given to a news story or picture—size and place in the newspaper of the story; typeface and size of headline.

P.M. Afternoon or evening newspaper.

pool Arrangement whereby limited numbers of reporters and photographers are selected to represent all those assigned to the story. Pooling is adopted when a large number of people would overwhelm the event or alter its nature. The news and film are shared with the rest of the press corps.

press release Publicity handout, or a story given to the news media for publication.

proof Reproduction of type on paper for the purpose of making corrections or alterations.

puff or puffery Publicity story or a story that contains unwarranted superlatives.

quotes Quotation marks; also a part of a story in which someone is directly quoted.

rewrite To write for a second time to strengthen a story or to condense it.

rewrite man Person who takes the facts of stories over the telephone and then puts them together into a story and who may rewrite reporters' stories.

rowback A story that attempts to correct a previous story without indicating that the prior story had been in error or without taking responsibility for the error.

running story Event that develops and is covered over a period of time. For an event covered in subsequent editions of a newspaper or on a single cycle of a wire service, additional material is handled as follows:
> New lead—Important new information.
> Add and insert—Less important information.
> Sub—Material that replaces dated material, which is removed.

sell Presentation a reporter makes to impress the editor with the importance of his or her story; also, editors sell stories to their superiors at news conferences.

shirttail Short, related story adapted to the end of a longer one.

short Filler, generally of some current news value.

situationer Story that pulls together a continuing event for the reader who may not have kept track as it unfolded. The situationer is helpful with complex or technical developments or on stories with varied datelines and participants.

slant To write a story so as to influence the reader's thinking. To editorialize, to color or misrepresent.

slug Word or words placed on all copy to identify the story.

source Person, record, document or event that provides the information for the story.

source book Alphabetical listing, by name and by title, of the addresses and the office and home telephone numbers of persons on the reporter's beat and some general numbers—FBI agent in charge in town, police and fire department spokesmen, hospital information, weather bureau.

split page Front page of an inside section; also known as the break page, second front page.

stringer Correspondent, not a regular staff member, who is paid by the story or by the number of words written.

style Rules for capitalization, punctuation and spelling that standardize usage so that the material presented is uniform. Most newspapers and stations have stylebooks. The most frequently used is the common stylebook of the United Press International and the Associated Press.

stylebook Specific listing of the conventions of spelling, abbreviation, punctuation, capitalization used by a particular newspaper, wire service. Broadcast stylebooks include pronunciations.

sub See running story.

subhead One-line and sometimes two-line head (usually in boldface body type) inserted in a long story at intervals for emphasis or to break up a long column of type.

text Verbatim report of a speech or public statement.

thumbnail Half-column-wide cut or portrait.

tight Full, too full. Also refers to a paper so crowded with ads that the news space must be reduced. It is the opposite of the wide open paper.

tip Information passed to a reporter, often in confidence. The material usually requires further fact gathering. Occasionally, verification is impossible and the reporter must decide whether to go with the tip on the strength of the insider's knowledge and reliability. Sometimes the reporter will not want to seek confirmation for fear of alerting sources who will alter the situation or release the information to the competition. Tips often lead to exclusives.

titles Mr., Mrs., Miss, Ms., Secretary of State, Police Chief, Senator are formal designations and may be used before the person's name. Usage depends upon the station's or newspaper's policy. False titles—Vietnam war hero, actress, leftfielder—are properly used after the name: For instance, Nate Thurmond, the center . . . instead of Center Nate Thurmond. . .

trim to reduce or condense copy carefully.

update Story that brings the reader up to date on a situation or personality previously in the news. If the state legislature appropriated additional funds for five new criminal court judges to meet the increased number of cases in the courts an update might be written some months later to see how many more cases were handled after the judges went to work. An update usually has no hard news angle.

VDT Video display terminal, a part of the electronic system used in news and advertising departments that eliminates typewriters. Copy is written on typewriter-like keyboards and words appear on attached television screens rather than on paper. The story is stored on a disk in a computer. Editing is done on the terminals.

verification Determination of the truth of the material the reporter gathers or is given. The assertions, sometimes even the actual observation, do not necessarily mean the information is accurate or true. Some of the basic tools of verification are: the telephone book, for names and addresses; the city directory, for occupations; *Who's Who,* for biographical information. For verification of more complex material, the procedure of Thucydides, the Greek historian and author of the *History of the Peloponnesian War,* is good advice for the journalist: "As to the deeds done in the war, I have not thought myself at liberty to record them on hearsay from the first informant or on arbitrary conjecture. My account rests either on personal knowledge or on the closest possible scrutiny of each statement made by others. The process of research was laborious, because the conflicting accounts were given by those who had witnessed the several events, as partiality swayed or memory served them."

wire services Synonym for press associations, the Associated Press and the United Press International. There are foreign-owned press services to which some newspapers subscribe: Reuters, Tass, Agence France-Presse.

Broadcast Terms

actuality An on-the-scene report.
audio Sound.

closeup (broadcast) Shot of the face of the subject that dominates the frame so that little background is visible.
cover shot A long shot usually cut in at the beginning of a sequence to establish place or location.

cue A signal in script or by word or gesture to begin or to stop. Two types: incue and outcue.
cut Quick transition from one type of picture to another. Radio: a portion of an actuality on tape used on broadcast.
cutaway Transition shot—usually short—from one theme to another, used to avoid jump cut. Often a shot of the interviewer listening.

dissolve Smooth fading of one picture for another. As the second shot becomes distinct, the first slowly disappears.
dub The transfer of one videotape to another.

FI or **fade in** A scene that begins without full brilliance and gradually assumes full brightness. **FO** or **fade out** is the opposite.

graphics All visual displays, such as art work, maps, charts and still photos.

jump cut Transition from one subject to a different subject in an abrupt manner. Avoided with cutaway shot between the scenes.

mix Combining two or more sound elements into one.
montage A series of brief shots of various subjects to give a single impression or communicate one idea.

O/C On camera. A reporter delivering copy directly to the camera without covering pictures.
outtakes Scenes that are discarded for the final story.

pan or **pan shot** Moving the camera from left to right or right to left.

remote A taped or live broadcast from a location outside the studio. Also, the unit that originates such a broadcast.
SOT Sound on tape. Recorded simultaneously with picture on tape.

V/O Reporter's voice over pictures.
VTR Videotape recording.

zoom Use of a variable focus lens to take closeups and wide angle shots from a stationary position. By using a zoom lens an impression can be given of moving closer or farther away from the subject.

Computer Terms

These definitions were provided by Merrill Perlman of *The New York Times*.

busy light or working light Tells the user that the computer is working on the function requested. Most computer systems prevent any other functions being performed while the light is on.

change case A key that allows a lowercase letter to be turned into an uppercase letter. The function is particularly useful when the user has forgotten to unlock the shift key.

control, command, supershift Usually a key that allows an extra function to be programmed onto a single key. For example, an x will yield a lowercase x with no extra key pressed, an uppercase x when the shift is pressed and perhaps a + mark when the supershift key is pressed. The control key also may act as a safety key that must be pressed simultaneously with another function key to, for example, erase an entire story.

crash The system "locks up" and the terminals stop functioning. This is the bane of computerized newsrooms, since in most cases all the copy that was on the screen when the system crashed is either lost or frozen. Most computer systems have a key or function that allows the user to protect or save copy from crashes by taking it off the screen for a moment so it can be entered into computer memory.

CRT Cathode ray tube.

cursor The square of light that indicates the place in the copy where the changes will be made. The user positions the cursor using directional keys before adding or deleting matter.

delete Just that. Most computer systems have keys for deleting characters, words, sentences, lines, paragraphs or blocks of copy that are defined by the user.

directory, file, basket Designations for the storage of stories, notes, memos, etc. The computerized equivalent of a file holder. Each reporter will have a file or directory; the copy desk will have another, etc.

film Terminology on some computer systems for setting a story into type.

format A specific set of instructions telling the computer to do something. Many systems have common formats built in; others require the user to format each story individually. The formats usually consist of the type size, the leading, the type face, the column width and any special instructions, such as cut-ins for the copy, to allow for half-column graphics or other special typographical set-ups. In some systems, formatting is called styling.

home In most systems, a single key allows the user to return the cursor "home" to the top left-hand corner of the screen, or to the start of the text, depending on how the system is programmed.

hyphenate and justify A function to have a story appear on the screen with the words lined up and hyphenated in the proper column width, just as they will appear in type.

keystroke Pressing one key one time. Functions are often expressed in terms of keystrokes.

load When the computer terminal is being programmed, either by the user or by the systems people, this is called loading.

program To give instructions to the computer. Keys on various systems are programmable as well, so often-used functions or phrases can be entered into them. For example, a programmable key may have "By The ASSOCIATED PRESS" programmed into it, so the person working at the terminal can press just the programmed key to get all those characters.

scope Jargon for video display tube or terminal.

scroll To move the text on the screen up or down, to bring the next lines into view. Most computer systems allow users to scroll through the entire story; some limit scrolling to a certain number of characters.

terminal An individual work station.

tube Jargon for video display tube or terminal.

VDT Video display tube or video display terminal.

Name Index

New York University Graduate School of
Business Office of Public Affairs,
400
Nietzke, Ann, 379
Noble, Joseph 38, 92, 101, 158, 239, 278
Nolan, Martin, 144
Norfolk *Virginian-Pilot,* 270

Oceanside, Calif. *Blade-Tribune,* 413
Ochs, Adolph S., 371
Ogilvy, David, 379
Orlando, Fla. *Sentinel,* 223
Orwell, George, 32, 100, 145, 172
Othman, Frederick C., 142
Oxford, Mona, 79

Papaleo, Ken, 257, 341, 342
Patinkin, Mark, 37, 210, 424
Peck, Robert, 144
People, 37, 292
Pepperdine University, 70, 140
Peritz, Ingrid, 311
Pett, Saul, 101, 123, 204
Philadelphia Inquirer, 427
Pitts, Beverley, 202, 393–95
Plageman, Susan, 80, 116, 268
Planned Parenthood Foundation of
America, Inc., 421
Plimpton, George, 243
Poe, Edgar Allan, 142
Pope, Edwin, 23
PRADS, Inc., 396
Price, Larry C., 41–44, 429
Providence Journal, 14–17
Public Relations News, 385
Public Relations Society of America, 386,
391, 399
Pyle, Morris, 323

Quigg, H. D., 214
Quill, 34

Rago, Rosalinde, 373
Raines, Howell, 242, 248
Rather, Dan, 9–12, 32, 35, 145, 194, 221
Reader's Digest, 387
The Record, 288
Reichard, Hank, 428
Reston, James, 169
Revson, Charles, 375
Riedel, Charlie, 56, 81, 107, 212, 319, 362
Rivest, Jean Pierre, 89
Robbins, Neal, 6–9, 19
Roberts, Gene, 165, 222
Roberts, Steven V., 94
Robertson, Alex, 69

Robinson, Mike, 391
Rose, Bob, 76, 132, 209
Rosenthal, A.M., 30
Ross, Lillian, 242
Rothstein, Arthur, 57, 131, 158, 340, 343
Rowan, Paul, 41–44

St. Louis Post-Dispatch, 277
St. Petersburg Times, 26, 80, 248, 424
Sandburg, Carl, 144
San Diego *Evening Tribune,* 413
Sanford, Bruce W., 412
San Francisco Examiner, 168
Sartore, Joel, 158, 360, 366, 368
Savannah Morning News, 167
Scanlan, Christopher, 37, 424
Schumann, Robert, 71
Seago, Les, 295
Sears, Phil, 22
Selcraig, Bruce, 241
Seligman, Kathy, 239
Shaw, David, 169, 172
Shulins, Nancy, 183
Simers, T. J. 301
Simpson, Kevin, 413
Sinclair, Upton, 95
Sluder, Rick, 134–37
Smith, H. Allen, 317
Smith, Red, 148
Society of Professional Journalists
code of ethics of, 457–59
Solomon, George, 23
Sommer, Jeff, 216–17
Spargo, John, 386
Sperling, Stacy, 388
Stacks, David, 84
Stahl, Lesley, 10
Stamford, Conn. *Advocate,* 126, 280, 305
Stanton, Mike, 129
Stinnett, Caskie, 164
Storm, William J., 141
Strasser, Joel, 60, 109, 220
Sullivan, Margaret, 124
Surfside News, 168
Szulc, Nicole, 259

Teagarden, Becky, 296
Terkel, Studs, 150, 243
Thayer, Bob, 15, 17
Thomas, Helen, 24
Thoreau, Henry David, 164
Time, 421
Titchen, John, 2
Tocqueville, Alexis de, 111
Toledo *Blade,* 133, 209
Tombstone Epitaph, 99

Subject Index